Financial Reporting in the West Pacific Rim

During recent years the West Pacific Rim has bee economic growth and has attracted considerable in investors. Yet there has been very little up-to-d financial reporting practices followed by companie

In a region of great diversity, both politic accounting environment has been variously shape colonialism and foreign occupation. *Financial Rep Rim* provides information about current practic places them in their respective historical, econor contexts.

After a general introduction covering the whol country studies which follow consider the busi accounting regulatory framework, company and t regulations, the accountancy profession and standa generally accepted accounting principles and e reports.

The description and analyses, written in the provide a framework for researchers and analysts important and fast-changing area.

T.E. Cooke is Professor of Accounting at the Un and visiting professor at the Free University, Ar lands. He has published several studies in in **R.H. Parker** is Professor of Accounting at the Univ Professorial Research Fellow of the Institute of Ch Scotland. He has published widely in interna accounting history and is a frequent visitor to the W

Financial Reporting in the West Pacific Rim

Edited by T.E. Cooke and R.H. Parker

ROUTLEDGE

London and New York

First published 1994
by Routledge
11 New Fetter Lane, London EC4P 4EE

Simultaneously published in the USA and Canada
by Routledge
29 West 35th Street, New York, NY 10001

Typeset in Times by
Solidus (Bristol) Limited
Printed and bound in Great Britain by
Biddles Ltd, Guildford and King's Lynn

British Library Cataloguing in Publication Data
A catalogue record for this book is available from the British Library

ISBN 0–415–10223–5

Library of Congress Cataloging in Publication Data
Cooke, Terence E., 1952–
Financial reporting in the West Pacific rim / T.E. Cooke and R.H. Parker.
p. cm.
Includes bibliographical references and index.
ISBN 0–415–10223–5
1. Financial statements–Pacific Area. 2. Corporations–Pacific Area–Accounting. 3. Financial statements–Law and legislation–Pacific Area. I. Parker, R.H. (Robert Henry) II. Title.
HF5681.B2C5944 1993
657'.3'099–dc20 93-13081
CIP

Contents

Figures

Tables

Contributors

S.T. Chiang is a partner in Chiang, Lai, Lin & Co., certified public accountants, and adviser to Deloitte Ross Tohmatsu, Taipei, Taiwan.

T.E. Cooke is Professor of Accounting, University of Exeter, and visiting professor at the Free University, Amsterdam.

Foo See Liang is Sub-Dean and Senior Lecturer, the School of Accountancy and Business, Nanyang Technological University, Singapore.

In Ki Joo is Professor of Accounting, College of Business and Economics, Yonsei University, Seoul, Republic of Korea.

Jee Hong Kim is Associate Professor of Accounting, College of Business and Economics, Yonsei University, Seoul, Republic of Korea.

Joon Seuk Kim is Associate Professor of Accounting, College of Business and Economics, Yonsei University, Seoul, Republic of Korea.

M.C. Miller is Associate Professor, School of Accounting, University of New South Wales, Sydney, Australia and member, Australian Accounting Standards Board.

S. Newby is a Senior Lecturer in Accounting, Department of Accounting and Finance, University of Auckland, New Zealand.

Ng Shwn Yng was a research scholar, the School of Accountancy and Business, Nanyang Technological University, Singapore.

R.H. Parker is Professor of Accounting, University of Exeter and part-time professorial fellow, Institute of Chartered Accountants of Scotland.

P. Phenix is head of the compliance division of the Stock Exchange of Hong Kong.

P. Tan is a Senior Lecturer in the School of Accountancy and Business, Nanyang Technological University, Singapore.

J.S.W. Tay is a Senior Lecturer in the School of Accountancy and Business, Nanyang Technological University, Singapore.

Preface

Interest in the West Pacific Rim stems mainly from the high rates of economic growth that have been achieved there since the Second World War. As a result, international investors have been attracted to the region and researchers have been interested in analyzing how the area has achieved its success, and in assessing whether the rest of the world can benefit therefrom.

The political, economic, and social environments which have helped to shape accounting in the region are very diverse. Consequently financial reporting practices differ considerably, and the extent and form of accounting regulation varies greatly. The implication of this diversity for the writing of this book is that while a framework was provided the chapters have not been standardized. This approach was thought to be the best way to reflect the variety of environments and to avoid unnecessary rigidity.

There is a dearth of material about the West Pacific Rim so the approach adopted is largely descriptive. We hope that our descriptive research will help others (and ourselves) to create theories and hypotheses for future research. This book covers most of the major countries of the region, moving from north to south from Japan to New Zealand. Japan dominates the region and so the coverage of this country is more extensive than that of the others.

The gestation period of the book has been substantial, reflecting the difficulty of co-ordinating this type of project and the variety of publication problems encountered. The editors would like to thank each of the contributors (at least two of whom found the time to increase the size of their families as well as write for us) and the Research Board of the Institute of Chartered Accountants in England and Wales for its financial support.

T.E. Cooke
R.H. Parker
Exeter, August 1993

1 Context, diversity and harmonization

R.H. Parker

INTRODUCTION

The description 'West Pacific Rim' is used in this book as shorthand for the major capitalist countries of the West Pacific and includes, moving from north to south, Japan, the Republic of (South) Korea, Taiwan, Hong Kong, Thailand, the Philippines, Malaysia, Singapore, Australia and New Zealand (see Figure 1.1).[1] A journey of equivalent distance in the East Atlantic would take one from the UK to South Africa. We do not discuss the countries of the East Pacific Rim in this book but the United States is a major trade partner, source of investment, and influence on financial reporting practices for all the West Pacific countries. A chapter is devoted to each country and it is these chapters which form the core of the book. This introductory chapter looks at the region as a whole, explaining why West Pacific countries are of interest from the point of view of corporate financial reporting, setting that financial reporting in context and providing some basic facts and figures. It then looks at the diversity of financial reporting in the region and discusses the prospects for harmonization.

The main reason for the outside world's interest in the capitalist countries of the West Pacific is their record of economic growth in recent decades and the openness of many of their economies to outside investment. Table 1.1 summarizes growth rates, including, for purposes of comparison, those of the US and the UK. The Asian countries of the West Pacific have in recent years been the fastest-growing region in the world. The West Pacific's share of world output has doubled and, because the growth has been export oriented, its share of world trade has trebled during the past three decades (Anderson 1991: 1540). Some of the reasons for growth are discussed below.

POLITICAL AND ECONOMIC DIVERSITY

The West Pacific Rim is, much more than North America or even Europe, a region of great diversity, both political and economic. One common political factor has been an experience of colonialism or occupation. This is relevant in a financial reporting context as many of the colonial or

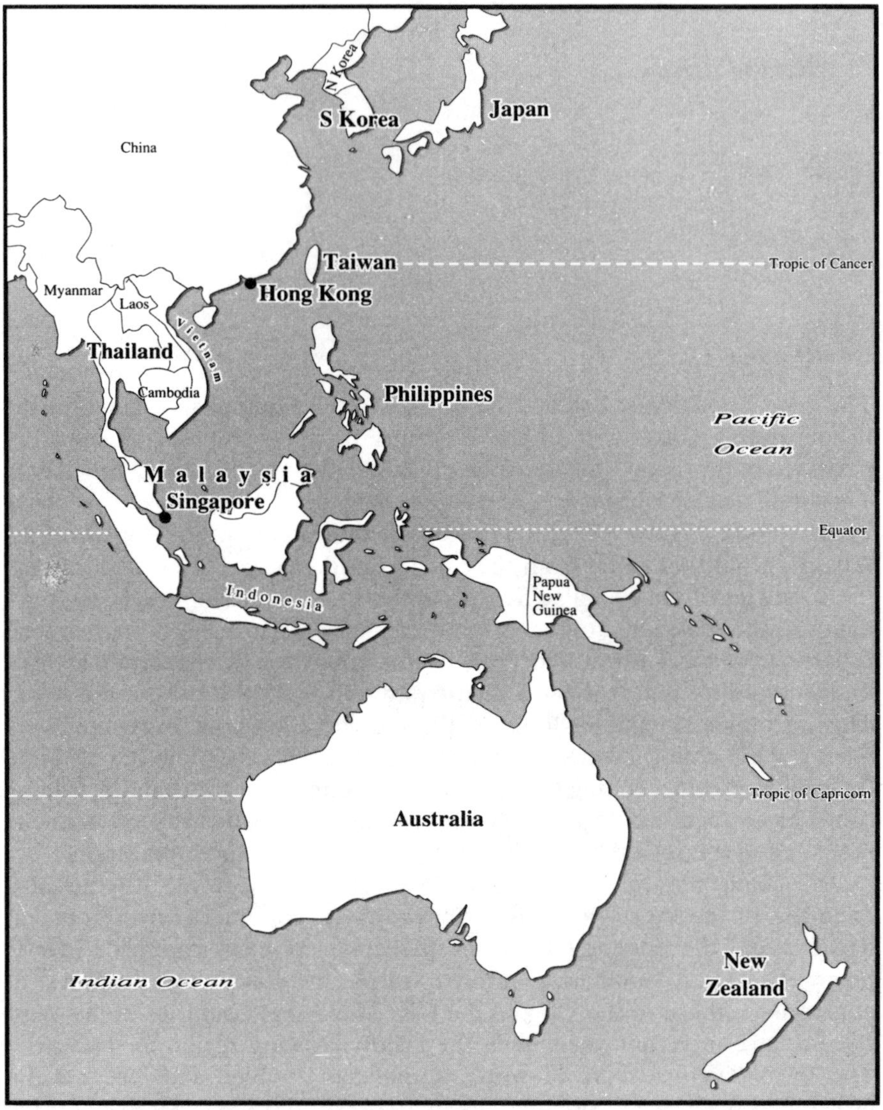

Figure 1.1 The West Pacific Rim

Note: Based upon a Mercator projection, therefore the scale increases in the higher latitudes.

Table 1.1 Growth in gross domestic product (per cent per annum)

	Average			
	1960–70	*1970–80*	*1980–90*	*1991*
Australia	5.6	3.0	3.4	−1.2
Hong Kong	10.0	9.3	7.1	4.0
Japan	10.4	5.0	4.1	4.4
South Korea	8.6	9.5	9.7	8.3
Malaysia	6.5	7.8	5.2	8.6
New Zealand	3.6	2.3	1.9	−1.8
Philippines	5.1	6.3	0.9	−1.0
Singapore	8.8	8.5	6.4	7.0
Taiwan	10.0	9.7	8.5	7.3
Thailand	8.4	7.2	7.6	7.5
UK	2.9	1.9	3.1	−2.2
US	4.3	3.0	3.4	−1.2

Sources: World Bank, *World Development Report*, Table 2 (1982, 1984, 1992); Asian Development Bank, *Asian Development Outlook* 1992; OECD *Economic Outlook*, December 1992; Mackie (1988), p. 286.

occupying powers imposed their own ideas of accounting on the countries they colonized or occupied. The region as a whole has never experienced any semblance of overall political unity. Political control has been exercised in the region at one time or another by all the major European and North American colonizing powers but no one of them succeeded in imposing its exclusive imprint. A brief summary of the political history and current political status of each West Pacific Rim country is given below:

- *Australia.* Settled by British from 1788 onwards. Separate colonies federated as the Commonwealth of Australia from 1 January 1901. Independent member of the British Commonwealth.
- *Hong Kong.* Acquired by Britain from China in three stages (1842, 1860, 1898). Occupied by Japanese 1942–5. A British colony until reversion to Chinese rule in 1997.
- *Japan.* After early European contacts in the mid-sixteenth century, closed to the outside world until 1853. Modernization and Europeanization began with the Meiji Restoration in 1868. Successful in war with Russia 1904–5. Annexed Korea 1910. Invaded Manchuria 1932. Entered Second World War 1941. Occupied by Allied forces 1945–51. Became member of United Nations 1956.
- *Korea (South).* Annexed by Japan 1910. Divided into South and North Korea 1945. Korean War 1950–3. Both Koreas became members of United Nations 1991.
- *Malaysia.* Malay states under British influence from nineteenth

century. Japanese occupation 1942–5. Malayan Federation (peninsular Malaya, including Singapore) independent state within the British Commonwealth from 1957. Malaysia formed by addition of Sarawak and Sabah 1963. Singapore seceded 1965.

- *New Zealand.* Treaty of Waitangi 1840 followed by British colonization. Dominion (self-governing) status from 1907. Independent member of the British Commonwealth.
- *Philippines.* Colonized by Spain from sixteenth century. Ceded to USA 1898 after Spanish American War. Occupied by Japan 1942–5. Independent republic from 1946. Dominated by Ferdinand Marcos 1965–86.
- *Singapore.* Ceded to Britain (represented by Sir Stamford Raffles) 1819. Centre of government for the Straits Settlements 1832. Occupied by Japan 1942–5. Internal self-government 1959. Part of Malaysian Federation 1963–5. Independent republic within the British Commonwealth since 1965.
- *Taiwan.* Island territory (also known as Formosa) ceded to Japan by China after Sino–Japanese War 1894. Returned to China 1945. Did not become part of People's Republic of China in 1949.

Table 1.2 Some basic economic indicators

	Population 1990 (millions)	*Urban population as % of total population 1990*	*Area (thousands of sq. km)*	*GDP 1990 (US$m)*	*GNP per capita 1990 (US$)*
High-income economies:					
Japan	123.5	77	378	2,942,890	25,430
US	250.0	75	9,373	5,392,200	21,790
Australia	17.1	86	7,687	296,300	17,000
UK	57.4	89	245	975,150	16,100
New Zealand	3.4	84	269	42,760	12,680
Hong Kong	5.8	94	1	59,670	11,490
Singapore	3.0	100	1	34,600	11,160
Upper-middle-income economy:					
South Korea	42.8	72	99	236,400	5,400
Lower-middle-income economies:					
Malaysia	17.9	43	330	42,400	2,320
Thailand	55.8	23	513	80,170	1,420
Philippines	61.5	43	300	43,860	730

Source: World Bank, *World Development Report 1992*, Tables 1, 3, 31.

Table 1.3 Structure of merchandise exports (percentage shares)

	Fuels, minerals and metals	*Other primary commodities*	*Machinery and transport equipment*	*Textiles and clothing*	*Other manufactures*
Australia	34	29	6	1	29
Hong Kong	1	3	23	34	39
Japan	1	1	66	2	30
South Korea	2	5	37	22	35
Malaysia	19	37	27	5	12
New Zealand	10	65	5	2	18
Philippines	12	26	10	7	45
Singapore	19	8	48	5	20
Taiwan	3	5	36	15	42
Thailand	2	34	20	16	28

Source: World Bank, *World Development Report 1992*, Table 16.

- *Thailand*. Independent kingdom (formerly known as Siam) never under colonial rule. Commercial treaty with Britain 1855. After Second World War much influenced by USA.

The only regional inter-country political organization of importance is the Association of South-East Asian Nations (ASEAN) which has as members Indonesia, Malaysia, the Philippines, Singapore, Thailand and (since 1984) Brunei. ASEAN was established in 1967 and is generally accepted as having increased the region's political stability. Economic co-operation among ASEAN countries has been less successful but is increasing.

Table 1.4 Structure of merchandise imports (percentage shares)

	Food	*Fuels*	*Other primary commodities*	*Machinery and transport equipment*	*Other manufactures*
Australia	5	5	4	42	44
Hong Kong	6	2	5	26	60
Japan	14	25	16	16	30
South Korea	5	16	15	34	29
Malaysia	11	5	6	45	33
New Zealand	7	8	4	41	41
Philippines	10	13	7	20	50
Singapore	5	16	5	42	32
Taiwan	6	9	14	37	34
Thailand	5	9	8	41	37

Source: World Bank, *World Development Report 1992*, Table 15.

Economically, the countries of the region can be classified, as the World Bank does, into high-income economies (Japan, Australia, New Zealand, Hong Kong and Singapore), upper-middle-income economies (Republic of Korea) and lower-middle-income economies (Malaysia, Thailand and the Philippines). Some basic economic indicators are given in Table 1.2. The US and the UK are included to provide a comparison. Tables 1.3 to 1.5 provide data relating to the structure of merchandise exports and imports and each country's major trading partners.

A combination of both political and economic factors provides four groupings:

1 *Japan*, the economic giant of the region, with a GDP about four times greater than all the other West Pacific countries combined; a GDP per capita income exceeding that of the USA and the countries of the EC; a stock exchange in Tokyo comparable in size to that in New York; and a very large share of the world's largest industrial corporations and banks;
2 the *settler economies* of Australia and New Zealand dependent upon the export of primary products (see Table 1.3) with relatively high GNP per capita but low growth rates compared with the other countries of the region;
3 the *newly industrializing economies* (NIEs) of Hong Kong, Singapore, the Republic of Korea and Taiwan which have attained relatively high GDP per capita quite recently by means of export-led industrial growth;
4 the *emerging industrializing economies* (sometimes referred to as the new NIEs) of Malaysia, Thailand and the Philippines, growing fast but still largely agricultural (the growth rate of the Philippines has been slowed by political instability).

Japan, Australia and New Zealand, but not the others, are members of the Organisation for Economic Co-operation and Development (OECD) which represents the world's developed economies.

The division of ten countries into four groups underlines the region's diversity. It must be further noted that there is diversity within each group. Australians and New Zealanders have always been at pains to point out the differences between them, although to many outside observers these are more apparent than real. Tables 1.3 and 1.4 demonstrate the dependence of both countries (much more than the other countries of the region other than Malaysia) on the export of primary commodities and the import of manufactures. They differ in that Australia has much greater resources of minerals, including oil.

The four newly industrializing economies are more heterogeneous. As Bollard *et al.* (1989: 7) point out, the differences include size of economy, domestic market and natural resources, as well as historical background and political and socio-cultural characteristics. Hong Kong and Singapore

Table 1.5 Direction of trade

	Imports	*Exports*
Australia	USA Japan UK	Japan USA South Korea
Hong Kong	China Japan Taiwan	China USA Germany
Japan	USA China Australia	USA Germany South Korea
Malaysia	Japan Singapore USA	Singapore USA Japan
New Zealand	Australia USA Japan	Australia Japan USA
Philippines	Japan USA Hong Kong	USA Japan Germany
Singapore	Japan USA Malaysia	USA Malaysia Hong Kong
South Korea	Japan USA Germany	USA Japan Hong Kong
Taiwan (1987)	Japan USA Hong Kong	USA Japan Hong Kong
Thailand	Japan USA Singapore	USA Japan Singapore

Sources: International Monetary Fund, *Direction of Trade Statistics* December 1992; Choo and Ali (1989), Table 10.

are densely populated city states with few natural resources other than geographical situation and the enterprise of their people. Both have open economies. They differ in the role of government (Fong 1988: 226–33). The colonial government of Hong Kong has limited itself to providing political stability and economic conditions permitting the free operation of market forces. The government of Singapore has, unlike the other NIEs, actively encouraged foreign direct investment: almost three-quarters of the republic's manufactures are produced by fully or majority owned foreign enterprises. The Singapore government is much more interventionist than that of Hong Kong and there has been a considerable amount of government investment. The Korean and Taiwanese economies have been less open and, until recently, foreign direct investment has not been encouraged. Public ownership is relatively more important in Korea than in the other three NIEs. The small firm is characteristic of Hong Kong; conglomerates (*chaebol*) of Korea. The three emerging industrializing countries have differences and similarities. All three continue to depend to a considerable degree upon the export of primary commodities – much more so than the NIEs but less than Australia and New Zealand (see Table 1.3). Malaysia is predominantly Muslim, Thailand Buddhist and the Philippines Roman Catholic. Malaysia is the most multiracial; Thailand is prone to military *coups d'état*; and the Philippines is the most politically unstable.

The trade of the West Pacific is increasingly intra-regional, having grown from about 40 per cent in the early 1960s to about 50 per cent in the late 1980s (Anderson 1991: 1540–1). There has been a strengthening of trade linkages among the NIEs (including Malaysia and Thailand) and between them and Japan (Choo and Ali 1989: 9). Table 1.5 provides data on the direction of trade.

The regional economic giants of the Pacific as a whole are the USA and Japan and this is reflected in both trade and investment flows. In broad terms a trade pattern has developed in which Japan supplies consumer and capital goods to the USA and to the West Pacific countries (Japan trades more with Asia than with North America but the USA is its largest single trade partner); the USA supplies both manufactured goods and agricultural goods to the West Pacific; the commodity producers supply Japan with raw materials; and the NIEs (old and new) send consumer goods to the USA and, increasingly, to Japan. At the same time, for good historical and geographical reasons, there is much trade between Hong Kong and China, between Singapore and Malaysia, and between New Zealand and Australia.

There has been much discussion recently of the possibility of a West Pacific free trade area (FTA). Anderson (1991: 1549) argues that the likelihood of a West Pacific FTA is remote for three reasons. First, the smaller countries would be unwilling to form a trade bloc with Japan for fear of Japanese domination in the absence of a North American counterweight. Second, even if North America were invited to join a Pacific FTA it would be unlikely to do so because of domestic political pressures. Third, Asian governments would find it difficult politically (despite the economic benefits) to remove their high barriers to agricultural imports from North America or even from Australia and New Zealand.

The alternative is to continue to strive for a strong open global trading system through the medium, *inter alia*, of the Asian–Pacific Economic Cooperation (APEC) group established in the late 1980s, which now includes all the countries dealt with in this book plus the USA, Canada,

Communist China and North Korea. The division of the world into three economic trade blocs (Europe, North America, West Pacific) is not in the interests of the countries of the West Pacific whose economic growth continues to depend on exports, whether industrial or agricultural.

The major sources of inward foreign direct investment throughout the region are Japan and the United States. Japanese industry, in order to remain competitive, is increasingly moving its plants into the other Asian West Pacific countries. At the same time the NIEs (old and new) are progressing beyond being merely assemblers of Japanese supplied parts and are manufacturing low-cost components for export to Japan and to Japanese-owned factories in the region. The old NIEs are investing in the new NIEs. Labour-intensive manufacturing is being relocated from higher-wage to lower-wage Asian economies (Riedel 1991).

EXPLANATIONS FOR ECONOMIC GROWTH

The post-Second World War economic success of Japan, the newly industrializing economies and the emerging industrializing economies has naturally given rise to great debate and a search for explanations amongst economists, sociologists and political scientists. No consensus has been reached and we can do no more here than briefly note some of the arguments. Both economic and cultural factors have been emphasized.

Economists have, not surprisingly, stressed economic explanations. ‘It is now widely accepted’, claims Hughes (1989: 128), ‘that the success of the Asian NIEs is not the result of cultural factors but of economic policy choices.’ According to Little (1981, cited in Riedel 1988: 23), ‘cultural factors cannot be more than contributory factors, which may play their part, but only when other conditions are favourable’. On the other hand, writers such as Kahn (1979) and Morishima (1982) have stressed the influence of the Confucianist values of respect for authority, loyalty to good leaders, preference for order, and a taste for education and hard work. To these the Japanese have added a preference for harmony (Lehmann 1988: 14). The Confucian work ethic has been compared with Max Weber’s concept of a Protestant work ethic, in spite of the fact that Weber himself viewed Confucianism as stressing the maintenance of tradition rather than favouring economic and social progress. However, the cultural values that relate to growth in one historical period may not, it is claimed, do so in another (Bond and Hofstede 1990: 389). Hirono (1988: 243) is sceptical of this line of reasoning, arguing that the way in which ideologies are interpreted in business behaviour is mainly a reflection of economic policies: ‘the Confucian ideology, like others, was suited either to stagnation or to growth: actual outcomes depended on the particular combination of economic circumstances and policies’. Fong (1988: 235) suggests that the cultural arguments are based on a selective interpretation of Confucianism, but also points out that purely economic factors cannot fully explain why the right growth-inducing policies came both to be chosen and to be effectively implemented (ibid.: 224). Sociologists and political scientists tend to regard purely economic explanations as insufficient and have constructed concepts of 'economic culture' and 'industrial culture', arguing, for example, that economic processes operate within a 'social, political, and cultural matrix or context' (Berger 1987: 7) and that each country has its own industrial culture which helps to determine the relationship between industry and the state (Wilks 1990). The recent experience of New Zealand demonstrates the difficulties of achieving growth merely by adopting the 'right' economic policies. Reynolds (1983: 976), looking at the historical evidence 1850–1980, concluded that the single most important explanatory variable was political organization and the administrative competence of government.

The minimal role of government is to supply public goods and infrastructure or, as Adam Smith (*Wealth of Nations*, Book V) put it, protection from external 'violence and invasion' and internal 'injustice or oppression' plus those 'public works and ... public institutions, which it can never be for the interest of any individual, or small number of individuals, to erect and maintain'. All the Pacific Rim countries (with the possible exception of Hong Kong) have, however, gone beyond this minimal role. They have established systems of industrial incentives; claimed exclusive responsibility for maintaining macroeconomic stability; and (perhaps less successfully) established not only public utility enterprises but also public enterprises to produce private goods.

Hughes's conclusion (1988: xv–xvi) is that 'unshackling exports' has been the key to success and that political stability and the rule of law are necessary preconditions. Governments must practise successful macroeconomic management and invest in social and physical infrastructure. Governments in the capitalist countries of the Asian Pacific Rim have provided the environment for growth, she argues, but private enterprise has produced it by making the necessary investments and becoming efficient and profitable through exposure to international competition. It could be counter-argued that economic growth in Japan, Korea and Taiwan has been based on tariff protection. Japan has now reduced its tariffs in areas where it can compete successfully, but not with agricultural products where it cannot compete.

Why have the emerging industrializing economies (Malaysia, Thailand and the Philippines) not yet achieved the growth rates of the NIEs of Singapore, Hong Kong, Taiwan and Korea? Mackie (1988) suggests five reasons:

1 They all have relatively large rural hinterlands not yet drawn into the orbit of a modern, capital intensive, commercialized economy. (Column 2, Table 1.2, which shows urban population as a percentage of total population, strikingly illustrates this point.)

2 The economic structures and policies inherited from the former colonial rulers of Malaysia and the Philippines have had distorting effects inappropriate to the requirements of rapid growth. The economic and political costs of dealing with these have been much greater than in the NIEs.
3 The dominance of investment from the former colonial power has posed difficulties and created constraints.
4 The dominant position of Chinese businessmen has led governments to implement measures disadvantageous to ethnic Chinese which have sacrificed the maximization of economic efficiency to the imperatives of economic nationalism.
5 Domestic savings rates have been relatively low. Hence local businessmen have had to rely relatively heavily on the state for credit and subsidies.

FINANCIAL SYSTEMS AND FINANCIAL REPORTING

Part of each country's industrial culture is its financial system. This provides yet another way of classifying the ten countries, and one which is highly relevant to financial reporting. Zysman (1983) distinguishes between three types of financial system: (1) a capital market-based financial system, in which prices are established in competitive markets; (2) a credit-based financial system in which prices are administered by the government; and (3) a credit-based financial system dominated by financial institutions. In his view, the UK and the USA have a type 1 system; France and Japan a type 2 system; and Germany a type 3 system.

In a capital market system, securities are the main source of external long-term finance. There is a wide range of capital and money market instruments and a large number of specialized financial institutions competing in terms of price and service. Prices are largely determined by supply and demand and financial institutions have arm's-length relations with particular companies. In credit-based financial systems the capital market is relatively small and companies depend heavily on credit for raising finance beyond retaining earnings and are thus dependent on whoever controls credit. The main suppliers of credit are usually banks which may be either relatively dependent or independent of government. If they are dependent it is the government which sets financial prices and, through these prices and through its control of the allocation of bank lending, exercises a powerful influence over investment.

In a capital market-based financial system investors make their entrances and exits through the mechanism of secondary markets in which securities can be readily bought and sold. In a credit-based system, on the other hand, entrance and exit is more difficult. Investors (especially financial institutions) are therefore less likely to sell their holdings and more likely to attempt to influence the actions of management.

There are several potential advantages of a credit-based market system over a capital market-based system for a developing country suffering from 'capital market failure' (Wade 1988). First, a credit-based system in a developing country permits faster investment because it is not dependent upon the growth of retained profits or the inevitably slow development of a securities market. Second, a credit-based system encourages more rapid mobility between sectors of the economy and permits the government to guide that mobility. Third, a credit-based system helps to avoid a bias towards 'short-termism'. Fourth, governments can more easily pursue a consistent industrial strategy through their control of credit.

These advantages are potential only and some of them rely heavily on the ability of governments and civil servants 'to pick winners', an ability which experience in many countries suggests cannot be taken for granted. Nevertheless, the examples of Japan, Korea, Taiwan and, outside the region, Germany show that a credit-based financial system can be used to deliver economic growth. It is also clear, however, that a capital market-based financial system may be equally effective.

The distinction between capital market-based and credit-based financial systems is not an absolute one. In particular, an expanding economy with a credit-based financial system may seek to move in part towards a capital market-based financial system. As pointed out by Cooke in Chapter 2, Zysman (1983) was correct in arguing that Japan before the 1980s had a credit-based financial system in which prices were administered by the government. More recently some liberalization has occurred and a wide variety of instruments have emerged that are akin to a capital market-based

Table 1.6 West Pacific stock exchanges (compared with New York and the UK)

	Number of domestic companies	*Market value of domestic equity (£m)*	*Market value of domestic equity as % of Tokyo*
Australia	968	77,465	4.79
Hong Kong	333	65,415	4.05
South Korea	686	51,504	3.19
Kuala Lumpur	321	30,816	1.91
Makati (Philippines)	161	5,701	0.35
New Zealand	139	7,642	0.47
Osaka	1,158	1,324,197	81.96
Singapore	157	31,219	1.93
Taiwan	221	66,127	4.09
Thailand	276	19,843	1.23
Tokyo	1,641	1,615,683	100.00
New York	1,780	1,895,717	117.33
UK	1,915	541,165	33.49

Source: London Stock Exchange, *Stock Exchange Quarterly*, July–September 1992, Table F.1.

financial system. These market-based innovations do not, however, fit easily with a financial system in which brokerage houses have sometimes guaranteed returns to corporate clients. Guaranteed returns were possible because of the dominant position of brokerage houses and an economy with surplus savings and growth in the money supply. The revelation of scandals on the Tokyo Stock Exchange may reflect the difficulties of transition from one financial system to another but it is more likely that the credit-based financial system will become more sophisticated. In addition, the tightening of monetary policy by the Bank of Japan has been very influential in terminating what had seemed to be perpetual growth in prices. The 38 percentage decrease in share prices in 1990 provided a shock to the system.

Table 1.6 provides data on West Pacific stock exchanges. In terms of market capitalization, the overwhelming predominance of Japan is again apparent and Tokyo is, of course, along with New York and London, one of the world's three leading stock exchanges. On the other hand, comparison of the number of domestic companies with equity shares suggests that the relative importance of the stock market is greater in other countries than in Japan. Table 1.7 sets out the number of companies in each country with sales in excess of £1,000 million.

Countries in the West Pacific region most likely to have a capital market-based system are those which have inherited one (or the concept of one) from a former colonial power and those which are relatively open to external investment. In the West Pacific Rim region, Australia, New Zealand, Hong Kong, Singapore and Malaysia fall into both these categories. Japan, Korea and Taiwan provide good examples of type 2

Table 1.7 Number of companies (excluding Japan) with sales in excess of £1,000 million

	Number of companies
Australia	18
South Korea	13
Hong Kong	6
Taiwan	4
Singapore	3
Malaysia	1
New Zealand	0
Philippines	0
Thailand	0

Source: *The Times 1,000, 1991/92* (*1990/91* for Korea, Taiwan, New Zealand, Philippines and Thailand).

Note: Japan has 58, Australia 3 and Korea 2 companies with sales in excess of £4,000 million.

credit-based systems. The Philippines inherited a capital market-based system from its US colonizers but its stock markets have not been a significant source of funds because most corporations are closely held. Thailand was never a colony but has encouraged foreign direct investment. Its stock market remains relatively underdeveloped.

Whether or not a country has a capital market-based or a credit-based financial system will influence its corporate financial reporting. A capital market-based system is likely to lead to a greater emphasis on public disclosure and external audit than a credit-based system since investors are shareholders rather than creditors and will demand credible information – to which as outsiders they will not otherwise have access – to help them make their decisions to buy and sell. To the extent that shareholders are not outsiders, however (because, for example they are large and powerful financial institutions as in the UK, as well as Japan, but not in the US), the pressure for public rather than private disclosure may be less. The market, however, may not produce an agreed set of measurement rules nor will these necessarily be provided directly by government. The gap may be filled by professional accountancy bodies who have a vested interest in maintaining the credibility of financial reporting.

In a credit-based system there are few perceived virtues in a system of public disclosure since the major investors are governments or financial institutions which are likely to have privileged access to accounting information and will see no need to share it with outsiders. In the West Pacific, as elsewhere (Nobes and Parker 1991), a broad distinction can be made between, on the one hand, 'Anglo-Saxon'-type corporate financial reporting which is commercially driven, dependent on business practice and professional rules, emphasizing the needs of shareholders and lacking in uniformity, and, on the other hand, 'Continental European'-type corporate financial reporting which is government-driven, dependent on tax rules, emphasizing the needs of creditors rather than shareholders and insistent on uniformity. Readers of the chapters which follow who are familiar with European and North American accounting should easily recognize the similarity of Japanese and Korean accounting to that in Germany and France, and that of accounting in most of the other countries

Table 1.8 Differences in gearing, profitability and liquidity

	USA	*Japan*	*South Korea*
Total debt to total assets	47%	84%	78%
Times interest earned	6.50	1.60	1.80
Return on net worth	13.9%	7.1%	13.1%

Source: Choi *et al.* (1983), Exhibit 1.

Note: Ratios refer to 902 US manufacturing firms, 976 Japanese and 354 Korean.

Table 1.9 Evolution of gearing ratios (USA and Japan)

	1970 (%)	*1975 (%)*	*1980 (%)*	*1985 (%)*	*1986 (%)*	*1987 (%)*
USA	45	52	50	50	49	51
Japan	86	83	84	73*	63	59

Source: Cooke and Kikuya (1992), p. 46.

Note: *Indicates a break in the series. Gearing is measured by ratio of gross debt to total assets (market values).

to that in the UK and the USA. These similarities remain despite the great post-Second World War influence of US accounting throughout the West Pacific and especially in Japan, Korea and Taiwan. We discuss later in this chapter the importance of these similarities in the context of harmonization.

One would expect companies operating under a credit-based financial system to be more highly geared (levered) than those operating under a capital market-based system. They may also have lower profitability ratios both because of a lack of short-termism and because of more conservative tax and creditor-oriented accounting policies. That this is, in fact, the case is illustrated by Choi *et al.*'s (1983) analysis of US, Japanese and Korean companies. Table 1.8 shows comparative ratios relating to total debt as a percentage of total assets, times interest earned and return on net worth. In the 1980s, however, the gap between US and Japanese gearing ratios narrowed (see Table 1.9).

Capital market-based corporate financial reporting requires a larger and more developed accountancy profession than does credit-based financial reporting. The size of a national accountancy profession also depends on the extent to which it is composed of accountants working in commerce and industry as well as in professional accountancy firms. The employment of professionally qualified accountants in companies is high in the UK, less high in the US and very low in Japan and Germany. Table 1.10 provides data regarding the age and size of public accountancy bodies within the West Pacific Rim. The largest and oldest bodies are to be found in Australia, the Philippines and New Zealand. New Zealand probably has more accountants per head of population (approximately five persons in every thousand) than any other country in the world. Unlike Australia, however, it is too small to have been a founder member of the International Accounting Standards Committee or the venue of an international congress of accountants. The only other West Pacific country to share these distinctions has been Japan. This has been in recognition of the importance of its economy rather than of that of its accountancy profession which like that of the Republic of Korea and Taiwan is small relative to the size of its economy (and, indeed, smaller than that of New Zealand). A sign of the

Table 1.10 Age and size of public accountancy bodies

Country	*Body*	*Founding date*	*Approx. membership 1990 (thousands)*
Australia	Australian Society of Certified Practising Accountants;	1952 (1887)	57
	Institute of Chartered Accountants in Australia	1928 (1886)	19
Hong Kong	Hong Kong Society of Accountants	1973	5
Japan	Japanese Institute of Certified Public Accountants	1948 (1927)	9
South Korea	Korean Institute of Certified Public Accountants	1954	2
Malaysia	Malaysian Association of Certified Public Accountants;	1958	2
	Malaysian Institute of Accountants	1967	6
New Zealand	New Zealand Society of Accountants	1909 (1894)	17
Philippines	Philippine Institute of Certified Public Accountants	1929 (1923)	23
Singapore	Institute of Certified Public Accountants of Singapore	1963	6
Taiwan	National Federation of CPA Associations of the Republic of China	1946	2

Table 1.10 (continued)

Thailand	Institute of Certified Accountants and Auditors of Thailand	1948	1

Notes: The date of the earliest predecessor body appears in brackets. The titles of some of the bodies have changed from time to time.

increasing importance of the region in accounting terms is the holding of international congresses of accountants in Sydney (1972) and in Tokyo (1987).

This suggests that, to accountants, the leading countries of the region are Japan and Australia. Although Nobes and Parker (1991: ch. 1), following Mason (1978), argue that Japan is a 'vital' country without whose support the international harmonization of financial reporting cannot be achieved (the other vital countries are the USA, the UK, Germany, France and The Netherlands) it cannot be said that Japan has yet had any strong influence on the development of corporate financial reporting world-wide.[2] Australia is not regarded by these authors as a 'vital' country, on the grounds that it is unlikely to take any action to forestall any accounting endeavour supported by both the USA and the UK. Whilst this is true, Australian accountants, so long as they do not stray too far from the US/UK consensus, do have an influence, especially through the International Accounting Standards Committee. Moreover, Australian accounting rules and practices influence those of Malaysia and Singapore.

The total personnel (partners plus professional and administrative staff)

Table 1.11 Relative importance of sources of rules on corporate financial reporting practice

	Company law or commercial code	*Tax law*	*Stock exchange requirements*	*Regulatory body*	*Accounting standards body*
Australia	/	×	+	+	/
Hong Kong	/	×	+	+	/
Japan	/	/	/	×	/
South Korea	/	/	×	/	/
Malaysia	/	×	+	×	/
New Zealand	/	×	+	×	/
Philippines	+	×	+	/	/
Singapore	/	×	+	×	/
Taiwan	/	/	×	+	/
Thailand	/	×	/	+	+

Key: / very important; + of some importance; × of little importance.

Table 1.12 Accounting standards-setting bodies of the Pacific Rim countries

	Body	*Membership*	*Remarks*
Australia	Australian Accounting Standards Board	Appointed by federal attorney-general from the profession, commerce, stock exchange and academia. In practice, are qualified accountants.	Issues accounting standards which have legal backing. Standards are prepared by Australian Accounting Research Foundation.
Hong Kong	Accounting Standards Committee (of the Hong Kong Society of Accountants)	Members of HKSA from large and small audit firms, industry and stock exchange.	Issues both Standards (mandatory for members of HKSA) and Guidelines (recommended practice).
Japan	Business Accounting Deliberation Council (of the Ministry of Finance)	Members from industry, accountancy profession, government, universities.	Prepares Business Accounting Principles which are issued by the Ministry of Finance.
South Korea	Accounting System Deliberation Committee (of the SEC)	Representatives of the SEC, KICPA, and business and academic associations concerned with accounting practice.	Prepares Accounting Standards for Business Enterprises for approval by the Ministry of Finance.
Malaysia	Accounting and Auditing Standards Committee (of MACPA and MIA)	Members of MACPA and MIA.	Issues Malaysian Accounting Standards (MAS); also adopts IASs with a local foreword.
New Zealand	Accounting Standards Committee (of the New Zealand Society of Accountants)	Members of NZSA.	Issues Statements of Standard Accounting Practice (SSAPs).

Philippines	Accounting Standards Council (autonomous body set up by the Philippine Institute of Certified Public Accountants and supported by regulatory agencies)	Four members from PICPA plus one each from Securities and Exchange Commission, Central Bank, Financial Executives Institute, and Professional Regulation Commission.	Issues Statements of Financial Accounting Standards (SFASs).
Singapore	Accounting Standards Committee (of the Institute of Certified Public Accountants of Singapore)	Members of the ICPAS.	Issues Statements of Accounting Standards based on IASs. Also issues Statements of Recommended Accounting Practice. Compliance is monitored by the Financial Statement Review Committee of ICPAS.
Taiwan	Financial Accounting Standards Committee (of the Accounting Research & Development Foundation)	Government officials, practising CPAs, academics, representatives of commercial and industrial organizations.	Issues Statements of Financial Accounting Standards and Auditing Standards. Compliance is mandatory for public companies; monitored by Securities and Exchange Commission.
Thailand	Committee on Financial Accounting Standards (of the Institute of Certified Accountants and Auditors of Thailand)	Members from ICAAT, practice, academia and the Ministry of Finance.	Issues Statements of Financial Accounting Standards, compliance with which is required by the Board of Supervision of Auditing Practices and the Stock Exchange of Thailand.

of the Big Six international accountancy firms in the region is dependent upon the size of the national accountancy bodies as well as the size of the economies. In 1989 there were about 12,800 staff in Australia, 5,400 in Japan, 4,100 in Hong Kong, 3,200 in Malaysia, 2,500 in Singapore and 800 in Thailand (Ernst & Whinney 1989: 3).

DIVERSITY IN FINANCIAL REPORTING

There are great differences in the styles of corporate financial reporting in the ten countries of the West Pacific Rim, but there are also similarities and incentives for a narrowing of the differences. The differences and similarities relate both to the ways in which accounting rules are established and to the content of those rules. Table 1.11 summarizes the relative importance of the various influences (company law or commercial code, tax law, stock exchange requirements, regulatory body, accounting standards body) on financial reporting in each country. In interpreting this table it is important to realize that the strength of an influence may vary with the type of company. In particular, stock exchange requirements apply only to public listed companies and the requirements of regulatory bodies and accounting standards bodies may not apply in full or at all to small companies. The table demonstrates that the provisions of company law (or of a commercial code) are important in all countries but that tax law is influential only in Japan, Korea and Taiwan. Stock exchange requirements are of major importance in Japan and Thailand. A regulatory body is of major importance in the Philippines (because of US influence) and of some importance in Australia. An accounting standard-setting body is important in all countries but the table fails to capture their great variety. Information on this is given in Table 1.12. Since accounting standard-setting bodies need both technical skills and powers of enforcement, all tend to be influenced by both government and professional accountants. The extent to which each predominates varies considerably as the table shows.

There are several ways in which corporate financial reporting can be regulated. If the process is left entirely to market forces, each company will choose its own rules, influenced only by pressures from, in particular, the capital market. At another extreme the whole process can be in the hands of the state, an organ of which decrees which practices are to be followed and provides an enforcement mechanism. Puxty *et al.* (1987) distinguish a continuum of regulatory modes: 'liberalism', in which regulation is provided exclusively by the discipline of the market; 'legalism' in which accounting practice follows the letter of the law, which is enforced by the state's monopoly of the means of coercion; 'associationism' in which regulation is accomplished through the development of organizations (e.g. professional accountancy bodies) that are formed to represent and advance the interests of their members; and 'corporatism' in which the state not only licenses the existence of organized interest groups but incorporates them into its own centralized, hierarchical system of regulation. The difference between corporatism and associationism lies in the extent to which the state 'leans' on interest groupings to achieve public (i.e. state) as contrasted with private (i.e. market) purposes.

Puxty *et al.* suggest that the UK has an associationist system of accounting regulation whereas the US is both legalist and associationist, with the latter subordinated to the former. Applying their concepts to the countries of the Pacific Rim, a study of Tables 1.11 and 1.12 and of the detailed information provided in the chapters that follow suggests the following:

- Legalistic: Japan, Korea, Taiwan.
- Corporatist: Malaysia, Singapore, Thailand, Philippines.
- Corporatist/associationist: Australia.
- Associationist: Hong Kong, New Zealand.

Technical skills can be borrowed from other countries. The extent to which national accounting standards are influenced by those of the International Accounting Standards Committee and those of other countries is indicated below:

- *Australia.* Influenced by accounting standards in, especially, the US and UK. Takes account of IASs. Founder member of the IASC.
- *Hong Kong.* Strongly influenced by UK SSAPs; IASs of increasing importance but not adopted as such.
- *Japan.* Founder member of the IASC but national accounting standards not much influenced by foreign standards or IASs.
- *South Korea.* Influenced by US accounting standards. Takes account of IASs.
- *Malaysia.* IASs adapted to local conditions. Influenced by accounting standards in the UK, Australia, the US.
- *New Zealand.* Influenced by accounting standards, in, especially, the US and UK. Takes account of IASs.
- *Philippines.* Influenced by US accounting standards. Takes account of IASs.
- *Singapore.* IASs adapted to local conditions. Influenced by accounting standards in the UK, Australia, the US.
- *Taiwan.* Mainly influenced by US accounting standards. IASs used only for reference.
- *Thailand.* Influenced by US accounting standards. Takes account of IASs.

Again there is diversity: Malaysia and Singapore use IASs as the starting point for almost all their standards; Hong Kong relies heavily on UK standards; Australia, New Zealand and the Philippines set their own standards but are influenced by IASs and the standards of the US and the

UK; Japan, Korea, Taiwan and Thailand are much less influenced by external standards.

Diversity in measurement rules is illustrated below by reference to tax effect accounting (deferred taxation):

- *Australia.* Tax effect accounting required by accounting standard. Comprehensive allocation and liability method.
- *Hong Kong.* Tax effect accounting required by accounting standard. Partial allocation and liability method.
- *Japan.* Tax effect accounting not practised, except in annual reports published in English for international consumption.
- *South Korea.* Tax effect accounting not required or practised.
- *Malaysia.* Tax effect accounting required by accounting standard, but no requirements as to whether comprehensive or partial allocation, deferral or liability method.
- *New Zealand.* Tax effect accounting required by accounting standard. Comprehensive allocation more common than partial allocation. Liability method.
- *Philippines.* Tax effect accounting not required by law or accounting standard but recommended by PICPA. Infrequent in practice. When used, comprehensive allocation and deferral method.
- *Singapore.* Tax effect accounting required by accounting standard, but no requirements as to whether comprehensive or partial allocation, deferral or liability method.
- *Taiwan.* Tax effect accounting not practised.
- *Thailand.* Tax effect accounting recommended by accounting exposure draft, but no requirements as to whether comprehensive or partial allocation, deferral or liability method.

This reveals major differences. Those countries (Japan, Korea, Taiwan) in which tax legislation is a major influence on financial reporting practice do not normally practise tax effect accounting. Those that do vary in the methods used. Despite US influence on its accounting, tax effect accounting is not required by law or accounting standard in the Philippines and is infrequent in practice. Malaysia and Singapore follow the permissive international standard which allows both comprehensive and partial allocation and both the liability and deferral methods. Hong Kong follows the UK standard. In Thailand tax effect accounting is recommended but there are no specific requirements. Australia and New Zealand have requirements very similar to those in the US.

CLASSIFICATION OF FINANCIAL REPORTING

Earlier in this chapter the countries of the West Pacific were classified on economic and political criteria into four groups: Japan; settler economies (Australia, New Zealand); newly industrializing economies (Hong Kong,

Singapore, South Korea, Taiwan); and emerging industrializing economies (Malaysia, Philippines, Thailand). One possible alternative classification follows the concept of 'culture areas'. According to Hofstede (1980), Australia and New Zealand are in an 'Anglo' culture area; Japan in a 'more developed Asian'; Taiwan, Thailand, Malaysia and the Philippines in a 'less developed Asian'; and Hong Kong and Singapore in a 'colonial Asian'. (South Korea was not included in Hofstede's study.) The two classifications differ only in their treatment of the NIEs, whose heterogeneity has already been recognized.

Gray (1988), in an extension of Hofstede's work, has developed the following pairs of contrasting 'accounting values':

- professionalism v. statutory control;
- uniformity v. flexibility;
- conservatism v. optimism;
- secrecy v. transparency.

The first two relate to authority and enforcement. Here Gray (1988: 12) sees a clear contrast between the Anglo culture area on the one hand and the more and less developed Asian areas on the other, with the colonial Asian representing a mixture of influences. The second two relate to measurement and disclosure. Here Gray (1988: 13) sees a contrast between the Anglo and colonial Asian culture areas on the one hand and the less and more developed Asian culture areas on the other.

A study of the subsequent chapters in this book suggests that neither of these classifications holds for financial reporting, where a more useful classification would be based on the political histories summarized on pp. 3–5:

- *UK influence.* Australia, Hong Kong, Malaysia, New Zealand, Singapore.
- *US influence.* Philippines, Thailand.
- *Continental European influence modified by US influence.* Japan, South Korea, Taiwan.

The Philippines are classified as US- rather than Continental European-influenced since although they were under Spanish political rule much longer than they were under that of the US, the Spanish seem to have left no lasting influence on Filipino accounting.

This classification is close to that of Donleavy (1990), who calls the third group 'cloud-pine' and divides the first into two on cultural grounds into Anglo (Australia, New Zealand) and Commonwealth (Hong Kong, Malaysia, Singapore). It is consistent with the principles set forth by David and Brierley who suggest, in the context of comparative law, first of all the pragmatic test that systems are said to be in the same group if 'someone educated in ... one law will then be capable ... of handling [the other]', and second, that the two systems must not be 'founded on opposed philosophical, political or economic principles' (David and Brierley 1985: 21).

It is certainly true that a British-trained accountant will have little difficulty in adapting to financial reporting in Australia, Hong Kong, Malaysia, New Zealand and Singapore. Similarly, a US-trained accountant will feel at home in the Philippines. Moreover, both UK and US accountants will feel familiar with the type of professional accountancy practised and the institutional structure of the professional accountancy bodies. Those who have studied German accounting will find much that is familiar in Japanese and Korean accounting.

The above classification is also consistent with the 'spheres of influence' model suggested by the American Accounting Association (1977). An empirical study based on 1973 measurement (as distinct from disclosure) practices produced four models of financial reporting: British Commonwealth, Latin American, Continental European and United States. Australia, New Zealand and Singapore were placed within the British Commonwealth model, and Japan and the Philippines within the United States model (Nair and Frank 1980). The inclusion of Japan within the United States model probably arose from the use of Japanese financial reports intended for external consumption. A different classification might have resulted if financial reports intended for domestic consumption had been used. Nobes, using 1980 data, classifies Australian and New Zealand financial reporting systems as macro-fair-judgemental, commercially driven, based on business practices and professional rules, of British origin and UK influenced. Japan's financial reporting is characterized as macro-uniform, government-driven, tax-dominated and statute-based (Nobes and Parker 1991: 49). Berry (1987: 91), in an extension of Nobes's work, classifies Malaysia and Singapore identically to Australia and New Zealand and characterizes financial reporting in the Philippines as similar with the substitution of US influence for UK influence.

An argument against the spheres of influence model is that it is based on the past rather than the present and that the imported institutions have only been superficially adopted. Tricker (1990), for example, discussing the 'reality of corporate governance', points out that patterns of ownership, sources of authority to govern, and group structures in the North Pacific are not the same as those in the North Atlantic. Investors in the former equate the public companies in which they buy shares with the family groups of which they are a part:

> The investment is not so much in the specific public company as in the reputation of the owner–entrepreneur, the network of family businesses and the future good-fortunes of that family. The exact legal entity, in which the public invest, is less significant.
>
> By contrast, the Anglo-American expectation of disclosure and regulation for the protection of investors and, ultimately, of the power of these shareholding owners to determine the state of affairs, are rooted in the concept of the joint-stock, limited liability company itself.
>
> (Tricker 1990: 201)

As Tricker (1990: 203) recognizes, however, it could be argued that what can be observed in the North Pacific today is not inherent in the Chinese conception of family and business but represents a state through which large North Atlantic business has already passed. In this case, the imported financial reporting rules and practices are not so much alien as more appropriate to larger businesses which have not yet developed.

HARMONIZATION

Now that the colonial empires have passed away is there any point in retaining a diversity of accounting practices based in part at least on spheres of influence which have lost much of their former importance? Are there market forces at work leading towards *de facto* harmonization? Should governments and professional accountants direct their energies towards achieving *de jure* harmonization? If so should the aim be to harmonize Pacific Rim practices with those elsewhere in the world or should the emphasis be on regional harmonization as it has been within the EC?

Harmonization will only take place if a sufficient number of persons or organizations perceive themselves as likely to benefit from it in any given context. Nobes and Parker (1991: ch. 5) argue that the major beneficiaries from harmonization are likely to be investors in foreign companies and the financial analysts who serve them, multinational companies, international accountancy firms, intergovernmental transnational bodies, revenue authorities, international credit grantors and labour unions. They note that the most fundamental obstacle to harmonization is the size of the present differences between the accounting practices of different countries, especially the dichotomy between shareholder/fair view presentation and creditor/tax/conservative presentation. The Pacific Rim, like the EC, has important economies with a tradition of creditor and tax-based accounting. The political drive towards greater harmony of company and other business laws in the EC has led to a series of directives which have consciously tried to compromise between this type of accounting and the shareholder-oriented accounting of the UK. No such political imperatives have operated within the Pacific Rim. There has been no impetus towards accounting harmonization from Japan, the region's major economic power. The relatively small Japanese accountancy profession has made no attempt – in the way that the much larger British profession has in Europe – to influence financial reporting developments elsewhere in the Pacific Rim. The professional accountancy bodies of the region (see Table 1.10) have come together in two associations: the Confederation of Asian and Pacific Accountants (CAPA) and the ASEAN Federation of Accountants (AFA). CAPA covers the whole Asia Pacific area, not just the West Pacific Rim. Its origins go back as far as 1957 although it was not formally organized until 1976. Choi (1979: 64) has suggested that its membership is too heterogeneous. AFA was established in Bangkok in 1977 as a sub-set of CAPA. Choi (1981: 31) saw it as an organization that would 'buffer individual ASEAN countries against the wholesale adoption of international accounting pronouncements that may not be suitable to local circumstances', but Donleavy (1990) comments that with hindsight it can be seen that the effect on regional or global harmonization of CAPA and AFA 'has been zero'. Both CAPA and AFA have, however, been successful in making professional accountants throughout the region better known to each other and in disseminating technical knowledge and ideas.

More important than CAPA or AFA from the point of view of harmonization has been the International Accounting Standards Committee (IASC). The IASC provides a ready made set of accounting standards that can be adapted to local conditions and are the more acceptable in that they are not the accounting standards of any foreign country. As is shown on p. 21, this is the route followed by Malaysia, Singapore and, to a lesser extent, Hong Kong. Australia and New Zealand, with more professional resources, have developed their own standards, although always with an eye on the relevant international standard. For all these countries, of course, adopting and adapting international standards has been facilitated by the UK derivation of their legal and commercial structures.

Nobes and Parker (1991: 72) argue that harmonization is only desirable in the context of multinational companies. Even here there is as yet no empirical evidence that foreign investors, who, it may be assumed, need to be provided with financial statements whose accounting principles they can understand, are better served by harmonization than by equipping themselves with what Choi and Levich (1990) call 'multiple principles capabilities' – that is, with the capability to understand foreign accounting principles, especially where the financial statements have been made credible by the process of audit by an accountancy firm associated with a Big Six international firm. These outside investors may make judgements of the quality of corporate financial reporting in particular countries. For example, the International Finance Corporation (IFC), in *Emerging Stock Markets Factbook 1990* (p. 160), has made the following judgements:

- *South Korea.* Good, of internationally acceptable quality.
- *Philippines.* Good, of internationally acceptable quality.
- *Taiwan.* Poor, requires reform.
- *Malaysia.* Good, of internationally acceptable quality.
- *Thailand.* Adequate.

The IFC does not categorize the other countries considered in this book but would presumably accept their financial reporting as being of internationally acceptable quality.

Multinational companies from outside the region originate mainly from the United States. They are likely to favour US-style accounting principles or international accounting standards, which can be regarded as a more flexible variant of US accounting. Within the region, the largest multinationals are Japanese. For external consumption many Japanese companies follow US accounting principles. International accountancy firms generally favour US/UK type accounting for which international accounting standards are a reasonable surrogate.

SUMMARY

Corporate financial reporting in the West Pacific Rim is of interest because of the recent successful economic growth of most countries in the region. The countries of the region display great political and economic diversity and can be classified in a number of different ways. There are competing explanations of the region's economic success, some writers emphasizing the choice of suitable macroeconomic policies and others laying great stress on cultural variables. From the point of view of financial reporting an important distinction can be made between countries with capital market-based financial systems and those with credit-based financial systems. The former (notably Australia, New Zealand, Hong Kong, Singapore and Malaysia) have the largest professional accountancy bodies and, relative to the size of their economies, the largest stock exchanges. Japan, by far the largest economy in the region, has the largest stock exchange but a relatively small accountancy profession.

The countries of the West Pacific Rim have financial reporting practices as diverse as their political, economic and cultural contexts. The extent and manner in which financial reporting is regulated varies considerably from country to country. By comparison with Europe, little has been attempted or achieved by way of harmonization.

Notes

1 The principal West Pacific countries not discussed in this book are Brunei, Cambodia, China, Indonesia, North Korea, Laos, Macao, Papua New Guinea, Russian Asia and Vietnam. The major omission is Indonesia for which we were not able to obtain a contributor. For a brief discussion of Indonesian accounting see Briston (1990), pp. 204–9.

2 On the other hand, US and other accountants have shown considerable interest in Japanese management accounting. For a survey of surveys see M.D. Shields *et al.* (1991).

REFERENCES

American Accounting Association (1977) *Accounting Review* (Supplement to vol. 52).

Anderson, K. (1991) 'Europe 1991 and the Western Pacific economies', *Economic Journal*, November.

Berger, P.L. (1987) *The Capitalist Revolution*, Aldershot: Wildwood House.

Berry, I. (1987) 'The need to classify worldwide practices', *Accountancy*, October.

Bollard, A., Holmes, F., Kersey, D. and Thompson, M.A. (1989) *Meeting the East Asia Challenge: Trends, Prospects and Policies*, Wellington: Victoria University Press for the Institute of Policy Studies.

Bond, M.H. and Hofstede, G. (1990) 'The cash value of Confucian values', in S.R. Clegg and S.G. Redding (eds), *Capitalism in Contrasting Cultures*, Berlin: Walter de Gruyter.

Briston, R.J. (1990) 'Accounting in developing countries: Indonesia and the Solomon Islands as case studies for regional cooperation', *Research in Third World Accounting*, vol. 1.

Choi, F.D.S. (1979) 'ASEAN Federation of Accountants: a new international accounting force', *International Journal of Accounting*, Fall.

—— (1981) 'A cluster approach to accounting harmonization', *Management Accounting* (USA), August.

—— , Hino, H., Min, S.K., Nam, S.O., Ujiie, J. and Stonehill, A.I. (1983) 'Analyzing foreign financial statements: the use and misuse of international ratio analysis', *Journal of International Business Studies*, Spring/Summer.

—— and Levich, R.M. (1990) *The Capital Market Effects of International Accounting Diversity*, Homewood, Ill.: Dow Jones-Irwin.

Choo, H. and Ali, I. (1989) 'The newly industrializing economies and Asian development: issues and options', *Asian Development Review* 7(2).

Cooke, T.E. and Kikuya, M. (1992) *Financial Reporting in Japan*, Oxford: Blackwell.

David, R. and Brierley, J.E.C. (1985) *Major Legal Systems in the World Today*, London: Stevens.

Donleavy, G.D. (1990) 'Prospects for accounting harmonization in the Asia Pacific Region in the 1990s', Unpublished paper, University of Hong Kong Department of Management Studies.

Ernst & Whinney (1989) 'Ernst & Whinney and Arthur Young Merge', *Quarterly Account*, Summer.

Fong, P.E. (1988) 'The distinctive features of two city states' Development: Hong Kong and Singapore', in P.L. Berger and H.-H.M. Hsiao (eds), *In Search of an East Asian Development Model*, New Brunswick, N.J.: Transaction Books.

Gray, S.J. (1988) 'Towards a theory of cultural influence on the development of accounting systems internationally', *Abacus*, March.

Hirono, R. (1988) 'Japan: model for East Asian industrialization?', in H. Hughes (ed.), *Achieving Industrialization in East Asia*, Cambridge: Cambridge University Press.

Hofstede, G. (1980) *Culture's Consequences*, Beverly Hills, California: Sage Publications.

Hughes, H. (ed.) (1988) *Achieving Industrialization in East Asia*, Cambridge: Cambridge University Press.

—— (1989) 'Catching up: the Asian newly industrializing economies in the 1990s', *Asian Development Review* 7(2).

Kahn, H. (1979) *World Economic Development: 1979 and Beyond*, London: Croom Helm.

Lehmann, J.-P. (1988) 'Themes and theories in modern Japanese history', in S. Henny and J.-P. Lehmann (eds), *Themes and Theories in Modern Japanese History*, London: The Athlone Press.

Mackie, J.A.C. (1988) 'Economic growth in the ASEAN region: the political underpinnings', in H. Hughes (ed.) *Achieving Industrialization in East Asia*, Cambridge: Cambridge University Press.

Mason, A.K. (1978) *The Development of International Financial Reporting Standards*, Lancaster, ICRA Paper No. 17.

Morishima, M. (1982) *Why Has Japan Succeeded?*, Cambridge: Cambridge University Press.

Nair, R.D. and Frank, W.G. (1980) 'The impact of disclosure and measurement practices on international accounting classifications', *Accounting Review*, July.

Nobes, C. and Parker, R. (eds) (1991) *Comparative International Accounting* (3rd edn), London: Prentice-Hall International.

Puxty, A.G., Willmott, Hugh C., Cooper, D.J. and Lowe, A. (1987) 'Modes of regulation in advanced capitalism: accountancy in four countries', *Accounting, Organizations and Society* 12(3).

Reynolds, L.G. (1983) 'The spread of economic growth to the Third World: 1850–1980', *Journal of Economic Literature*, vol. 21.

Riedel, J. (1988) 'Economic development in East Asia: doing what comes naturally?', in H. Hughes (ed.), *Achieving Industrialization in East Asia*, Cambridge: Cambridge University Press.

—— (1991) 'Intra-Asian trade and foreign direct investment', *Asian Development Review* 9(1).

Shields, M.D., Chow, C.W., Kato, Y., and Nakagawa, Y. (1991) 'Management accounting practices in the U.S. and Japan: comparative survey findings and research implications', *Journal of International Financial Management & Accounting*, Spring.

Tricker, R.I. (1990) 'Corporate governance: a ripple on the cultural reflection', in S.R. Clegg and S.G. Redding (eds), *Capitalism in Contrasting Cultures*, Berlin: Walter de Gruyter.

Wade, R. (1988) 'The role of government in overcoming market failure: Taiwan, Republic of Korea and Japan', in H. Hughes (ed.), *Achieving Industrialization in East Asia*, Cambridge: Cambridge University Press.

Wilks, S. (1990) 'The embodiment of industrial culture in bureaucracy and management', in S.R. Clegg and S.G. Redding (eds), *Capitalism in Contrasting Cultures*, Berlin: Walter de Gruyter.

Zysman, J. (1983) *Government, Markets and Growth: Financial Systems and the Politics of Industrial Change*, Ithaca: Cornell University Press.

2 Japan

T.E. Cooke

INTRODUCTION

Like any other nation, the Japanese have been shaped, in part, by the location, climate and natural endowments of their country (Reischauer 1988: 1). The Japanese archipelago lies off the north-east coast of Asia and consists of four main islands – Hokkaido, Honshu, Shikoku and Kyushu – and over 3,900 smaller islands. The island chain stretches some 2,800 kilometres (1,700 miles) from north to south and has a combined surface area of 377,728 square kilometres (147,200 square miles). Whilst the country ranks 42nd in the world in terms of geographical size, its population ranks seventh. The country, therefore, is densely populated (ranking fourth in the world in this respect), but as approximately 67 per cent of the countryside is mountainous and largely uninhabitable, the country is probably the most densely populated nation-state (as opposed to city-state) in the world.

Historically, the division of the country into geographical units encouraged decentralized government and feudalism in medieval times and even today prefectural boundaries are influenced by terrain. 'Despite the natural division of the country, however, unity and homogeneity characterize the Japanese. Today few if any large masses of people are as homogeneous as the Japanese' (Reischauer 1988: 8). Such assertions are based on relativity to other nations, since Japan's population, which is in excess of 122 million, includes 670,000 Koreans and 130,000 other non-Japanese.

The country is situated in the temperate zone of the northern hemisphere and the temperatures are commensurate with those in Central America and Southern Europe, although Japan receives plentiful rainfall even in summer. As a result agriculture thrives even though the soil is not inherently fertile. Not only is the climate kind during the growing season but artificial fertilizers and substantial labour input produce good arable returns, particularly rice. Only a small proportion of agricultural land is set aside for pasture. Nevertheless, agricultural land is in short supply, not only because of the natural terrain but also because of the country's large population. To meet its needs for protein, Japan has become a major fishing nation and exploited its island position in which no part of the country is more than 70 miles away from the sea. However, this is not sufficient to meet its needs and so the country relies on the importation of basic foodstuffs.

In addition to its inherent agricultural problems, Japan is poor in other natural resources. Whilst the country has some coal and precious metal resources, Japan has virtually no oil and so is heavily dependent on imported energy supplies. In an endeavour to reduce this dependency Japan has developed nuclear and hydroelectric power. The lack of natural resources has stimulated the country into becoming a principal trading nation and one of the world's major exporting nations.

The background information at the beginning of this chapter should be of interest to those unfamiliar with Japan and, in addition, the detail also serves to place accounting in its context and highlights influences on financial reporting.

THE ECONOMIC AND POLITICAL ENVIRONMENT

The economy

The Japanese character, based on Chinese Confucianism, has been described as filial piety, family solidarity and loyalty to the ruler as well as to authority in general. Such characteristics have been used by government to improve the efficiency of Japanese business organizations.

> The modern Confucian ethic (as opposed to the earlier Protestant ethic) is superbly designed to create and foster loyalty, dedication, responsibility and commitment and to intensify identification with the organization and one's role in the organization. All this makes the economy and society operate much more smoothly than one whose principles of identification and association tend to lead to egalitarianism, to disunity, to confrontation, and to excessive compensation or repression.
>
> (Kahn 1979: 122)

However, such assertions fail to explain why there are Confucian-based societies that are economically weak, and why such an ethic did not prove effective in early periods. The explanation may be that post-war Japanese governments have been more effective than their predecessors in harnessing those ethics to achieve economic success.

This ability to use Confucian ethics, coupled with a mutual understanding between industry and central government based on a strong bureaucracy, has assisted in bringing Japan to its position as the second biggest economy in the world. However, the phenomenal growth rate in gross national product during the 1960s has slowed down, particularly since the oil crisis of 1973. The average growth rate of 7.5 per cent between 1970 and 1973 was noticeably smaller than the rate during the 1960s. Despite this, Japan's growth rate in the early 1970s was still noticeably better than its major trading competitors.

Ohkawa and Rosovsky (1973) have argued that Japan lagged far behind western technology at the end of the Second World War. The country absorbed foreign technology at an extraordinary rate, demonstrating its dynamic ability at assimilating and improving on foreign products. In order to grow rapidly there had to be a pool of available labour which was forthcoming from the agricultural sector. Success at importing technology and improving upon it gave Japanese industry the incentive to invest heavily. Investors preferred their money going into industry rather than agriculture because it gave a better return. With capital stock growing so quickly economies of scale were readily achieved. Domestic investment was financed by domestic savings rather than by foreign borrowings, mainly because the household sector was, and still is, a net saving group reflecting the high propensity of the Japanese to save.

Lincoln (1988: 18–21) lists a number of contributing factors to high economic growth in Japan:

- improved education since the end of the Second World War;
- political stability;
- supportive government policies using tight fiscal policies and expansionary monetary policies with public works being industrially oriented rather than the provision of social amenities;
- government imposition of high import barriers;
- a favourable world environment characterized by changing world trade patterns as a result of the end of colonization;
- only moderate union activity;
- reforms implemented by the Allied Forces, specifically land reforms, the legalization of labour unions and the dissolution of the *zaibatsu* (family combines).

In addition to the above factors 'strict control of imports and capital flow was also strongly influenced by economic xenophobia' (Lincoln 1988: 74). The phenomenal growth of the 1960s was ended not only by the oil crisis of 1973 but also by the revaluation of the yen at the end of August 1971. Furthermore, in 1973 the US began its continuing campaign of trade restrictions on Japan with a complete embargo on the export of soybeans. Whilst the embargo was short-lived concern over US–Japanese trade has not been. These factors contributed towards the recession of 1974. Demonstrating its remarkable ability to adapt to new circumstances, Japan has not suffered any further recessions, despite substantial increases in the value of the yen.

Such economic success has generated great confidence in the private sector and at times this may appear to border on the arrogant. For example, the Japanese sometimes question whether the US has anything of value to export that the Japanese would want to buy (Lincoln 1988: 41). Furthermore, Yoshihiro Inayama is quoted in the *Sydney Morning Herald* (3 August 1985) as saying that 'there is nothing Japan really wants to buy from foreign countries except, possibly, neckties with unusual designs' (James and Parker 1990: 203). The Japanese would counter such arguments with the view that US executives emphasise short-term goals and effects on share prices rather than long-term investment which tries to secure future growth.

Japan entered the 1990s as a major economic power, with many multinational enterprises, some of which have overseas quotations, and with a domestic stock exchange in its capital city that has the second largest market capitalization in the world (Morgan Stanley *Capital International Perspective*, May 1991). According to the OECD (1989), Japan's per capita income exceeds that of the US and all other OECD countries except Iceland and Switzerland. In addition, Japan has a massive trade surplus which rose from $18.6 billion (US terminology throughout) in 1982 to $96.3 billion in 1987 ($76.9 billion in 1989). The ten largest banks in the world in terms of total assets are all Japanese (de Carmoy 1990, based on data for 1988–9); 350 of the world's top thousand companies are Japanese; and the world's biggest creditor nation is Japan (Nester 1990: 4). The economic significance of Japan is one reason why Mason (1978) included it in his concept of vital countries to achieve harmonization of financial reporting.

Japanese politics

Superficially, Japan's political system seems similar in many ways to those that prevail in the west. Indeed the administration of the Meiji period (1868–1912) sought to develop a government machine based more on merit than on ancestry. The foundation of this new parliamentary system was a bicameral structure influenced by Britain, France and Germany. The system was thoroughly revised in 1946 with the promulgation of the Constitution of Japan, which was effective from 3 May 1947. In order to maintain political stability in Japan the Allied Forces considered that the retention of the Emperor was important. However, the Emperor's role was restricted to a diplomatic and ceremonial one – a symbolic head of state like the British Queen.

The national government is headed by the Prime Minister who leads the majority party in the Diet (The House of Representatives). Administrative power is vested in the Cabinet consisting of nineteen ministers appointed by the Prime Minister. The Cabinet is responsible to the National Diet (elected parliament), which consists of 512 members from 130 districts who are elected for a period of four years. The House of Representatives can vote for no confidence in the cabinet if it chooses and this House has power over the House of Councillors, the second elected body of parliament. The House of Councillors consists of 252 members appointed from the prefectures (152) and from a national constituency (100). Members are elected every six years – half the members every three years.

There are five main political parties in the Diet: the Liberal Democratic Party (LDP), similar in many respects to Britain's Conservatives and America's Republicans; the Japanese Socialists, the main opposition party; the Komeito (the 'Clean Government' Party); the Japanese Communists; and the Democratic Socialists. Ignoring ten months from 1947 to 1948, the LDP governed without interruption since 1955. However, concerns over 'money politics' and corruption scandals have led to changes including the formation of the Japan New Party. In the July 1993 election the LDP secured the most seats, 228, in the House of Representatives but was ousted from office by a coalition commanding 260 seats. The coalition is a seven-party alliance of neo-conservatives, socialists, social democrats and Buddhists (known as the 'Not-LDP coalition'). However, the majority of the Diet is conservative and so radical changes in policies are not expected.

The judicial power of the country is based on a court system headed by the Supreme Court. The Cabinet appoints judges with the exception of the Chief Justice, whose appointment is conferred by the Emperor. As well as general responsibility for the laws the courts can rule on constitutional matters.

In essence then, the character of the political system in Japan is familiar to westerners. However, the system has been moulded to fit with Japanese culture. For example, like the hierarchical structure of employees in Japanese firms, a young politician will seek a relationship with an established politician in which the former offers loyalty and the latter offers opportunities for advancement. The young politician is introduced to new circles whose members, in the long run, may become his supporters. Despite the modernization of the Japanese political system in the Meiji period, ancestry is still an important factor in developing support. A political candidate chosen mainly on the grounds of education and merit may well be at a severe disadvantage. However, this may be compensated by the distribution of wealth, possession of which may well be based on ancestry. An aspiring politician will need to distribute funds to local charities and organizations and be seen to do so. The objective of this is in fact to buy loyalty. Reciprocal relations prevail throughout Japanese life.

Since the Second World War Japan has been, in effect, a one-party state dominated by the Liberal Democratic Party. Its support stems from industrialists, professionals and those involved in agriculture. The LDP party, like Japan itself, has been dominated by men. Perhaps a feature of the Japanese political system is that the 'institutions are quite recognisable, but the behaviour within them is not so clear. Indeed, some integral parts of the Japanese version of the system are quite corrupt by the standards of the societies from which the framework was adopted' (Hendry 1987: 183).

INFLUENCES ON ACCOUNTING

One reason why Japan is a country of interest is because there is substantial literature that emphasises the uniqueness of the country, particularly its culture. This literature is referred to as the *nihonjinron* (literally, discussions of the Japanese) and is characterized by three major assumptions. First, that the Japanese constitute a culturally and socially homogeneous racial entity; second, that they differ radically from all other known peoples; and third, they are nationalistic and hostile to analysis from non-Japanese sources (Dale 1986: ix). Examples of the *nihonjinron* are given in Buck (1966), Suzuki (1975), Watanabe (1978), and Clark (1979). In addition, Cooke (1991) has argued that shame, rather than guilt, is an important characteristic of Japanese people.

This section explores cultural aspects in relation to business organizations and the regulatory environment. To understand the regulatory environment in Japan requires an understanding of the relationship between parliament and the bureaucracy (McKinnon 1986: 98). The aim is to highlight these major issues by considering both bureaucratic control and the fundamental structure of Japanese business organizations. This involves a consideration of the relationship between stakeholders in Japanese companies and their influence on financial reporting.

Culture and control

Bureaucratic control

Japan has a strong bureaucratic system, developed in the nineteenth century and based on German authoritarian institutions (Cooke 1991: 254). The three most important ministries as far as accounting, finance and economics are concerned are the Ministry of Finance, the Ministry of Justice and the Ministry of International Trade and Industry (MITI). The role of the first two Ministries will be dealt with later in this chapter, whilst the role of MITI will be discussed here.

Wakiyama (1986: 467) argues that there is a spectrum of views about Japan. Some believe that MITI controls every aspect of the Japanese economy as if it were chief executive officer of 'Japan Inc.'. Others view Japan's industrial policy as a mysterious black box, about which outsiders know very little in detail. There is no doubt that the Japanese government has been instrumental in assisting in the development of the economy in its own interests. It has assisted by influencing industrial policy in a number of ways (Wakiyama 1986: 469–70):

- to achieve an appropriate industrial structure;
- to assure a stable and economical supply of natural resources and energy;
- to promote research and development;

- to develop small/medium-sized firms;
- to promote trade and other international transactions;
- to encourage appropriate industrial location.

Furthermore, Wakiyama (1986: 467) states that the major tools to achieve its objectives are:

- administrative guidance;
- tax incentives;
- fiscal investments/loans;
- subsidy;
- legal power;
- direct execution by MITI or its affiliates.

The mysteries of the Japanese bureaucratic system revolve, in particular, around the nature of administrative guidance (*gyosei shido*). 'Administrative guidance' is neither an academic nor legal term but is used by government offices and the mass media and may be defined as follows:

> Administrative guidance might indicate that series of operations by which administrative organs, in those matters which fall within their own specific duties, exercise influence over specific individuals, public and private juristic persons and associations through non-authoritative and voluntary means, and guide parties by means of their own agreement and cooperation toward the formation of a definite system, the goal which the administrative organs seek. Some of the operations of this nature which are carried on have clear statutory authority; others do not.
>
> (Tanaka and Smith 1976: 353)

There must be effectiveness of control if administrative guidance is to achieve its objectives. Like the City Code on Takeovers in the UK, effectiveness depends on consensus since there are no legal powers to enforce administrative guidance. Also, like the City Code, the lack of legal enforcement powers can be an advantage when consensus exists since flexibility and, consequently, timeliness can be more readily achieved. However, lack of compliance with the Rules can always be a problem.

The nature of administrative guidance in Japan reflects the close relationship that exists between the bureaucracy and business, a characteristic based on the German model. However, many countries, including the UK, US and Germany, have a form of administrative guidance that affects its citizens at either the local or national level. The view in Japan is that administrative guidance is important 'to form social order in response to the demands of the people, even if it means exceeding the law on occasion' (Tanaka and Smith 1976: 361). This is not altogether surprising since it was necessary for some control and planning to be undertaken centrally after much of Japanese industry had been devastated after the Second World War. How administrative guidance is carried out is complex since the methods and contents vary from one ministry to another.

Whilst liaison between MITI and the major companies has been close in the past the significance of the collaboration has sometimes been overestimated. For example, Fransman's (1990) account of the relationship between MITI and the computer and semiconductor industries suggests that the extent of collaboration has been exaggerated. Furthermore, there have been occasions when the Fair Trade Commission has come into conflict with MITI's administrative guidance although the Commission has stated that such instructions are not illegal provided there is no collusion between industry members.

In summary, MITI seeks to ensure that Japanese industrial policy is conducted in an orderly manner. Like the Ministry of Finance, administrative guidance assists the process of achieving a mutually agreed long-term strategy assumed by Nagourney (1988: 3) to be 'independence of action within the American sphere of global hegemony and where "business is the fountainhead of values".' Such administrative guidance has been found to be particularly successful in a country where the bureaucracy and the Liberal Democratic Party are extraordinarily close. Relationships in Japan are typically reciprocal so that whilst the bureaucracy serves the ruling party well, by exercising a dominant position in the formulation of policy and legislation, the LDP provides the bureaucracy with increased jurisdictional power and generous budgets (Fukui 1981: 286–8).

Economic culture and welfare corporatism

'Corporatism' is a concept that has been assigned a number of interpretations. For example, George (1988) states that the 'essence of corporatism is a pattern of interest group–state bureaucracy relations of interdependence'. This is achieved by the inclusion of interest groups in government administration to establish policy, and in return access is provided to the administration. The result of this is co-operation between the public and private sectors. As Nester (1990: 17) has argued, the state not only acts as the referee and a player in policy issues but it also determines the other players. In contrast, in the UK and the US the state acts in a less interventionist manner, often restricting its activities to the provision of a regulatory framework.

Whilst the post-war economic and political environment has been characterized by corporatism it is noticeable that the Japanese government has reduced its interventionism since the mid-1970s. This is due mainly to the fact that intervention is not needed so much, but also it reflects a response to external criticism, particularly from the US. Nevertheless, Japan's political and economic environment may be described as neo-corporatism (Nester 1990: 24).

The concept of 'corporatism' has also been applied to organizational structures. For example, Dore (1973: 370) refers to 'welfare corporatism' to denote organizational form which includes the following:

- factory- and company-based trade union and bargaining structures;
- enterprise welfare and security;
- stability of employment;
- integration of manual workers as valuable members of the organization;
- bureaucratization;
- co-operative or corporate ideology;
- status hierarchies;
- deference to organizational superiors;
- devotion to work in which an individual's personal family is subordinated to the corporation as the 'family'.

Dore's explanation for economic success is not based on cultural attributes but on late development. The late-development hypothesis is based on the notion that a country has the opportunity to use modern equipment and techniques because there are no sunk costs. In contrast, early industrial developers such as Britain have substantial sunk costs not only in equipment but also in organizational structures.

Some aspects of Dore's hypothesis will be reconsidered later but it is important to note that a number of alternative or complementary explanations have been advanced. For example, Ouchi's (1981) 'Theory Z' maintains that the secret of Japan's success is in organizational structure and culture. Aspects of this management system include consensus decision-making, long-term staff development, and a strong corporate culture. However, such highly developed internal structures have been developed in some US companies such as IBM. An alternative view, expressed by Edwards (1979), is that bureaucratic control is a sophisticated means of controlling labour by advancing loyalty to the company and suppressing class and occupation allegiances. Edwards argues further that this is not unique to Japan but is a characteristic of a corporatist form of business organization. These views are supported by Burawoy (1983), who refers to such developments as 'hegemonic despotism' in which loyalty to the organization is enhanced by paternalism and supported by the threat of plant closure or the subcontracting of source materials.

An alternative explanation has been advanced by Abegglen (1958) who considered that Japanese practices stem from communalism that would eventually inhibit the growth of companies. However, history has shown this early assertion to be inaccurate and has led to revisions to such views. For example, Abegglen and Stalk (1985) have argued that Japanese companies succeed because of their competitive fundamentals, which include a bias towards growth, a preoccupation with the actions of competitors, exploitation of their competitive advantage, and the choice of both corporate financial and personnel policies that are consistent with these objectives.

What is likely is that the government has selected macroeconomic policies that suit its own needs at any particular time and has successfully utilized the country's resources.

The company and employees

It is difficult to generalize about companies in Japan that range in size from the very small to some of the largest in the world. Rewards differ significantly between the large companies and the smaller companies (Morishima 1982: 173). The rewards offered by the large companies extend to the provision of better pensions, higher bonuses, better health care and, in many cases, accommodation too. In addition, large companies extend their role to the provision of sports facilities, hobby clubs, and holiday homes.

As a result of the duality of employment there is fierce competition to join large firms. Competition to join large companies takes place only once in a lifetime, after leaving school or college.

> Since in a Confucian society people are ranked in the hierarchy according to the education they have, or have not, received, the large enterprises wish to recruit graduates from what one might term the more prestigious institutions, as this is clearly the most appropriate way to preserve the standing of the enterprise.
>
> (Morishima 1982: 174)

Such rankings are not unique to Japan since they often occur in non-Confucian societies (e.g. France and the UK). In return for greater rewards, based on a seniority system, large Japanese companies expect loyalty through a lifetime's work. Leaving a large company without agreement with his employer would render a person a 'traitor' and make him unfit to work for another large company.

The contractual relationship between a company and employee is formalized by the signing of a document which pledges the individual to obey company rules. However, the rules are not stated so contractual obligations are implicit rather than explicit. Consequently, disagreements are resolved by reaching a consensus through negotiation rather than by resort to litigation. Alston (1986) argues that since the contractual obligations are so vague a resolution through litigation is not appropriate. 'This is one reason why America has more lawyers and litigation than Japan' (Alston 1985: 243). A feature of the contractual relationship between employers and employees is flexibility. Rohlen (1974: 19) states that there is an obligation on an employee to be flexible in the type of job undertaken and he must be flexible with respect to pay, attributes which allow large companies to respond quickly to changing circumstances. In return the company offers lifetime employment.

Another important difference between a Japanese company and a western corporation can be seen in their responses to an economic depression. 'During times of economic depression all workers will receive reduced pay if necessary, and since higher-level employees receive higher pay, they will also be expected to receive larger percentage pay decreases than the lower-level workers' (Alston 1985: 244). In times of economic prosperity employees would receive not only increased bonuses but also improved fringe benefits. Thus, members of the 'family' gain or lose according to the performance of the company, thereby enhancing the concept of *wa* (harmony) within the group. The concept of harmony is

> a salient social characteristic of Japan. This emphasis on harmony, it is generally alleged, is derived from Confucianism; it is, however, a Japanese variant of Confucianism, for such emphasis on 'harmony' cannot be found in other Confucianist societies such as China or Korea.
> (Lehmann 1988: 14)

Flexibility in the type of job an employee undertakes means that the employer is acquiring the services of an individual rather than a particular skill. In a western company if an employee is dissatisfied or if his skill is no longer needed an employee will leave or perhaps be dismissed. The Japanese employee is perceived to have a lifetime obligation to serve and be served by the company. Such a perception is promoted by industrial organizations nd government. However, whilst the concept of lifetime employment is often viewed as a characteristic of Japan, the system is not as prevalent as some believe. First, as already pointed out, there is a substantial difference between large Japanese companies where lifetime employment exists and medium and small firms where such practices are not common. In reality the majority of employees work in medium and small companies, a situation more prevalent in Japan than many other major countries. Information from a government white paper (*Chusho Kigyo Hakusho* 1986) and a Statistics Bureau publication (*Nihon no Tokei* 1986) reveal that the majority of employees work in companies with a maximum of 300 employees. In the manufacturing sector 74.3 per cent of those employed work in firms with less than 300 employees and 87 per cent of organizations in this sector employ less than 20 people (Hendry 1987: 139).

Second, women are expected to marry and in many cases leave their jobs to concentrate on the home:

> Japanese women take very seriously the roles of wife and mother and probably a majority feel that they should be at home during the early child-rearing years. The business of rearing children is regarded almost as a profession in itself by some mothers.
> (Hendry 1987: 148).

Thus, the concept of lifetime employment does not apply to most women, a fact which can prove advantageous to a large Japanese corporation. For example, about 60 per cent of Matsushita's Japanese employees are women, the majority of whom work in relatively unskilled jobs in the factories. Thus, girls leave school, join the company and then in their early to mid-twenties leave to concentrate on the home. Such women are often employed in assembly work where they are still more dexterous than robots. Consequently, the corporation has a pool of loyal women workers for a relatively short period of time to be replaced by other young, agile and nimble women.

Third, those employees who have lifetime employment are usually expected to retire between the ages of 55 and 60; and fourth, it is common practice for companies to have a pool of 'temporary' workers who may work for the company for several years but are excluded from the lifetime employment system. As a result of these features, Sumiya (1981: 2) has estimated that only about 20 per cent of Japanese workers are part of the lifetime employment system.

Emphasis is placed on the enterprise as a family in which there is a strong desire for consensus. However, labour participation in management through unions and councils is not common, particularly since most unions are company unions rather than skill (trade) unions. Consensus within a Japanese company is reached by disseminating information widely. Information is disseminated to individuals within the firm even if they are not directly concerned. The *ringi* (suggestions and proposals) involves suggestions that are sent to collateral departments so that agreement is reached with junior managers before being shown to senior management. Senior management hold regular discussion groups with junior staff which provide details of performance. Such information flows enhance corporate understanding, team spirit and participation in the decision-making process (Clark 1979).

It is a characteristic of Japanese companies, particularly large companies, that employees are kept fully informed, not only of developments in the corporation but also of its financial position. Consequently, there is no need for information to be disseminated through special employee publications or in the corporate annual reports. Furthermore, employees can exert considerable influence over decision-making despite the lack of works councils, such as in Sweden, or board representation as in Germany. The labour unions in Japan are different from those common in the UK or US because they represent employees of only one company. Japanese unions have a feeling of belonging towards the company where their members are employees. This feeling of belonging is important and Ishizumi (1988) has argued that the success of a merger or acquisition is largely determined by the extent to which co-operation is obtained from the work-force.

It should be apparent from the above discussion that employees of Japanese companies, particularly large companies, can be a significant force within a company. This is achieved not by strong trade unions but by the acceptance that a company is a family of employees, including its management. The company is a community in which there is usually no major distinction between managers and workers, since managers usually come from the ranks of the work-force, and where shareholders are associated with the company for a long period of time. Consequently, short-term profits and dividends are not reasons for share purchase, unlike western companies where shareholders are primarily interested in the company as a financial investment – particularly a short-term investment. Shareholders obtain returns in the form of long-term capital gains and in some cases enhanced business relations which serve mutual interests. Profits in a Japanese company are pursued to ensure the financial viability and expansion of the corporation rather than for the benefit of shareholders. In summary,

> companies in Japan are said to be essentially 'communal organizations'. Large companies in particular seem to exist for their workers; workers have lifetime ties to their firms, for which they seem to work incessantly. This factor is said to be a reason for Japanese companies' entertainment expenses (spent largely by management on employees and viewed as an important fringe benefit) often exceeding shareholder dividends.
>
> (Ames 1986: 551)

Shareholders

In practice Japanese companies are largely unconcerned about the small shareholder. In contrast, the institutional shareholder can exert considerable influence, but as a business associate rather than as a shareholder.

The directors of most Japanese companies emerge from the ranks of employees after having spent some 20 to 30 years working through various levels of management. The fact that they have served the company for many years may mean that they favour employees' interests rather than shareholders' interests. Such behaviour is reinforced by the fact that most Japanese directors also own part of the business. Non-executive directors form only a small minority of the board of directors and often consist of company allies. Sometimes individuals are appointed because of their connections and contacts. 'Notable among these are retired civil servants who have "come down from heaven" from Ministries concerned with the company's business' (Clark 1979: 100). Such appointments are not uncommon in the west. In Japan, non-executive directors are often sympathetic to the management directors unless the company is unprofitable in which case dissatisfaction may be expressed that is consistent with shareholders' interests. In reality, therefore, ordinary shareholders may have little real impact on the board of directors.

What is different between the UK and Japan is the objective of the major institutions. In the UK the objective of an investing institution is to receive a return in the form of a dividend plus capital gain. Consequently, the objective of the financial institutions is the same as that of individual shareholders. In Japan institutional shareholdings, consisting of banks, their associates and trading partners, often hold investments in the form of cross-holdings. 'In general, therefore, Japanese institutional shareholders invest as a means of doing business with companies' (Clark 1979: 102). Since the objective of such institutions is to foster business relations they are unlikely to support any conflict with management that could endanger that relationship.

At a general meeting directors are not very forthcoming when questioned by shareholders. Indeed there is almost a tacit understanding that no questions will be asked. Voting invariably occurs on a 'follow-the-leader' basis where the leader is the institution with the largest shareholding. Where there is the potential for embarrassing questions directors can make use of *sokaiya* (a general meeting fixer – a form of gangster) who, for a fee, will discourage the inquisitive. In effect, therefore, small shareholders have been disenfranchised. Large shareholders wish to maintain their existing business relations so shareholders in reality are very passive.

Management

Management of Japanese companies is the responsibility of the board of directors, subject, in theory, to the rights of shareholders, creditors and other interested parties. An essential difference between the management structure of a western corporation and a Japanese company is the decision-making process. In the west the process may be described as 'top to bottom' whereas in Japan emphasis is on 'bottom to top'. In a Japanese corporation those on the bottom rung of the management structure are required to prepare a *ringisho* (*ringi* report) and submit it to the next rung of management. The *ringisho* is a corporate document recommending a particular course of action and which requires approval from the immediate superior. The document is modified where necessary and submitted to the next rung of the management ladder. Such a procedure suggests that decision-making is a collective responsibility rather than that attributable to a particular individual. However, whilst Clark (1979: 127) provides some evidence for this assertion he states that a comparison between companies in Japan and those in the west is not at all simple.

One of the inherent difficulties of a hierarchical management structure based on a 'bottom-up' process is that managers at the bottom may put forward ideas and policies that they believe will be acceptable to their immediate superiors even if alternative courses of action may be more beneficial to the company.

In this way, when things go wrong, they can still be safe and avoid

> responsibility for any detrimental consequences by saying that under the objective circumstances in which they were forced to make the decisions they made, they had no alternative but to do what they did.
>
> (Ishizumi 1988: 127).

In essence, then, a Japanese company belongs to its work-force from which most of the members of the board of directors will emerge. The 'insider' group includes not only employees but extends to the banks, insurance companies and other companies with cross-shareholdings, and all are likely to have access to information in excess of that reported in the corporate annual report. Indeed, some argue that the very essence of Japanese stock markets is the availability of market-sensitive information to brokers, bankers and large shareholders.

> This means that altering the system [to establish effective insider dealing legislation] would prejudice the interests of a very large section of the Japanese business community, and not only a few individuals who make spectacular profits by flouting the law. And in a market moved more by fundamentals, the Japanese brokers' inside track on the news is clearly a major selling point with clients.
>
> (Waldmeir 1989)

Since Japanese companies have generally been more highly geared than western companies the banks have been more influential and are likely to support management provided interest and principal repayments on debt are fully met. Thus, management, employees and major shareholders have sufficient inside information for their purposes and, consequently, there will be little lobbying for an increase in disclosure in corporate annual reports beyond meeting their obligations. Continuity of the enterprise is all-important and in some ways 'the company itself has taken over the traditional role of the *ie*' (Hendry 1987: 35). (The *ie* was the preindustrial social unit.) There is little internal pressure to extend disclosures in corporate annual reports since information is for family members, not outsiders. In contrast in the 'United States as well as other countries, the board of directors is a powerful policy-making group that can have a strong impact on the nature and quality of reported information' (Radebaugh 1975: 44).

The objectives of management also differ between Japanese and western companies. Japanese companies pursue policies of long-term market share and growth based on development research and efficiency, whereas Anglo-Saxon companies often pursue goals, including asset-stripping, to achieve short-term profits and dividends for short-term investors. Reischauer argues that,

> whereas the American executive must keep his eye on stock prices and the quarterly bottom line, his Japanese counterpart can take a more Olympian view, seeking to maintain a sound company and to lay the

> basis for growth that may not pay off for a decade, long after he himself has retired. This longer time horizon for Japanese business permits a wiser strategy for growth and is probably the single greatest advantage it has over business in the West.
>
> (Reischauer 1988: 332)

The above summary has provided considerable support to the hypothesis advanced by Dore (1973) that organizational structures in Japan may be described as 'welfare corporatism'. Important empirical work by Lincoln and Kalleberg (1990) has shed some light on the transferability of Japan's management practices, organizational structures and employment systems to other countries. They conclude that such structures could increase workforce commitment in US factory settings as well as being successful in Japan. Thus success could be achieved without Japan's so-called unique culture. As a result convergence may occur if western companies adopt Japanese styles of work organization. Perhaps such convergencies could occur in accounting.

What is important from this discussion is that there is a close relationship between government and business. The post-war institutional framework is based on the logic of developing the manufacturing sector which can serve the country best in achieving its objective of export-led growth. The institutional framework of the national economy shapes the economic culture and thereby influences accounting, whose practice tends to serve the national interest.

Culture and accounting

Gray (1988: 8) has attempted to identify accounting value dimensions based on a review of the accounting literature and practice. Four main value dimensions were identified:

1. *Professionalism versus statutory control.* Professionalism emphasizes the exercise of individual professional judgement based on a self-regulated profession whereas statutory control involves compliance with statutory accounting and legal requirements.
2. *Uniformity versus flexibility.* Uniformity involves the enforcement of uniform accounting practices on a consistent basis as opposed to flexibility based on the needs of individual entities.
3. *Conservatism versus optimism.* Conservatism emphasizes a cautious measurement approach in dealing with uncertain future events whereas optimism is characterized by *laissez-faire* and risk-taking.
4. *Secrecy versus transparency.* Secrecy demonstrates a preference for confidentiality and the restriction of disclosure of information about the business to those closely involved with management and financing operations, whereas transparency naturally provides a more open and publicly accountable approach.

Whilst each of the above dimensions are considered to be a function of culture it is possible to argue that they are really functions of the financial system. For example, Zysman (1983) has argued that Japan had a credit-based financial system in which prices were administered by the government. This was certainly true up to 1980, but subsequently some liberalization occurred and a wide variety of instruments emerged that were akin to a capital market-based financial system. These market-based innovations did not fit easily with a financial system in which brokerage houses sometimes guaranteed returns to corporate clients. Guaranteed returns were possible because of the dominant position of brokerage houses and an economy with surplus savings and growth in the money supply. The revelation of scandals on the Tokyo Stock Exchange may reflect the difficulties of transition from one financial system to another but it is more likely that the credit-based financial system will become more sophisticated. In addition, the tightening of monetary policy by the Bank of Japan was very influential in terminating what had seemed to be perpetual growth in prices. The 30 per cent decrease in share prices in 1990 provided a shock to the system.

Each of the value dimensions identified by Gray (1988) will be discussed further to see the extent to which they are relevant to the development of the Japanese accounting system.

Professionalism versus statutory control

A strong independent accounting profession is a characteristic of both the UK and the US, whereas in Japan the profession is small and is effectively controlled by the government. Gray (1988: 9) argues that 'a preference for independent professional judgement is ocnsistent with a preference for a loosely knit social framework where there is more emphasis on independence, a belief in individual decisions and respect for individual endeavour'. Early on in this chapter we highlighted the importance of the 'inside' group (*uchi*), a concept that children joining a kindergarten are introduced to probably for the first time. From that early stage collectivism becomes more important than individualism and continues throughout school and university education and characterizes human resource management in Japanese firms. And yet throughout the period of compulsory education the individual is subject to an extremely competitive examination-oriented environment followed later by substantial competition to obtain a place with a large firm. These seemingly contradictory features are common throughout society but the Japanese choose not to see such internal contradictions. For example, it is perfectly acceptable, and not considered contradictory, for an individual to choose a Christian or Shinto wedding and a Buddhist burial. The ethics of the Japanese stem, in the main, from Confucianism and popular religious customs are derived mostly from traditional Shinto and Bhuddism (Reischauer 1988: 215). Such diversity contrasts with western monotheism.

Internal contradictions such as those described above have led many authors, including accounting authors such as Takatera and Yamamoto (1987: 10), to offer a dynamic explanation for the coexistence of both individual responsibility and collective responsibility and co-operation and competition. However, in reality an aspect of culture is chosen to fulfil the requirements of a particular occasion, for in Japan nothing is quite as it seems. Both the Japanese accounting profession (8,474 qualified Certified Public Accountants at 1 February 1990) and the legal profession (about 14,000 in 1986) are kept small by the state since droves of highly qualified mobile professionals is against the principle of company loyalty and a threat to stability. It is the state that controls the development of accounting in Japan, a characteristic which is not likely to change in the near future.

Uniformity versus flexibility

Consistent with state control of accounting in Japan is the requirement to be uniform rather than flexible. For example, the Code and the SEL stipulate the format for financial statements, the schedules that should accompany such statements and the content of the business report. However, flexibility does exist since measurement requirements often offer alternatives which allow companies to exercise judgement and indeed to indulge in creative accounting from time to time. Gray suggests that a preference for uniformity is consistent with concern for law and order and rigid codes of behaviour with

> a need for written rules and regulations, a respect for conformity and the search for ultimate, absolute truths and values. This value dimension is also consistent with a preference for collectivism, as opposed to individualism, with its tightly knit social framework, a belief in organization and order, and respect for group norms.
>
> (Gray 1988: 9)

Conservatism versus optimism

Since the 1899 Code was largely influenced by Germany, which in turn was influenced by France, it is not surprising that Japanese accounting is strongly conservative. Consequently, assets may not be revalued upwards and legal earned reserves must be provided.

Secrecy versus transparency

'Secrecy would also seem to be closely related to conservatism in that both values imply a cautious approach to corporate financial reporting in general; but with secrecy relating to the disclosure dimension and conservatism relating to the measurement dimension' (Gray 1988: 11). Work undertaken by Cooke and Kikuya (1992) suggests that Japanese accounting is conservative with respect to measurement and secretive with respect to disclosure. Despite having the world's second largest stock market in terms of turnover and market capitalization (as at 31 July 1991), Cooke and Kikuya (1992) found that levels of corporate disclosure were noticeably lower than in the UK and the US. The Code accounts, which are sent to shareholders, are in most instances a poor excuse for an annual report since they constitute little more than a pamphlet with minimum levels of disclosure. More extensive disclosure is provided in the SEL accounts, but these are not distributed to shareholders and are produced by listed companies only and filed with the Ministry of Finance. However, these accounts may be scrutinized at head office and copies may be ordered through many bookshops. Furthermore, Cooke and Kikuya (1992) found that the extent of isclosure in the SEL accounts differed significantly between those with a domestic listing only and those with at least one overseas quotation.

In summary, disclosure by all companies is characterized by secrecy, uniformity and compliance. Such features, particularly secrecy, may appear somewhat inconsistent with the size of the Tokyo Stock Exchange. However, characteristics such as interlocking shareholders and directorships and the fact that dividend payments to shareholders are very low, are factors which must not be ignored.

Japanese equity markets

There is no doubt that the financial institutions are important investors in Japanese listed companies. Table 2.1 shows the percentage breakdown of shareownership in terms of market value over the period 1986 to 1990. It is noticeable that the financial institutions and business companies together hold in excess of 70 per cent of shares. According to Hodder and Tschoeg (1985: 178) the shareholdings of private domestic institutions increased

Table 2.1 Share ownership by market value (percentages)

	Gov't and Local Gov't	*Financial institutions*	*Business companies*	*Securities companies*	*Individuals and others*	*Foreigners*
1986	0.3	39.8	28.8	1.9	22.2	7.0
1987	0.9	41.5	30.1	2.1	20.1	5.3
1988	0.5	42.5	30.2	2.3	20.4	4.1
1989	0.4	44.1	29.0	2.3	19.9	4.3
1990	0.3	43.5	29.5	2.0	20.5	4.2

Source: Tokyo Stock Exchange Fact Book 1991.

fairly consistently from 28.1 per cent of total shares in 1950 to 66.7 per cent in 1983. The comparable figure for 1990 is 73 per cent.

An issue of some importance is the extent to which financial institutions and business companies are active in trading securities. Hodder and Tschoeg, when referring to trading in 1983, state that

> the majority of institutional holders (banks, insurance companies, and non financial business companies) collectively held 61.2 per cent of listed shares, but engaged in only 10.7 per cent of trades. By contrast, member security firms, individuals, and foreigners accounted for 81.5 per cent of trading, despite holding less than 35 per cent of the listed shares. If we exclude trades by member security firms acting as dealers (23.9 per cent of the total), individuals and foreigners accounted for 75.7 per cent of remaining trades. Thus, we get a rather clear picture of an economy where over 60 per cent of listed shares are held by institutions that do very little trading.
>
> (Hodder and Tschoeg 1985: 178).

Franklin (1988) estimates that the non-trading sector may be as high as 75 per cent, and Sakakibara *et al.* (1988: 138) suggest that 'on the average, less than 30 per cent of outstanding shares of Japanese common stocks are available to the ordinary investor'. The extent of the non-trading sector is important since for a given level of demand the supply is somewhat restricted, thereby pushing up share prices. The total market capitalization of the Tokyo market may not, in reality, be as high as the sum of the value of the individual share prices. This may provide one explanation as to why the P/E ratios of Japanese companies are much higher than those in the west (see Table 2.2). In addition, it may explain why Japan can have a large capital market without the requirement of extensive corporate disclosure that one might expect.

A feature of Japanese companies has been the ability to sustain high

Table 2.2 International equity markets

	(1) *P/E ratio**	*(2)* *P/CE ratio†*	*(3)* *(1)/(2)*	*(4)* *(3)/1.92‡*	*Adj. P/E* *(1)/(4)*
UK	11.1	6.6	1.68	87.50%	12.69
US	14.6	7.6	1.92	100.00%	14.60
France	9.5	4.7	2.02	105.21%	9.03
Germany	12.7	4.0	3.18	165.63%	7.67
Japan	31.3	10.5	2.98	155.21%	20.17

Source: Columns (1) and (2), Morgan Stanley Capital International Perspective, no. 1, 1991.

Notes:
* P/E ratio = price/earnings ratio.
† P/CE ratio = price/cash earnings ratio (cash earnings = earnings before depreciation).
‡ The divisor is 1.92 using the US as the base.

levels of debt compared with Anglo-Saxon companies. To some extent this may be explained by the close relationship between the banks and the companies in which it is common for financial institutions to hold shares in client companies. The simultaneous holding of debt and equity facilitates not only the monitoring of performance, through access to inside information, but also the influencing of the borrowers' policies. An important trend in the 1980s has been the substantial decrease in the ratio of gross debt to total assets (defined by the Bank for International Settlements as gross debt plus equity at market value) in Japanese companies, whereas there has been only a modest increase in the US ratio (see Table 1.9).

In addition to lower gearing levels in Japanese companies, earnings growth has often been achieved as a result of '*zaitech*' manipulation of their financial assets. *Zaitech* funds are cash reserves held for the specific purpose of speculation on the stock exchange. Returns including capital gains on such investments may be included in income anywhere in the profit and loss account.

One of the problems with making comparisons with P/E ratios is that there are fundamental differences between Japanese and UK/US financial reporting practices which affect both price and EPS. These differences are considered later in this chapter (see pp. 71–80).

International accounting standards

Although the JICPA was a founder member of the International Accounting Standards Committee and has agreed to make every effort to acquire and harmonize its rules and regulations with international accounting standards this is not apparent in Japanese corporate annual reports. It is very rare for a company to make any mention of international accounting standards in its Japanese reports but occasionally this may occur in their English version accounts. Only one company, Sasebo Heavy Industries, prepares a report which it describes as being consistent with international accounting standards.

THE ACCOUNTING AND FINANCIAL REGULATORY FRAMEWORK

The evolution of Japanese financial reporting

From 1639 the *shogun* cut off Japan from the rest of the world and the country continued to be isolated for a further 200 years. Whilst some changes began towards the end of the Tokugawa period (1603–1867) the start of the Meiji period in 1868 heralded the beginning of a concerted attempt to catch up and overtake the west.

It is possible that a feeling of shame and backwardness in relation to the west could have been one of the catalysts. However, whilst there was a feeling of political, economic and military inferiority when compared to the west (Reischauer 1988: 78–9), it is undeniable that the despatch of a substantial US naval fleet in 1853, under the command of Commodore M.C. Perry, was significant in forcing the Japanese to allow the Americans into their ports.

An important aspect of this process of catching up was the Iwakura Mission. In November 1871 a large party (in excess of 100 officials) left Japan to visit both Europe and the US with a view to revising the unequal treaties and to find out as much as possible about the west (Soviak 1971: 7). When they returned in September 1873 they realized that the process of catching up with the west would involve 'drastic political, judicial, and social reforms along Western lines, in addition to technological innovation and knowledge of international law ... That the Iwakura Mission was one significant factor in the development of modern Japan is unquestionable' (Soviak 1971: 7–8).

Introduction of double-entry bookkeeping in Japan

Before 1870 a variety of bookkeeping methods were used by merchants and some of these systems were specific to a particular firm (Ogura 1982). The development of western business beyond merchanting, to encompass industrial activity, became apparent to Japan in the latter part of the Tokugawa period. And it was in order to advance and compete with its adversary that Japan copied from the west such devices as the limited liability company. The first Japanese companies were established in 1867 but most of these companies failed quickly as a result of managerial inexperience and government interference, and in the early Meiji period the government had to coerce the merchants to form companies (Clark 1979: 30).

With the country embarking on a programme of modernization, which included the importation of European machinery and equipment, 'accounting for business transactions [became] so complicated that the hereditary Japanese system could hardly do justice to the business methods, so considerable impetus was given to the introduction of European accounting methods' (Shimme 1937: 291).

As Fujita (1966: 50–1) has noted, western bookkeeping was introduced into Japan through the simultaneous importation of books from Britain, France, Germany, Russia and the US. Indeed, the whole education system was vulnerable to western ideas (Shively 1971: 87). In addition to the importation of western books on bookkeeping, a number of accounting experts – including Vincente Braga from Portugal, Alexander Shand from Britain, and William Whitney from the US – were invited to train Japanese accountants based on western models (Fujita 1966: 51). In addition, the translation of western accounting textbooks, for example by Fukuzawa, played a vital role in the acceptance of double-entry bookkeeping in Japan (Someya 1989: 78).

The development of improved accounting systems was associated with the coming of big business. Some of the major businessmen that emerged at that time included Iwasaki of Mitsubishi, Minomura of Mitsui, and Yasuda – all of whose business activities were encouraged by the government through financial subsidies and materials, with the added advantage that profits were tax-free (Clark 1979). In addition, some non-strategic state-owned industries were sold off cheaply during the recession of the 1870s. Entrepreneurs, particularly from the same family, founded companies in several different industries but principally in heavy industry such as engineering, chemicals, iron and steel, and shipbuilding. With common origins and common ownership, together with money from the same bank, the core of the *zaibatsu* (financial combines) was formed. The banks received deposits from the public and recycled them in the interests of the group. Throughout this period the financial system was relatively under-developed. Even though the Tokyo and Osaka stock exchanges were formed in 1878, they traded almost exclusively in bonds, principally government bonds.

Four main groups developed – Mitsubishi, Mitsui, Sumitomo and Yasuda. They were characterized by inter-company trading on favourable terms and continuing benefits from government influence. The structure of each *zaibatsu* was hierarchical, with a central holding company controlled by a founding family. The holding company owned the majority of shares in a number of core companies including the bank, the trust company, trading company and insurance. Limited liability status as an aspect of modern western commercial culture was considered to be crucial and clearly assisted the development of the *zaibatsu.* Double-entry book-keeping was not only considered to be modern, but appropriate for complex transactions, often involving the group, that were well beyond the simple methods of record keeping used by the early merchants.

One factor that hindered the formation and development of companies was the lack of an appropriate legal framework and, consequently, regulation was on an *ad hoc* basis. The determination to improve matters in this area must be attributed, however, not only to the desire to improve economic performance, but also because the Japanese government gave priority to the revision of the unequal treaties, and success in this respect rested on acceptance by the west that sufficient legal reform had occurred (Shively 1971: 90).

Disagreements between French-trained and English-trained jurists occurred with the development of both the Civil Code and the Commercial Code. In 1881 the government tried to resolve the disagreement over the Code by employing a German, Hermann Roesler, to draft the Code. Perhaps not surprisingly he used the draft German Code as his foundation (Henderson 1973: 167–9). A version modified by Japanese jurists became law in 1890, demonstrating the country's ability to absorb western ideas and apply them to different environmental conditions. The Code was substantially amended in 1899 and most notably permitted the formation of joint-stock companies without special arrangements, provided there was a mechanism for dissolution when considered necessary. The emphasis of the Code was on the provision of information for creditors rather than shareholders, reflecting the European continental influence in its drafting (Choi and Hiramatsu 1987: 35).

Important developments in the twentieth century before the Second World War included the issue, in 1934, of the 'Working Rules for Preparing Financial Statements' by the Temporary Industrial Rationalization Bureau with the aim of providing guidance to those preparing financial statements as well as assisting national planning. This was important because it represented a break from the legalistic approach to financial reporting based on the Code towards consistency and uniformity.

Central planning was increased further during the inter-war period, particularly by the 'Tentative Standards for Financial Statements of Manufacturing Companies' that were issued in 1941. The 'Tentative Standards', issued by the Uniform Financial Statements Council of the Central Planning Board, were aimed at enhancing macroeconomic control by the provision of specific information on pricing and production policies, rather than integrating standards with the CC.

The Allied Occupation

The Allied Occupation proved to be a significant development in Japanese financial reporting. The driving force behind the Occupation Forces was the US which sought to democratize Japan, which involved, amongst other things, the breakup of the *zaibatsu* and the sale of their shares to the public, and the protection of investors by increased disclosure based on a regulatory system modelled on that prevailing in the US. Thus, the interests of shareholders were considered for the first time to be as important as those of creditors.

The US disbanded the Temporary Industrial Rationalization Bureau and the Planning Board in an attempt to reduce the influence of government bodies and to reflect anticipated changes, but retained the Code, which continued to be controlled by the Ministry of Justice. However, the Occupation Forces recognized deficiencies in the Code, particularly with respect to the extent of information disclosure for investors. Consequently, the Code was revised in 1947, 1948, 1949 and twice in 1950. The 1950 amendments revised certain provisions which related to the role of auditors, the rights and duties of shareholders, the general meeting and the individual shareholder (McKinnon 1986: 180). In addition, the 1950 revision included the following new accounting provisions:

1 *Article 286–4.* Expenses involved in a new share issue may be treated as an asset and amortized over a three-year period.
2 *Article 288.* A company shall set aside an amount equivalent to at

least 10 per cent of cash dividends paid with respect to each fiscal period until this legal reserve equals 25 per cent of stated capital.

3 *Article 288–2.* A transfer should be made to a capital surplus reserve when shares are either issued in excess of their face value or when shares are issued without a par value the amount not credited to share capital.
4 *Article 293–2.* A company may make the whole or a part of a distribution of profits in the form of newly issued shares (i.e. a stock dividend).
5 *Article 293–3.* A company may capitalize legal reserves provided a resolution has been approved by the board of directors.
6 *Article 293–4.* A company has the power to introduce a share split provided a resolution has been approved by the board of directors.
7 *Article 293–6.* Any shareholder holding not less than 10 per cent of the total number of the issued shares may demand to inspect the books, records and documents of the account.

In addition to modifying the Code, the Occupation Forces introduced a completely new system of regulation, based essentially on that prevailing in the US. This involved the formation of the Securities Exchange Commission in 1948, the introduction of the Securities and Exchange Law (SEL) (promulgated first in 1947 and subsequently amended in 1948 and 1950), the formation of the Japanese Institute of Certified Public Accountants (JICPA) in 1949, the formation of the Investigation Committee on Business Accounting Systems in 1949 and the establishment of the Tax Bureau and National Tax Administration Agency. Other than the dissolution of the Securities Exchange Commission in 1953, the regulatory system introduced by the US still exists (see Figure 2.1). The aim of the new regulatory system was to protect investors in what the Occupation Forces anticipated would be a shareholding democracy. As part of this programme, an independent thriving professional accountancy body, like that in the US, was considered essential. The role of each of these important organizations will be considered separately.

THE POST-WAR REGULATORY FRAMEWORK

The Securities Exchange Commission (SEC) and the Securities and Exchange Law (SEL)

The SEC and the SEL were based on the Securities and Exchange Commission and the Securities and Exchange Act in the US. The US considered that these elements of control were essential aspects of the democratization programme. This programme involved the liquidation of the *zaibatsu* holding companies and the distribution of their shares to the public, thereby creating the middle class that Japan had lacked in its feudal society. However, within a few months of the departure of the Allied

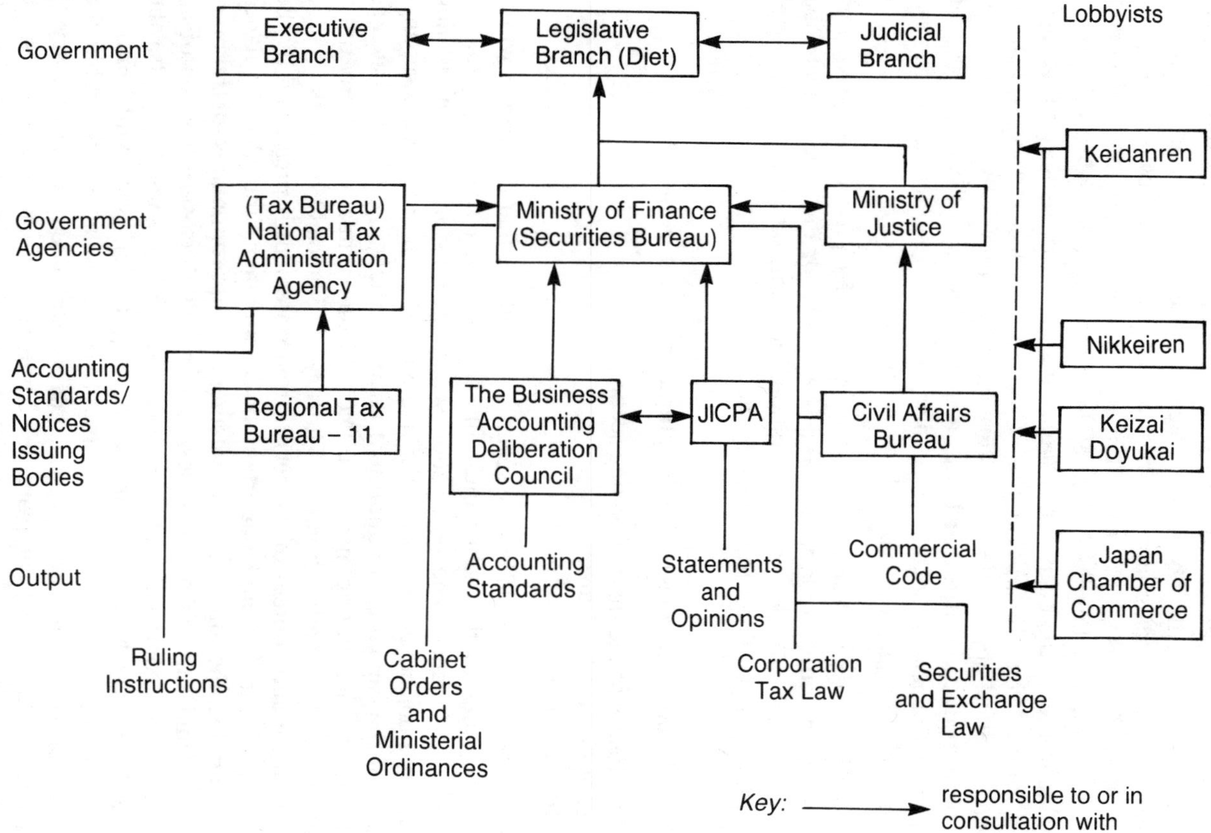

Figure 2.1 Institutional framework governing financial reporting in Japan

Forces the SEC had been abolished and its role transferred to the Finance Bureau of the Ministry of Finance (effective from 1 August 1953).

Thus, within a very short period of time, a regulatory body, independent of government, had been fundamentally changed by its incorporation into the bureaucracy. McKinnon (1986: 186) argues that the abolition of the SEC was not a reaction to its external imposition since other requirements introduced during the occupation remained intact, rather it reflects an aspect of Confucianist philosophy of the existence of the 'ruled' and 'ruler'. 'This cultural philosophy is realized in a greater level of active involvement of government and bureaucracy at all levels of social and economic policy formulation and administration in Japan than in Anglo-American nations' (McKinnon 1986: 186). That this is indeed the case can be seen from Japan's political and intellectual history (see Dale 1986: 39).

The introduction of the SEL was a major change in the orientation of corporate financial reporting since disclosures were oriented to general investors. The original purpose of the Act was:

> to permit and facilitate fair issuance and transfer procedures, as well as other transactions in securities and to provide for the orderly exchange of securities to make possible a rational administration of the national economy, in addition to protecting the investors.
>
> (Article 1)

The disclosure requirements fall into three major categories:

- disclosure at the time of issuing securities;
- continuous disclosure;
- further disclosure of reports.

Disclosure at the time of issuing securities stipulates that companies which issue securities to the public must file a registration statement with the Ministry of Finance. The registration statement must include: the issuing company's objectives for a securities issue; the trade name of the company; details of the capital issue; important issues surrounding the issue, such as business and accounting matters; officers of the company; and any other matters considered appropriate by Ministry of Finance Ordinances.

The form and content of the registration statement is prescribed by the Ministry of Finance and important disclosure items include: a balance sheet, an income statement, a statement of appropriations of retained earnings, and supporting schedules. Continuous disclosure consists of an obligation on companies to file semi-annual and annual reports, the contents of which are similar to the registration statement. Further disclosure of reports requires companies to make available to the public the registration statement and other documents, stipulated by the Ministry of Finance, at the issuing company, the Ministry of Finance, and the stock exchange, and must be made available for purchase at government publication centres.

The Japanese Institute of Certified Public Accountants (JICPA)

In 1907 the first group of professional accountants organized themselves as a group (probably as a reaction to the requirements of the Code), although the first formal body of accountants was not established until 1927 by the Registered Accountants Law. However, such was the economic significance of the *zaibatsu*, and outside shareholders were of such little consequence as a result, that there was little pressure to introduce the concept of independent external audit of financial statements at that time.

The Occupation Forces considered the registered accountants body to be inadequate for the new regulatory environment (Fujita 1966: 67). Consequently, the Registered Accountants Law was repealed and replaced by the Certified Public Accountants Law 1948. JICPA was formed the following year as a voluntary body and in 1953 the Institute became incorporated under the Civil Code. However, both the profession and the professional body were of little importance until 1966 when the Certified Public Accountants Law was amended to make it compulsory for all CPAs to be members. One of the reasons for the introduction of the Certified Public Accountants Law was a feeling that the Japanese profession was not as competent as those of its counterparts.

> The Certified Public Accountants Law was designed to ensure the quality of professional accountants at a level of competence comparable with the United States, the United Kingdom, etc. As a result, the Law requires that Japanese accountants be comparable in status with Japanese lawyers.
>
> (JICPA 1987: 1)

JICPA has no authority to issue accounting standards, that role being given to the Business Accounting Deliberation Council (BADC). In essence the JICPA offers a sort of administrative guidance in the form of statements, opinions or working rules. Such guidance is not backed by law (as in the US) but, as in the UK, the JICPA has authority over its members.

The Investigation Committee on Business Accounting Systems

Due to the lack of detail and variety of practices in Japanese accounting, the Occupation Forces established the Investigation Committee on Business Accounting Systems (ICBAS) of the Economic Stabilization Board in 1948. The following year ICBAS issued the 'Working Rules for Preparing Financial Statements' and the 'Business Accounting Principles', which were based on *A Statement of Accounting Principles* written by Sanders, Hatfield and Moore (1938) for the American Institute of Certified Public Accountants. There was considerable US influence over these accounting statements which continued with the issuance of a 'Tentative Statement of Auditing Standards' in 1950. In July 1952 the government changed the role of ICBAS away from its independent structure to become, in effect, part of the Ministry of Finance. Thus, within a short period of time both the Securities and Exchange Commission and ICBAS had become part of the government machinery, the bureaucracy.

ICBAS was renamed the Business Accounting Standards Deliberation Council in 1950 and then the Ministry of Finance changed its name to the Business Accounting Deliberation Council (BADC) with the role of sole originator of accounting standards in Japan. Like all Japanese deliberation councils, BADC acts as an advisory body to the Ministry. Membership of BADC comes from business, academe, and the professional accounting community as well as the Ministry of Finance itself. The Ministry has to approve the appointment of all members of the Council.

The purpose of the Business Accounting Principles issued by ICBAS in 1949 was threefold:

- accounting conventions should be followed, even if they are not covered by Ministerial Ordinance, because they are considered to be 'fair and proper';
- CPAs should follow these standards in the audit of financial statements under the SEL and the requirements of the Certified Public Accountants Law;
- accounting standards should be given full consideration in any amendments to the law affecting financial statements (e.g. the Code or tax law).

The purpose of the statement on financial accounting standards is to provide a guide to the establishment of generally accepted accounting principles which should be adhered to by all business enterprises. The Principles consist of three main sections, covering general principles, income statement principles and balance sheet principles. The general principles provide a summary of the seven key principles which in essence are as follows:

- financial accounts should provide a true report of the financial position of the company and its operational results;
- financial accounts should be based on accurate accounting records in accordance with the principles of orderly bookkeeping;
- capital surplus and earned surplus should be separately disclosed;
- the financial statements should incorporate accounting which should not mislead users;
- accounting principles and practices should be consistently applied and only changed if there is good reason;
- a prudent approach to accounting should be adopted in providing for possible unfavourable effects upon the financial condition of a business enterprise;
- accounts should be prepared on a consistent basis in accordance with

the accounting records and facts and not with regard to the receiver of the statements (e.g. shareholders, creditors, tax authorities).

Tax Bureau and National Tax Administration Agency

The introduction of the Tax Bureau and National Tax Administration Agency to the regulatory system was the result of recommendations of the Shoup Committee, which in turn were based on tax theory in the US. One important aspect, which still prevails today, was the introduction of a dual system of tax returns that encourage good bookkeeping and honest self-assessment. Privileged taxpayers (blue tax returns) receive additional tax deductions in the form of reserves – particularly in the areas of losses, research and development and accelerated depreciation – and the authorities can only adjust tax assessments for errors in the books of accounts and records. In contrast, white form taxpayers are only eligible for tax relief on provisions.

In order to obtain tax relief for provisions and reserves they must, as in most of Continental Europe, be incorporated into the financial statements. As a result, deferred taxation is rarely practised although permanent and timing differences do occur. Tax law is based on the Corporation Tax Law, the Income Tax Law and the Special Taxation Measures Law. The latter provides the government with special measures considered necessary to achieve its social and economic goals.

The power to tax and make people responsible for payment is vested in the Diet as provided by the Japanese Constitution. Proposed legislation is drafted by the Tax Bureau which is part of the Ministry of Finance. The actual administration of the tax laws rests with the National Tax Administration Agency (NTAA) which is part of the Ministry of Finance. The Ministry issues regulations and rules called Cabinet Orders or Ministerial Ordinances which in effect implement the national tax laws. The director of NTAA issues ruling instructions or directives to the regional tax bureaux, with the aim of ensuring uniformity in the interpretation of tax law. However, as with all legal matters definitive interpretation rests with the courts.

Ministry of Finance

This Ministry is the most important body which influences accounting in Japan by the major companies, a position gained since the Second World War. Previously the Ministry of Justice had been the most important, since it administered financial reporting based on the Code of 1899 and as subsequently amended.

The underlying objective of financial statements prepared in accordance with Code requirements is to protect creditors and current investors.

> Accordingly, disclosures as to the availability of earnings for dividend distributions, creditworthiness and earning power are of prime importance. The emphasis is on proper presentation of the Company's financial position and results of operations in accordance with law.
>
> (JICPA 1984: 4–5)

Consequently, the Ministry of Justice has an important role which had been well established before the imposition of a new regulatory environment by the US.

The imposed regulatory environment gave the Ministry of Finance new powers which elevated it to its predominant position. The purpose of reporting under the SEL is 'adequate and appropriate disclosure for the protection of general investors' (JICPA 1984: 38). Whilst reporting under SEL is mainly limited to listed companies, such companies represent a significant proportion of economic activity. The Ministry of Finance must be kept informed, not only through disclosures at the time of issuing securities by a registration statement for which Ministry approval must be obtained by the issuing corporation, but also by continuous disclosure. The form and content of the registration statement and securities report are prescribed by the Ministry of Finance Ordinance.

Since both the form and content of the financial statements prepared under SEL is more detailed than under the Code (Cooke 1993a) there has been considerable uneasiness between the two Ministries. Furthermore, there are, at times, contradictions between SEL and the Code. In addition, SEL accounts must be filed with the Ministry of Finance. Control over BADC and the Tax Bureau and National Tax Administration Agency, together with effective control over JICPA, places the Ministry of Finance in a particularly strong position. Discussions have taken place between the two Ministries to reconcile some of the differences between accounting standards and the Code. Whilst conflict was common in the 1950s and 1960s the two Ministries now enjoy a stable relationship based on mutual distrust.

Ministry of Justice

The Code established in 1899 provided companies with their legal status. Consequently the Ministry of Justice has been influential in the setting of minimum levels of disclosure in the annual reports of Japanese companies. The Code tries to ensure a reasonable level of disclosure in the annual reports distributed to shareholders. Emphasis is placed on financial position, although a statement of changes in financial position has never been a requirement of the Code. Whilst the Ministry of Finance is a more significant body in terms of accounting disclosure and filing arrangements as far as the major companies are concerned, the Ministry of Justice is of more significance to the vast number of Japanese companies. Indeed, the

Ministry of Finance is of no consequence to the majority of companies unless it is envisaged that securities will be issued to the public in the future.

Civil Affairs Bureau

The Civil Affairs Bureau is part of the Ministry of Justice and is responsible for the Legal Affairs Bureau and the District Legal Affairs Bureau. It is the responsibility of the Civil Affairs Bureau to draft both laws and Ministerial Ordinances which relate to commercial or civil matters. Consequently, it is the responsibility of this bureau to draft both amendments to the Code and Ministerial Ordinances.

Lobbyists

The four major business lobbyists, in descending order of importance, are Keidanren, Nikkeiren, the Keizai Doyukai and the Japan Chamber of Commerce and Industry. Keidanren is a powerful body of major industrialists, particularly automobile manufacturers, ship builders, iron and steel, petrol companies, the chemical industry, as well as trading companies, wholesale businesses, banks, insurance companies and securities companies. So powerful and influential is this employers' organization that the chief of Keidanren is often referred to as the 'prime minister of business' (van Wolferen 1989: 354).

Keidanren is brought within the political system by regular consultation with the most important ministries. Furthermore, Keidanren is able to appoint members to BADC in order to ensure that the interests of its federation are protected. Whilst this organization has been influential in determining changes in accounting principles it does not always get its own way. For example, Keidanren has never been in favour of extending the nature and scope of the audit function. Despite such opposition the 1974 amendment to the Code involved an extension of the scope of audit and consequently an increase in responsibility for auditors.

The other lobbying bodies pale into insignificance when compared with Keidanren. For example, Nikkeiren, the Japan Federation of Employers' Association, was set up by 'business bureaucrats formerly in the forefront of wartime industrial organisations, for the specific purpose of combating the labour movement' (van Wolferen 1989: 68). The organization has been successful in lobbying for changes in the national education curriculum as well as influencing business policy.

The Keizai Doyukai, Committee for Economic Development, 'has provided a forum in which elite *zaikai* (*the broad circle of top business functionaries*) members can formulate a theoretical basis for business policies; it attracted attention in the mid-1950s with proposals for a Japanese style "reformed capitalism"' (van Wolferen 1989: 34). Keizai

Doyukai has emphasised the need for economic mobilization and the interplay between companies, effectively public institutions, and the administration. Furthermore, this organization has consistently taken a national interest point of view in which profit may not be consistent with that objective. Like all these lobbying organizations former bureaucrats serve in senior positions, not least because of their good connections. The Japan Chamber of Commerce and Industry, the last of the four lobbyists, protects the interests of small businesses. It is important to realize that these lobbying organizations are not independent of each other but interdependent. Consequently, each organization can influence accounting by lobbying the most effective body. For example, the Chamber of Commerce and Industry may try to protect the interests of its members by lobbying Keidanren, which has direct access to the appropriate regulatory authority.

DISCLOSURE REQUIREMENTS

The Commercial Code and the Securities and Exchange Law (SEL)

Every *Kabushiki-Kaisha*, which is similar to the public limited company in the UK and the joint-stock company in the USA, must prepare financial statements in accordance with the Code. The accounts, prepared at the end of each fiscal year, must include the following:

- a balance sheet;
- a profit and loss account;
- a business report;
- a proposal for appropriation of retained earnings;
- supporting schedules.

Both the form and contents of the accounts are prescribed by the Ministry of Justice. The accounts are prepared for a single year only and on an individual company basis (i.e. not consolidated), the traditional form of presentation in Japan.

As well as preparing accounts in accordance with the Code, all listed companies, and companies that publicly offer shares or bonds amounting to ¥100m or more, must file a registration statement under SEL rules and submit it to the Ministry of Finance. The form and content of these statements is prescribed by an Ordinance of the Ministry of Finance and in accordance with the SEL an annual securities report must be filed. This securities report includes the articles of association, financial statements prepared in accordance with the SEL and consolidated financial statements for the most recent fiscal years.

The accounts are presented in more detail than that required under the financial regulations of the Code. Whilst the general content of the two sets of accounts is very similar, the

> terminology, form and content of these financial statements and supporting schedules are more precisely defined in the SEL financial regulations. This will require, in most instances, additional detail of certain items or, in certain instances, the reclassifying of items as presented in the Code financial statements in order to comply with the SEL financial regulation requirements. However, the reported net income and shareholders' equity would not change as the result of the reclassifications.
>
> (JICPA 1984: 39)

A feature of Japanese accounting is that major companies are required to produce two sets of annual reports – one that complies with the requirements of the Code and another that complies with the requirements of the SEL. In addition, some major companies, including those that file a 20-F report in the US, prepare another annual report for the international reader, which as far as the Japanese are concerned is a US reader. This report is in English using US terminology and often complies with US GAAP. Invariably those companies that file a 20-F report in the US include a consolidated set of accounts based on US GAAP and these are filed in the US with the SEC and also with the Ministry of Finance in Japan. As a consequence, such companies do not prepare consolidated accounts in accordance with Japanese GAAP, although this is considered to be acceptable in Japan. The accounting details provided in this chapter refer to Japanese GAAP (Cooke 1993b).

THE BALANCE SHEET

The Commercial Code

The Code specifies certain items of disclosure, including significant accounting policies and any information necessary for understanding the financial position and results of operations. Table 2.3 shows an example of balance sheet reporting under the Code. The English translations shown in Tables 2.3 to 2.7 are those published by the JICPA. It is noticeable that the translations of items included in the Code tend to have a UK and European orientation, whereas the SEL accounts are US oriented. The format shown in Table 2.3 has a continental European influence although presentation based on the current arrangement method (descending order of liquidity) is similar to that in the US. Note also that whilst IAS 1 (paragraphs 16 and 21) requires the disclosure of comparative financial statements and the disclosure of the facts and reasons if the going concern assumption has not been followed, there are no equivalent requirements under the Code. Furthermore, disclosure in the notes to the financial statements is more limited than that envisaged by IAS 5 (paragraphs 10–16) – for example, disclosure of items such as pensions and retirement plans.

Table 2.3 The balance sheet prepared in accordance with the Commercial Code as at 31 March 19X1

ASSETS		**LIABILITIES**	
Current assets	**xxx**	**Current liabilities**	**xxx**
Cash in hand and at bank	xx	Notes payable	xx
Notes receivable	xx	Trade accounts payable	xx
Trade accounts receivable	xx	Short-term borrowings	xx
Marketable securities	xx	Accounts payable	xx
Treasury stock	xx	Deferred income	xx
Finished goods	xx	Accrued expense	xx
Work in progress	xx	Accrued corporation and	
Raw materials		inhabitants taxes	xx
and consumables	xx	Accrued enterprise tax	xx
Advance payments	xx	Allowance for product	
Prepaid expense	xx	warranty	xx
Short-term loans	xx	Other current	xx
Other current assets	xx	liabilities	xx
Allowance for doubtful		**Long-term liabilities**	**xxx**
accounts	(xx)	Bonds payable	xx
Fixed assets	**xxx**	Convertible bonds	xx
Tangible fixed assets	**xxx**	Long-term borrowing	xx
Buildings and structures	xx	Allowance for	
Machinery and equipment	xx	severance payment	xx
Vehicles	xx	Allowance for special repair	xx
Tools, fixtures and fittings	xx	Others	xx
Land	xx	**Allowances**	**xxx**
Construction in		Allowance for	
progress	xx	exchange losses	xx
Intangible fixed assets	**xxx**	Others	xx
Land rights	xx		——
Lease tenant rights	xx	**Total liabilities**	**xxxx**
Patents	xx		
Telephone rights	xx	**CAPITAL**	
Goodwill	xx	**Share capital**	**xxx**
Investment etc.	**xxx**	**Legal reserve**	**xxx**
Long-term cash at bank	xx	Capital reserve	xx
Investment in		Legal earned reserve	xx
subsidiaries	xx		
Investment securities	xx	**SURPLUS**	**xxx**
Long-term loans	xx	Reserve for overseas	
Loans to affiliates	xx	investment losses	xx
Long-term prepaid		Reserve for dividend	
expense	xx	equalization	xx
Other investments	xx	Reserve for expansion	
Allowance for doubtful		of business	xx
accounts	(xx)	Other voluntary reserve	xx
Deferred charges	**xxx**	General reserve	xx
Pre-operating costs	xx	Unappropriated retained	
Research and development		earnings	xx
costs	xx	(Current net income)	(xx)
Bond discounts	xx		
Bond issuing costs	xx	**TOTAL LIABILITIES**	
TOTAL ASSETS	**xxxx**	**AND CAPITAL**	**xxxx**

The Securities and Exchange Law (SEL)

The Ministry of Finance Ordinance specifies the form and content of the registration statement that must be filed by all public companies. Consequently, the financial statements, notes and relating supporting schedules are laid down in this Ordinance. The following requirements are important:

1 Assets and liabilities must be listed in descending order of liquidity under the SEL. There is no similar requirement in the Code although in practice such a presentation is normal.
2 Balances and transactions with related parties must be separately stated (there is no similar requirement in the UK or US). Four out of the 14 mandatory supporting schedules under the SEL require information on investments in and balances with related parties.
3 Under the SEL, *any* balance sheet item which exceeds 1 per cent of total assets must be disclosed separately.

Table 2.4 The balance sheet prepared in accordance with the Securities and Exchange Law as at 31 March 19X1

ASSETS		
I CURRENT ASSETS		
Cash in hand and at bank		xx
Notes receivable	xx	
Allowance for bad debts	x	xx
Trade accounts receivable	xx	
Allowance for bad debts	x	xx
Notes and accounts receivable from affiliates	xx	
Allowance for bad debts	x	xx
Marketable securities		xx
Treasury stock		xx
Finished goods		xx
Semi-finished goods		xx
Work in progress		xx
Raw materials and consumables		xx
Advance payments		xx
Prepaid expenses		xx
Accounts receivable		xx
Accounts receivable from affiliates		xx
Short-term loans	xx	
Allowance for bad debts	x	xx
Short-term loans to affiliates	xx	
Allowance for bad debts	x	xx
Other current assets		xx
Total current assets		**xxx**

II FIXED ASSETS		
1 Tangible fixed assets		
Buildings	xx	
Accumulated depreciation	x	xx
Structures	xx	
Accumulated depreciation	x	xx
Machinery and equipment	xx	
Accumulated depreciation	x	xx
Vehicles	xx	
Accumulated depreciation	x	xx
Tools, fixtures and fittings	xx	
Accumulated depreciation	x	xx
Land		xx
Construction in progress		xx
Total tangible fixed assets		**xxx**
2 Intangible fixed assets		
Mining rights		xx
Land rights		xx
Trade mark rights		xx
Patents		xx
Telephone rights		xx
Goodwill		xx
Total intangible fixed assets		**xxx**
3 Investment and other assets		
Long-term cash at bank		xx
Investment in securities		xx
Investment in subsidiaries		xx
Investment in associates		xx
Investment in partnerships		xx
Long-term loans	xx	
Allowance for bad debts	x	xx
Long-term loans to shareholders, officers and employees	xx	
Allowance for bad debts	x	xx
Long-term loans to affiliates	xx	
Allowance for bad debts	x	xx
Doubtful receivables		xx
Long-term prepaid expenses		xx
Other		xx
Total investment and other assets		**xxx**
Total fixed assets		**xxxx**

III DEFERRED CHARGES		
Organization expenses		xx
Pre-operating costs		xx
Experimental research costs		xx
Development costs		xx
Stock issuing costs		xx
Bond discounts		xx
Interest during construction		xx
Total deferred charges		**xxx**
Total assets		**xxxx**
LIABILITIES		
I CURRENT LIABILITIES		
Notes payable		xx
Trade accounts payable		xx
Notes and accounts payable to affiliates		xx
Short-term borrowings		xx
Current portion of long-term borrowings		xx
Current portion of bonds with warrants		xx
Accounts payable		xx
Deposits received		xx
Deferred income		xx
Accrued expenses		xx
Accrued corporation and inhabitants taxes		xx
Accrued enterprise tax		xx
Allowances		
Allowance for bonus payments	x	
Allowance for damages	x	
Allowance for repairs	x	
Allowance for warranty	x	xx
Other current liabilities		xx
Total current liabilities		**xxx**
II LONG-TERM LIABILITIES		
Bonds payable		xx
Bonds with warrants		xx
Convertible bonds		xx
Long-term borrowings		xx
Long-term borrowings from shareholders, officers and employees		xx
Long-term borrowings from affiliates		xx
Allowances		
Allowance for severance payments	x	
Allowance for special repairs	x	xx
Other		xx
Total long-term liabilities		**xxx**
Total liabilities		**xxxx**

CAPITAL		
I SHARE CAPITAL		xx
II CAPITAL RESERVE		xx
III LEGAL EARNED RESERVE		xx
IV OTHER SURPLUSES		
1 Other capital surpluses		
Reserve for government grants	x	
Reserve for gain on insurance claims	x	xx
2 Voluntary reserves		
Reserve for overseas investment losses	x	
Reserve for dividend equalization	x	
Reserve for business extension	x	
Reserve for additional equipment	x	
Reserve for sinking fund	x	
General reserve	x	xx
3 Unappropriated		xx
Total capital		**xxx**
Total liabilities and capital		**xxxx**

Additional balance sheet disclosures considered necessary for the protection of general investors include accrued income; short-term loans; loans to officers and employees; other assets; taxes payable; dividends payable; loans from officers and employees; and transactions with related parties. An example of a balance sheet prepared in accordance with SEL is shown in Table 2.4.

The requirements for the disclosure of information in the notes to the financial statements prepared in accordance with the SEL are similar to those of the Code. Additional disclosure includes information on significant events after the balance sheet date, net assets per share and differences in the accounting policies of foreign companies.

THE PROFIT AND LOSS ACCOUNT

The Commercial Code

Ordinary income (or loss) is calculated by adding non-operating income to operating profit (or loss) and deducting non-operating expenses. Ordinary profit is generally regarded as being the most reasonable and fair indicator of the result of operations for the current period. Unlike the UK, there is no concept of exceptional items. Profit before income taxes, which indicates the distributable income as at the balance sheet date, is to be calculated by adding extraordinary gains to ordinary income and deducting extraordinary losses from the above total. The extraordinary gains or losses include prior year adjustments, gains or losses on the sale of fixed assets, gains or losses from the disposal or sale of securities or other assets initially acquired for purposes other than for resale, and other losses arising from economic events such as calamities that are considered unusual. The nature and the amount of each unusual gain or loss must be shown as separate items.

In the UK, FRS (paragraph 7) defines prior year adjustments as material adjustments applicable to prior years arising from changes in accounting policies or from the correction of fundamental errors. In Japan, the Business Accounting Principles list the following items as prior year adjustments:

- adjustments to allowances/reserves;
- adjustments to depreciation charges;
- correction to the valuation of inventories;
- recovery of bad debts written off in prior years.

It is apparent from the above examples that most items included in prior year adjustments in Japan would not qualify as such in the UK. Furthermore, the presentation of prior year adjustments also differs between the two countries.

Another important difference between Anglo-Saxon accounting and Japanese accounting lies in the definition of extraordinary items. Whereas in the UK and the US extraordinary items are identified by their unusual nature and by the infrequency of their occurrence, this is not so in Japan. Consequently, even events or transactions which are expected to recur frequently may be considered to be extraordinary in Japan because they are not ordinary items by their nature. Such a wide definition is probably contrary to the approach adopted in IAS 8 (paragraph 3).

After determining income before income taxes, net income must be stated by deducting corporate income tax and inhabitants tax and other taxes that are assessable to the current fiscal year. Enterprise tax, fixed property tax, automobile tax, excise tax, and liquor tax are not reported as part of the tax charge for the year but are included in administrative expenses. Tax effect accounting may not be provided for and is optional only when the timing differences arise on consolidation. The pro-forma profit and loss account under the Code is shown in Table 2.5.

The Securities and Exchange Law (SEL)

The profit and loss account prepared in accordance with SEL (Table 2.6) is similar in format to that required by the Code. However, the extent of disclosure is greater under the SEL, and certain items disclosed in the Code accounts require classification. A materiality standard for disclosure is specified at 10 per cent of a major category of the profit and loss account or 20 per cent of total sales. For example, if sales to related parties exceed

Table 2.5 The profit and loss account prepared in accordance with the Commercial Code from 1 April 19X0 to 31 March 19X1

ORDINARY ITEMS			
Operating revenue and expenses			
Sales			xxx
Cost of sales	xxx		
Distribution costs and administrative expenses	xx		xxx
Operating profit			**xx**
Non-operating income and expenses			
Non-operating income			
Interest and dividend income	xx		
Gain on foreign currency exchange	xx		
Other non-operating income	xx	xx	
Non-operating expenses			
Interest and discount charges	xx		
Other non-operating expenses	xx	(xx)	
Ordinary income			**xx**
EXTRAORDINARY ITEMS			
Extraordinary gains			
Gains on sale of fixed assets	xx		
Recovery of bad debts written off	xx		
Gain on sale of shares of subsidiary	xx	xx	
Extraordinary losses			
Adjustment of depreciation provided in prior years	xx		
Fire loss	xx		
Loss on sale of fixed asset	xx	(xx)	xx
Income before income taxes			**xx**
Income taxes			xx
Net profit			**xx**
Opening balance of retained earnings brought forward	xx		
Reversal of reserve for self-insurance	xx	xx	
Interim dividends	xx		
Legal earned reserve appropriated in relation to the interim dividends	xx	xx	xx
Unappropriated retained earnings as at the end of the year			**xx**

20 per cent of total sales that item must be disclosed separately. If losses from the sale of trade investments exceed 10 per cent of total non-operating expenses then that item must be separately disclosed.

Statement of appropriations of retained earnings

The proposal for appropriation of retained earnings must be prepared by the board of directors and is subject to approval by shareholders at the annual general meeting. The appropriation statement specified by the Code is similar to that in the SEL (see Table 2.7).

The Business Report

Until 1982 the Code had not prescribed the content of the 'Business Report'. In practice most companies had followed US practice and disclosed business information with their 'Reporting Review' or 'Financial Review'. The amended Code prescribes that all companies, with the exception of small companies, must prepare a business report disclosing information on the company's business activities, main shareholders and main lenders, etc.

ACCOUNTING PRACTICES AND PRINCIPLES

Consolidated financial reports

During the 1960s there were several cases where a large number of investors sustained losses as a result of profit manipulation or window dressing through subsidiary companies. In particular, the bankruptcy of Sanyo Special Steel Ltd in 1965 led to considerable criticism of accounting practices in Japan, even though Japan is used to a relatively high level of corporate bankruptcies. However, the case of Sanyo Steel did receive more public criticism than many previous cases.

> The strength of the public outcry, based on the social and political ramifications and the potential of fraudulent reporting to prejudice the operations of the Japanese securities markets, created intense pressure on [the] Diet and the Ministry of Finance to improve corporate disclosure under the Securities Exchange Law.
>
> (McKinnon and Harrison 1985: 210–11)

As a consequence, from 1970 the Japanese stock exchanges began to delist the shares of companies which issued fraudulent financial statements.

There was also concern about the level of bankruptcies, and consequently the quality of information disclosed, that arose from the oil crisis of 1973. This had the effect of increasing the pressure on government. As Clark notes:

> Equipment was idle to an extent unparalleled in previous recessions. For most of 1973 firms were working at about ninety per cent of capacity; by the winter months of 1974–5 they were working at only about seventy per cent. Company profits were vastly reduced. In the first half of fiscal 1973 the profits of large firms represented 3.76 per cent of their turnover. Two years later the ratio was 0.84 per cent. In fiscal 1973, 9,349 firms went bankrupt. Two years later there were more than 13,000 bankruptcies, and the debts involved had doubled, to more than 2,000 billion yen.
>
> (Clark 1979: 244–5)

A factor of considerable importance which stimulated the development of consolidated accounts in Japan was the growth of multinational companies.

Table 2.6 The profit and loss account prepared in accordance with the Securities and Exchange Law from 1 April 19X0 to 31 March 19X1

I TURNOVER		
Turnover to affiliates	XX	
Turnover to other customers	XX	XXX
II COST OF SALES		
1 Opening stock	XX	
2 Purchases	XX	
Sub-total	XXX	
3 Closing stock	XX	XXX
Gross profit		**XXX**
III DISTRIBUTION COSTS AND ADMINISTRATIVE EXPENSES		
Packing and freight	XX	
Commission	XX	
Warehouse	XX	
Advertising	XX	
Directors' remuneration	XX	
Payroll	XX	
Bonuses	XX	
Welfare benefits	XX	
Travelling	XX	
Postage, telephone, fax and telex	XX	
Utilities	XX	
Insurance and maintenance	XX	
Taxes and dues	XX	
Provision for accrued enterprise tax	XX	
Depreciation	XX	
Provision for allowance for doubtful accounts	XX	
Research and development	XX	
Others	XX	XX

OPERATING PROFIT			**xx**
IV NON-OPERATING INCOME			
Interest income and dividends	xx		
Interest income from affiliates	xx		
Interest income on securities	xx		
Dividend income	xx		
Dividend income from affiliates	xx		
Gain on sale of marketable securities	xx		
Others	xx	xx	
V NON-OPERATING EXPENSES			
Interest and discounts	xx		
Interest on bonds payable	xx		
Amortization of deferred charges	xx		
Valuation loss on marketable securities	xx		
Exchange loss	xx		
Others	xx	(xx)	xx
ORDINARY INCOME			**xx**
VI EXTRAORDINARY GAINS			
Gain from sale of fixed assets	xx		
Recovery of bad debts written off	xx		
Gain on sale of shares in subsidiary	xx		
Gain from sale of investment securities	xx	xx	
VII EXTRAORDINARY LOSSES			
Adjustment of depreciation provided in prior years	xx		
Fire loss	xx		
Loss on sale of fixed assets	xx	(xx)	xx
Income before income taxes			**xx**
Corporate income tax and inhabitants tax			xx
Net profit			**xx**
Unappropriated retained earnings brought forward	xx		
Reversal of reserve for self-insurance	xx	xx	
Interim dividends	xx		
Legal earned reserve appropriated in relation to the interim dividends	xx	xx	xx
Unappropriated retained earnings as at the end of the year			**xx**

Table 2.7 Statement of appropriations of retained earnings under the Securities and Exchange Law

I	Unappropriated retained earnings at the end of year		xxx
II	Reversals of voluntary reserves		
	Reversal of reserve for overseas investment losses		xx
	TOTAL		xxx
III	Appropriations		
	Legal earned reserve	xx	
	Cash dividend (i.e. final dividend)	xx	
	Directors' bonuses	xx	
	Reserves for business expansion	xx	
	Reserve for government grants	xx	
	General reserve	xx	xx
IV	Unappropriated retained earnings to be carried forward		xxx

In the early 1960s the entry of Japanese companies on to the New York Stock Exchange was barred by the US since their accounts were based on the parent company only. The first listing of a Japanese corporation on the New York Stock Exchange did not occur until 1970. As McKinnon and Harrison (1985: 211) point out, 'the Ministry of Finance came to perceive that Japan's parent-only financial statements carried relatively low international status'. In addition, US companies and the US government lobbied the Japanese government to allow US companies to be listed in Japan and file consolidated accounts. The Japanese government agreed to this and in 1973 foreign shares were listed on the Tokyo Stock Exchange for the first time. Three US companies obtained a quotation on the Tokyo Stock Exchange on 18 December 1973 but it was not until 1976 that a non-US company obtained a listing. At 31 December 1988 there were 112 foreign companies listed on the Tokyo Stock Exchange of which nearly 60 per cent were from the US and a further 16 per cent from the UK.

The BADC was asked by the Ministry of Finance to consider the introduction of consolidation accounting closely and in 1975 it published the 'Accounting Principles for Consolidated Financial Statements'. The Ministry of Finance itself issued the 'Regulations Concerning Consolidated Financial Statements' in 1976 and the related interpretative rules in 1977. Consequently, consolidated financial statements became a requirement for listed companies for the financial year beginning on or after 1 April 1977. An important point is that consolidated accounts need only be prepared by companies reporting under the SEL and even then the consolidated accounts have been supplementary to the main set of accounts which have been prepared on an individual basis. Since 1992 consolidated accounts have been recognized as having the same importance as individual accounts. A detailed discussion of events in the formulation of the consolidation Ordinances is given in McKinnon (1984), and McKinnon and Harrison (1985).

Segmental reporting

The issue of segmental information is allied to that of consolidation accounting since there is a loss of underlying detail in consolidated financial reports. To compensate in part for the loss in detail, US generally accepted accounting principles require segment information concerning the company's operations in different industries, its foreign operations and its export sales. Similar provisions have existed in Companies Acts and stock exchange requirements in the UK, and SSAP 25 was published on 1 August 1990. The standard brings together and extends the existing rules and ensures that it complies with the requirements of the International Accounting Standard. SSAP 25 requires segmental disclosure for accounting periods beginning on or after 1 July 1990 (see Cooke and Kikuya 1992b).

Despite the requirements in the US, foreign issuers of securities have been able to claim an exemption from such disclosure requirements in the Securities and Exchange Act 20-F filing with the US Securities and Exchange Commission. As a result, the accounts of Japanese companies prepared for the international reader that have an independent audit report invariably have a 'subject to' paragraph which highlights the omission of segment information. Thus, there is a conflict of two concepts. On the one hand the shame of being thought of as somehow inferior by foreigners would lead to disclosure of the required information, but on the other hand corporate secrecy and resistance to disclosure often prevails (Aida 1972, Ballon *et al.* 1976, Someya 1989).

Tax

In Japan, tax rules are not separated from financial accounting regulations, a characteristic probably reflecting German influence. An extensive range of tax-related reserves have been used in the past although these are not so prevalent today. Corporate income taxes include a national corporation tax and local taxes contain the enterprise (business) tax and municipal inhabitants tax. These taxes are based on income. Deferred taxation is not normally accounted for in Japanese accounts except in consolidated financial statements.

Leases

SSAP 21, FAS 13 and IAS 17 all require finance leases to be capitalized in the balance sheet of the lessee but there has not been a similar requirement in Japan until fairly recently. Consequently, whilst reporting practices have not yet reflected these changes, Section 18-2 of the Regulations Concerning Accounts, which was amended in June 1988, makes it compulsory for lessee companies to either capitalize finance leases or disclose the information in the accounts. These requirements have been effective from April 1990. However, the leasing business in Japan is nowhere near as big as that in the UK and US.

Annual bonuses

It is common for Japanese companies, particularly large ones, to pay bonuses to their employees on an annual or semi-annual basis. Such payments are considered to be part of the remuneration package and may amount to several months' wages. The computation of such bonuses is often stipulated in the company's working regulations. Tax law prescribes the maximum bonuses that may be offset against tax. Bonuses paid to employees are included in the SEL accounts as a separate item under selling, general and administrative expenses but they are not separately disclosed in the Code accounts. In contrast, bonuses paid to directors and statutory auditors are not allowable against tax and are included in appropriations of retained earnings.

Cash (funds) flow statements

There is no requirement in Japan to prepare a funds statement in either the Code or SEL accounts. This differs from the UK and the US and is not consistent with IAS 7. However, whilst a funds statement is not required, a Ministry of Finance Ordinance stipulates that a cash flow statement must be included in the company's securities report and registration statement but only as a supplementary statement. Consequently, the statement falls outside the basic financial statements and supplementary schedules and outside the scope of audit. The cash flow statement was introduced in 1953 and consists of a quarterly cash receipts and disbursements statement for the last twelve months and a planned quarterly statement for the subsequent six months. Such information is disclosed under the heading 'accounting status' which is not part of the financial statements in the Securities Registration Statement. The introduction of the cash flow statement was an important development and well ahead of accounting practice in Anglo-Saxon countries.

Pensions

It is common for Japanese companies to provide for employee retirement and severance benefits. In general, employees are usually entitled to a lump-sum payment based on the current rate of pay and length of service.

In practice it is normal to use base pay to apply the service multiple since this excludes various allowances and any bonuses. Many schemes for employees have not been fully funded although in recent years some companies have decided to partially fund their schemes. Where schemes do exist it is common to try to obtain the maximum tax advantage on the unfunded element which is set at 40 per cent of the voluntary retirement and severance liability as at the balance sheet date. Contributions to the pension fund are charged to income as incurred, whereas those costs that relate to past service are treated as a liability and amortized.

Provisions and reserves

Designated provisions (e.g. provision for bad debts) are allowable against tax and available to all companies. Other than the provision for retirement allowance, all provisions allowed in one accounting period must be reversed in the following period. In addition to provisions there are a number of reserves that are tax-deductible provided they are recorded in the books of account.

Inventories

Considerable flexibility is offered, both in terms of accounting and tax regulations, to Japanese companies in valuing inventories. Unit cost, FIFO, LIFO, weighted-average cost, moving-average cost, straight-average cost, latest purchase price, and the retail inventory cost method are all acceptable methods of valuing inventories. In the UK, in contrast, SSAP 9 stipulates that the base stock method, LIFO and the latest purchase price method are not acceptable (although they are allowed by Companies Act 1985), whereas in Japan only the base stock method is not acceptable.

When valuing stocks at the year-end the rule is either cost or the lower of cost (applying one of the above methods) and market value. Companies may interpret market value to be either current replacement cost or net realizable value. In contrast, IAS 2 and SSAP 9 stipulate that inventories should be valued at the lower of cost and net realizable value. In the US the rule is the lower of cost or market value as in Japan. However, market value in the US means current replacement cost which should not exceed net realizable value and must not be less than realizable value reduced by the normal profit margin.

In Japan, where there is a substantial and irrevocable decline in the market value of inventories it is necessary to value inventories on the basis of the new market value, in accordance with the provisions of the Code.

Depreciation of tangible fixed assets

The use of accelerated rates of depreciation is far more common in Japan than in the US and the UK. This is mainly because of tax considerations.

The effect is to artificially reduce earnings of Japanese companies thereby increasing the P/E ratio. To compensate for this some analysts add back depreciation. For example, Thompson, of Barclays de Zoete Wedd, states in general that

> the easiest way to hide earnings is to make excess provisions and the largest and most manipulable provision is that for depreciation. The relationship between cash earnings and published earnings is probably as good a 'rule of thumb' measurement of the degree of conservatism of different accounting systems as is available.
>
> (Thompson 1989: 5)

Table 2.2 shows that US cash earnings were 192 per cent of published earnings and Japanese cash earnings were 298 per cent of published earnings for 1990. To compensate for this UK and US investment analysts adjust Japanese earnings by 298/192=155.21 per cent of the published figure and calculate an adjusted P/E ratio which in the case of Japan would have the effect of reducing it from 31.3 to 20.17. Using the US P/E ratio as the base the adjusted P/E ratios of the countries under consideration are lower than the unadjusted figure, with the exception of the UK.

Some would argue that this is a poor proxy of the degree of conservatism of accounting systems and that the adjustment creates a further distortion since Japanese depreciation charges are high, not only to obtain the maximum tax advantage but also because the purchase and scrapping of plant and equipment is more rapid than in the west. This is important when comparing Japanese P/E ratios with those in the UK since depreciation in Japan is based on historical cost whereas depreciation in the UK is sometimes based on revalued amounts.

When depreciating tangible assets, it is permissible in Japan to use the straight-line, the declining-balance, the unit-of-production method or the sum-of-the-year digits method. In practice, it is common to use the declining-balance method applying the rates prescribed by the tax regulations. Land is not normally depreciated in Japan and there is no requirement to review the useful lives of assets periodically as specified in IAS 4 (paragraph 16).

Intangible fixed assets

Intangible fixed assets such as goodwill, patent rights and trade marks must be stated at their unamortized amount. Goodwill may be recognized as an intangible fixed asset in the balance sheet only when purchased or acquired through a business transfer or merger. Purchased goodwill must be valued at acquisition cost. Consistent with international practice, internally generated goodwill is not accounted for in Japan.

Purchased goodwill must be amortized to income on a systematic basis over its estimated useful life and is allowable against tax. However, the

Code provides that goodwill must be amortized within five years of the acquisition and the Corporation Income Tax Law permits voluntary amortization of goodwill. In practice, purchased goodwill is amortized within five years in accordance with the requirement of the Code. Such an approach is consistent with the prudent accounting policies common in Continental Europe. In contrast, APBO 17 in the US stipulates that goodwill, like other intangible assets, must be amortized over its useful life which must not exceed 40 years.

Earnings per share (EPS)

Whereas EPS figures have been disclosed by listed companies for many years it was not until October 1982 that there was a requirement to disclose such information in the Code and SEL accounts. The computation of EPS must be based on the weighted-average number of shares outstanding during the year, although the effect of dilution caused by a free-share distribution is not to be taken into consideration. In calculating EPS, common stock equivalents such as convertible bonds and warrant bonds must be ignored.

Deferred charges

Certain costs may be accounted for as deferred charges in the balance sheet and, in accordance with the Code, must be stated at their unamortized amounts. Such costs include organization costs, pre-operating costs, new share issuing costs, bond issuing costs, bond discounts, and research and development costs.

Deferred charges have to be amortized to income on a systematic basis over their estimated useful life or any other basis. Notice the flexibility in approach permitted under Japanese GAAP; often an option is provided which permits alternative methods of accounting. In accordance with the provisions of the Code, organization costs, pre-operating costs and research and development costs are amortized within five years and share-issuing costs and bond-issuing costs are normally amortized over a period of three years, or in the case of bonds, the life of the bond if shorter.

Foreign currency translation

The Japanese Standard requires that a transaction denominated in a foreign currency should normally be translated at the actual exchange rate prevailing on the transaction date or the rates of exchange at which the transaction is contracted to be settled in the future. Exchange differences arising on settlement of short-term monetary items must be recognized as part of income for the current period. Such an approach is consistent with IAS 21.

Table 2.8 Translation methods of foreign currency financial statements, foreign enterprises

Method	*Foreign branches*	*Foreign subsidiaries and associates*
Principal application	Temporal method. Long-term monetary items must be translated at the historical rates. Exchange differences must be included in current income.	Modified temporal method. Long-term monetary items must be translated at the historical rates. Current net income and retained earnings at the year-end must be translated at the closing rate. Exchange differences must be treated as deferred assets/liabilities.
Exceptional application where long-term monetary and non-monetary items are not material	Current rate method. Exchange differences must be included in current income.	Current rate method. Exchange differences must be treated as deferred assets/liabilities.

Table 2.8 summarizes the translation methods which must be applied to foreign currency financial statements when preparing consolidated accounts in Japan. An important point is that the translation of financial statements differs between a foreign branch operation and a foreign subsidiary or associated company.

Audit requirements

The extent and type of audit under the Code depend upon the type and size of the company. The Code classifies companies into three size groups:

- *large* – those whose capital stock is not less than ¥500 million *or* whose total liabilities are not less than ¥20 billion;
- *medium* – those whose capital stock exceeds ¥100 million but is less than ¥500 million *and* whose total liabilities are below ¥20 billion;
- *small* – those whose capital stock does not exceed ¥100 million *and* whose total liabilities are below ¥20 billion.

The financial statements and supporting schedules of large corporations are subject to audit by both statutory auditors – a 'member' of the corporation – and by an independent external auditor (a CPA or audit corporation) whose appointment is confirmed at the annual general meeting. There is no requirement for small and medium-sized companies to be audited. In addition to the Code audit, public corporations have their financial accounts that are prepared in accordance with the SEL, audited.

The statutory audit is, in effect, an internal audit by individuals who may not also serve as a director, manager or employee. Statutory auditors are not qualified CPAs, so in technical terms they are unqualified investigators. The nature of the audit is to ensure that fraud has not and does not take place, that directors have fulfilled their responsibilities and complied both with the law and the articles of association.

In contrast, the CPA audit is undertaken by a highly qualified individual whose role is to express an opinion on the financial statements. To achieve this, CPAs must at all times be free and independent and must exercise due professional care and proper judgement in rendering their services.

In the past an auditor's ability to be truly independent has been compromised by the inequality in size of audit practices and the corporation being audited. It was not until 1966 that the CPA Law was amended to enable joint accounting practices to be developed. The 1966 amendment enabled five or more CPAs to form an audit corporation with unlimited liability. Whilst the size of audit corporations has grown over time (in 1990 there were 98 audit corporations compared with 50 in 1978) the imbalance in size between Keidanren and the JICPA means that the fixing of the CPA fee schedule may have an effect on independence.

Whilst accounting standards have evolved over the last century auditing standards have developed more recently. In addition to auditing standards issued by BADC, the JICPA has issued a series of audit releases covering a range from audits in general to specific aspects on confirming receivables and observing inventories. Such aspects are similar to those in the west although differences are apparent, particularly in respect of representation letters from management and confirmation of balances. Standard audit reports are produced by the JICPA for both the Code and SEL audits. An example of a corporate annual report prepared for the international reader is provided at the end of this chapter (see Appendix). As well as extracts from the financial statements and notes to the accounts of Matsushita Electric, the audit report is shown as an example of that included in an English version of an annual report prepared by a Japanese company.

SUMMARY

It was not until the 1860s and 1870s that limited liability companies developed in Japan and even then most of them failed quickly. In the main, this form of business organization was alien to the Japanese whose enterprises had traditionally been based on family mercantile houses. Nevertheless, the Meiji government encouraged the formation of corporations to demonstrate to the rest of the world that Japan was modern and had imported western ideas.

As well as importing western ideas, Japanese politicians, together with the bureaucracy and military men, saw an opportunity to highlight cultural aspects that would improve the efficiency of their business organizations. For example, Confucian ethics were highlighted with an emphasis on loyalty, dedication, responsibility and commitment to the goals of business organizations.

In the late nineteenth and early twentieth centuries the *zaibatsu* emerged as a major commercial force. The early *zaibatsu* were based on individual families and were assisted by government incentives, but other industrial capitalists were developed which were loyal to the military. Not surprisingly, the post-Second World War Occupation Forces sought to purge the *zaibatsu* and distribute their shareholdings more widely. While holding companies were made illegal and the *zaibatsu* were dismembered they were replaced after the Occupation Forces left Japan by the *keiretsu*, companies with interlocking shareholdings and directorships.

Post-Second World War Japan had been characterized by corporatism (i.e. interdependence between interest groups and the state). While developments in accounting in the first forty-five years of the twentieth century were dominated by the requirements of the military for consistent information, disclosure of information after the Second World War was influenced by the democratization programme. Since the shares of the dismembered *zaibatsu* were distributed to shareholders, the US introduced a new regulatory framework modelled on its own which was based on the provision of information to shareholders. From 1890 to 1952 the information needs of creditors had been predominant in the Commercial Code that was based on the German Commercial Code. While the Code still exists (although it has been substantially amended), and remains the major influence on accounting for most companies, the Securities and Exchange Law is more significant than the Commercial Code for companies that issue securities to the public. This is because the disclosure requirements of the Securities and Exchange Law are considerably more extensive than those of the Commercial Code.

The US hopes that the imposed regulatory framework would encourage the development of a thriving independent accounting profession has not materialized. The CPA examinations are controlled, in effect, by the state, and this has led to a very low examination pass rate and only 8,500 qualified accountants. The accountancy profession is not unique in this sense and is mirrored by the legal profession which only consists of 14,000 qualified lawyers. To a large extent the existence of large, thriving professional bodies is somewhat alien to Japan. Whereas such professionals have a great deal of potential job mobility in the west, this concept is foreign to a nation that continues to emphasize loyalty to company and country. Companies requiring accountants and lawyers recruit from universities and train the graduates themselves with the objective of meeting the skilled needs of the entity and only that entity and thereby loyalty to that entity. For most men in the large corporations the company represents the surrogate family, often to the detriment of their real families.

Another important aspect of regulation in Japanese accounting is that, while the examination pass rate to become a CPA is extremely low, subsequent rewards for qualification are not particularly high. This is because audit fees are negotiated between the JICPA and Keidanren with the two sides being unequal. The power of Keidanren leads to relatively modest audit fees and, as a consequence, modest professional accountancy salaries.

Accounting in Japan is dominated by statute, thus disclosure is uniform rather than flexible, although flexibility does exist in measurement. Furthermore, with the origins of financial reporting in Japan being based on the German Commercial Code it is not surprising that Japanese accounting is conservative rather than optimistic. While conservatism applies to the measurement dimension secrecy applies to disclosure.

APPENDIX

Extracts from the accounts of Matsushita Electric

CONSOLIDATED BALANCE SHEETS

Matsushita Electric Industrial Co., Ltd. and Subsidiaries
March 31, 1991 and 1990

	Yen (millions)		U.S. dollars (thousands) (note 2)
Assets	**1991**	1990	**1991**
Current assets:			
Cash and cash equivalents (note 6)	**¥1,657,525**	¥2,010,848	**$11,755,496**
Short-term investments, at cost, which approximates market	**182,829**	335,406	**1,296,660**
Trade receivables (notes 5 and 6):			
Notes	**148,161**	120,873	**1,050,787**
Accounts	**1,159,172**	1,015,719	**8,221,078**
Allowance for doubtful receivables	**(27,622)**	(24,251)	**(195,900)**
Net trade receivables	**1,279,711**	1,112,341	**9,075,965**
Inventories (notes 4 and 6)	**931,090**	846,005	**6,603,475**
Other current assets (note 8)	**351,774**	308,364	**2,494,851**
Total current assets	**4,402,929**	4,612,964	**31,226,447**
Non-current receivables	**423,741**	344,261	**3,005,255**
Investments and advances (notes 3 and 5)	**2,460,042**	1,647,575	**17,447,106**
Property, plant and equipment:			
Land	**177,004**	163,481	**1,255,348**
Buildings	**683,477**	605,201	**4,847,355**
Machinery and equipment	**1,993,747**	1,769,704	**14,140,050**
Construction in progress	**108,374**	56,530	**768,610**
	2,962,602	2,594,916	**21,011,363**
Less accumulated depreciation	**1,804,350**	1,637,274	**12,796,809**
Net property, plant and equipment	**1,158,252**	957,642	**8,214,554**
Other assets (note 8)	**316,179**	288,769	**2,242,404**
	¥8,761,143	¥7,851,211	**$62,135,766**

Liabilities and Stockholders' Equity	Yen (millions) 1991	Yen (millions) 1990	U.S. dollars (thousands) (note 2) 1991
Current liabilities:			
Short-term bank loans, including current portion of long-term debt (note 6)	**¥1,478,056**	¥1,045,848	**$10,482,666**
Trade payables (note 5):			
Notes	**97,140**	72,839	**688,936**
Accounts	**497,138**	439,358	**3,525,801**
Total trade payables	**594,278**	512,197	**4,214,737**
Accrued income taxes (note 8)	**173,916**	168,281	**1,233,447**
Accrued payroll	**157,877**	144,087	**1,119,695**
Other accrued expenses	**411,213**	372,599	**2,916,404**
Deposits and advances from customers	**130,995**	117,344	**929,043**
Employees' deposits	**116,345**	125,504	**825,142**
Other current liabilities	**114,607**	116,638	**812,816**
Total current liabilities	**3,177,287**	2,602,498	**22,533,950**
Long-term debt (note 6)	**1,223,740**	1,197,082	**8,679,007**
Retirement and severance benefits (note 7)	**289,317**	269,070	**2,051,894**
Minority interests	**636,052**	581,658	**4,511,007**
Stockholders' equity:			
Common stock of ¥50 ($.35) par value (notes 3, 6 and 9):			
Authorized—5,000,000,000 shares			
Issued—2,093,403,004 shares (2,080,234,037 shares in 1990)	**195,258**	184,940	**1,384,808**
Capital surplus (note 6)	**561,872**	541,786	**3,984,908**
Legal reserve (note 9)	**57,057**	52,181	**404,660**
Retained earnings (notes 6 and 9)	**2,718,549**	2,487,093	**19,280,489**
Cumulative translation adjustments (note 1(e))	**(97,989)**	(65,097)	**(694,957)**
Total stockholders' equity	**3,434,747**	3,200,903	**24,359,908**
Commitments and contingent liabilities (note 12)			
	¥8,761,143	¥7,851,211	**$62,135,766**

CONSOLIDATED STATEMENTS OF INCOME

Matsushita Electric Industrial Co., Ltd. and Subsidiaries
Years ended March 31, 1991, 1990 and 1989

	Yen (millions)			U.S. dollars (thousands) (note 2)
	1991	1990	1989	**1991**
Net sales (note 5)	**¥6,599,306**	¥6,002,786	¥5,504,250	**$46,803,589**
Cost of sales (note 5)	**4,393,502**	4,009,590	3,670,885	**31,159,589**
Gross profit	**2,205,804**	1,993,196	1,833,365	**15,644,000**
Selling, general and administrative expenses	**1,733,214**	1,540,475	1,416,176	**12,292,298**
Operating profit	**472,590**	452,721	417,189	**3,351,702**
Other income (deductions):				
Interest and dividend income	**266,634**	213,242	177,857	**1,891,021**
Interest expense	**(161,371)**	(109,202)	(88,932)	**(1,144,475)**
Other, net	**19,583**	14,969	23,333	**138,887**
	124,846	119,009	112,258	**885,433**
Income before income taxes	**597,436**	571,730	529,447	**4,237,135**
Provision for income taxes (note 8):				
Current	**330,846**	309,664	309,938	**2,346,426**
Deferred	**(25,852)**	(8,717)	(23,023)	**(183,348)**
	304,994	300,947	286,915	**2,163,078**
Income before equity in earnings of associated companies and minority interests	**292,442**	270,783	242,532	**2,074,057**
Equity in earnings of associated companies (note 5)	**13,040**	11,272	11,650	**92,482**
Minority interests	**46,568**	46,494	40,720	**330,269**
Net income	**¥ 258,914**	¥ 235,561	¥ 213,462	**$ 1,836,270**

	Yen			U.S. dollars (note 2)
Net income per share of common stock (note 1 (j))	**¥ 117.12**	¥ 108.34	¥ 99.94	**$ .83**

CONSOLIDATED STATEMENTS OF SURPLUS

Matsushita Electric Industrial Co., Ltd. and Subsidiaries
Years ended March 31, 1991, 1990 and 1989

	Yen (millions)			
	Retained earnings	Capital surplus	Legal reserve	Cumulative translation adjustments
Balance at March 31, 1988	¥ 2,094,625	¥ 324,478	¥ 43,397	¥ (117,242)
Net income for year	213,462			
Increase in capital surplus arising from merger of a consolidated subsidiary (note 9)		141,750		
Increase in capital surplus and transfer to minority interests arising on conversion of debentures (note 9)	(1,190)	20,325	(24)	
Cash dividends (note 9)	(19,043)			
Transfer to legal reserve (note 9)	(4,544)		4,544	
Exercise of stock purchase warrants (note 9)		1		
Translation adjustments (note 1(e))				1,726
Balance at March 31, 1989	2,283,310	486,554	47,917	(115,516)
Net income for year	235,561			
Increase in capital surplus and transfer to minority interests arising on conversion of debentures (note 9)	(2,279)	42,007	(225)	44
Allocation related to detachable warrants (note 6)		13,225		
Cash dividends (note 9)	(25,010)			
Transfer to legal reserve (note 9)	(4,489)		4,489	
Translation adjustments (note 1(e))				50,375
Balance at March 31, 1990	2,487,093	541,786	52,181	(65,097)
Net income for year	**258,914**			
Increase in capital surplus and transfer to minority interests arising on conversion of debentures (note 9)	**(1,676)**	**20,086**	**(52)**	**1**
Cash dividends (note 9)	**(20,854)**			
Transfer to legal reserve (note 9)	**(4,928)**		**4,928**	
Translation adjustments (note 1(e))				**(32,893)**
Balance at March 31, 1991	**¥ 2,718,549**	**¥ 561,872**	**¥ 57,057**	**¥ (97,989)**

	U.S. dollars (thousands) (note 2)			
	Retained earnings	Capital surplus	Legal reserve	Cumulative translation adjustments
Balance at March 31, 1990	$ 17,638,957	$3,842,454	$370,078	$ (461,681)
Net income for year	**1,836,270**			
Increase in capital surplus and transfer to minority interests arising on conversion of debentures (note 9)	**(11,887)**	**142,454**	**(368)**	**7**
Cash dividends (note 9)	**(147,901)**			
Transfer to legal reserve (note 9)	**(34,950)**		**34,950**	
Translation adjustments (note 1(e))				**(233,283)**
Balance at March 31, 1991	**$ 19,280,489**	**$3,984,908**	**$404,660**	**$(694,957)**

CONSOLIDATED STATEMENTS OF CASH FLOWS

Matsushita Electric Industrial Co., Ltd. and Subsidiaries
Years ended March 31, 1991, 1990 and 1989

	Yen (millions)			U.S. dollars (thousands) (note 2)
	1991	1990	1989	**1991**
Cash flows from operating activities (note 10):				
Net income	**¥ 258,914**	¥ 235,561	¥ 213,462	**$ 1,836,270**
Adjustments to reconcile net income to net cash provided by operating activities:				
Depreciation	**273,418**	237,749	217,789	**1,939,135**
Deferred income taxes	**(25,852)**	(8,717)	(23,023)	**(183,348)**
Minority interests in income	**46,568**	46,494	40,720	**330,269**
Increase in trade receivables	**(198,826)**	(283,270)	(105,937)	**(1,410,113)**
Increase in inventories	**(116,538)**	(4,236)	(123,640)	**(826,511)**
Increase in other current assets	**(31,758)**	(13,124)	(9,624)	**(225,234)**
Increase in non-current receivables	**(79,480)**	(63,479)	(72,413)	**(563,688)**
Increase in trade payables	**89,893**	103,258	58,388	**637,539**
Increase (decrease) in accrued income taxes	**7,934**	(897)	(36,159)	**56,270**
Increase in accrued expenses and other current liabilities	**42,125**	72,561	20,846	**298,759**
Increase in retirement and severance benefits	**21,305**	21,216	20,126	**151,099**
Other	**20,523**	92	3,025	**145,553**
Net cash provided by operating activities	**308,226**	343,208	203,560	**2,186,000**
Cash flows from investing activities:				
Proceeds from sale of short-term investments	**356,272**	85,686	284,076	**2,526,752**
Purchase of short-term investments	**(207,562)**	(217,805)	(142,326)	**(1,472,071)**
Proceeds from disposition of investments and advances	**562,386**	427,830	185,268	**3,988,553**
Increase in investments and advances (note 3)	**(1,382,574)**	(543,599)	(447,895)	**(9,805,489)**
Capital expenditures	**(478,412)**	(346,371)	(318,210)	**(3,392,993)**
Other	**5,722**	(2,737)	(6,544)	**40,582**
Net cash used in investing activities	**(1,144,168)**	(596,996)	(445,631)	**(8,114,666)**
Cash flows from financing activities (note 10):				
Increase in short-term borrowings	**464,641**	167,658	176,205	**3,295,326**
Increase (decrease) in deposits and advances from customers and employees	**4,492**	13,512	(7,253)	**31,858**
Proceeds from long-term debt	**257,223**	769,739	196,543	**1,824,277**
Repayments of long-term debt	**(173,198)**	(134,021)	(38,282)	**(1,228,355)**
Dividends paid	**(20,854)**	(25,010)	(19,043)	**(147,901)**
Dividends paid to minority interests	**(11,055)**	(10,679)	(9,528)	**(78,404)**
Other	**—**	1,418	2	**—**
Net cash provided by financing activities	**521,249**	782,617	298,644	**3,696,801**
Effect of exchange rate changes on cash and cash equivalents	**(38,630)**	41,875	1,003	**(273,972)**
Net increase (decrease) in cash and cash equivalents	**(353,323)**	570,704	57,576	**(2,505,837)**
Cash and cash equivalents at beginning of year	**2,010,848**	1,440,144	1,382,568	**14,261,333**
Cash and cash equivalents at end of year	**¥1,657,525**	¥2,010,848	¥1,440,144	**$11,755,496**

NOTES TO CONSOLIDATED FINANCIAL STATEMENTS

1 Summary of Significant Accounting Policies

(a) Basis of Presenting Consolidated Financial Statements
The Company and its domestic subsidiaries maintain their books of account in conformity with financial accounting standards of Japan, and its foreign subsidiaries in conformity with those of the countries of their domicile.

The consolidated financial statements presented herein have been prepared in a manner and reflect the adjustments which are necessary to conform them with United States generally accepted accounting principles.

(b) Principles of Consolidation (See Notes 3 and 5)
The consolidated financial statements include the accounts of the Company and its subsidiaries. Significant intercompany accounts and transactions have been eliminated in consolidation.

Investments in certain associated companies in which the Company's ownership is 20% to 50% are stated at their underlying net equity value after elimination of intercompany profits. The difference, not significant in amount, between the cost and underlying net equity at acquisition date of investments in subsidiaries and companies accounted for on an equity basis is being amortized over a ten-year period.

(c) Leases
Certain subsidiaries of the Company lease machinery and equipment. Leases of such assets are principally accounted for as direct financing leases and included in trade receivables-accounts and non-current receivables in the accompanying balance sheets.

(d) Inventories (See Note 4)
Finished goods and work in process are stated at the lower of cost (average) or market. Raw materials are stated at cost, principally on a first-in, first-out basis, not in excess of current replacement cost.

(e) Foreign Currency Translation
Foreign currency financial statements are translated in accordance with Statement of Financial Accounting Standards (SFAS) No. 52, "Foreign Currency Translation," under which all assets and liabilities are translated into yen at year-end rates and income and expense accounts are translated at weighted average rates. Adjustments resulting from translation of financial statements are reflected under the caption, "Cumulative translation adjustments," a separate component of stockholders' equity.

Foreign currency transaction gains and losses included in the consolidated statements of income for the three years ended March 31, 1991 were not significant.

(f) Property, Plant and Equipment
Property, plant and equipment is stated at cost. Depreciation is computed primarily by the declining-balance method based on the estimated useful lives.

(g) Investments and Advances (See Note 5)
The portfolio of marketable equity securities, which is included in investments and advances, is carried at the lower of cost or market, cost being determined by the average method. Other items included in investments and advances, including other marketable securities, are carried at cost or less.

(h) Income Taxes (See Note 8)
Provision is made in the accounts to reflect the interperiod allocation of income taxes resulting from certain income and expenses being treated differently for financial reporting purposes than for tax computation purposes.

Income taxes have not been accrued for undistributed earnings of subsidiaries and associated companies, as taxes resulting from distributions of such earnings would not be significant.

SFAS No. 96, effective for fiscal year beginning after December 15, 1991 with earlier applications permitted, requires the use of the asset and liability approach in accounting for income taxes.

If SFAS No. 96 had been implemented without any amendments, a certain portion of the Company's cumulative deferred income tax assets would probably not be sustainable, with a corresponding effect on retained earnings.

The Company is examining the impact of the alternatives, including amendments currently under consideration by the Financial Accounting Standards Board, and has not yet determined the period or method of adoption.

(i) Retirement and Severance Benefits (See Note 7)
During the year ended March 31, 1990, the Company adopted the provisions of SFAS No. 87, "Employers' Accounting for Pensions," for unfunded retirement and severance benefit plans covering substantially all of its employees. Previously, provision was made in the consolidated balance sheets for the estimated unfunded liability. The adoption of SFAS No. 87 had no material effect on the consolidated financial statements.

(j) Net Income Per Share (See Notes 6 and 9)
In computing net income per share, the average number of shares outstanding during each period has been used, appropriately adjusted for free distributions of common stock and the number of shares issuable upon conversion of common share equivalents and exercise of stock purchase warrants.

(k) Cash Equivalents
Cash equivalents include all highly liquid debt instruments purchased with a maturity of three months or less.

(l) Foreign Exchange Contract (See Note 11)
The Company entered into forward foreign exchange contracts to hedge the impact of foreign currency fluctuations on certain monetary assets and liabilities denominated in foreign currencies and certain firm foreign currency commitments. Gains and losses on foreign currency monetary assets and liabilities are recognized and reported currently in income. With respect to firm commitments, gains and losses are recognized when the transactions are settled and accounted for as part of the transactions.

KPMG Peat Marwick

The Board of Directors
Matsushita Electric Industrial Co., Ltd.

We have audited the accompanying consolidated balance sheets (expressed in yen) of Matsushita Electric Industrial Co., Ltd. and subsidiaries as of March 31, 1991 and 1990 and the related consolidated statements of income, surplus and cash flows for each of the years in the three-year period ended March 31, 1991. These consolidated financial statements are the responsibility of the Company's management. Our responsibility is to express an opinion on these consolidated financial statements based on our audits.

We conducted our audits in accordance with generally accepted auditing standards. Those standards require that we plan and perform the audit to obtain reasonable assurance about whether the financial statements are free of material misstatement. An audit includes examining, on a test basis, evidence supporting the amounts and disclosures in the financial statements. An audit also includes assessing the accounting principles used and significant estimates made by management, as well as evaluating the overall financial statement presentation. We believe that our audits provide a reasonable basis for our opinion.

The segment information required to be disclosed in financial statements under United States generally accepted accounting principles is not presented in the accompanying consolidated financial statements. Foreign issuers are presently exempted from such disclosure requirement in Securities and Exchange Act filings with the United States Securities and Exchange Commission.

In our opinion, except that the omission of the segment information discussed above results in an incomplete presentation, the consolidated financial statements referred to above present fairly, in all material respects, the financial position of Matsushita Electric Industrial Co., Ltd. and subsidiaries at March 31, 1991 and 1990, and the results of their operations and their cash flows for each of the years in the three-year period ended March 31, 1991, in conformity with United States generally accepted accounting principles.

The consolidated financial statements as of and for the year ended March 31, 1991 have been translated into United States dollars solely for the convenience of the reader. We have recomputed the translation and, in our opinion, the consolidated financial statements expressed in yen have been translated into United States dollars on the basis set forth in note 2 of the notes to consolidated financial statements.

Osaka, Japan
May 21, 1991

KPMG Peat Marwick

REFERENCES

Abegglen, J.C. (1958) *The Japanese Factory: Aspects of its Social Organisation*, Glencoe, Ill.: The Free Press.

—— and Stalk, G. (1985) *Kaisha: The Japanese Corporation*, New York: Basic Books.

Aida, Y. (1972) *Nihonjin no ishiki kozo*, Tokyo: Kodansha Gendai Shinsho.

Alston, J.P. (1986) *The American Samurai*, Berlin: Walter de Gruyter.

Ames, W.L. (1981) *Police and Community in Japan*, London: Routledge and Kegan Paul.

Ballon, R.J., Tomita, I. and Usami, H. (1976) *Financial Reporting in Japan*, Tokyo: Kodansha International.

Buck, P. (1966) *The People of Japan*, London: Robert Hale.

Burawoy, M. (1983) 'Between the labour process and the state: factory regimes under advanced capitalism', *American Sociological Review*, 48.

Choi, F.D.S. and Hiramatsu, K. (eds) (1987) *Accounting and Financial Reporting in Japan*, Wokingham: Van Nostrand.

de Carmoy, H. (1990) *Global Banking Strategy*, Oxford: Basil Blackwell.

Clark, R.G. (1979) *The Japanese Company*, Princeton: Princeton University Press.

Cooke, T.E. (1991) 'The evolution of financial reporting in Japan: a shame culture perspective', *Accounting, Business and Financial History*, Autumn.

—— (1993a) 'Disclosure in Japanese corporate annual reports', *Journal of Business Finance and Accounting*, June.

—— (1993b) 'The impact of accounting principles on profits: the US versus Japan', *Accounting and Business Research*, forthcoming.

—— and Kikuya, M. (1992a) *Financial Reporting in Japan: Regulation, Practice and Environment*, Oxford: Basil Blackwell.

—— and —— (1992b) 'International comparison of segmental reporting in the US, UK and Japan', *Accounting Research (Tokyo)*, Autumn.

Dale, P.N. (1986) *The Myth of Japanese Uniqueness*, London: Routledge.

Doi, T. (1971) *'Amae' no kozo*, Tokyo: Kobundo.

Dore, R. (1973) *British Factory–Japanese Factory: The Origins of Diversity in Industrial Relations*, Berkeley, California: University of California Press.

Edwards, R. (1979) *Contested Terrain*, New York: Basic Books.

Franklin, G. (1988) *Japanese Price–Earnings Ratios*, London: UBS–Philips and Drew.

Fransman, M. (1990) *The Market and Beyond: Cooperation and Competition in Information Technology in the Japanese System*, Cambridge: Cambridge University Press.

Fujita, Y. (1966) 'The evolution of financial reporting in Japan', *International Journal of Accounting*, vol. 2.

Fukui, H. (1981) 'Bureaucratic power in Japan', in B. Drysdale and H. Kitaogi (eds) *Japan and Australia: Two Societies and their Interaction*, Canberra: Australian National University Press.

George, A. (1988) 'Japanese interest group behavior', in J.A.A. Stockwin, *Dynamics and Immobilist Politics in Japan*, London: Macmillan.

Gray, S.J. (1988) 'Towards a theory of cultural influence on the development of accounting systems', *Abacus*, March.

Henderson, D.F. (1973) *Foreign Enterprise in Japan: Law and Politics*, Chapel Hill, N.C.: The University of North Carolina Press.

Hendry, J. (1987) *Understanding Japanese Society*, London: Croom Helm.

Hodder, J.E. and Tschoeg, A.E. (1985) 'Some aspects of Japanese corporate finance', *Journal of Financial and Quantitative Analysis*, June.

Ishizumi, K. (1988) *Acquiring Japanese Companies*, Tokyo: *The Japan Times*.

James, S. and Parker, R.H. (1990) *A Dictionary of Business Quotations*, London: Routledge.

Japanese Institute of Certified Public Accountants (JICPA) (1984) *Corporate Disclosure in Japan: Reporting*, Tokyo: JICPA.

—— (1987) *Corporate Disclosure in Japan: Overview*, Tokyo: JICPA.

Kahn, H. (1979) *World Economic Development*, London: Croom Helm.

Lehmann, J.-P., (1988) 'Themes and theories in modern history', in S. Henny and J.-P. Lehmann (eds), *Themes and Theories in Modern History*, London: The Athlone Press.

Lincoln, E.J. (1988) *Japan Facing Economic Maturity*, Washington, DC: The Brookings Institution.

Lincoln, J.R. and Kalleberg, A.L. (1990) *Culture, Control, and Commitment*, Cambridge: Cambridge University Press.

McKinnon, J.L. (1986) *The Historical Development and Operational Form of Corporate Reporting Regulation in Japan*, New York: Garland Publishing.

—— and Harrison, G.L. (1985) 'Cultural influence on corporate and governmental policy determination in Japan', *Journal of Accounting and Public Policy*, 4.

Mason, A.K. (1978) *The Development of International Financial Reporting Standards*, ICRA Paper No. 17, Lancaster: Lancaster University.

Morishima, M. (1982) *Why Has Japan Succeeded?* Cambridge: Cambridge University Press.

Nagourney, S.H. (1988) *Japan – Parts 1 and 2: The World's Largest Capital Exporter*, New York: Shearson Lehman Hutton.

Nester, W.R. (1990) *The Foundation of Japanese Power*, London: Macmillan.

Ogura, E. (1982) 'The Nakai family's bookkeeping system', *Accounting and Business Research*, Spring.

Ohkawa, K. and Rosovsky, H. (1973) *Japanese Economic Growth: Trend Accelerator in the Twentieth Century*, Oxford: Oxford University Press.

Organisation for Economic Co-operation and Development (OECD) (1989) *Economic Surveys: Japan*, Paris: OECD.

Ouchi, W.G. (1981) *Theory Z*, Reading, Mass.: Addison-Wesley.

Radebaugh, L.H. (1975) 'Environmental factors influencing the development of accounting objectives, standards and practices in Peru', *International Journal of Accounting Education and Research*, Fall.

Reischauer, E.O. (1988) *The Japanese Today*, Cambridge, Mass.: The Belknap Press of Harvard University Press.

Rohlen, T.P. (1974) *For Harmony and Strength: Japanese White Collar Organization in Anthropological Perspective*, Berkeley, California: University of California Press.

Sakakibara, S., Yamaji, H., Sakurai, H., Shiroshita, K. and Fukuda, S. (1988) *The Japanese Stock Market*, Westport, Conn.: Praeger.

Sanders, T.H., Hatfield, H.R. and Moore, U. (1938) *A Statement of Accounting Principles*, New York: American Institute of Accountants.

Shimme, S. (1937) 'Introduction to double-entry bookkeeping in Japan', *The Accounting Review*, September.

Shively, D.H. (1971) *Tradition and Modernization in Japanese Culture*, Princeton, N.J.: Princeton University Press.

Someya, K. (1989) 'Accounting "revolutions" in Japan', *Accounting Historians Journal*, vol. 16.

Soviak, E. (1971) 'On the nature of Western progress: the journal of the Iwakura Embassy', in D.H. Shively (ed.), *Tradition and Modernization in Japanese Culture*, Princeton, N.J.: Princeton University Press.

Sumiya, M. (1981) 'Reconstruction of the Theory of Japanese Labour Relations', *Nikon Rodo Kyokai Zasshi*, vol. 262, January.

Suzuki, T. (1975) *Tozasareta Gengo – Nihongo nosekai*, Tokyo: Shincho Sensho.

Takatera, S. and Yamamoto, M. (1987) 'The cultural significance of accounting in Japan', Paper presented at the European Institute for Advanced Studies in Management, Brussels, December.

Tanaka, H. and Smith, M.D.H. (eds) (1976) *The Japanese Legal System*, Tokyo: University of Tokyo Press.

Thompson, P. (1989) *The Valuation of International Equity Markets*, London: Barclays de Zoete Wedd.

Wakiyama, T. (1986) 'The nature and tools of Japan's industrial policy', *Harvard International Law Journal*, 27, special issue.

Waldmeir, P. (1989) 'Japanese financial markets: walls improve view from abroad', *Financial Times*, 13 March.

Watanabe, S. (1978) *Bunka no jidai*, Tokyo: Bunshun Bunko.

van Wolferen, K. (1989) *The Enigma of Japanese Power*, London: Macmillan.

Zysman, J. (1983) *Government, Markets and Growth: Financial Systems and the Politics of Industrial Change*, Ithaca: Cornell University Press.

3 South Korea

In Ki Joo, Jee Hong Kim and Joon Seuk Kim

INTRODUCTION

Geography and population

The Republic of Korea occupies the southern half of a peninsula which juts down from the northeastern part of Asia. To the east and south lie the Japanese islands. The area of the Republic is 38,000 square miles or 97,000 square kilometres. The terrain is mostly mountainous with only 20 per cent of the land arable. Korea seldom has earthquakes and even when they occur they have not been as strong as those that Japan experiences.

After Japan surrendered unconditionally to the United States in the Second World War, Korea was divided into North Korea (the Democratic People's Republic of Korea) and South Korea (the Republic of Korea). Because Japan occupied Korea for 35 years before and during the Second World War, both North Korea and South Korea refused to have diplomatic relationships with Japan – although the latter did eventually open diplomatic relationships with Japan in 1962 and North Korea is planning to have diplomatic relationships with Japan soon.

The population of Korea[1] was over 43 million in November, 1988 and it is one of the most densely populated countries in the world. The annual growth of population in the urban area has averaged 5 per cent in recent years. Seoul, the capital city, with more than one-quarter of the country's population, is not only the focus of the administrative and cultural activities but the centre of the largest industrial concentration. The headquarters of corporations and government offices are largely located in and around Seoul.

Government

Korea has a constitutional form of government with the greatest power in the hands of the President. Under the Constitution as revised in late 1987, the President is directly elected to serve a single five-year term.

Legislative powers are from the National Assembly which consists of

299 members. National Assembly approval is required to pass the national budget, ratify treaties, review administrative activities, as well as initiate and approve legislation. The Assembly may require testimony from government officials and is empowered to remove them from office. The Constitution also grants the National Assembly the power to impeach the President.

The judiciary is a separate institute of government which is composed of four levels. Cases are tried in the family courts or district courts and then in appellate courts. The Supreme Court is the highest judicial court and its chief justice is appointed by the President with the consent of the National Assembly.

The economy

The economy of Korea has been one of the outstanding successes of international development. By the end of 1992, real GNP had grown at an average rate of 8.5 per cent annually since 1970. However, the annual growth rate during the period from 1990 to 1992 averaged 7.5 per cent. The per capita GNP, in current prices, substantially increased from US$248 in 1970 to US$6,749 in 1992. Such an improvement may be attributed to the nation's will to industrialization based on the human resources of a well-educated, highly motivated and industrious people. Like most other nations where Confucianism used to dominate their cultural development, Koreans respect scholars and teachers. They are highly motivated to educate their children. Koreans may also have been inspired by Japan's successful economy. The government announced in January 1993 that Korea planned to join the Organisation for Economic Co-operation and Development (OECD) in 1996, projecting that the per capita GNP would be over US$10,000 by then. To comply with the OECD requirements, the Korean government may take cautious steps towards trade and foreign exchange liberalization. Also, Korea has gradually upgraded its position in the General Agreement on Tariffs and Trade (GATT) to an Article 11 member which lifts the quantitative import restrictions permitted to developing countries. Korea also became an Article 8 member of the International Monetary Fund (IMF) in 1989.

Relative importance of public sector companies

The Korean economy is basically and largely directed by private sector companies. However, it is in part affected by public sector companies, including government business and firms whose equity has been wholly or partially invested and controlled by the government. In 1986, the formation of tangible fixed assets in the public sector totalled 3.3 trillion (trillion = 1,000,000,000,000) *won* or 12.6 per cent of the whole formation of fixed assets (see Table 3.1). The public sector enterprises

Table 3.1 The relative importance of public sector companies in the national economy

	1981	*1984*	*1985*	*1986*
The formation of tangible fixed assets (unit: trillion *won*):				
Public sector (a)	1.63	3.24	3.51	3.29
Total (b)	12.93	20.79	22.43	26.24
(a)/(b) × 100	12.60	15.58	15.65	12.54
Employment (unit: 1,000):				
Public sector (c)	76	126	132	138
Total (d)	14,023	14,429	14,970	15,505
(c)/(d) × 100	0.54	0.87	0.88	0.89
Budget (unit: trillion *won*):				
Public sector (e)	7.6	11.7	13.0	14.5
Government general budget (f)	8.0	11.0	12.4	13.8
(e)/(f) × 100	95.0	106.4	104.8	105.1
Value added (unit: trillion *won*):				
Public sector (g)	1.4	3.7	4.0	–
GNP (h)	45.1	66.4	72.8	83.8
(g)/(h) × 100	3.10	5.57	5.49	–

Source: Korea Institute for Economics & Technology, *Performance Evaluation of Government Invested Enterprises* (in Korean), December 1987, pp. 15–18.

employed 140,000 which was 0.7 per cent of the total employed population. The total budget of the public sector companies in 1986 was 14.5 trillion *won*, which was in excess of the national budget. The value added by the public sector was about 4 trillion *won* or 5.5 per cent of the GNP in 1985. Overall, the public sector has never dominated the Korean economy but the relative importance of the public sector is by no means negligible.

Size of private sector companies

At the end of December 1989, the number of companies in Korea was over 1.2 million as shown in Table 3.2. According to the Small and Medium Enterprise Law, companies employing less than 300 employees belong to the category of small and medium companies. The number of small and medium companies was about 1.2 million or 98.7 per cent of the whole, while the number of large companies was 16,512 or 1.3 per cent.

In addition, small and medium companies may be compared with large companies in terms of the total number of employees, production amount and value added. The small and medium companies number about 4.8 million employees or 63 per cent of the whole, and the large companies number about 2.8 million or 37 per cent. The production amount by large

Table 3.2 Comparison between small and medium companies and large companies

	Number of companies		*Number of employees*		*Production amount*		*Value added*	
Size of companies	*Unit: 1,000*	*Per cent*	*Unit: 1,000*	*Per cent*	*Unit: trillion* won	*Per cent*	*Unit: trillion* won	*Per cent*
Small and medium	1,208	98.7	4,820	63	85.9	46.3	21.8	40.2
Large	16	1.3	2,827	37	99.6	53.7	32.4	59.8
Total	1,224	100	7,647	100	185.5	100	54.2	100

Source: Korea Federation of Small Business, *The Small Industry Statistics of Major Countries*, December 1989, p. 11.

companies totals 99.6 trillion *won* or 53.7 per cent, while the production amount by small and medium companies totals 85.9 trillion *won* or 46.3 per cent. Finally, the value added by large companies was 32.4 trillion *won* or 59.7 per cent and the value added by small and medium companies was 21.8 trillion *won* or 40.3 per cent.

Ownership structure of private sector companies

Korean companies are largely young because most of them have been established since the Korean War in 1950. Most were run by single proprietors or by their families and were not open to the public until the end of 1972 when the government adopted the Special Promotion Act. According to the Act, the government was empowered to force privately run and financially healthy companies to go public by offering some form of incentive such as preferential treatment in corporate taxation and credit allocations. With the government's efforts, the number of companies open to the public has gradually increased from 352 in 1980 to 647 as of 30 April 1990.

The ownership of listed companies in Korea has been substantially concentrated on single proprietors who are the founders of the companies or founders' family members. As Korean companies become mature, the ownership is expected to be spread over small investors. As shown in Table 3.3, the proportion of family ownership, ranging from a low of 0.35 per cent to a high of 88.4 per cent, was 28.8 per cent on average. The firms whose single proprietors or their family members owned over 20 per cent made up three-quarters of the sampled companies. Almost two-thirds of sampled firms belong to the category of minority control with a proportion of family ownership between 20 and 50 per cent. Yet it should be admitted that these figures of family ownership may be somewhat biased downward in many cases because traders in current security transactions do not have to identify themselves by their real names. Thus, it is possible that the real proportion of family ownership may be higher.

A group of companies owned by the same individual or his or her family members is known as a *chaebol. Chaebols* have played a very important role in the Korean economy. For instance the top 30 *chaebols*' total assets, equities, and sales are 45, 41 and 48 per cent respectively, of those of all Korean corporations.

The structure of Korean *chaebols* can be characterized as follows:

- The major owners of a *chaebol* are usually top managers who actively participate in the management. In other words, ownership and management are not separated from each other.
- Member firms of a *chaebol* are very diverse in terms of industry specification.

Sources of finance

Throughout the 1980s the proportion of internal funds has steadily grown and surpassed that of external funds in 1988 as shown in Table 3.4. One of the major factors contributing to such improvement was the increase of retained earnings due to the booming economy since the mid-1980s.

Table 3.3 Proportion of family ownership of 411 listed industrial corporations

*Proportion of family ownership (%)**	*Number of companies*	*Relative frequency (%)*	*Cumulative frequency (%)*
Under 10.0	47	11.4	11.4
10–19.9	60	14.6	26.0
20–29.9	112	27.4	53.4
30–39.9	106	25.8	79.2
40–49.9	55	13.4	92.6
50–59.9	17	4.1	96.7
60–69.9	12	2.9	99.6
70–79.9	1	0.2	99.8
80–89.9	1	0.2	100.0
90–100	0	0.0	100.0
Total	411†	100.0	

Source: Ungki Lim, *Ownership and Control Structure of Korean Listed Firms* (Korea Listed Companies Association), November 1989, p. 15.

Notes: *Average = 28.8 per cent; minimum = 0.35 per cent; maximum = 88.4 per cent.
† As of December 1988 the number of listed companies was 502, from which 411 companies were sampled in this study.

Table 3.4 Financing structure of manufacturing firms (%)

	1970–4	*1975–9*	*1980–4*	*1985*	*1986*	*1987*	*1988*
Internal Funds	19.5	22.8	30.0	39.2	41.5	37.1	56.0
Retained Earnings	5.4	8.2	5.0	7.5	13.4	10.7	21.3
Depreciation	14.1	13.5	21.8	28.0	24.6	22.4	28.7
Reserve	–	1.1	3.2	3.7	3.5	4.0	6.0
External funds	80.5	77.2	70.0	60.8	58.5	62.9	44.0
Stock*	12.9	7.9	7.7	6.7	5.3	10.7	9.5
Loan	41.6	41.3	34.1	46.3	31.4	25.7	9.6
Others†	26.1	28.0	28.2	7.8	21.8	26.5	24.8
Total financing demands	100.0	100.0	100.0	100.0	100.0	100.0	100.0

Source: The Bank of Korea, *Monthly Bulletin*, March 1990, pp. 9–10.

Notes: *The paid-in capital in excess of stated value was excluded.
† Others include the paid-in capital in excess of stated value, accounts payable, and notes payable.

Another major factor was the augmentation of capital surplus due to paid-in capital in excess of stated value after firms were allowed to issue shares at current prices in a buoyant securities market.

On the other hand, the proportion of external funds which include the issuance of stock, loans, accounts payable, etc. has become lower. One thing to note is that the composition of external funds has been changed as compared to that in the 1970s. Direct financing by the issuance of stock has steadily increased while the loans have substantially decreased. For instance, the proportion of loans in 1988 was only 9.6 per cent of the total financing demands. In the 1970s and early 1980s it was difficult to raise corporate funds by direct financing because there were not many small investors and the Korean securities market was not well developed. As the Korean economy develops, the number of small investors is increasing and now many Korean companies can raise corporate funds through direct financing.

The securities market

The Korean securities market which reached the record index of 1,007 on 1 April 1989 has since declined as shown in Table 3.5. The market value of shares declined from US$ 110.2 billion in 1990 to US$ 96.4 billion in 1991. The primary factors behind the market's sluggish performance in 1991 were twofold: a worsening economic situation and a supply/demand imbalance. Poor economic figures such as a record trade deficit, high inflation and high interest rates led to poor corporate earnings, resulting in poor market sentiment throughout the year and a serious imbalance of

Table 3.5 Securities market statistics

At year-end	*1985*	*1988*	*1989*	*1990*	*1991(E)*	*1992(E)*
Market index (CSPI) (4 Jan. 1980 = 100)	163.4	907.2	909.7	696.1	610.9	800
PER (times)*	5.7	13.6	22.9	18.5	14.8	12.6
Market cap (US $ billion)	7.4	94.3	140.9	110.2	96.4	133
Market cap/GNP (%)	8.2	54.6	67.1	46.3	36	44
No. of listed companies	342	502	626	669	686	720
No. of listed stocks (1,000 shares)	796	2,511	4,242	4,796	5,102	5,700
Daily trading volume (US$ million)	14.2	289.2	413	256	282	500
No. of investors (% of population)†	1.9	6.1	13.9	5.6	6.0	7.0
Ownership of institutional investors	47.5	37.0	45.4	54.2	55.0	60.0
Corporate earnings growth (%)‡	−24.1	27.5	−0.7	−5.3	10.0	15.0
Funds raised through equity (US$ million)	331	11,358	21,585	4,073	3,216	5,000
Dividend yield (%)	4.6	1.1	1.2	1.7	1.9	2.2

Source: Baring Securities, *Korean Monthly Report*, April 1990, p. 16.

Notes: * Figures for 1985–9 are official figures based on arithmetic averages; figures for 1989–92 are weighted based on Baring Securities estimates.
† Fluctuations are partly due to changes in survey methods. Gross number of investor accounts.
‡ All non-individual investors.

funds due to a sharp increase in margin loans. Positive factors include the inflow of foreign capital (the Korean stock market was opened to direct foreign investment on 3 January 1992), South–North *rapprochement*, declining real estate prices and generous money supply growth. But poor corporate earnings will remain a burden on market recovery.

The requirements for listing are laid down by the Korea Stock Exchange. To be eligible for listing, the issuer must meet the following conditions: (a) the time lapsed since incorporation must be more than five years; (b) the capital stock must exceed two billion *won*; (c) the number of shares to be listed should be more than 200,000; (d) the number of shares publicly offered must be higher than 30 per cent of the total shares. In addition, the issuer of the securities is required to publicize and make available its annual and semi-annual reports. The issuer also must notify the Exchange of all important information necessary to protect investors and maintain a fair and orderly market.

The Securities and Exchange Law, enacted in 1962 and last amended in 1987, provides the legal basis for the regulation of both the issuing and the secondary markets. A Presidential Decree and Ministry of Finance Regulations were promulgated to supplement the Securities and Exchange Law. The law on Fostering the Capital Market, enacted in 1968 and amended in 1987, stimulates firms to offer their shares to the public. The Securities Investment Trust Business Law, enacted in 1969, controls the issuance and sales of investment trusts and the administration of management companies.

REGULATORY FRAMEWORK AFFECTING KOREAN GAAP

The Korean Institute of Certified Public Accountants (KICPA), established in 1954, is the centre of accounting in Korea. The Institute has over 2,000 members, of whom about 1,600 were in practice at the end of 1988. The Securities and Exchange Commission (SEC) controls the examination process for the CPA licence. Because the Korean securities market used to be small, there was not so much need for CPAs. As the number of listed companies grows, the pass rate for the CPA examination is increasing. There are about 250 new CPAs each year.

KICPA is a private organization for Korean CPAs. The SEC controls the quality of CPAs' external auditing work and has the authority to summon and review working papers of external auditors. Apart from this quality control KICPA is quite independent of the SEC. The Ministry of Finance does not have any direct control of KICPA.

The SEC and the Accounting System Deliberation Committee (ASDC) under the Ministry of Finance are the chief rule-making authorities for the accounting profession (see Figure 3.1). The SEC, established in 1977, is authorized to make decisions on major issues related to both the issuance and fair transaction of securities and the supervision of securities institutions. The SEC is composed of nine commissioners: three *ex officio* commissioners and six commissioners appointed by the President of Korea. Under the law, all decisions made by the SEC must be reported to the Minister of Finance, who may repeal any decision or suspend its enforcement in whole or in part if it is found to be illegal or inappropriate to the best interests of the public or investors.

The ASDC, affiliated with the SEC, drafts accounting standards applicable to the preparation of financial statements. The ASDC consists of the representatives of the SEC, the KICPA, and a number of business and academic associations concerned with the practice of accountancy. Subject to review by the Ministry of Finance, the ASDC promulgates accounting

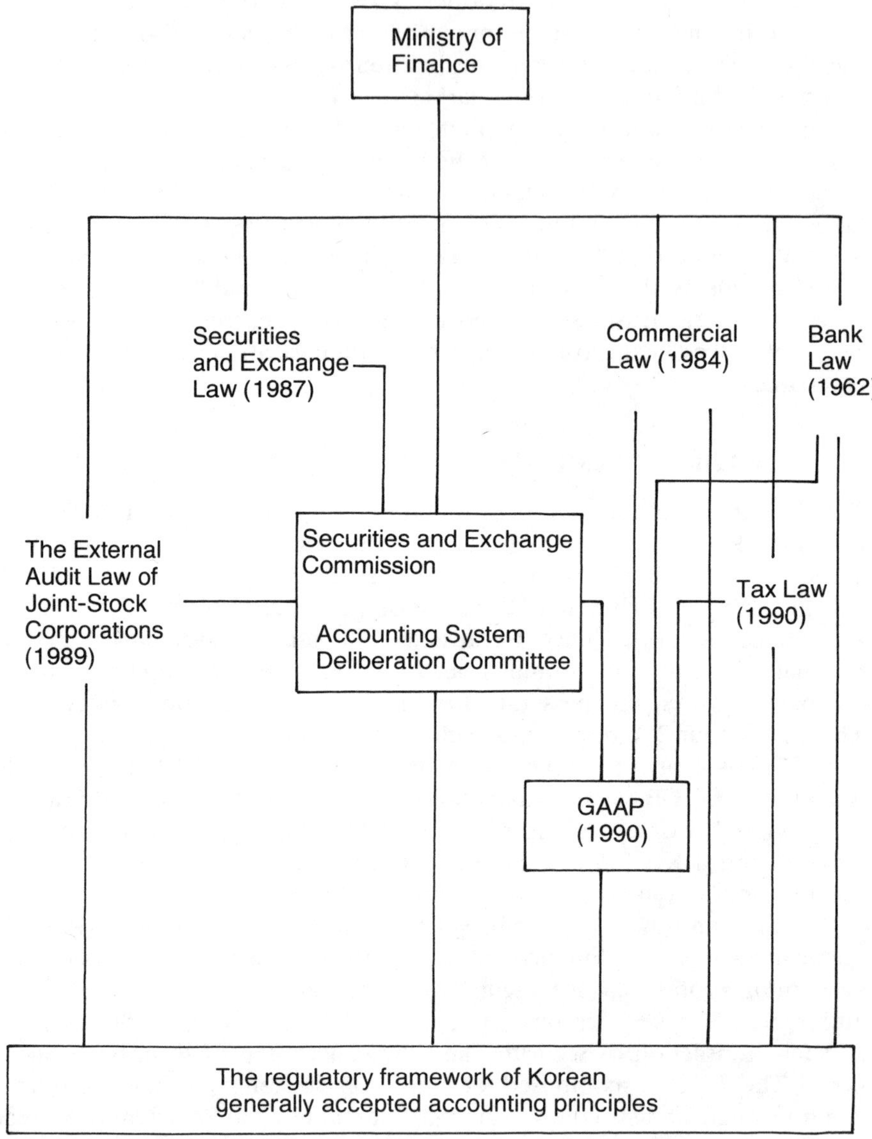

Figure 3.1 The regulatory framework of Korean GAAP

standards as official rules in the form of a regulation with which Korean companies must cmply.

Joint-stock corporations are required by the commercial laws to prepare four financial statements for stockholders. They are a balance sheet, an income statement, a statement of changes in financial position, and a proposal for retained earnings appropriations. These financial statements are attested to by the company's statutory auditor, an officer of the company who need not be a certified public accountant. The statutory auditor's legal duty is to examine the statements prior to the general meeting of stockholders and to monitor the performance of company directors in doing their jobs.

The External Audit Law of Joint-Stock Corporations, enacted in 1981, dictates that independent audits by certified public accountants be conducted for companies with beginning-of-year total assets in excess of 3 billion *won.* In addition, independent audits are also required in most regulated industries and apply to not only domestic corporations but also branch offices of foreign corporations.

Audit procedures are laid down by the Korean Institute of Certified Public Accountants. These procedures are called 'generally accepted auditing standards', and are comparable in most instances to those in western countries. There are four types of audit opinions: unqualified, qualified, adverse and disclaimer.

Accounting practice in Korea has developed rapidly, stimulated by the tremendous growth in the economy. Joint ventures with foreign corporations in the early 1970s, for instance, prompted the necessity of revisions in Korean generally accepted accounting principles to accommodate more sophisticated accounting techniques and standards for foreign currency transactions and translation.

Tax and commercial laws have also strongly affected accounting practice. For example, the depreciation methods as well as the inventory valuation methods selected by the firm are largely the alternatives that result in the most favourable tax consequences. Companies are also required by law, in order to protect creditors, to set up a legal reserve out of retained earnings until its amount reaches one-half of par value of the capital stock.

Korean GAAP has been largely influenced by those in western countries, especially the US. There exist, however, certain differences between Korean and western accounting practices. For example, the amount of notes receivable or payable by Korean firms is much more than that of western firms. This reflects the business practice that the promissory note is the typical form of payment for commercial transactions. Korean companies typically have relatively high debt–equity ratios. However, they are not as risky as most western financial analysts may think because most bank loans are customarily renewed even when the companies are financially in trouble. Since Korean business practice and accounting procedures are in part different from those of western countries (Choi *et al.* 1983), care is needed in analysing and evaluating the soundness and profitability of Korean companies.

COMPANY LAW

The seven types of business organization in Korea are based on Continental European models. Two types carry corporate attributes: the stock corporation (*chusik hoesa*) and the private limited liability company (*yuhan hoesa*). The former is an entity very similar to an American corporation or joint-stock company with corresponding rules governing organization, administration, and dissolution. The latter is a private limited liability company also formed under Art. 543 *et seq.* of the Commercial Code, having attributes of both a partnership and an ordinary corporation. There are three Korean entities with partnership attributes: the *hap myung hoesa* (unlimited liability company), the *hap ja hoesa* (company with limited and unlimited liability partners), and the *johap* (partnership). The *hap myung hoesa* is a partnership company which is a legal entity whose members have unlimited liability for the firm's obligations. The *hap ja hoesa* is a limited partnership company similar to the *hap myung hoesa* except that it includes both limited and general partners. The *johap* is a partnership formed under the Civil Code which does not have a separate legal personality. Finally, there are two other types of business entities recognized in Korea: the branch of a foreign business and the sole proprietorship.

Chusik hoesa (stock corporation)

By far the most important type of business organization is the stock corporation. The stock corporation corresponds most nearly to the American corporation, with the most significant attributes being the representation of the individual's interest by shares of stock and liability for company debts being limited to the amount of investment. It is a separate legal entity and as such can transact business, enter into contracts, and sue or be sued in its own name. For enterprises requiring financing through public offerings, the use of the stock corporation as a form of doing business is unavoidable.

Due to potential problems concerning the presence of limited liability, management participation, and regulations under the Korean foreign exchange control legislation, joint ventures in Korea are usually formed by the establishment of a stock corporation which is the general corporate form for major companies in Korea. The requirements relating to the incorporation, administration, and dissolution of a stock corporation are governed by the Commercial Code.

The Commercial Code requires any person who engages in business in Korea to keep accounting books and records. The books of account include general ledgers, subsidiary ledgers, journals and cash books. An accounting period, which may be prescribed in the articles of incorporation, must not exceed twelve months. Many companies choose a one-year period ending 31 December. The Commercial Code provides detailed regulations for the preparation of a balance sheet and income statement. Besides the regulations relating to the Commercial Code, the financial statements of stock corporations for reporting under the Securities and Exchange Law must be prepared in accordance with regulations issued by the Ministry of Finance. 'Financial Accounting Standards for Business Enterprises' issued by the Ministry of Finance prescribes accounting practices to be followed by business enterprises.

Yuhan hoesa (private limited liability company)

This company is basically a simplified limited stock corporation and it is compared generally with the private company form in Britain and also the Gesellschaft mit beschränkter Haftung (GmbH) under German law. It is regulated by Articles 543 *et seq.* of the Commercial Code. This company has the characteristics of both partnership and corporate entities.

On the corporate side it can transact business, enter into contracts, and sue or be sued in its own name. With regard to the company's debt, the potential liability of the owners, who are called 'members' rather than 'shareholders', is limited to their capital contribution. On the partnership side, the procedural requirements for formation, management, and termination of this entity are less stringent and formalistic than those for a stock corporation. Furthermore, there are significant restrictions on the transfer of capital interests, comparable to those attaching to partnership interests. The private limited liability company, however, is seldom utilized in Korea.

Hap myung hoesa (unlimited liability company)

The *hap myung hoesa* is similar in many respects to a modern US partnership in that as a legal entity it can transact business, enter into contracts, and sue or be sued in its own name. Because of its partnership nature, all members are jointly and severally liable for the excess of the company's debt over its net assets. Nevertheless, the *hap myung hoesa* is taxed as an entity under the Corporate Tax Law.

The Commercial Code prohibits a company from becoming a member with unlimited liability in another company, therefore only natural persons may be members in a *hap myung hoesa.* Formation and capitalization, though governed by the Commercial Code, are loosely regulated, the primary requirement being the execution of the articles by all the members before a notary and subsequent registration in the Commercial Registry. Contributions by the members are not limited in amount or as to type of property.

Unless the articles provide otherwise, representation of the company and participation in its management is a right of all members; however, the customary practice is to delegate management responsibilities to one or more representative members. Profits and losses are apportioned in accordance with the members' equities.

Hap ja hoesa (limited partnership)

The limited partnership is similar in most respects to the *hap myung hoesa*, but differs principally in that it includes both limited and general partners. The limited partner's liability is confined to the amount of his or her capital contribution; the general partner's potential liability is restricted only to the amount of company debts. The advantages of limited liability are offset by the prohibition against making non-cash contributions, and exclusion from managerial participation and authorized representation of the company. A limited partner is not, however, precluded from engaging in similar business enterprises nor prevented from participation in other companies.

Despite the restrictive scope of activity, a limited partner may, under the doctrines of misrepresentation and estoppel, incur general liability if his or her acts reasonably suggest to third persons the status of a general partner. Unanimous consent of the general partners is required to effect the transfer of a limited liability interest or a portion thereof.

Johap (partnership)

The business association known as a *johap* does not have a separate legal personality and therefore cannot do business as an entity. Although formed under the Civil Code rather than the Commercial Code, the *johap* is still subject to the Commercial Code in a number of ways. The *johap* is comparable, therefore, in many primary aspects, to the traditional common law view of partnerships in the United States.

The primary provisions of the Civil Code relating to the *johap* postulate an organizational structure where the partners take contributions as co-owners, and share profits and losses in proportion to their equity interests. In addition, the management and administration of the firm are governed by majority rule, except as to removal of partners for reasonable cause, in which case unanimous consent is required. In a manner that resembles the law governing joint ventures in the US, the *johap* is dissolved on completion of its purpose, when existing circumstances impede or prohibit attainment of its objective, or upon fulfilment of the terms of the partnership agreement.

TAX LAW

Present tax system

There are many different taxes in Korea (see Figure 3.2), but they can be grouped into two broad categories – national taxes and local taxes. Taxes

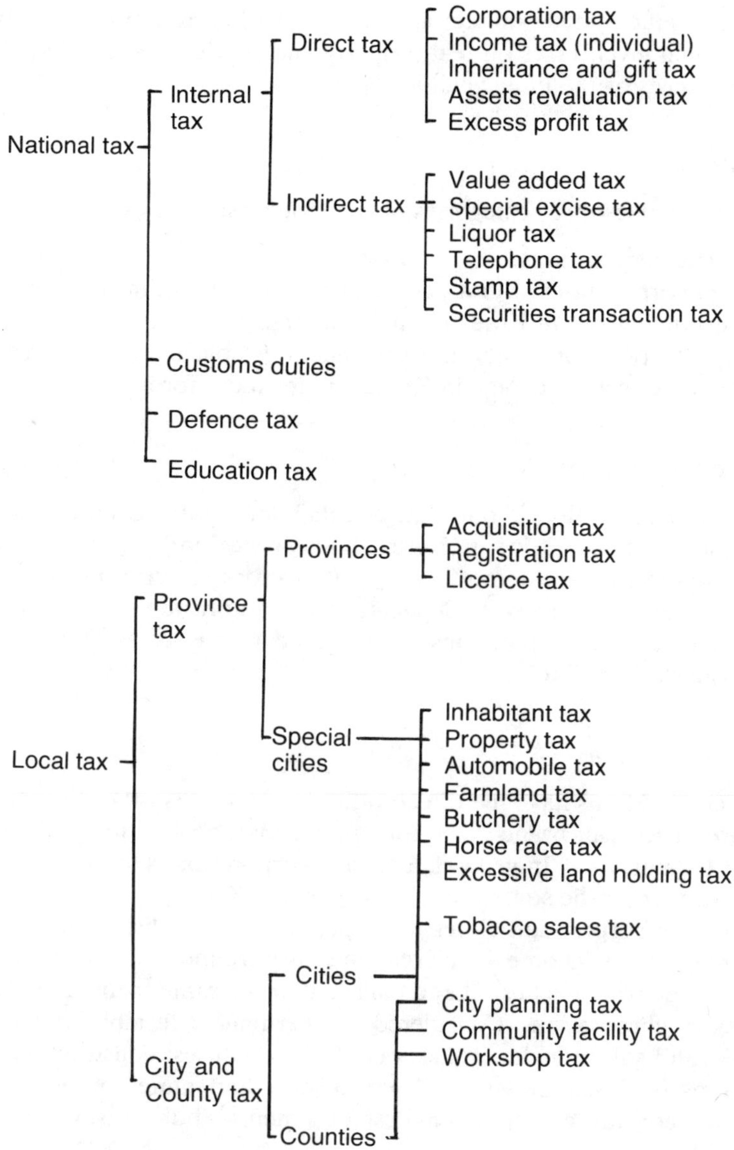

Figure 3.2 Taxation in Korea

on income, value added, and certain categories of consumption are levied at the national level; taxes on real property and residence are levied either by the provinces or the municipalities.

Corporate tax

The law recognizes three categories of corporations:

- domestic corporations;
- foreign corporations with a permanent establishment in Korea or with real estate income in Korea (resident foreign);
- foreign corporations without a permanent establishment in Korea and without real estate income in Korea (nonresident foreign).

Domestic corporations

A domestic corporation is one that is either incorporated under Korean laws or has its head office in Korea. Subsidiaries and joint ventures of foreign corporations are domestic corporations for tax purposes, since they are separate entities formed under Korean law and have their head offices in Korea. Domestic corporations are required to pay corporation tax on their world-wide income.

Foreign corporations

Foreign corporations have their head offices in countries other than Korea. Therefore, a Korean branch of a foreign corporation is a foreign corporation for tax purposes. In general, a foreign corporation is taxed only on its income from domestic sources, or sources within Korea.

If a foreign corporation either has a permanent establishment in Korea or has real estate income in Korea, the corporation tax on its Korean source income will be assessed and collected in the same manner as that of a domestic corporation. Considered as permanent establishments are branches (and sub-branches); sales outlets, warehouses; construction sites, installations or assemblies including factories; and mines. Many agency operations constitute permanent establishments, but liaison activities generally do not.

Foreign corporations without permanent establishments or real-estate income in Korea are classified as nonresident foreign corporations and are subject only to withholding tax on their Korean source income.

Taxable income

The taxable income of corporations is generally determined on an accrual basis; for banks, insurance companies, and other financial institutions, the cash basis is acceptable, although the accrual method is still the norm. Taxable income is defined as assessable income less allowable deductions. Assessable income is simply gross income adjusted to include receipts deemed to be income by the Corporation Tax Law and to remove tax-exempt income items. Allowable deductions include most expenses recognized for financial accounting purposes.

Income tax allocation

Taxable income and income before income taxes for a corporation may differ significantly for a number of reasons. In fact, the tax return may show a loss, while the income statement shows positive pre-tax income. However, Korean Accounting Standards do not recognize income tax allocation. Therefore the amount of income tax payable determined in tax returns equals the amount of the income tax expense to be reported in the income statement. Items which create differences between taxable income and income before income taxes are as follows:

Tax incentives

The Tax Exemption and Reduction Control Law provides for a number of tax incentives designed to promote technological development, benefit key industries and encourage certain types of business activity. The following corporations are examples of those which may be entitled to tax benefits under this law:

- small and medium-sized corporations engaged in manufacturing, mining, construction, transportation, or fishery;
- corporations developing technology and manpower in the manufacturing, mining, banking or insurance industry;
- new corporations using certain new technology;
- technology service corporations;
- corporations earning foreign currency;
- corporations operating overseas business;
- corporations in the resource development business (including mining, forestry, and livestock);
- corporations moving from major cities to provincial areas;
- small and medium-sized corporations planning to consolidate;
- corporations investing in:
  facilities for increasing productivity,
  energy-saving facilities,
  anti-pollution facilities,
  facilities for prevention of industrial accidents,
  mine safety facilities, etc.;
- certain corporations operated for public benefit.

The tax incentives set out in the Tax Exemption and Reduction Control Law are of the following types:

- Special depreciation: This is an additional annual depreciation deduction ranging from 30 to 100 per cent of the ordinary depreciation amount. If the provision of this law and the Corporation Tax Law with respect to special depreciation are both applicable, a corporation may select only one for application.
- Tax credit for investment: This is a one-time credit against the corporation's income tax liability of an amount ranging from 3 to 10 per cent of the target investment. Generally, investments using domestically produced materials will generate larger credits.
- Tax-free reserves: Within specified limitations, a corporation may be able to deduct amounts appropriated to certain reserves, including:
  reserve for investment;
  reserve for technological development;
  reserve for export losses;
  reserve for overseas market development;
  reserve for overseas business losses;
  reserve for investment losses.
- Tax-exemption of income: This type of incentive has limited applications. The income of a few types of corporations is tax-exempt in whole or in part. Also, a few types of income are tax-exempt (e.g. income from the lease of patent).

Corporations may be eligible for more than one type of incentive. However, if more than one benefit is available from a given type of incentive, the corporation may choose only one benefit. The aggregation of special depreciation charges and appropriations to reserves prescribed by this law may not exceed 50 per cent of taxable income in any year. Tax credits prescribed by this law are limited to 30 per cent of the calculated tax for the year.

The Foreign Capital Inducement Law (FCIL) offers incentives to foreign corporations to invest in certain small and medium-sized industries and to bring advanced technology to Korea. Such foreign-invested enterprises are exempt from corporation tax for the five-year period elected from the first ten tax years after the registration of the enterprise. However, these exemptions apply only to a portion of the tax liability, based on the percentage of stock owned by the foreign investors.

Corporate tax rates

Corporate taxes depend on which of three classifications a corporation falls into. A non-listed large corporation is one whose capital stock exceeds 5 billion *won*, or whose shareholders' equity exceeds 10 billion, and which is not listed on the stock exchange. A second classification is the not-for-

Table 3.6 Corporate taxes: the three classifications

Income	*Non-listed large*	*Not-for-profit*	*Other*
First 80 million	20%	20%	20%
Amount over 80 million	33%	27%	30%

profit organization which engages in certain activities which produce taxable income. All other corporations, including branches of foreign corporations, comprise the third classification (see Table 3.6).

In addition, corporations are liable for defence tax and inhabitants tax, which are 20 per cent (25 per cent when taxable income is 500 million or more) and 7.5 per cent, respectively, of the corporate tax amount. The tax liability of a foreign subsidiary having taxable Korean source income of 100 million would be 28.05 million, an effective tax rate of 28.05 per cent, as follows:

Corporate tax on 100 million	22,000
(80 million × 20 per cent) + (20 million × 30 per cent)	
Defence tax	
22 million × 20 per cent	4,400
Inhabitants tax	
22 million × 7.5 per cent	1,650
Total	28,050

SECURITIES LAW

Public institutions related to the securities industry

The government agency responsible for security-related administration is the Bureau of Securities in the Ministry of Finance. The Ministry of Finance is the highest policy-making and regulatory institution. It:

- establishes and implements the overall security policies;
- controls the Securities and Exchange Commission, the Securities Regulation Bureau, and the Stock Exchange;
- approves the incorporation of security-related organizations such as security firms, security financing firms, security trust firms, and public accounting firms, etc.

The Securities and Exchange Commission and the Securities Supervision Bureau were established under the Securities Exchange Law, revised in December 1976.

Securities and Exchange Commission

The SEC is composed of six commissioners. Three of them are part-time: the president of the Bank of Korea, the chief executive officer of the Korea Stock Exchange and the vice minister of MOF. The remaining three are full-time, appointed by the President of the Republic of Korea, and one of them is designated by the President to serve as a chairman of the SEC as well as the chairman of the Securities Regulation Bureau.

The SEC is responsible for securities and accounting matters in connection with the regulation of (a) the initial offerings and management of securities, (b) the fair trading of securities, and (c) the supervision of the securities-related organizations.

Securities Supervision Bureau

The Securities Supervision Bureau is the implementing institution under the jurisdiction of the Securities and Exchange Commission. Its main activities are:

- management and guidance of registration of securities and registered firms;
- evaluation of securities reports;
- oversight of listed corporations;
- administration of over-the-counter stock trading;
- management and control of the credit granting activities of securities firms;
- examination of insider trading, intercompany stockholdings within conglomerates, excessively large stock holdings.

The stock market

In 1981, the stock market received its first foreign investments. Foreigners were allowed to purchase certificates in two open-end investment trusts valued at $15 million each. Currently there are five trusts valued at $135 million. Further, a $40 million closed-end Korea Fund was established in the New York Stock Exchange in 1984 whose value is about $150 million. A $60 million Korea Euro Fund was established in Europe in 1985. From July 1989, foreigners who purchase convertible bonds issued overseas were able to convert them to stocks.

Data relating to the stock market are given in Table 3.5. To increase the market size and to widen investment opportunities, some unlisted corporations have been recommended to go public if they meet certain requirements set by the Securities and Exchange Commission.

The Foreign Currency Trading Law and the Securities Trading Law

Under the Foreign Currency Trading Law, nonresident foreigners are permitted to acquire securities of Korean corporations in the following cases:

- acquisition of domestic securities of foreign investment companies;
- investment of international revenue securities;
- acquisition of foreign currency securities issued overseas.

Under the Securities Trading Law, the Securities and Exchange Commission sets limits on items of securities to be purchased – maximum amounts of acquisition within each industry in case of the stock acquisition by nonresident foreigners. For example, when a foreign investment company invests in Korean securities, (a) the investment in an industry cannot exceed 25 per cent of net assets of the investee companies, and (b) for each stock, investment cannot exceed the acquisition limit set by the Minister of Finance, which is within 5 per cent of total shares issued, and the total portion of foreign acquisition should be less than 10 per cent of total shares issued.

ESTABLISHMENT OF ACCOUNTING STANDARDS

Relevant laws and regulations

All limited liability companies are subject to the requirements of the Korean Commercial Code which requires only the publication of periodic balance sheets. Companies whose securities are listed on the stock exchange in Seoul are subject to the much more comprehensive provisions of the Securities and Exchange Law.

Before 23 December 1981 there were two sets of accounting principles. One was for listed companies and the other was for all other types of business enterprises. These two sets of accounting principles were actually the same and, therefore, they were combined into a new set of accounting principles entitled 'Accounting Standards for Business Enterprises' on 23 December 1981. These standards have been revised several times since by the Securities and Exchange Commission; the latest being made on 29 March 1990.

The latest revision was made to reflect the recent development of the Korean capital market. As a result of the continuous success of the series of five-year economic plans and the continuous effort to promote the securities market by government, the Korean stock market has been growing fast with increasing numbers of small investors. The stock market is allowing direct foreign investments from 1992. To make Korean accounting standards more compatible with those of other countries, some standards, especially in relation to evaluation of marketable securities, inventories, foreign exchange gains and losses, and investment securities were revised in March 1990.

Korea has been a board member of the International Accounting Standard Committee (IASC) since 1 January 1988 and is moving fast to accommodate and adopt more international accounting standards.

Establishment of accounting standards

'Accounting Standards for Business Enterprises' constitutes generally accepted accounting principles in Korea. These standards were established by the Securities and Exchange Commission, with the approval of the Minister of Finance, under Article 13 of the Law on Outside Audit of Corporations. Therefore, the Securities and Exchange Commission is the official body responsible for accounting standards. However, accounting principles are not valid unless approved by the Minister of Finance.

The Securities and Exchange Commission maintains an advisory body called the Accounting System Deliberation Committee. This committee recommends accounting standards. KICPA provides information and official comments on exposure drafts of accounting standards which will be issued by the Accounting System Deliberation Committee but the KICPA does not have authority to establish accounting standards. After due approval by the Ministry of Finance, the recommended accounting principles are codified and become enforceable standards. These standards are applicable not only to corporations but to sole proprietorships as well.

The standards are supplemented by three other accounting principles including 'Working Rules Related to Accounting Standards for Business Enterprises', and 'Specialized Industry Accounting Standards'.

Korean Institute of CPAs

The Korean Institute of CPAs operates like similar institutes in other countries. To practise as a professional accountant one must pass two levels of professional examinations. These examinations are governed by the Securities and Exchange Commission and are very competitive. One out of ten applicants on average passes the first examination and one out of three applicants passes the second examination.

The Korean Institute of CPAs at present has about 2,000 members. Among its major functions are the maintenance of the political and social interests of the members and advising the Securities Exchange Commission on financial accounting, reporting and auditing matters.

SUMMARY OF SELECTED ACCOUNTING STANDARDS

Basic financial statements

- Balance Sheet;
- Income Statement;
- Statement of Appropriation of Retained Earnings;
- Statement of Changes in Financial Position.

Significant accounting policies and other necessary accounting information should be parenthetically disclosed or incorporated in footnotes to the financial statements.

Valuation of marketable securities

Marketable securities held for temporary purposes (short term) must be valued at cost. However, short-term marketable securities whose market value has declined below cost should be valued at the market value. The market price of securities should be determined at the average closing price of the one-month period preceding the balance sheet date.

Valuation of inventory

The lower of cost or market basis is required. The method for the determination of cost can be chosen from among: individual identification, first-in, first-out, last-in first out, average cost and retail inventory. The market price is defined as an average wholesale price for the one-month period preceding the balance sheet date determined by a price survey index published by a reputable price survey institute.

Long-term investments in stocks

The valuation of long-term investments in stocks is the same as the valuation of marketable securities, as explained above. One difference is that while the valuation of marketable securities is allowed only on a portfolio basis, both the individual basis and the portfolio basis are allowed for the valuation of long-term investments.

A company with ownership, directly or indirectly, of over 50 per cent of the outstanding voting shares of another enterprise is required to prepare consolidated financial statements. However the unconsolidated financial statements of a parent company are the prime financial statements, and consolidated statements are sometimes shown as unaudited special supplementary schedules in the parent financial statements. In the unconsolidated financial statements of a parent company the equity method is not applied to account for changes in net equity.

Property, plant, and equipment

Tangible fixed assets are recorded at cost, except for upward revaluation in accordance with the Asset Revaluation Law to give accounting recognition to some extent to the loss in purchasing power of the Korean *won*. The revaluation is permitted if the wholesale price index has increased by 25 per cent or more from the date the related assets were acquired or from a previous revaluation. In the case of fixed assets which were revalued within the past three years, the details must be disclosed in footnotes.

Interest cost incurred on long-term debt and other related financial charges directly connected with manufacturing, purchase or construction of fixed assets may be capitalized as part of the cost until such acquisition activities are completed.

Estimation of service lives is required in principle, but service lives as specified in the Corporation Tax Law are commonly used for accounting purposes.

Research and development costs

All research and development costs are required to be expensed except:

- non-ordinary research and development costs incurred in relation to a particular product or technology for which costs are identifiable and for which future benefits are expected to be sufficient to recover the related costs;
- prepaid royalties, patents and similar rights/intangibles which have future benefits from which to recover their cost.

These items are, in general, treated as deferred charges (or prepaids) and amortized accordingly – mostly over five years.

Valuation of assets and liabilities denominated in foreign currency

Monetary assets and liabilities denominated in foreign currency should be converted into Korean *won* at the appropriate exchange rate in effect at the balance sheet date, while non-monetary assets and liabilities should be converted into Korean *won* at the appropriate exchange rate in effect at the time of the related acquisition or borrowing. All translation gains and losses should be accounted as ordinary gains and losses in the income statement.

The balance sheet items of overseas places of business may be translated at the exchange rate at the balance sheet date; the average exchange rate of the current fiscal year is to be applied to translation of the income statement items. The net amount of overseas business translation debit (or credit), after first offsetting the amount against any overseas business translation credit (or debit), should be subtracted (or added) in the owner's equity section of the balance sheet.

Pension liabilities

Liabilities for employee pensions and special benefits like lump sum severance obligations are to be fully accrued based on salaries and length of service, computing as if employees are all voluntarily terminating their employment at the balance sheet date. The pension liabilities are, however, not funded in most cases.

Appropriation of retained earnings

In an effort to protect outside creditors and small investors various legal reserves are required by the Korean Commercial Code and government regulations. For example, the Korean Commercial Code requires a company to appropriate as legal reserve an amount equal to at least 10 per cent of cash dividends for each accounting period until the reserves equal 50 per cent of stated capital. The legal reserves can be used only to reduce a deficit. Reserves for business rationalization and for financial structure improvement are also examples of other statutory reserves.

Extraordinary items and prior period adjustments

Extraordinary gains and losses include gain or loss on disposal of investments, gain or loss on disposal of fixed assets, recoveries of bad debts written off, casualty loss, and others. Debits or credits of errors attributable to prior years' financial statements.

Corporation income tax

Net operating losses may be carried forward to offset future income for up to three years but are not carried back. The differences between accounting income and taxable income should not be deferred for allocation over future fiscal years. Deferred tax accounting is not used in Korea.

Accounting treatment of accounting changes

Changes in accounting principles and accounting estimates should only be applied on a current and prospective basis. In other words, financial statements of prior periods are not restated, nor is the cumulative effect on prior years of retroactive application of new principles or estimates presented in the current year statements. Current and future financial statements are presented on the basis of the new principles and estimates.

COMPARISON WITH THE USA

		Korea	*USA*
	Financial statements		
1	Comparative	Comparative financial statements are mandatory	Comparative financial statements are recommended
2	Consolidated financial statements	They are not primary statements	They are mandatory as the primary statements
3	Statement of cash flows	Working capital concept	Cash or cash equivalent concept
4	Segment information	Not required	Required for publicly held companies
	Balance sheet items		
1	Investments	The equity method is not allowed in the primary statements	The equity method is required where ownership is between 20 and 50 per cent
2	Property, plant and equipment	Asset revaluation is permitted under certain conditions	Historical cost principle
3	Deferred charges	Capitalization of pre-incorporation expenses, stock issuing expenses, bond issuing expenses, R&D expenses and other deferred cost items are permitted. Amortization period is from 3 to 5 years	Most items are expensed as incurred. Bond issuing costs are amortized as an interest adjustment over the loan terms
4	Retained earnings	A legal reserve is required to be set up in relation to cash dividends	No legal reserve required

5	Leased assets	Leases meeting the US GAAP 90 per cent fair market value test are not capitalized	Leases whose present value of minimum lease payments exceed 90 per cent of the fair market value of the leased equipment are capitalized
6	Product warranty costs	No specific GAAP. In practice they are generally recorded on a cash basis	Accrued in the year of related product sale
7	Contingent liabilities	Contingent liabilities are not accrued. They are recognized when realized	Losses accrued when the occurrence of the loss becomes probable and the amount of the loss is estimatable
	Income statement		
1	Translation method for foreign currency financial statements	Monetary–non monetary method is used in principle	Functional currency concept is used
2	Income taxes	Taxes payable concept is used	Comprehensive inter-period income tax allocation is required. Deferred taxes are recorded
3	R&D costs	Non-ordinary R&D costs relating to the future benefits of specifically identifiable projects can be deferred	All R&D costs are required to be expensed
4	Business combinations	Distinction between 'pooling' and 'purchase' not used	Definitive rules distinguish between 'pooling' and 'purchase' combinations
5	Positive goodwill	Amortized over 5 years	Amortized over no more than 40 years
6	Negative goodwill	Negative goodwill should be treated as capital surplus in the owner's equity section	Negative goodwill is first allocated to non-current assets with any residual being deferred and amortized over no more than 40 years

7	Extraordinary items	Specific predetermined transactions are to be disclosed separately as extraordinary items without the related tax effect	Both the unusual in nature and infrequency in occurrence tests must be met. Separate disclosure, net of tax, is required
8	Accounting changes	Accounting changes are accounted for prospectively from the year of change	Accounting changes are made through a cumulative adjustment to operations in the year of change. Certain limited accounting changes are effected through the restatement of prior period statements

Interim reports

Listed companies should prepare semi-annual financial statements. Seasonal fluctuations of sales volume and inventories are to be explained if they are material.

SUMMARY

The South Korean economy has grown rapidly in recent years. Private sector companies, including the *chaebol* (conglomerate groups) are still largely dominated by family ownership. Although Korean companies are still relatively highly geared the percentage of debt to equity has been falling. The stock market was opened to direct foreign investment in 1992. Types of business organization include the stock corporation, the private limited liability company, the unlimited liability company, the limited partnership and the partnership.

Accounting practice is influenced by the Commercial Code, tax law and accounting standards. The main external influence is US GAAP. All business organizations are subject to the accounting provisions of the Commercial Code. Companies whose securities are listed on the stock exchange are also subject to the Securities and Exchange Law. The depreciation and inventory valuation methods used are usually those that result in the most favourable tax consequences.

Accounting standards are established by the Accounting System Deliberation Committee of the Securities and Exchange Commission. The standards must be approved by the Ministry of Finance. The Korean Institute of Certified Public Accountants plays an advisory role.

Unlike in the USA and the UK, consolidated financial statements are not the primary statements, segment information is not required, a legal reserve must be established, and deferred taxation accounting is not practised.

APPENDIX

Extracts from the accounts of Kia Motors

BALANCE SHEETS

December 31, 1991 and 1990

	In thousands of Korean Won		In thousands of U.S. Dollars	
Assets	**1991**	1990	**1991**	1990
Current assets:				
Cash and deposits	**₩308,660,341**	₩264,192,717	**$405,705**	$368,778
Marketable securities, at cost which approximates market	**22,502,842**	31,287,578	**29,578**	43,673
Notes and accounts receivable	**1,070,127,365**	639,890,384	**1,406,582**	893,203
Less allowance for doubtful accounts	**(12,946,019)**	(7,899,193)	**(17,016)**	(11,026)
Net	**1,057,181,346**	631,991,191	**1,389,566**	882,177
Inventories (Note 2)	**208,419,875**	154,257,731	**273,948**	215,324
Prepaid expenses and other	**92,710,073**	63,268,140	**121,858**	88,313
Total current assets	**1,689,474,477**	1,144,997,357	**2,220,655**	1,598,265
Investments in affiliated companies (Notes 3 and 6)	**80,850,163**	70,196,685	**106,270**	97,985
Property, plant and equipment (Note 5):				
Land	**87,435,047**	81,241,214	**114,925**	113,402
Buildings and structures	**230,691,694**	176,819,379	**303,223**	246,817
Machinery and equipment	**719,352,460**	646,603,401	**945,521**	902,573
Tools, furniture and fixtures	**220,765,522**	207,927,305	**290,176**	290,239
Vehicles	**13,333,828**	10,377,422	**17,526**	14,486
Construction in-progress	**344,338,489**	74,952,816	**452,600**	104,624
	1,615,917,040	1,197,921,537	**2,123,971**	1,672,141
Less accumulated depreciation	**(464,997,903)**	(357,501,169)	**(611,196)**	(499,024)
Net property, plant and equipment	**1,150,919,137**	840,420,368	**1,512,775**	1,173,117
Other assets:				
Deposit for severance and retirement benefits	**87,240,844**	68,254,047	**114,670**	95,274
Long-term savings deposits and other (Notes 6 and 7)	**464,716,322**	319,296,654	**610,826**	445,696
Total other assets	**551,957,166**	387,550,701	**725,496**	540,970
Deferred charges	**19,363,370**	12,266,907	**25,451**	17,123
Total assets	**₩3,492,564,313**	₩2,455,432,018	**$4,590,047**	$3,427,460

Won/Dollar exchange rate: ₩716.40 in 1990, ₩760.80 in 1991.

	In thousands of Korean Won		In thousands of U.S. Dollars	
Liabilities and Stockholders' Equity	**1991**	1990	**1991**	1990
Current liabilities:				
Short-term borrowings (Note 6)	**₩427,596,710**	₩211,100,088	**$562,036**	$294,668
Notes and accounts payable	**729,543,487**	575,047,457	**958,916**	802,690
Income taxes payable (Note 11)	**962,786**	9,990,317	**1,266**	13,945
Unearned income	**113,568,341**	90,295,624	**149,275**	126,041
Current portion of long-term debt (Note 7)	**165,909,390**	147,680,653	**218,072**	206,143
Accrued liabilities and other	**165,091,615**	127,631,925	**216,997**	178,157
Total current liabilities	**1,602,672,329**	1,161,746,064	**2,106,562**	1,621,644
Employees' severance and retirement benefits	**175,302,315**	130,198,846	**230,418**	181,740
Guarantee deposits	**1,261,855**	1,179,608	**1,659**	1,647
Long-term debt, less current portion (Note 7)	**900,180,207**	488,190,626	**1,183,202**	681,450
Deferred gains	**4,738,282**	9,030,775	**6,228**	12,606
Total liabilities	**2,684,154,988**	1,790,345,919	**3,528,069**	2,499,087
Commitments and contingent liabilities (Note 9)				
Stockholders' equity (Note 10):				
Common stock ₩5,000 par value Authorized: 80,000,000 shares Issued and outstanding: 57,403,633 shares in 1991 and 48,318,265 shares in 1990	**287,018,165**	241,591,325	**377,258**	337,230
Capital surplus	**406,488,990**	298,847,088	**534,292**	417,151
Retained earnings:				
Appropriated	**97,200,000**	82,100,000	**127,760**	114,601
Unappropriated	**15,886,326**	42,547,686	**20,881**	59,391
	113,086,326	124,647,686	**148,641**	173,992
Conversion right adjustment	**1,815,844**	—	**2,387**	—
Total stockholders' equity	**808,409,325**	665,086,099	**1,062,578**	928,373
Total liabilitis and stockholders' equity	**₩3,492,564,313**	₩2,455,432,018	**$4,590,647**	$3,427,460

* See accompanying notes to financial statements.

Statements of Income and Unappropriated Retained Earnings

For the years ended December 31, 1991 and 1990

	In thousands of Korean Won		In thousands of U.S. Dollars	
	1991	1990	**1991**	1990
Net sales	**₩2,744,776,709**	₩2,540,389,186	**$3,607,751**	$3,546,049
Cost and expenses:				
Cost of sales	**2,408,613,108**	2,216,928,304	**3,165,895**	3,094,540
Selling, general and administrative expenses	**263,500,715**	220,767,714	**346,347**	308,163
	2,672,113,823	2,437,696,018	**3,512,242**	3,402,703
Operating income	**72,662,886**	102,693,168	**95,509**	143,346
Other income (expenses):				
Interest income	**132,807,239**	59,991,958	**174,563**	83,741
Interest expense	**(145,938,581)**	(83,160,894)	**(191,823)**	(116,082)
Dividend income	**12,498,165**	7,202,795	**16,428**	10,054
Foriegn currency exchange gain (loss)	**(11,895,889)**	(7,399,725)	**(15,636)**	(10,329)
Amortization	**(53,485,171)**	(35,145,870)	**(70,301)**	(49,059)
Others, net	**10,099,389**	13,669,450	**13,274**	19,081
	(55,914,848)	(44,842,286)	**(73,495)**	(62,594)
Income before income taxes	**16,748,038**	57,850,882	**22,014**	80,752
Provision for income taxes (Note 11)	**962,786**	15,523,778	**1,266**	21,669
Net income	**15,785,252**	42,327,104	**20,748**	59,083
Unappropriated retained earnings at beginning of year, as adjusted	**101,074**	220,582	**133**	308
Unappropriated retained earnings at end of year	**₩15,886,326**	₩42,547,686	**$20,881**	$59,391
Per share data (Note 13)				
Earnings per share	**₩314**		**$0.412**	

Won/Dollar exchange rate: ₩716.40 in 1990, ₩760.80 in 1991.

Statements of Proposed Appropriations of Unappropriated Retained Earnings

For the years ended December 31, 1991 and 1990
Proposed appropriation date: February 28, 1992
Appropriated date: February 26, 1991

	In thousands of Korean Won		In thousands of U.S. Dollars	
	1991	1990	**1991**	1990
Unappropriated retained earnings:				
Balance carried forward	**₩230,923**	₩220,582	**$304**	$308
Prior period adjustments — loss	**129,849**	—	**171**	—
Balance carried forward, as adjusted	**101,074**	220,582	**133**	308
Net income	**15,785,252**	42,327,104	**20,748**	59,083
Unappropriated retained earnings at end of year	**15,886,326**	42,547,686	**20,881**	59,391
Appropriations proposed (Notes 10 and 12)				
Legal reserve	**1,000,000**	2,800,000	**1,314**	3,909
Reserve for improvement of financial position	**2,200,000**	4,300,000	**2,892**	6,002
Business rationalization reserve	**—**	7,000,000	**—**	9,771
Reserve for overseas market development	**2,500,000**	1,000,000	**3,286**	1,396
Reserve for technology development	**2,300,000**	—	**3,023**	—
Dividends	**7,614,395**	27,216,763	**10,009**	37,991
	15,614,395	42,316,763	**20,524**	59,069
Balance to be carried forward after appropriations	**₩271,931**	₩230,923	**$357**	$322

• See accompanying notes to financial statements.

Statements of Changes in Financial Position

For the years ended December 31, 1991 and 1990

	In thousands of Korean Won		In thousands of U.S. Dollars	
	1991	1990	**1991**	1990
Working capital provided from operations:				
Net income	**₩15,785,252**	₩42,327,104	**$20,748**	$59,083
Items not affecting working capital:				
Depreciation	**117,243,367**	102,722,515	**154,105**	143,387
Amortization	**53,485,171**	35,145,870	**70,301**	49,059
Provision for employees' severance and retirement benefits	**51,197,971**	40,895,311	**67,295**	57,085
Unrealized foreign currency exchange loss	**—**	6,218,177	**—**	8,680
Loss (gain) from disposal of properties	**(3,224,773)**	(566,405)	**(4,238)**	(791)
Others, net	**360,390**	191,204	**474**	267
	234,847,378	226,933,776	**308,685**	316,770
Working capital provided from investing and financing activities:				
Disposal of investment in affiliated companies	**—**	4,626,084	**—**	6,457
Disposal of properties	**7,199,523**	11,886,039	**9,463**	16,591
Decrease in deposits for severance and retirement benefits	**6,044,034**	5,041,971	**7,944**	7,038
Decrease in long-term savings deposits and other	**145,409,158**	50,853,685	**191,127**	70,985
Increase in guarantee deposits	**116,932**	1,019,825	**154**	1,424
Increase in long-term debt	**592,884,747**	272,436,819	**779,291**	380,286
Issurance of common stock	**45,426,840**	26,500,000	**59,709**	36,990
Increase in capital surplus	**107,641,903**	62,010,000	**141,485**	86,558
	904,723,137	434,374,423	**1,189,173**	606,329
Total source of working capital	**₩1,139,570,515**	₩661,308,199	**$1,497,858**	$923,099

Won/Dollar exchange rate: ₩716.40 in 1990, ₩760.80 in 1991.

	In thousands of Korean Won		In thousands of U.S. Dollars	
	1991	1990	**1991**	1990
Applications of working capital:				
Acquisition of investment in affiliated companies	**₩10,653,478**	₩13,195,635	**$14,003**	$18,419
Additions to property, plant and equipment	**431,716,885**	243,186,287	**567,451**	339,456
Increase in deposits for severance and retirement benefits	**25,030,832**	19,339,662	**32,901**	26,996
Increase in long-term savings deposits and other	**290,916,540**	206,558,921	**382,382**	288,329
Increase in deferred charges	**65,072,531**	26,267,633	**85,532**	36,666
Decrease in long-term debt	**179,153,595**	167,366,270	**235,480**	233,621
Decrease in guarantee deposits	**34,684**	22,886	**45**	32
Payment of employees' severance and retirement benefits	**6,094,503**	5,203,816	**8,011**	7,264
Payment of dividend	**27,216,763**	21,576,011	**35,774**	30,117
Prior year adjustment	**129,849**	—	**171**	—
Total applications of working capital	**1,036,019,660**	702,717,121	**1,361,750**	980,900
Increase (decrease) in working capital	**103,550,855**	(41,408,922)	**136,108**	(57,801)
Working capital at end of year:				
Total current assets	**₩1,689,474,477**	₩1,144,997,357	**$2,220,655**	$1,598,265
Total current liabilities	**1,602,672,329**	1,161,746,064	**2,106,562**	1,621,644
	86,802,148	(16,748,707)	**114,093**	(23,379)
Working capital at beginning of year:				
Total current assets	**1,144,997,357**	873,536,381	**1,504,991**	1,219,341
Total current liabilities	**1,161,746,064**	848,876,166	**1,527,006**	1,184,919
	(16,748,707)	24,660,215	**(22,015)**	34,422
Increase (decrease) in working capital	**₩103,550,855**	₩(41,408,922)	**$136,108**	$(57,801)

* See accompanying notes to financial statements.

Notes to Financial Statements

December 31, 1991 and 1990

1. Summary of significant accounting policies.

Organization and business — The Company was organized in December 1944 under the Laws of Republic of Korea to manufacture and distribute bicycles, and now produces the passenger car "Pride", "Capital" and "Concord"; as well as various kinds of trucks and minibuses. Of praticular importance the Company manufactured the passenger car "Brisa" first in Korea and developed the gasoline engine with endless endeavor of technical development. The production facilities of the company are at an international level with completion of the construction of second plant in Asan Industry Complex, Hwa Sung, Kyonggido, Korea. The Company became a public company upon listing its shares of common stock on the Korea Stock Exchange in 1973. As of December 31, 1991, Ford Motor Co., U.S.A., Mazda Motor Corp. and C. Itoh Co., Japan owned 10%, 8% and 2%, respectively, of the total outstanding shares of the Company.

Basis of financial statement presentation — The official accounting records of the Company are maintained in Korean won in accordance with the relevant laws and regulations of the Republic of Korea. Certain amounts in the accompanying financial statements have been regrouped and reclassified for the convenience of the reader, and certain amounts for prior year have been reclassified to conform with current year classifications.

Foreign currency translation — Assets and liabilities denominated in foreign currencies have been translated into Korean won at year-end exchange rates. The resulting exchange gains or losses have been charged to current income in the accompanying statements of income except that unusual and significant losses and gains on long-term foreign currency debt, which exceed 5% of capital stock, are deferred and amortized over five years using the straight-line method.

Allowance for doubtful accounts — The Company provides allowance for possible losses on notes and accounts receivable as of balance sheet date based on an analysis of the current status of the receivables and collection experience.

Inventories — Inventories are stated at weighted average cost for finished products and work-in-process, moving average cost for raw materials, supplies and purchased merchandise, and specific unit cost for materials in-transit.

Investments in affiliated companies — Investments in affiliated companies are carried at weighted average cost except for investments in existence in 1981 which were revalued under the Assets Revaluation Law.

Depreciation — Property, plant and equipment are stated at cost except for assets in existence in 1981 which were revalued under the Assets Revaluation Law. Depreciation, including depreciation of the revaluation increases, has been computed on the straight-line method over the following estimated useful lives:

	Years
Buildings and structures	34 — 47
Machinery and equipment	2 — 7
Tools, furniture and fixtures	2 — 20
Vehicles	4 — 5

Maintenance and repairs are charged to expense accounts in the year in which they are incurred. Expenditures which result in the enhancement of the value of facilities are accounted for as additions to property, plant and equipment. Interest incurred on loans used to finance construction projects is being capitalized as part of the cost of the assets. Capitalized interest in 1991 is ₩16,925 million.

Accounting for leases — Lease contracts covered by non-cancellable terms and which satisfy one of the following conditions are accounted for as financing leases:

— The ownership of the leased property shall be transferred to lessee at the end of the lease term.
— A bargain purchase option is included.
— The lease term is more than the estimated economic life of the leased property.

All other leases are accounted for as operating leases.

For financing leases, the leased assets are stated at the minumum lease payments less interest to be incurred during the lease term. The leased assets under financing leases are depreciated on the straight-line method over the estimated useful lives of the assets.

For operating leases, the lease rentals are recognized as an expense when paid in accordance with the lease contracts.

Deferred charges — Deferred experimentation and research costs incurred prior to December 31, 1989 are being amortized using the straight-line method over five years commencing with the year in which such costs are incurred. Experimentation and research costs incurred after January 1, 1990, stock, debenture and convertible bond issuing costs are amortized in the year incurred.

Employees' severance and retirement benefits — Under the Korean Labor Standard Law, employees terminating their employment are entitled to severance payments based on the rates of pay at the time of termination, years of service and certain other factors. The annual provision is sufficient to state the liability at the estimated obligation arising from services performed to and at rates of pay in effect at December 31, 1991. No funding is required by law. Since 1983, the Company insured a portion of its obligation for employees' severance and retirement benefits in order to obtain tax benefit by making a deposit with a life insurance company. The deposit including accrued interest is refundable on demand. However, since refunding of the deposit would result in loss of current tax benefit, the Company has no intention of seeking a refund.

Translation of foreign currency statements — Accounts of overseas branches are maintained in currencies of the countries in which they conduct their operations. In translating the foreign currency financial statements of the overseas branches into Korean won, income and expense accounts were translated at average exchange rates in effect during the year, and assets and liabilities were translated at year end exchange rates. The resulting translation gain of ₩247,4 million for 1991 was recorded to the deferred gains, liability account in the balance sheet.

Sales — Domestic sales consist primarily of long-term installment sales, ranging from 12 — 36 months, for which revenue is recognized at the time of sale, while related finance charges are recognized as interest income over the installment periods.

Income taxes — The Company provides for income taxes on income that are currently payable.

Report of Independent Public Accounts

CHONG-UN ACCOUNTING CORPORATION
CERTIFIED PUBLIC ACCOUNTANTS

A Member of
HORWATH INTERNATIONAL
with Affiliated Offices Worldwide

Room 704, Sampoong Building
310, 4-Ka, Eulji-Ro, Choong-Ku, Seoul

Tel: (822) 272-7211/4
Fax: (822) 265-5214

The Stockholders and Board of Directors
Kia Motors Corporation

We have examined the accompanying balance sheets of Kia Motors Corporation for the periods ending Dec. 31, 1991 and Dec. 31, 1990, and the related statements of income and unappropriated retained earnings, proposed appropriations of unappropriated retained earnings and statements of changes in financial position for the years then ended. Our examinations were made in accordance with auditing standards generally accepted in the Republic of Korea.

In our opinion, the statements mentioned above present fairly the financial position of Kia Motors Corporation on December 31, 1991 and 1990, and the results of operations, proposed appropriations of unappropriated retained earnings and changes in financial position for the years then ended, in conformity with accounting principles generally accepted in the Republic of Korea.

Chong Un Accounting Corporation

February 14, 1992

NOTE

1 References to 'Korea' in the remainder of this chapter are to South Korea only.

BIBLIOGRAPHY

Bank of Korea, The (1990) *Monthly Bulletin*, March, pp. 9–10.
Baring Securities (1990) *Korean Monthly Report*, April, p. 16.
Choi, F.D.S. *et al.* (1983) 'Analysing foreign statements: the use and misuse of international ratio analysis', *Journal of International Business Studies*, Spring.
Korea Federation of Small Business (1989) *The Small Industry Statistics of Major Countries*, December.
Korea Institute for Economics & Technology (1987) *Performance Evaluation of Government Invested Enterprises* (in Korean), December, pp. 15–18.
KPMG San Tong & Co. (1989) *Taxation in Korea* (3rd edn), June.
—— (1989) *Investment in Korea* (4th edn), August.
—— (1990) *The Accounting Profession in South Korea*, Seoul: AICPA.
Samil Accounting Corporation (1988) *Generally Accepted Accounting Principles in the Republic of Korea and United States of America, A Review and Comparison.*
—— (1989) *A Guide to Foreign Investment in the Republic of Korea*, May.
—— (1989) *A Guide for Business and Investors.*
Ungki Lim (1989) *Ownership and Control Structure of Korean Listed Firms* (Korea Listed Companies Association), November, p. 15.

4 Taiwan

S.T. Chiang

INTRODUCTION

Taiwan, formerly known in the west as Formosa, is an island of 36,000 square kilometres (13,900 square miles) in the East China Sea about 200 kilometres (120 miles) off the south-eastern coast of mainland China. With the Taiwan Strait in the west and the Pacific Ocean in the east, Taiwan is on the crossroads between north-east and south-east Asia, and midway between Japan and Korea to the north and Hongkong and the Philippines in the south. Straddling the Tropic of Cancer, Taiwan stretches about 386 kilometres (240 miles) from north to south and 137 kilometres (85 miles) across its widest points from east to west. It includes the satellite islands of the Penghu archipelago, formerly known as the Pescadores, consisting of 64 islets situated in the Taiwan Strait, and 22 other islands.

Under Japanese rule for fifty years, Taiwan was restored to the Republic of China (ROC) in 1945 at the end of the Second World War as an island province. The government of the Republic, also called the Nationalist Chinese government, moved to Taiwan in the wake of the communist conquest of the mainland and established its provisional capital in Taipei, Taiwan, in 1949.

ECONOMIC BACKGROUND

Taiwan was mainly an agricultural economy when it was restored to the Republic of China in 1945, and agriculture is still important. The sub-tropical climate permits year-round farming and multi-cropping of a wide variety of crops.

In the early stage of economic development, a US Aid programme in a gross amount of US$1,482.2. million for a period of 14 years starting in 1951 and terminating in 1965 played an important role in accelerating Taiwan's economic growth. Since then, a series of four-year economic plans have continuously been instituted. In its economic policy, the government has always emphasized growth with stability and respect for free enterprise. For Taiwan's future development, the government has committed itself to the liberalization and internationalization of the economy. Liberalization essentially refers to the removal of tariff and non-tariff barriers in such areas as trade, foreign exchange transactions and business, while internationalization emphasises the desire of the government to open Taiwan to foreign technology and expertise, particularly in high-tech industry and the service sector of the economy.

During its post-war rehabilitation, Taiwan had a time of economic difficulties such as inflation, unemployment and loss of markets in Japan and mainland China. To cope with these problems, the government instituted a series of economic policies. First, a land reform programme for redistribution was carried out in three stages. During the 1950s, Taiwan emphasized the development of labour-intensive import-substitution industries, such as textiles, plastics, plywood, consumer electronics, etc., and social and economic stability was promoted.

In the 1960s, the government implemented an export-expansion strategy and the encouragement of investment and savings. Export processing zones, a combination of free ports and industrial parks, were established, and a Statute for the Encouragement of Investment was promulgated. Exports of labour-intensive manufactured goods and new farm products were vigorously promoted. In the 1970s, the government increased infrastructural investment to build new ports, highways, power plants and airports, and developed basic and heavy or upstream industries, such as steel and petrochemicals. From 1980, with the industrial base well developed, the government and private industry have moved together to promote the growth of technology-intensive strategic industries related to energy, material, information and bio-technology, and to strengthen the development of science and technology.

With successful government planning and hard-working people, Taiwan has, after three decades of development under an export-oriented trade policy, built up an enormous amount of foreign exchange reserves and a strong economic infrastructure with a wide range of supporting industries. By 1991, Taiwan's GNP had grown to NT$4,431.2 billion (US$179.4 billion) with a per capita income of NT$217,730 (US$8,815).

BUSINESS ENVIRONMENT

Under the government policy of encouragement of investment with an emphasis on incentives to private industry, Taiwan's private sector growth started in the early 1960s when former landlords, through the land reform programme, received full compensation from the government and made investments in manufacturing industries. The multitude of small and medium-sized family-run companies they established have been the foundation for Taiwan's economic growth.

The funding of this private sector, which was heavily dependent on an unorganized money market, has been greatly improved since the inauguration of the Export–Import Bank (Eximbank) in February 1979. The Eximbank, an independent corporate agency, was set up specifically to assist in financing the export and import trade. In addition, there are a score of local banks and a large number of foreign banks and representative offices providing a full range of trade, development and operational financing for all companies in Taiwan.

Through trade surpluses and with a high savings propensity, Taiwan has been able to finance its capital investment by its own means since 1971 and has maintained a ratio of capital formation to GNP of 20 to 30 per cent for almost three decades.

For the state-run government enterprises such as China Steel Corporation, Taiwan Sugar Corporation, China Petroleum Corporation, Taiwan Power Company and banking institutions, adequate financing under government planning is available by inclusion in the government's fiscal budgets. There is a small foreign loan or debt raised by Taiwan Power Company for its expansion of nuclear power plants.

Taiwan set up a Securities and Exchange Commission (SEC) in September 1960. The Taiwan Stock Exchange was formed in 1961, but the stock market was not in operation until February 1962. The Taiwan Stock Exchange is the sole stock exchange in the Republic of China, and no brokers or dealers are allowed to make a market in any security or to trade shares off-market, except the OTC market for trading shares of OTC companies. Since January 1986 stock trading has been completely computerized. The stock market has grown steadily. Record highs for the TSE index were recorded in late 1989 but the index collapsed in 1990. It has remained very volatile since.

At the end of November 1992, a total of 424,960 companies with a total capital amount of NT$4,867.1 billion (US$194.6 billion) were registered with the Ministry of Economic Affairs (MOEA). At the end of December 1992, 1,070 companies having a capital of over NT$200 million each were mandatorily required to go public. Of these 1,070 public companies, only 257 were listed on the stock exchange. It is quite common for companies to go public without ever applying for a stock exchange listing. The total capital of the 257 listed companies amounted to NT$761.0 billion (US$30.4 billion), or 15 per cent of the total capitalization of all companies in Taiwan.

All publicly held companies are required by the SEC to disclose publicly their financial information periodically after audit by independent certified public accountants (CPAs). For companies with a capital exceeding NT$30 million (US$1.21 million), an annual financial report audited by CPAs must be submitted to the MOEA once a year, while state-run government enterprises are subject to audit only by government auditors.

To promote the capital market, the government has established a special securities finance company, has issued compulsory measures requiring companies with paid-up capital amounting to NT$200 million to go public, and has offered tax incentives to public listed companies. There is no tax payable on the purchase of securities, but a securities transaction tax of 0.6 per cent has been levied on the sale of securities as from January 1990. Dividends are subject to a 15 per cent withholding tax, while capital gains are exempt from taxation.

As foreign exchange controls prevent non-ROC residents from investing directly in the Taiwan stock market, a mutual fund, called Taiwan (ROC) Fund, was launched for indirect foreign investment in the Taiwan securities market in 1983, which was followed by three more funds issued by three local firms in 1986, called Formosa Fund, Taipei Fund and Taiwan Fund, Inc., respectively.

COMPANIES AND COMPANY LAW

Company law in Taiwan provides for four different forms of companies: the unlimited company, the limited company (approximately equivalent to the UK private company), the unlimited company with limited liability shareholders, and the company limited by shares (approximately equivalent to the UK public company). All companies must be registered with the MOEA and public listed companies must be further approved by the SEC.

Unlimited companies are organized by two or more shareholders who bear unlimited joint and several liabilities for the obligations of the company and half of whom must be domiciled in the Republic of China. The articles of incorporation of the company must be adopted and agreed upon unanimously by all shareholders.

A limited company must have not less than five shareholders and not more than 21 shareholders, at least half of whom must be Chinese nationals domiciled in the country and holding more than 50 per cent of the total capital. Each shareholder is liable for his or her capital contribution only, and is entitled to one vote, irrespective of the amount of capital contribution, unless the articles of incorporation prescribe that the votes shall be allocated in proportion to the amount of capital contribution.

An unlimited company with limited liability shareholders is a company incorporated both by shareholders with unlimited liability and by shareholders with limited liability. Shareholders with unlimited liability are jointly and severally liable for all obligations of the company, whereas shareholders with limited liability are liable only for their capital contribution.

A company limited by shares must be incorporated by at least seven promoters, more than half of whom must be domiciled in the country. A government and a legal entity such as a company can be a promoter. The capital must be divided into shares and each share must have the same par value. A part of the share capital may be special shares, such as preferred stocks. The issue price of shares must not be less than the par value, and all shares of an issue must be of the same par value. A shareholder's liability is limited to the payment in full of his or her subscription.

The business of a company limited by shares must be conducted by a board of directors which comprises at least three directors with a term of office of no more than three years, but who are eligible for re-election. The 'supervisors' of the company hold office for a term of three years or less but may be re-elected; at least one of them must be domiciled within the country. Supervisors review and verify all statements and records prepared by the board of directors and submit a report on the verification to the shareholders' meeting. Such verification of statements and records may be done by certified public accountants engaged for the purpose. A supervisor must not concurrently serve as a director, managerial officer or any other staff member of the company.

A company limited by shares may issue debt such as corporate bonds, debentures and notes by resolution of a directors' meeting and with the approval of the SEC. The aggregate amount of secured debt issued must not exceed the balance of the company's current total assets less the total amount of liabilities and intangible assets, and the aggregate amount of the issue of unsecured debt must not exceed 50 per cent of the same balance.

When new shares are issued, a company limited by shares must set aside 10 to 15 per cent of its new shares for purchase by its employees, and the balance thereof for public subscription.

Public listed companies, whose stocks are listed on the Taiwan Stock Exchange (TSE), are of three categories, A, B and C. Category A companies are those with relatively higher capitalization, profitability, capital structure (net worth/total assets ratios) and distribution of shares than categories B and C at the time of filing applications for going public. At present, only stocks of categories A and B are traded on the stock exchange.

In November 1989, the government permitted the establishment of an over-the-counter (OTC) market for trading the shares of those companies, called OTC companies, which have, in accordance with the regulation for trading shares over the counter, been approved for going public with a lower capitalization than category A, B or C companies, and which are not qualified to list their stocks on the stock exchange but to list their shares with the Taipei Securities Traders Association for trading over the counter through its member brokerage firms.

A foreign company must translate its name into Chinese and must not do business in the Republic of China until duly granted a certificate of recognition and a company licence as a branch office. A duly recognized foreign company may acquire such real estate as may be required for its business operations, provided that prior approval of the acquisition has been obtained from the central competent authority and on condition that the laws of its home country permit a Republic of China company to have the same rights. Where a foreign company does not contemplate establishing a branch office, it may register a representative office with the

Ministry of Economic Affairs for sending its representative to perform juristic acts in the Republic of China.

A FIA company is one established by a foreign investor who has received Foreign Investment Approval (FIA) status and is entitled to tax incentives and privileges offered by the government in accordance with a number of laws and regulations, including the Statute for Encouragement of Investment, the Statute for Investment by Foreign Nationals and the Statute for Investment by Overseas Chinese. A foreign investor may co-operate with a local partner to form a joint venture in any one of the four forms of companies. However, foreign investors cannot receive FIA privileges and benefits unless they have obtained FIA status for investment in the joint venture. FIA companies may also apply to go public and to list their stocks on the market in accordance with the relevant laws and regulations.

A branch is a part of the foreign company which must first be recognized and registered with the MOEA, and which is operated in the same way as a local company.

SECURITIES AND EXCHANGE LAW

The Securities and Exchange Law, first promulgated in April 1968, and amended in 1981, 1983 and 1988, prescribes the public offering, issuance, buying and selling, administration and supervision of marketable securities. Marketable securities include government bonds and public offerings of shares and corporate bonds and debentures of a publicly listed company limited by shares.

Prior to public offering, a prospectus must be prepared and distributed to subscribers and signed by the responsible person of the company, the underwriter, certified public accountant and lawyer, all of whom are jointly liable for any claims of damages due to misrepresentation in any of the material facts specified in the prospectus.

A public listed company must publish its financial statements approved by its board of directors and supervisors and certified by an independent accountant as follows:

- annual financial statements within four months after the close of a fiscal year;
- semi-annual financial statements within two months after the close of a half year's operations;
- the first and third quarterly financial statements within one month after close of a quarter's operations;
- a monthly report on business sales income within ten days of the following month.

In addition, the following important information must be disclosed publicly within two days after occurrence:

- any corrections or rectifications of the financial statements which have been made by the SEC;
- any significant matters that affect the shareholders' equity or the price of securities.

The Securities and Exchange Commission supervises the operations of the stock exchange and all publicly listed companies, as well as the profession of certified public accountants.

INFLUENCES ON ACCOUNTING

Accounting is influenced by the Commercial Accounting Law, the Securities and Exchange Law, the Accountancy Profession and Tax Law. There are also external influences.

The majority of business enterprises in Taiwan keep their accounting records in compliance with the Commercial Accounting Law promulgated in 1948, brought into force in 1952 and amended in 1964 and 1968. To meet the rapid economic growth, the Commercial Accounting Law was drastically amended in 1987, with the new rules applying as from 1990. The law now requires both the private and public sectors to keep accounting records and prepare financial reports, and emphasizes financial accounting as distinct from tax accounting. The Commercial Accounting Law has been the mainstay of the accounting systems and practices of all business enterprises in Taiwan, while the private sector has generally regarded accounting record-keeping as just for the purpose of preparing income tax returns, and has usually put more emphasis on tax accounting than financial accounting.

The Law applies to all business enterprises established under the Business Regulation and Company Laws but is not applicable to small partnerships or sole proprietors. The financial year must run from 1 January to 31 December and accounting records and financial statements, if not kept in the national currency, must be translated into it. Accrual accounting and double entry bookkeeping must be used. If day-to-day accounting is on a cash basis, adjustments must be made at the year-end. A general accounting system, designed by the government, must be followed.

Every business enterprise must keep at least two account books: a general journal and a general ledger. The accounts kept must be classified into nine categories: assets, liabilities, owners' equity, operating revenues, operating costs, non-operating revenues and expenses, operating expenses, extraordinary items and income tax.

The prescribed annual financial statements are: balance sheet, income statement, statement of changes in financial position, statement of changes in owners' equity (or statement of appropriation of profit and loss), a list of property, plant and equipment. Corresponding figures for the preceding period must be shown. The notes to the financial statements must disclose:

significant accounting policies; changes in accounting policies; restrictions imposed on assets by creditors; material contingent liabilities and promises; restrictions on the appropriation of profit; material matters concerning owners' equity; material post balance sheet events; other explanations required to avoid misinterpretation by users and provide a fair representation.

The historical cost-accounting convention must be followed. In particular, inventories and marketable securities must be valued at the lower of cost (including FIFO, LIFO and weighted average cost) and net realizable value. An allowance for doubtful accounts must be deducted from accounts receivable. Fixed assets must be depreciated annually. The depreciation methods permitted include straight line, declining balance, and sum of the years' digits. Intangible assets must be amortized over the period of their estimated economic lives. Fixed assets, depletable assets and intangible assets may be revalued. If this is done a reserve for asset valuation must be established and depreciation calculated on the revalued amount. Liabilities must be shown at the amounts payable on maturity.

For publicly held companies, securities dealers and brokers, and stock exchange corporations, the SEC regulations for the preparation of financial reports govern accounting practices, while for government enterprises the Accounting Law applies.

Following the Security Transaction Act in 1968, the SEC issued 'Regulations for the Preparation of Financial Reports' for securities issuers, dealers and brokers and stock exchange corporations. The regulations have since been amended six times. They prescribe the installation of accounting systems and the preparation of financial reports including the balance sheet and its required schedules, the income statement and its required schedules, the statement of changes in shareholders' equity and the statement of changes in financial position. Standard forms of financial reports are also prescribed. The generally accepted accounting principles issued by the Accounting Research and Development Foundation (see p. 141) must be followed. Departures therefrom must be described in detail and their financial effect quantified. The prescribed forms of financial reports (balance sheet, balance sheet schedules, income statement, income statement schedules, statement of changes in stockholders' equity, statement of changes in financial position) are illustrated in the Appendix at the end of the chapter.

A company's annual financial reports must be reviewed by the supervisors of the company. For a publicly held company, the financial report must be audited and certified by a certified public accountant and published within one month after it has been duly certified.

A company must, after paying all taxes, transfer at least 10 per cent of its net profits to a legal surplus reserve before it declares dividends and bonuses, until the reserve equals the total authorized capital stock. Apart from the legal reserve, a special reserve may also be set aside by the company according to its articles of incorporation or a resolution adopted at a shareholders' meeting.

The following must be treated as capital reserves:

- any premium on capital stock;
- the net appraisal surplus of each fiscal year;
- any gain on the disposal of assets;
- the fair market value of assets received from a merged company in excess of assumed liabilities and payment for shares held by shareholders of the merged company;
- any donated surplus.

The legal reserve and capital reserve can only be used to cover corporate losses; capital reserves must not be used to cover capital losses unless the legal reserve is insufficient to cover such losses.

A company must not distribute dividends and bonuses when it generates no profits for an accounting period. For the purpose of maintaining the price of its shares, a company may declare dividends and bonuses out of the legal reserve to the extent that the amount of such reserve exceeds 50 per cent of its capital stocks, or that the amount of legal reserve set aside for a year exceeding 20 per cent of the profits, only the portion in excess of the 50 per cent and 20 per cent may be declared as dividends and bonuses. The percentage of bonuses to be allotted to the employees of a company must be provided in the articles of incorporation.

A company may declare dividends and bonuses payable in new shares issued by the company. The half of the legal reserve in excess of 50 per cent of the paid-in capital stock may be capitalized by issuing new shares for distribution to all shareholders proportionately.

ACCOUNTANCY PROFESSION AND ACCOUNTING STANDARDS

The accountancy profession in Taiwan has been organized since certified public accountants from various places in mainland China followed the Nationalist government to Taiwan in 1949. The first to be reactivated in Taipei was the National Federation of Certified Public Accountant Associations of the Republic of China. Subsequently, three more local associations of CPAs have been organized in Taiwan – namely, Taiwan Provincial, Taipei City and Kaohsiung City Associations of CPAs. At the end of 1992, there were 2,590 CPAs in Taiwan of whom 1,320 were members of CPA associations as practising CPAs and 1,270 were not in practice.

As early as the 1950s, American CPAs were working in the US Aid Agency in Taiwan and assisting in training Chinese government accounting personnel. Since the 1970s, the US 'Big Eight' (later the 'Big Six') have appointed local CPA firms as correspondent, affiliate, or member firms in

Taiwan. Except for a handful of Japanese-trained accountants, the majority of practising public accountants are US-oriented, as American accounting textbooks are generally used for accounting education in Taiwan.

The CPA qualification can be obtained by passing the full course of a CPA exam sponsored by the government. In addition, individuals possessing relevant qualifications and experience or a foreign CPA certificate and accreditations, which are recognized and accepted by the government, may apply for a CPA qualification by sitting one or more of the courses of the government CPA examination. A CPA must have two years' work experience and must be a member of a CPA association before he or she can practise either as a sole practitioner or in a firm of CPAs.

A practising CPA may offer, as permitted by law, services which include accounting, auditing and taxation and acting as a liquidator, receiver, executor, trustee and management consultant, and as an agent for filing applications for making investments into Taiwan and patent and trade mark registrations.

The National Federation of CPA Associations of the Republic of China is an organization of practising CPAs to co-ordinate with government regulatory authorities, to conduct continued professional education programmes and to keep contacts with foreign professional bodies. It has six committees – namely, the Ethics Committee, the Education Committee, the Publication Committee, the Peer Review Committee, the International Affairs Committee and the Legal (Laws & Regulations) Committee. The Ethics Committee has issued seven bulletins on professional ethics since its inauguration in 1982. The contents of the bulletins are based on the guidelines of professional ethics issued by the International Federation of Accountants.

The National Federation was the standards setting body until the end of 1983. The Accounting Research and Development Foundation took over the National Federation's Financial Accounting Committee and Auditing Standards Committee in 1984 to form an independent standards-setting body. The Foundation comprises government officials, representatives from industry, academics and practising CPAs. It is headed by the vice-minister of finance with a board of twenty-seven directors of whom nine are managing directors. The Foundation has four committees (Financial Accounting Standards, Auditing Standards, Accounting Systems, and Education and Training), three divisions, and an Accounting Research Centre.

The Financial Accounting Standards Committee has issued twenty pronouncements and two interpretations; the Auditing Standards Committee has issued twenty-three statements of auditing standards as at December 1992. The Accounting Systems Committee has issued five accounting systems for chemical, cement, banking and textile industries as well as a general commercial accounting system.

The eighteen statements of auditing standards cover the following

Table 4.1 A synopsis of financial accounting standards

	Statements	*Synopsis*
No. 1	The Inventory of GAAP (issued July 1982 by the National Federation and revised October 1984 by the Foundation)	This statement deals with the basic framework of financial accounting, including the objectives; fundamental principles such as separate legal entity, going concern, prudence, substance over form, materiality, consistency, and accruals are defined. Assets, liabilities, owners' equity, profit and loss, financial statements and disclosures are prescribed
No. 2	Accounting for Leases (issued October 1982 by the National Federation and revised October 1984 by the Foundation)	Operating and capital leasing, lessor and lessee, and leasing contracts are defined. Examples of sixteen accounting entries for operation and capital leasing are illustrated
No. 3	Capitalization of borrowing costs (issued December 1982 by the National Federation and revised March 1984 by the Foundation)	This deals with the capitalization of interest expenses and its presentation. Three examples of a purchase of capitalized assets, construction of an office building and purchase of machinery by instalment payments are illustrated
No. 4	Statement of changes in financial position (issued September 1983 by the National Federation)	Definition and preparation of statement of changes in financial position on working capital and cash bases are given together with two examples – one on the basis of working capital and the other on cash basis
No. 5	Long-term equity investments (issued April 1984 by the National Federation and revised by the Foundation)	Long-term equity investments are defined. Equity method, cost method and disclosures are prescribed. Altogether twenty-one accounting entries for long-term investments by cost method and equity method are illustrated
The following statements were all issued by the Foundation:		
No. 6	Related party transactions (issued June 1985)	This deals with the disclosure of related party transactions. An example of the notes to financial statement for disclosure of related party transactions is given

No. 7	Consolidated financial statements (issued December 1985)	Definition and preparation of consolidated financial statements including balance sheet, profit and loss, changes in financial position and notes to consolidated financial statements are presented with six examples of accounting entries for offsetting accounts, acquiring subsidiary's shares and special shares, sales to subsidiary, and sale of fixed assets and income taxes thereon
No. 8	Accounting changes and prior period adjustments (issued June 1986)	Definitions of accounting changes and prior period adjustments are prescribed. Six examples are given: three changing methods of depreciation, one for correction of inventories for the previous period, one for amendment of the income statement and retained earnings statement for the previous period, and the other for changing the method of long-term construction contracts
No. 9	Contingencies and subsequent events (issued September 1986)	Definition and accounting for contingencies and subsequent events are prescribed with illustration of the notes to financial statements
No. 10	Valuation and presentation of inventories (issued May 1987)	Definition, method and disclosure of inventories are prescribed with illustrations of production cost, replacement cost and the lower of cost or market
No. 11	Long-term construction contracts (issued July 1987)	Methods of recognition of profit and loss and presentation of long-term construction contracts are prescribed with illustrations of the percentage of completion method and the completed contract method
No. 12	Income tax credit (issued December 1987)	Income tax credit is defined as only applicable to purchase of equipment, research and development expenses and equity investments and other items as permitted by law. Examples of deferral method and liability method are presented

Table 4.1 (continued)

	Statements	*Synopsis*
No. 13	Reconstruction of debt in financial difficulties (issued June 1988)	This deals with accounting for debtors and creditors during structuring of debt in financial difficulties of the debtors. Illustrations of notes payable and interest payable thereof to be repaid by used machinery, or to be repaid by issuance of common stocks, or to be repaid by issuance of a promissory note with reduced interest rates and reduced amount of principal, or to be repaid by a promissory note by waiving the interest payment in arrears and with a reduced interest rate together with the original amount of principal
No. 14	Translation of foreign currencies (issued December 1988)	Dealing with translation of financial statements of foreign operations in foreign currencies and translations of foreign currency transactions. Definitions of functional currency and historical rate or spot rate are prescribed. Examples of foreign currency transactions with spot rate and forward rate are given. Also, the use of forward rate to avoid risks in foreign exchange rate fluctuations is illustrated
No. 15	Disclosure of accounting policies (issued June 1989)	Disclosure in the notes to financial statements is required for basic accounting principles and procedures used in preparation of the statements
No. 16	Financial forecasts (issued December 1989)	This statement deals with the preparation and disclosure of financial forecasts. Examples of projected income statement and statement of retained earnings, projected balance sheet and projected cash flow statement, together with financial forecasts on the summary of significant accounting policies and basic projections of sales, cost of sales, fixed assets, operating expenses,

		bank loans and interest expenses, income taxes and dividends, are given
No. 17	Cash flow statements (issued December 1989)	This statement deals with the preparation of cash flow statements. Illustrations of indirect method and direct method are presented

topics: outlines of GAAS, auditors' report, audit planning, working papers, clients' representation, audit evidence, internal control, confirmation, taking inventories, related party transactions, interim financial statements, analytical review, subsequent events, fraud and error, going concern, connections between superseding and previous accountants, the use of another CPA's work, and audit quality.

The financial accounting standards and auditing statements are prepared on the basis of national requirements and with reference to US standards and the statements issued by IFAC.

A synopsis of the financial accounting standards is given in Table 4.1.

The inventory of generally accepted accounting principles was prepared mainly on the basis of the US GAAP. The main differences are:

- For long-term investments, it is specifically prescribed that investments under 20 per cent holdings of common shares are without influence, that over 20 per cent and under 50 per cent are of significant influence, and that over 50 per cent are of controlling capability.
- Trade-in fixed assets with cash payment must be valued at book value plus cash payment or fair market price, whichever is the lower. Trade-in fixed assets with cash receipts must be valued at the book value of trade-off assets without any gain or loss, while the cash receipts are entered as sales revenue recognizing the profit.
- Intangible assets must be amortized within a period not exceeding twenty years.
- Fixed assets and intangible assets can be revalued, and depreciation, depletion and amortization thereof can be provided from the date of asset revaluation based on the revalued amount.
- Deferred revenue (unearned revenue) can be recorded as a contra account, a current liability or a non-liability.
- A legal profit reserve is mandatory.
- Accumulated losses may be made up by retained earnings, capital reserve and capital. The capital reserve for increment of asset revaluation can be used for making up losses, while it should be replenished by future profits of the company.
- Instalment sales must be presented by the percentage of gross margin method.

TAX LAWS

As in most countries, taxes in Taiwan take many forms. Only those taxes which principally affect accounting are described in any detail here.

Direct taxes in the Republic of China are administered by the Department of Taxation of the Ministry of Finance (MOF), while customs duties are collected and administered by a separate department of customs administration, the Inspectorate General of Customs of the MOF, and by various local customs offices in different locations. There are three categories of taxes: national taxes; provincial or municipal taxes; and prefectural or city taxes. National taxes, except customs duties, are collected by the National Tax Administration; provincial and prefectural taxes are collected by Tax Collection Offices in various cities.

National taxes consist of customs duties, income taxes (business enterprise income tax and individual income tax), estate and gift tax, commodity tax, securities transaction tax and mining lot tax. Provincial and prefectural taxes consist of business tax (VAT), stamp tax, house tax, deed tax, land tax (land-value increment tax, land-value tax, rural land tax), amusement tax and vehicle licence tax.

The four major taxes are: income tax, property tax, business tax and commodity tax. According to the 1992 *Essential Statistics on Taiwan, R.O.C.*, property tax formed the largest proportion of tax revenues at 23.1 per cent of the total tax revenue, followed by income tax 22.1 per cent, business tax 13.2 per cent and commodity tax 11.9 per cent. Other taxes produced 29.7 per cent.

There is no single consolidated code on taxation as each tax has a different law. Since 1976, a Tax Collection Law has been enacted, which, however, prescribes only general rules in addition to the provisions of special nature of each tax in different tax laws.

Thc Incomc Tax Law concerns all taxpayers the most, since it prescribes the individual income tax and business income tax to be levied on income from sources in ROC.

All business enterprises must register with the local tax collection office before commencement of business, and apply for cancellation or amendment of registration in case of dissolution, closure, merger, transfer or change of name, address, responsible person or nature of business. Sufficient account books, vouchers and accounting records must be kept. The accounting system must be on the accrual basis.

Inventories of merchandise, raw materials, supplies, goods-in-process, finished goods and by-products must be valued at cost or the lower of market or cost. Cost may either be the actual cost or the cost arrived at by FIFO, LIFO, the weighted average, moving average or single average methods or other methods approved by regulatory authority, but where LIFO is used, evaluation on the basis of the lower of market or cost must not be applied. Actual cost means the acquisition price plus all the necessary expenses incidental to acquisition and putting in use. Market value is the current price prevailing at the local market on the day of reporting the account.

The cost methods mentioned above may also be applicable to the valuation of short-term investments in marketable securities. Where the securities market value fluctuates violently at the close of a financial period, the average price during the immediately preceding month may be taken as the market value of the securities.

The valuation of accounts and notes receivable is net of their respective amounts less an allowance for doubtful accounts. Allowance for doubtful accounts is 1 per cent of the total amount of accounts and notes receivable, depending on whether with or without collaterals. An account or note receivable may be deemed as a loss of bad debt where the outstanding amount is uncollectable by reason of insolvency of the debtor or adjudication of bankruptcy or past due for over two years.

The valuation of buildings, fixtures, equipment, vessels, machinery, tools, apparatus, appliances and other fixed assets is at cost less prescribed depreciation. Depreciation may be calculated by the straight-line method, the fixed percentage on diminishing book value method or the working-hour method. In the computation of the depreciation of a fixed asset, the service life of the fixed asset shall not be shorter than the minimum years of service life as specified in the Table of Service Life of Fixed Assets, and a residual value equal to 10 per cent of the cost shall be first deducted from the cost.

Depletable assets are valued by deducting depletion charges from the cost. Depletion charges may be computed by dividing the cost of the asset by the quantity actually exploited during the year, or by setting aside annually a depletion charge from the gross sales of products according to the prescribed Table of Depletion Assets.

Intangible assets, such as trade marks, copyrights, patents and franchises are valued at cost less accumulated amortization. Amortization is computed in equal annual instalments according to the prescribed number of years. The amortization of organization cost must not exceed 20 per cent of the original amount per annum.

In case of dissolution, closure, merger or transfer, the assets are valued on the basis of current values or the actual prices of the transaction.

A long-term investment of all the shares or more than one half of the shares of a company is valued on the basis of the total net assets of the company or a part of the total net assets proportionate to the amount of shares held. Where the amount of long-term investment in a company is less than a majority of holdings, the valuation of the investment is based on the cost.

When the retained earnings of a company are equal to more than one half of its paid-in capital, the company must transfer in the following year the retained earnings to increase its capital and meantime distribute that

Table 4.2 Individual income tax rates

Net consolidated income (NT$)	*Tax rate (%)*
0– 300,000	6
300,000– 800,000	13
800,000–1,600,000	21
1,600,000–3,000,000	30
3,000,000 and over	40

portion of retained earnings transferred to capital increase as dividends to shareholders who shall, in turn, pay income tax on the dividend received therefor.

A taxpayer may appoint a registered accountant or other lawful agent to file his or her income tax return and applications for administrative remedy procedures for tax matters.

In 1960, the government issued the Statute for Encouragement of Investment which has been mainly by the use of tax measures to complement economic development, and which has been one of the major policies to make possible the rapid economic growth during the past three decades. The Statute was terminated at the end of 1990.

Individual income tax includes business and professional income, salaries and wages, interest, rental and royalties, self-employment in farming, fishery, forestry, animal husbandry and mining, gains on sales of property and securities, games and prizes, and other income such as subsidies, awards, compensations and life insurance payments.

Individual taxpayers are those who receive income from a ROC source and are divided into two categories: resident and nonresident taxpayers. Resident taxpayers are those who have a domicile or live in the country up to 183 days in a taxable year. Nonresident taxpayers include aliens or overseas Chinese who reside in the country less than 90 days within one tax year.

Various exemptions are prescribed for all the nine categories of income mentioned above, while deductions are allowed to choose either standard deduction or itemized deductions. Standard deduction is mandatory if the taxpayer is not required or fails to file an annual income tax return. Itemized deductions include donations amounting to 20 per cent of consolidated income; a prescribed amount of premiums for life and labour insurance; medical and maternity expenses; disaster losses; and mortgage interest expense. The individual income tax rates for 1990 are shown in Table 4.2.

The business enterprise income tax, or business income tax, is a levy on the income of a company, a sole proprietorship and a partnership. For sole proprietorship and partnership organizations, an individual income tax is also levied on the profits of individual proprietors and partners and there is thus double taxation.

As there are over 400,000 sole proprietorships, partnerships and small businesses, the great majority of which have a business income below the minimum for paying business income tax, double taxation, though it exists, is not serious.

Those paying business income tax comprise, in addition to companies, sole proprietorships and partnerships, co-operative organizations, and educational, cultural, public welfare and charitable institutions, all of which are required to file income tax returns regardless of whether they are tax-exempt or not.

Business enterprises are required to pay estimated tax within one month beginning 1 July in an amount equivalent to 50 per cent of the income tax paid for the previous year, together with a provisional tax return, except those without a fixed place of business in ROC, small-scale businesses, educational, cultural, public welfare, charitable organizations and branches of international financial banks.

Business income tax returns must be filed within two months beginning 1 February of each year, and may be extended no later than 31 May. There are four kinds of business income tax returns:

- Ordinary returns – used by business enterprises in general;
- Blue returns – used only with the approval of the tax office for encouraging honest reporting by businesses;
- Simplified returns – used by small-scale businesses;
- Report of final accounts of operational organizations – used by educational, cultural, public welfare and charitable organizations.

Losses are permitted to be carried over for three years; in other words, any losses incurred during the preceding three years may be deducted from the net profit of the current year, before payment of income tax. The business income tax rates for 1990 are shown in Table 4.3.

Business enterprises are also responsible for withholding tax on various payments to taxpayers, such as dividends, commission, interest, salaries and wages, and issue tax withholding certificates to the taxpayers. The tax withheld must be paid to the tax office within ten days of the following

Table 4.3 Business income tax rates

Net profit (NT$)	*Income tax rate (%)*
Under 50,000	Exempt
50,000–100,000	15
100,000 and over	25

month, and at the end of January each year an annual tax withholding report must be prepared and submitted to the tax authorities.

The tax withholding rates are of two categories, one applicable to resident taxpayers and the other for nonresident taxpayers. For resident taxpayers, the withholding tax rates are generally either 10 or 15 per cent according to various incomes, and for nonresident taxpayers withholding rates are either 20, 25 or 35 per cent.

The business tax, first enacted in July 1928, was, in theory, a kind of multiple-stage gross receipt tax. A VAT system has been adopted since the Business Tax Law was amended in November 1985. The current Business Tax Law was last amended in May 1988 supplemented by rules governing the collection of business tax and rules on uniform invoices. The ROC VAT system, like its counterparts in other countries, has two basic forms of exemptions – namely, zero rating and non-credit exemptions. All business enterprises must issue uniform invoices for doing business transactions. Only small businesses are permitted not to use uniform invoices but to issue ordinary receipts. On a uniform invoice, the amount of business tax must be specified.

The commodity tax is a single-stage sales tax levied on goods at the time of shipping out from a factory or at the port of import. The commodity tax began with the tax on cigarettes in 1927. The current Statute for Commodity Tax, promulgated in 1946, has been repeatedly amended with the last amendment in May 1979. The Customs Law, promulgated in August 1967, has been revised thirteen times with the last amendment in January 1989. Customs duties collected on imported goods are either on an *ad valorem* basis or on a specific basis in accordance with the Customs Import Tariff.

The land-tax system in China originated as early as 22 BC; land tax has always been a major source of fiscal revenue. The current Land Tax Law enacted in July 1977 provides a unified code on land tax, consolidating all the laws, rules and regulations concerning the collection of land tax in the past. The prevailing land-tax system includes land value tax, agricultural land tax and land value increment tax. The land value tax is imposed on land that has been assigned a value. Taxpayers are land owners or mortgagees of land. The agricultural land-tax system is the oldest system in the history of taxation in China and also in the world. Land value increment tax is collected on the natural increment value of lands within the area of city plannig at the time of selling, transfer or mortgage.

The house tax in China may be traced back to AD 618. The present House Dues Act, promulgated in 1943, was amended three times in 1950, 1955 and 1967. The house tax is levied on all houses and their attached constructions which increase the value of the house.

The current Estate and Gift Tax Law of 1981 was first drafted in 1915 and re-drafted and revised in 1929, 1940 and 1946. Estate tax started in 1940 under the Tentative Statute for Estate Tax. Estate includes moveable and immoveable properties having market values, such as cash, bank deposits, securities, land, house, rights of claim, mining rights and the like.

A gift tax is levied on a gift property which is transferred gratuitously from a donor to a donee who accepts the transfer. Another type of gift is the constructive gift which is a transfer of property as determined by tax authority according to law.

The Stamp Tax Law was introduced in the early years of ROC government and was first revised in 1927, a further eight revisions being made subsequently. The present Stamp Tax Law has been simplified since VAT business tax was adopted in January 1986. Stamp tax is levied by affixing revenue stamps on documents.

Securities transaction tax began with the Statute for the Stock Exchange in March 1922, which, however, was not enforced until the Securities Exchange Act was promulgated in September 1946 and revised in December 1955.

The collection of vehicle licence tax, then called licence plate tax, began in 1936. In February 1947, the General Provisions for Vehicle Licence Tax Collection Law was issued which, after several amendments, was replaced by the Vehicle Licence Tax Law in May 1950. The present Vehicle Licence Tax Law was last amended in 1979 with a progressive tax system according to the total cylinder displacement volume in cubic centimetres (CC) of the vehicle engine.

Deed tax in China originated in AD 400, and was first enacted in December 1940 as prescribed by the Statute for Deed Tax which has been amended seven times and has been in force since February 1952. Deed tax is levied on the value of deeds for buying and selling, mortgage, exchange, donation, dividing and legal possession of real estate outside the areas where land value increment tax is levied.

EXTERNAL INFLUENCES

In order to promote economic development, the government has realized that the improvement of the capital market is one of the important steps and that to improve the capital market requires upgrading the standard of accounting.

In 1973 and 1980 the government invited American advisers to hold seminars with local practising public accountants and to present recommendations for improving the capital market and upgrading the accountancy profession.

As early as the late 1960s, the American 'Big Eight' had, in fact, already used an overseas Chinese accounting firm in the Philippines and had appointed local accounting firms to set up operations in Taiwan.

As the inflow of US investments grows rapidly under the government policy of encouragement of investment, the US influence on local accountancy profession also grows. The 'Big Eight' (later the 'Big Six') have become more active either in establishing their own offices or by sending expatriates to work in local accounting firms.

Presently, the large national accounting firms in Taiwan, having between 200 to 500 staff, are all connected or operate together with one of the 'Big Six'.

SUMMARY

Taiwan has experienced strong economic growth in recent decades but the Taiwan Stock Exchange, which is supervised by the Securities and Exchange Commission, has remained relatively small despite government efforts to promote the capital market. Nonresidents are not able to invest directly in the market.

There are four different types of companies: the unlimited company, the private company, the unlimited company with limited liability shareholders and the company limited by shares. The last is economically the most important category and includes public listed companies.

Accounting is influenced by the Commercial Accounting Law, the Securities and Exchange Law, the accountancy profession (the National Federation of CPAs Association of the Republic of China), and tax law. The most important external influence is the United States. The Commercial Accounting Law applies to all business enterprises except small partnerships and sole proprietorships. The Securities and Exchange Law applies to listed companies. Accounting standards are set by the Accounting Research and Development Foundation, an independent standards-setting body whose membership includes government officials, representatives from industry, academics and practising CPAs.

APPENDIX

Extracts from the accounts of USI Far East

會計師查核報告書

臺灣聚合化學品股份有限公司財務報表會計師查核報告書

台灣聚合化學品股份有限公司民國八十年及七十九年十二月三十一日之資產負債表，暨民國八十年及七十九年一月一日至十二月三十一日之損益表、股東權益變動表及現金流量表，業經本會計師依照一般公認審計準則及會計師查核簽證財務報表規則，採用必要之查核程序，包括各項會計記錄之抽查在內，予以查核竣事。

據本會計師之意見，上開財務報表係依照證券發行人財務報告編製準則及一般公認會計原則，於前後一致之基礎上編製，足以公正表示台灣聚合化學品股份有限公司民國八十年及七十九年十二月三十一日之財務狀況，暨民國八十年度及七十九年度之營業成績及現金流量。

台灣聚合化學品股份有限公司已編製民國八十年度及七十九年度之合併財務報表，並經本會計師出具無保留意見之查核報告在案，備供參考。

此致

臺灣聚合化學品股份有限公司 公鑒

勤業會計師事務所

會計師 王小蕙

會計師 王景盆

中華民國八十一年一月十七日

監察人審查報告書

臺灣聚合化學品股份有限公司監察人審查報告書

董事會造送本公司八十年度（八十年元月一日至十二月三十一日）決算報告書表，經本監察人等依照公司法第二一九條之規定委託勤業會計師事務所查核，經該會計師事務所提出八十一年一月十七日查核報告書，據稱已全部查核竣事，足以公正表示本公司財務狀況，營業成績及現金流量。復經本監察人等會同審查認爲屬實，茲依規定檢同勤業會計師事務所查核報告書報告如上。

此上

本公司八十一年股東常會

臺灣聚合化學品股份有限公司

監察人：吳幼林

金克和

王錦旺

鄺仲棟

中華民國八十一年三月十日

AUDITORS' REPORT

The Board of Directors and Stockholders
USI Far East Corporation

We have examined the balance sheets of USI Far East Corporation as of December 31, 1991 and 1990, and the related statements of income, changes in stockholders' equity and cash flows for the years then ended. Our examinations were made in accordance with generally accepted auditing standards and the regulations governing such examinations and, accordingly, included such tests of the accounting records and such other auditing procedures as we considered necessary in the circumstances.

In our opinion, the financial statements referred to above present fairly the financial position of USI Far East Corporation as of December 31, 1991 and 1990, and the results of its operations and cash flows for the years then ended, in conformity with generally accepted accounting principles applied on a consistent basis.

For your information, we have examined the consolidated financial statements of USI Far East Corporation as of and for the years ended December 31, 1991 and 1990, and issued unqualified reports thereon.

T.N.Soong & Co.
(Signed)

Taipei, Republic of China
January 17, 1992

SUPERVISORS' REPORT

To: The 1992 Annual Stockholders Meeting
USI Far East Corporation

In accordance with Article 219 of the Company Law of the Republic of China, we have appointed Messrs. T. N. Soong & Co., Certified Public Accountants, to examine the 1991 (from January 1 to December 31, 1991) financial statements of the Corporation as transmitted to us for examination by the Board of Directors. Messrs. T. N. Soong & Co. have completed the examination and submitted their report, dated January 17, 1992, which states that the financial statements of the Corporation present fairly the financial position of the Corporation at December 31, 1991 and the results of its operations and cash flow for the period then ended. We have examined the report submitted by Messrs. T. N. Soong & Co. and found it to be correct.

Supervisors:

George Y. L. Wu (Sealed)
K. H. King (Sealed)
C. W. Wang (Sealed)
C. T. Li (Sealed)

March 10. 1992

台灣聚合化學品股份有限公司 USI FAR EAST CORPORATION

財務報表附註 NOTES TO FINANCIAL STATEMENTS

民國八十年及七十九年十二月三十一日
（除另予註明外，金額均以新台幣元爲單位）

(Expressed in New Taiwan Dollars, Unless Stated Otherwise)

一、組織及營業

本公司爲股票公開上市之公司，主要從事於聚乙烯塑膠粒之生產及銷售。

1. GENERAL

The Corporation is engaged mainly in the manufacture and sale polyethylene. Its capital shares are listed in the Taiwan Stock Exchang

二、會計政策摘要

2. SIGNIFICANT ACCOUNTING POLICIES

現金

本公司財務報表所稱之現金，係包括用途未受限制及未提供作質押、擔保之庫存現金、銀行及金融機構存款、信託資金存款及銀行定期存款。

Cash

Cash includes cash, cash in banks, deposits in financial institutions, tru funds and time deposits which have not been encumbered, or pledge

短期投資

短期投資於上市公司股票及證券投資信託基金之受益憑證，係按成本與市價總金額孰低計價；市價低於成本時，則提列備抵短期投資跌價損失；已提列之備抵短期投資跌價損失，若因短期投資之市價已告回升，則於提列金額內予以冲回。出售時其成本係按移動平均法計算。

Short-term investments

Short-term investments in stocks of listed companies and beneficial ce tificates of security investment trust funds are carried at the lower aggregate cost or market value. When the total carrying value excee the market value, allowance for losses is provided for the excess; wh the market value recovers, such allowance is reversed to the extent the loss provision. Cost of stocks and beneficial certificates sold is d termined by the moving average method.

備抵呆帳

備抵呆帳係按應收票據及帳款之收現可能性估列。

Allowance for doubtful receivables

Provision is provided based on the collectibility of notes and accoun receivable.

存貨

存貨係按加權平均成本與市價孰低計價。

Inventories

Inventories are stated at the lower of weighted average cost or mark value.

長期投資

長期股權投資按權益法計價者（擁有被投資公司20%以上普通股股票），以投資成本加（或減）按股權比例認列被投資公司之純益（或純損）計算。被投資公司發生純益或純損時，認列投資收益或損失；如有新增之資本公積應按比例貸記資本公積；發放現金股利時則作爲投資減項。

其他長期投資按成本法計價。當該項投資之價值確已減損，且回復之希望甚小時，則減少其帳面價值，認列投資損失。

在持有被投資公司普通股股權不超過百分之五十情況下，若未能及時取得被投資公司同年度之報表者，則於次一年度取得時，按上年度約當持股比例認列投資損益。

Long-term investments

Long-term investments in stocks representing 20% or more of each i vestee's common stocks are accounted for by the equity method. Su investments are stated at cost plus (or less) proportionate share of n earnings (or net losses). Share in net earnings or losses of investees recognized as investment income or loss; share in increase or decrea of the investee capital surplus is credited or debited to capital surplu cash dividends received are deducted from the investments.

Other long-term investments in stocks are carried at cost. When a d cline in value of an investment is considered not recoverable, the ca rying value of such investment is reduced with the resulting lo charged to current income.

Gain or loss on investments in investees of which USIFE's ownership below 50% and whose financial statements for the current years are n available is recognized in the following year when such financial stat ments are obtained.

固定資產

固定資產係按成本（或成本加重估增值）減累積折舊計價。重大改良及更新作爲資本支出；零星更換及維護修理支出則作爲當年度費用。

折舊係依照下列估計耐用年數，按直線法計算提列：土地改良，八至三十年；廠房建築及設備，三至五十五年；機器及設備，三至八年；交通及運輸設備，三至五年；生財器具，三至十年。

固定資產出售或報廢時，其相關成本、重估增值及累積折舊均自帳上予以減除，而所發生之盈益或損失，則以當年度收益或損失處理，並於當年底將處分收益於減除應負擔之所得稅後，自未分配盈餘轉列資本公積。

Property, plant and equipment

Property, plant and equipment are stated at cost (or cost plus apprec tion on certain assets) less accumulated depreciation. Major replac ments and improvements are capitalized, while minor renewals or r placements and maintenance and repairs are expensed currently.

Depreciation is determined by the straight-line method over estimate service lives which range as follows: land improvements, 8 to 30 yea buildings, 3 to 55 years; machinery and equipment, 3 to 8 years; tran portation equipment, 3 to 5 years; furniture and fixtures, 3 to 10 years.

Upon sale or disposal of properties, the related cost, appreciation a accumulated depreciation are removed from the accounts and any ga or loss is credited or charged to income. The gain, less applicable i come tax, is later transferred to capital surplus in the same years.

員工退休利益

每月提撥之退休準備金及香港分公司每月提列之退休利益均列入當年度費用，詳見附註十五。

Retirement benefits

Reference is made to Note 15. Monthly contributions to the retireme fund and provisions for retirement benefits of employees at the Ho Kong Branch are charged to expense when paid or accrued.

所得稅

所得稅係按當年度帳面稅前利益計算；其與依照所得稅法計算所得稅負間之差異，因若干損益項目列帳及認列時間之不同而發生者，列爲遞延所得稅。

以前年度所得稅之調整，包含於當年度之所得稅。

投資抵減於抵減時，列爲所得稅之減項。

以外幣為準之交易事項

以外幣爲準之交易事項係按交易發生時匯率折算之新台幣金額入帳。外幣資產及負債實際收付結清時，因適用不同匯率所產生之損失或盈益，列爲結清年度之損益。除外幣長期股權投資外之外幣資產及負債之年底餘額，再按年底之匯率予以換算調整，因而產生之兌換差額列爲當期損益；外幣長期股權投資按年底之匯率予以換算調整，因而產生之兌換差額處理如下：

1. 按權益法計價者——該項差額作爲累積換算調整數，並列於股東權益項下。
2. 按成本法計價者——若換算後之金額低於原始成本及回轉仍未超過原始成本時，則比照前述之權益法處理；若高於原始成本，則不予調整。

本公司香港分公司之財務報表，依下列方式換算爲新台幣金額：資產及負債科目——均按資產負債表日之匯率換算；期初未分配盈餘——以期初換算餘額結轉；損益科目——按加權平均匯率換算，外幣財務報表換算所產生之兌換差額列示於累積換算調整數項下。

科目重分類

七十九年度財務報表若干科目已予重分類，以配合八十年度財務報表之表達方式。

Income tax

Income tax is based on pre-tax financial statement income, which is different from the amount of tax currently payable because certain income and expenses are recognized in different periods for financial statement purposes and for tax reporting purposes; the difference is recorded as deferred income tax.

Adjustments of tax liabilities of prior years are added to, or deducted from, the current year's tax provision.

Investment tax credits are recognized in the year when they reduce income tax payable.

Foreign-currency transactions

Foreign-currency transactions are recorded in New Taiwan dollars at the rates of exchange in effect when the transactions occured. Gains or losses, caused by different foreign exchange rates applied when foreign-currency assets and liabilities are settled, are credited or charged to income in the year of actual settlement. At year-end, the balances of foreign-currency assets except long-term investments in stock, and liabilities are restated based on year-end exchange rates, and resulting differences are credited or charged to current income. Exchange differences resulting from restatement of the following foreign-currency long-term investments at year-end based on year-end exchange rate are recorded as follows:

a) Accounted for by the equity method—as a separate component of stocksholders' equity, namely, cumulative translation adjustment.

b) Accounted for by the cost method—same as a) above for the difference representing write-down of the investment from original cost and for any recoveries in subsequent years up to original cost. No adjustment is made for any difference representing write-up of the investment above original cost.

The accounts of the Hong Kong Branch are translated into New Taiwan dollars as follows: assets and liabilities—at year-end exchange rate; beginning balance of retained earnings—carried forward from prior period; income and expenses—at weighted average exchange rate. Resulting translation difference is classified as part of Cumulative Translation Adjustments.

Reclassifications

Certain reclassifications have been made to the 1990 financial statements to conform to classifications adopted in 1991.

三、質抵押資產

下列資產業已質抵押作爲應付帳款及部分長、短期借款之擔保品：

3. MORTGAGED OR PLEDGED ASSETS AND SECURED LIABILITIES

The following assets are pledged or mortgaged as collateral for accounts payable, long-term and short-term debts:

		八十年底 1991	七十九年底 1990
信託資金及銀行定期存款（附註八）	Trust funds and time deposits (Note 8)	$ 570,200,000	$ 570,200,000
固定資產	Fixed assets	873,737,105	1,090,651,762
		$ 1,443,937,105	$ 1,660,851,762

四、現金

4. CASH

		八十年底 1991	七十九年底 1990
現金	Cash	$ 34,405,846	$ 23,655,516
信託資金存款	Trust funds	1,870,000,000	1,710,000,000
銀行定期存款	Time deposit	270,000,000	379,744,381
		$ 2,174,405,846	$ 2,113,399,897

五、短期投資

5. SHORT—TERM INVESTMENTS

		八十年底 1991	七十九年底 1990
上市公司股票——美國量子化學公司	Listed Stocks—Quantum Chemical Co.	$ 15,325,495	$ —
減：備抵短期投資跌價損失	Less: Allowance for decline in value	(1,840,189)	—
		13,485,306	—
受益憑證	Beneficial certificates of security investment trust funds	25,000,000	—
		$ 38,485,306	—

台灣聚合化學品股份有限公司及其子公司 USI FAR EAST CORPORATION AND SUBSIDIARIES

合併資產負債表 CONSOLIDATED BALANCE SHEETS

民國八十年及七十九年十二月三十一日 December 31, 1991 and 1990

（單位：新台幣元） (Expressed in New Taiwan Dollars)

資產	ASSETS	八十年底 1991 金額 Amount	%	七十九年底 1990 金額 Amount	%
流動資產	**CURRENT ASSETS**				
現金(附註二及四)	Cash(Notes 2 and 4)	$ 2,204,423,328	30	$ 2,260,938,469	29
短期投資(附註二及五)	Short-term investments (Notes 2 and 5)	38,485,306	1	—	—
應收票據及帳款—淨額（附註二及六）	Notes and accounts receivable—net (Notes 2 and 6)	167,803,922	2	280,993,642	4
應收利息	Interest receivable	114,058,549	2	81,550,636	1
應收關係公司款項(附註十八)	Receivable from affiliates (Note 18)	—	—	61,994,244	1
存貨(附註二及七)	Inventories(Notes 2 and 7)	291,736,061	4	239,804,288	3
預付所得稅	Prepaid income tax	—	—	26,357,990	—
其他流動資產(附註三及八)	Other current assets(Notes 3 and 8)	599,394,330	8	1,098,182,733	14
流動資產合計	Total Current Assets	3,415,901,496	47	4,049,822,002	52
長期投資（附註二及九）	**LONG-TERM INVESTMENTS** (Notes 2 and 9)	1,568,212,281	22	1,218,423,086	16
固定資產（附註二、三及十）	**PROPERTY, PLANT AND EQUIPMENT** (Notes 2, 3 and 10)				
成本	Cost				
土地	Land	75,682,007	1	75,682,007	1
土地改良	Land improvements	50,475,723	1	51,815,913	1
廠房建築及設備	Buildings	318,920,455	4	318,954,235	4
機器及設備	Machinery and equipment	2,278,045,613	32	2,244,639,206	29
交通及運輸設備	Transportation equipment	38,664,194	—	37,443,659	—
生財器具	Furniture and fixtures	38,671,956	1	37,925,349	1
修護零件	Spare parts	112,982,316	2	106,938,438	1
在建工程	Construction in progress	14,919,849	—	24,494,911	—
		2,928,362,113	41	2,897,893,718	37
重估增值	Appreciation	534,328,547	7	535,367,905	7
		3,462,690,660	48	3,433,261,623	44
減：累積折舊	Less:accumulated depreciation	1,662,577,025	23	1,485,636,029	19
固定資產淨額	Net Property,Plant and Equipment	1,800,113,635	25	1,947,625,594	25
遞延費用—淨額(附註十一)	**DEFERRED CHARGES-NET**(Note 11)	222,120,873	3	271,400,397	3
其他資產(附註十二)	**OTHER ASSETS** (Note 12)	212,476,130	3	347,098,136	4
資產總計	**TOTAL ASSETS**	$ 7,218,824,415	100	$ 7,834,369,215	100
負債及股東權益	**LIABILITIES AND STOCKHOLDERS' EQUITY**				
流動負債	**CURRENT LIABILITIES**				
短期借款(附註三及十三)	Short-term debts (Notes 3 and 13)	$ 78,132,793	1	$ 280,135,270	3
應付帳款(附註三)	Accounts payable (Note 3)	156,627,424	2	297,764,946	4
預收貨款	Customers' prepayments	46,076,017	1	88,275,427	1
應付費用	Accrued expenses	49,527,924	1	59,870,707	1
應付所得稅(附註十六)	Income tax payable (Note 16)	31,049,317	—	—	—
一年內到期之長期借款（附註三及十四）	Long-term debts due within one year (Notes 3 and 14)	227,100,000	3	227,100,000	3
存入保證金	Guarantee deposits	5,814,783	—	6,714,038	—
其他流動負債	Other current liabilities	12,136,130	—	10,695,037	—
流動負債合計	Total Current Liabilities	606,464,388	8	970,555,425	12
長期負債	**LONG-TERM LIABILITIES**				
長期借款(附註三及十四)	Long-term debts (Notes 3 and 14)	454,200,000	6	991,300,000	13
土地增值稅準備(附註十)	Reserve for land value increment tax (Note 10)	106,050,179	—	106,050,179	1
長期負債合計	Total Long-Term Liabilities	560,250,179	6	1,097,350,179	14
其他負債(附註十五)	**OTHER LIABILITIES** (Note 15)	7,499,379	2	3,989,910	—
負債合計	Total Liabilities	1,174,213,940	10	2,071,895,514	20
股東權益	**STOCKHOLDERS' EQUITY**				
股本—每股面額10元；八十年額定及發行387,397,071股；七十九年額定及發行358,700,992股	Capital stock, $10 par value, authorized and issued-387,397,071 shares in 1991 and 358,700,992 shares in 1990	3,873,970,710	54	3,587,009,920	46
資本公積	Capital surplus				
股票發行溢價	In excess of par value	673,039,210	9	960,000,000	12
固定資產重估增值	Revaluation increment on fixed assets	179,445,897	2	179,445,897	3
因長期投資按權益法計價產生	Long-term investments accounted for by the equity method	61,866,915	1	71,908,208	1
處分固定資產淨益及受贈資本	Net gain on disposal of properties and other	17,858,464	—	17,087,173	—
資本公積合計	Total Capital surplus	932,210,486	12	1,228,441,278	16
保留盈餘	Retained earnings				
法定公積	Legal reserve	755,031,661	11	738,710,550	9
未分配盈餘	Unappropriated earnings	489,227,841	7	208,832,023	3
保留盈餘合計	Total Retained earnings	1,244,259,502	18	947,542,573	12
累積換算調整數	Cumulative translation adjustments	(5,830,229)	—	(520,070)	—
股東權益合計	**Total Stockholders' Equity**	6,044,610,469	84	5,762,473,701	74
負債及股東權益總計	**TOTAL LIABILITIES AND STOCKHOLDERS' EQUITY**	$ 7,218,824,415	100	$ 7,834,369,215	100

台灣聚合化學品股份有限公司及其子公司 USI FAR EAST CORPORATION AND SUBSIDIARIES

合併損益表 CONSOLIDATED STATEMENTS OF INCOME

民國八十年及七十九年一月一日至十二月三十一日 For the Years Ended December 31, 1991 and 1990

（單位：新台幣元） (Expressed in New Taiwan Dollars)

		八十年度 1991		七十九年度 1990	
		金額 Amount	%	金額 Amount	%
銷貨收入總額	GROSS SALES	$ 4,071,178,315	101	$ 4,425,540,603	101
減：銷貨退回及折讓	LESS: SALES RETURNS AND ALLOWANCES	46,512,392	1	43,037,297	1
銷貨收入淨額	NET SALES	4,024,665,923	100	4,382,503,306	100
銷貨成本	COST OF GOODS SOLD	3,083,323,404	77	3,653,940,157	83
銷貨毛利	GROSS PROFIT	941,342,519	23	728,563,149	17
營業費用	OPERATING EXPENSES				
行銷、實驗及運輸	Marketing, laboratory and shipping	263,431,652	6	285,271,257	7
總務、管理及其他	General, administrative and other	237,133,634	6	245,458,499	5
營業費用合計	Total Operating Expenses	500,565,286	12	530,729,756	12
營業利益	INCOME FROM OPERATIONS	440,777,233	11	197,833,393	5
營業外收入	NON-OPERATING INCOME				
利息收入	Interest income	275,218,753	7	341,887,935	8
兌換盈益	Foreign exchange gain	24,542,673	1	30,515,710	1
租金收入	Rental	9,065,789	—	9,498,974	—
按權益法認列之投資利益（附註二及九）	Gain on investments recognized under the equity method (Note 2 and 9)	4,227,028	—	3,532,427	—
其　他	Others	2,688,649	—	15,911,787	—
營業外收入合計	Total Non-Operating Income	315,742,892	8	401,346,833	9
營業外支出	NON-OPERATING EXPENSES				
利息支出	Interest expense	55,110,398	1	140,845,275	3
兌換損失（附註十二）	Foreign exchange loss (Note 12)	30,633,106	1	66,943,336	2
呂宋公司投資損失（附註十二）	Investment loss on other assets (Note 12)	29,940,978	1	135,000,000	3
閒置資產費用（附註十二）	Idle plant expenses (Note 12)	24,447,823	1	29,116,757	1
按權益法認列之投資損失（附註二及九）	Loss on investments recognized under the equity method (Notes 2 and 9)	12,292,202	—	21,597,396	—
長期債券投資損失（附註九）	Loss on investment of long-term bonds (Note 9)	10,236,815	—	—	—
其　他	Others	14,007,140	—	11,348,602	—
營業外支出合計	Total Non-Operating Expenses	176,668,462	4	404,851,366	9
稅前利益	INCOME BEFORE INCOME TAX	579,851,663	15	194,328,860	5
所得稅（附註二及十六）	INCOME TAX (Notes 2 and 16)	112,000,000	3	31,000,000	1
純　益	NET INCOME	$ 467,851,663	12	$ 163,328,860	4
每股純益	NET INCOME PER SHARE				
按各年發行之加權平均股數八十年387,397,071股及七十九年347,588,663股計算	Based on weighted average number of outstanding shares of 387,397,071 in 1991 and 347,588,663 in 1990	$ 1.21		$ 0.47	
按375,157,071股計算	Based on 375,157,071 shares			$ 0.44	

台灣聚合化學品股份有限公司及其子公司
USI FAR EAST CORPORATION AND SUBSIDIARIES

合併現金流量表
CONSOLIDATED STATEMENTS OF CHANGES IN FINANCIAL POSITION

民國八十年及七十九年一月一日至十二月三十一日
For the Years Ended December 31, 1991 and 1990

（單位：新台幣元）
(Expressed in New Taiwan Dollars)

		八十年度1991	七十九年度1990
營運活動之現金流量	**CASH FLOWS FROM OPERATING ACTIVITIES**		
純　益	Net income	$ 467,851,663	$ 163,328,860
調整項目	Adjustments to reconcile net income to net cash provided by operating activities:		
折　舊	Depreciation	206,415,468	215,599,126
攤　銷	Amortization	49,279,524	51,398,732
按權益法認列之長期投資損失—淨額	Loss on long-term investments recognized under the equity method—net	8,064,931	18,064,969
呂宋公司投資損失	Investment loss on other assets	29,940,978	135,000,000
投資長期債券及呂宋公司之兌換損失(盈益)	Foreign exchange loss (gain) on investment in long-term bonds and other assets	(3,691,682)	57,700,000
處分固定資產損失(利益)	Loss (gain) on disposal of properties	(767,855)	914,581
長期債券投資損失	Loss on disposal of investment in long-term bonds	10,236,815	—
短期投資跌價損失	Provision for loss on short-term investment	1,840,189	—
遞延所得稅減少	Decrease in deferred income tax	17,000,000	—
應收票據及帳款減少	Decrease in notes and accounts receivable	113,189,720	47,617,742
應收利息減少(增加)	Decrease (increase) in interest receivable	(32,507,913)	(9,123,055)
存貨減少(增加)	Decrease (increase) in inventories	(51,931,773)	(66,739,893)
預付所得稅減少(增加)	Decrease (increase) in prepaid income tax	26,357,990	(17,151,264)
其他流動資產減少(增加)	Decrease (increase) in other current assets	498,788,403	(495,454,779)
應付帳款增加(減少)	Increase (decrease) in account payable	(141,137,522)	53,621,153
預收貨款增加(減少)	Increase (decrease) in customers prepayments	(42,199,410)	26,486,012
應付費用增加(減少)	Increase (decrease) in accrued expenses	(10,342,783)	2,772,331
應付所得稅增加	Increase in income tax payable	31,049,317	—
存入保證金增加(減少)	Increase (decrease) in guarantee deposits	(899,255)	(5,619,420)
其他流動負債增加(減少)	Increase (decrease) in other current liabilities	1,441,093	(2,733,295)
營業活動之淨現金流入	Net Cash Provided by Operating Activities	1,177,977,898	175,681,800
投資活動之現金流量	**CASH FLOWS FROM INVESTING ACTIVITIES**		
增加短期投資	Increase in short-term investments	(40,325,495)	—
減少應收關係公司款項	Decrease in receivable from affiliates	61,994,244	28,688,729
增加長期投資	Increase in long-term investments	(458,263,151)	(677,259,667)
處分長期債券投資價款	Proceeds from disposal of investments long-tern bond	89,064,068	—
購置固定資產	Additions to properties	(34,748,970)	(54,722,629)
處分固定資產價款	Proceeds from disposal of properties	1,803,912	618,378
收回投資呂宋公司款項	Proceeds from recovery of other assets	62,735,838	—
增加其他投資—呂宋公司	Increase from recovery of other assets	—	(190,834,980)
減少(增加)其他資產	Decrease (increase) in other assets	875,283	(15,244,314)
投資活動之淨現金流出	Net Cash Used in Investing Activities	(316,864,271)	(908,754,483)
理財活動之現金流量：	**CASH FLOWS FROM FINANCING ACTIVITIES**		
發行商業本票	Issuance of commercial papers	—	129,927,763
增加(減少)短期借款	Increase (decrease) in short-term debts	(202,002,477)	25,639,998
償還一年內到期之長期借款	Repayment of long-term debts due within one year	(227,100,000)	(227,100,000)
償還長期借款	Decrease in long-term debts	(310,000,000)	—
增加其他負債	Increase in other liabilities	3,509,469	459,023
現金增資	Capital increase	—	1,200,000,000
發放現金股利、董監事酬勞及員工紅利	Cash dividends and bonuses to directors, supervisors and employees	(180,404,736)	(233,972,359)
理財活動之淨現金流入(流出)	Net Cash Provided by (Used in) Financing Activities	(915,997,744)	894,954,425
匯率影響數	**CUMULATIVE TRANSLATION ADJUSTMENTS**	(1,631,024)	2,020,902
本年現金增加(減少)數	**NET INCREASE (DECREASE) IN CASH**	(56,515,141)	163,908,644
年初現金餘額	**CASH AT BEGINNING OF YEAR**	2,260,938,469	2,097,029,825
年底現金餘額	**CASH AT END OF YEAR**	$ 2,204,423,328	$ 2,260,938,469
現金流量資訊之補充揭露：	**SUPPLEMENTAL DISCLOSURES OF CASH FLOWS INFORMATION**		
本期支付利息	Cash paid during the year for: interest	$ 66,063,847	$ 172,628,366
本期支付所得稅	Income tax	$ 54,592,674	$ 63,151,265
不影響現金流量之投資及理財活動：	**SUPPLEMENTAL DISCLOSURES OF NON-CASH INVESTING AND FINANCING ACTIVITIES**		
一年內到期之長期借款轉列流動負債	Long-term debts due within one year	$ 227,100,000	$ 227,100,000

5 Hong Kong

P. Phenix

BACKGROUND

Hong Kong is a group of 236 islands and a peninsula at the mouth of the Pearl River of Guangdong (Canton) Province of southern China. The estimated population is 5.8 million, living in 416 square miles (1,024 square kilometres) which is approximately half the size of Rhode Island in the USA or the size of Greater London in the UK. The main Hong Kong island where the central business district, most government offices and 22 per cent of the people live, is only 30 square miles (78 square kilometres) – a little larger than Manhattan.

Hong Kong is a British Dependent Territory with an administration appointed from London headed by a governor who is the representative of the Queen. He is advised by an appointed executive council which operates as a cabinet and by a partly elected legislative council which serves the function of a parliament. At a municipal level below these two bodies are the urban council, managing the built-up areas, and the regional council, for the rural and island areas. These councils are composed of a mixture of government appointees, elected persons and representatives of various organizations. In the lowest tier of government are nineteen directly elected district boards. Although most of the various legislators are appointed or are indirectly elected as representatives of various interest groups, the three levels of representation and consultation mean that Hong Kong is remarkably democratic. In many ways it is the most democratic, and certainly the most liberal, territory in Asia.

Political liberalism is mirrored in the economic liberal tradition which dictates that government involvement in economic and financial affairs is actively minimized – even the territory's bank notes are issued privately by the two leading banks. By consensus, government restricts itself to public order, fire services, immigration (because of the limited territory available) and the provision of a safety-net level of health, education and welfare services. However, there is a streak of paternalism in this policy as reflected in the provision of low-cost public housing (which houses approximately 47 per cent of the population), the minimal-cost public health system (87 per cent of all hospital beds), the extensive public recreational facilities, and in the strictly protected country park system which occupies 60 per cent of Hong Kong's crowded land area.

Hong Kong began its progress to a major global financial centre when Hong Kong island was ceded permanently by China to Britain under the 1842 Treaty of Nanking following the First Opium War. As a result of subsequent Anglo-Chinese conflicts the tip of the Kowloon peninsula was acquired on a permanent basis under the Convention of Peking in 1860. Finally, in 1898 the New Territories, including 235 other islands (91 per cent of the total area), were leased to the British on a 99-year lease which will expire on 30 June 1997.

In accordance with 'The Joint Declaration of the British and Chinese Governments on the Question of Hong Kong' of May 1985, the whole of Hong Kong, including the permanently ceded areas, will become a Special Administrative Region (SAR) of the People's Republic of China (PRC) from 1 July 1997. The Joint Declaration also guarantees that Hong Kong's 'lifestyle' (i.e. liberal capitalism) will continue for fifty years. The government and most other organizations, including the professional bodies, are working to ensure that this promised continuity can take place in the areas under their supervision.

THE BUSINESS ENVIRONMENT

Hong Kong's *laissez-faire* business environment and the entrepreneurial spirit of its people are well known and often cited as models for the development of other countries.

Private sector

The Territory has approximately 500,000 registered businesses of which about 220,000 are incorporated under the Companies Ordinance. In 1980 there was a mere 81,000 or so such companies. In addition, there are about 2,000 foreign incorporated companies registered under the Companies Ordinance. There are virtually no barriers to business entry except an annual Business Registration Fee (currently US$125 per annum) and nominal licensing for food and similar industries under public health regulations. There are also qualification and experience requirements for most of the professions.

There are 417 companies listed on the Stock Exchange of Hong Kong as at December 1992 of which about 200 are incorporated in Hong Kong. Ownership of listed companies is dominated by about 15 families (see Table 5.1) and most companies (listed or otherwise) are closely held by families. In recognition of this situation, the Stock Exchange requires that only 25 per cent or more of the issued share capital of listed companies should be held by unconnected persons and the general public.

Historically, business in Hong Kong has concentrated on trading (capitalizing on its geographic location) and labour intensive manufacturing (capitalizing on its abundant supply of cheap labour). However in the 1970s this began to change gradually and in the 1980s, since the opening-up of China, there has been a dramatic restructuring of Hong Kong business. The Territory's supply of cheap immigrant labour from China dried up as previously liberal immigration policies were tightened in the early 1970s to limit the Territory's population growth. In the early 1980s

Table 5.1 Family groupings in listed companies

Family		*Company*
Group 1	Li Ka Shing	Cavendish International; Cheung Kong; Hong Kong Electric; Hutchison Whampoa
Group 2	Keswick	Dairy Farm; Hong Kong Land; Jardine Matheson; Jardine Strategic; Mandarin Oriental; Zung Fu
Group 3	Swire	Cathay Pacific*; Haeco; Swire Pacific 'A'
Group 4	Li Shau Kee	Henderson Investment; Henderson Land; Hong Kong Ferry; Hong Kong & China Gas
Group 5	Y.K. Pao	Allied Investors; Harbour Center; Harriman; Hong Kong Realty 'A'; Lane Crawford 'A'; Realty Development 'A'; Wharf; World International
Group 6	Kadoorie	China Light*; Hong Kong Carpet; Hong Kong Hotel
Group 7	Kwok Tak Shing	Kowloon Motor Bus Ltd; Sun Hung Kai Properties
Group 8	Cheng Yu Tung	New World Development; New World Hotel
Group 9	Chen Tseng Tao	Amoy Properties; Hang Lung
Group 10	Lo Yuk Shui	Cathay City; Century City; Paliburg; Regal Hotel
Group 11	Lau Luen Hung, Joseph	China Entertainment; Chinese Estate; Evergo
Group 12	Ng Teng Fong	Sino Land; Sino Realty
Group 13	R.R. Shaw	Shaw Brothers; Television Broadcasts; TVB Holdings
Group 14	Karl C.L. Kwok	Wing On Co; Wing On (Holdings)
Group 15	Te Kan Chiu Deacon	Far East Consolidated; Far East Holdings; Far East Hotel

Note: *Significant PRC interests in the company.

the locally born population exceeded immigrants for the first time and currently stands at about 60 per cent of the total. Even with these restrictions about 100 illegal immigrants from China are apprehended each day and the conventional wisdom is that less than half the illegal immigrants are caught. Trade is still at the heart of Hong Kong's prosperity (about 23 per cent of GDP in 1988) but services (about 17 per cent of GDP), particularly in the financial sector, are displacing manufacturing (about 21 per cent of GDP) in importance.

This change in population pattern and the increasing affluence of the population has raised wage rates and led to a move to higher quality, up-market products and more capital intensive operations. The three most important manufactured products continue to be textiles, electronics and toys. However, since the open-door policy was instituted in the PRC in 1979/80 and with the development of Special Economic Zones (SEZ), the actual manufacturing operations have shifted to China, especially to the Shenzen SEZ which abuts Hong Kong. Hong Kong remains the centre of designing, international marketing and general management for the PRC-based operations.

The implications of these developments for accounting and financial reporting are that a significant proportion of manufacturing companies' profits come from direct investment or joint ventures in China. Hong Kong standards of accounting, reporting and auditing are applied as much as possible even if, in accordance with a particular joint venture agreement, a PRC Certified Public Accountant is engaged as the organization's accountant or auditor.

At the same time, the importance of Hong Kong as a base for China operations – if only as a form of rest and recreation centre – has greatly increased. This trend hesitated briefly following the June 1989 crackdown, but has accelerated anew notwithstanding the central government's attempts to rein in the economy.

The importance of China in the Hong Kong economy is highlighted by the relative size of the Territory's domestic exports (40 per cent of total exports) and of re-exports (60 per cent). Most of the re-exports consist of two-way trade between China and its trading partners (the USA, Japan, Taiwan, Singapore and the EEC) which passes through Hong Kong's port. Largely because of this trade, the Hong Kong port is the largest or one of two or three largest in the world, depending on which measurement criterion is used. In contrast, the trade and other services provided by the Territory generates about 40 per cent of China's foreign exchange.

Government participation

Government participation in the economy has always been minimal and its involvement in commerce is being eliminated as a matter of policy. The utilities, except water supply, the MTR (subway) and the railway, have always been private. The government has gradually sold its minority holdings in the telecommunication monopoly which was a subsidiary of the UK's Cable & Wireless Plc. and is committed to the privatization of its other commercial operations. The only other government commercial equity holdings have been the result of rescue operations of failed banks following the 1983–4 property crash but these have also been almost entirely re-privatized. On a macro level, government expenditure runs at about 12 per cent of GDP and government employees represent about 7 per cent of the total work-force. These proportions will reduce as the planned privatization of government services such as the Official Receiver (liquidations and bankruptcy), airport and water are implemented.

As noted earlier, the Territory's bank notes are issued by two private sector 'note issuing' banks: the Hongkong and Shanghai Banking Corporation (HSBC) and the Standard Chartered Bank Plc. In addition, until May 1988, the HSBC was effectively the Central Bank including the provision of a lender of last resort service. Exchange rate control, the management of money supply and the liquidity of the financial system became the sole responsibility of the Hong Kong Monetary Authority from April 1993.

Financial sector

The Territory is a major world financial centre and the thirteenth largest international trader. It is possible to produce an extensive litany of evidence of its importance such as: over three-quarters of the 100 largest banks operate in Hong Kong; it has the world's second largest gold market; the foreign exchange market has a turnover of over US$50 billion per day; and it is the world's third largest centre for fund management (all based on 1990 figures).

The key to this success has been its political liberalism and the openness of its economy. It is these two features which most strongly differentiate Hong Kong from all its neighbours in the Western Pacific. Again a recitation of indicative evidence supports this view: there is no exchange control; no restrictions on foreign ownership of companies or assets; of the 165 authorized banks in Hong Kong only 31 are locally incorporated; in addition there are about 60 representative offices of foreign banks; in the securities markets, of the 230 corporate registered dealers 60 per cent are foreign, whilst about 30 per cent of registered commodities dealers are from overseas.

The international aspects of the financial markets are also reflected in the asset structure of the authorized banks of which 80 per cent is held in foreign currency. In the same area, the size of loans for use outside Hong Kong and to finance trade (US$70 billion) exceeds the amount of loans for use within the Territory. Apart from bank loans and the Stock Exchange, the other main sources of finance are Certificates of Deposits and a growing market in commercial paper, both of which have heavy involvement by Japanese and American companies and to a lesser extent, European companies. There is also considerable interest in the newer financial products such as interest rate swaps.

Taxation

Taxation in Hong Kong is remarkably traditional and hence relatively simple and with very few exceptions relatively low.

There are two forms of direct taxation:

- a salaries tax based on employment income arising in Hong Kong on a sliding scale up to a top marginal rate of 25 per cent or at a standard (maximum effective) rate of 15 per cent;
- a profits tax at 17.5 per cent for incorporated and 15 per cent for unincorporated businesses on net profits arising in Hong Kong.

The rates cited are all those current at 31 July 1993.

There is no concept of residency or world income and hence both taxes are on a source (territorial) basis. They are collected on a partly lagged year-of-assessment basis with one-quarter paid in advance. There is a set of normal depreciation allowances and the usual other allowable business expenses. Dividends and interest income are not taxed. There is no capital gains tax and profits on trading in real estate and securities by individuals and by businesses not engaged in 'trading' are not taxable.

There is an Estate Duty on a sliding scale of 6–18 per cent with a threshold of estates valued at approximately US$310,000. A Stamp Duty (transaction tax) is payable on transfer of listed or unlisted shares (0.3 per cent) and real property. The other main sources of government revenue are horse-race betting duty, entertainment tax and duties on petroleum products, alcohol, tobacco and cosmetics. All other products are duty free.

There are no particular tax rules which have financial reporting requirements although, even with the low tax rates, financial statements, particularly those of private companies, are drawn up with tax considerations in mind. For example, the method of disclosure of profits on real estate and share transactions is sensitive to their being regarded as taxable trading profits rather than non-taxable capital gains.

THE ACCOUNTING REGULATORY FRAMEWORK

The regulatory framework for financial reporting in Hong Kong has the three-tiered structure familiar to most British Commonwealth jurisdictions:

- Companies legislation – mainly in the Companies Ordinance, but also the Banking, Insurance and Securities Ordinances if relevant to the reporting entity.
- Accounting standards – issued by the Hong Kong Society of

Accountants (HKSA): Statements of Standard Accounting Practice (HK SSAP); and Accounting Guidelines.

- Regulators' requirements – The Stock Exchange of Hong Kong Ltd (SEHK); the Banking Commission; and the Insurance Commission.

Companies legislation

The core companies legislation is the Companies Ordinance which dates from 1965 and which, although subject to frequent piecemeal revisions, is still essentially the UK 1948 Companies Act as far as reporting in the financial statements is concerned. More alarmingly, it is still essentially the UK 1929 Companies Act as far as accounting requirements and regulation of companies is concerned. In all respects it lags sadly behind the equivalent Companies Acts of other equivalent British Commonwealth countries in the Pacific basin. The term 'Ordinance' rather than 'Act' is used for legislation in Hong Kong as it does not have an independent legislature – at least in form or theory – although the Legislative Council is independent in substance.

In fairness, it should be said that the Ordinance appears to be what the business community wants, although there are occasional complaints from regulators and the larger audit firms about the continued existence of what are in effect exempt private companies, nominee shareholders and nominee directors. However, the Ordinance, and company law in general, is subject to constant review by a Standing Committee on Company Law Reform which is very receptive to suggestions for reforms from any quarter. The fact that reform is slow even with this active consultative process probably reflects the desires of the business community at large.

Types of companies

As would be expected, company law follows the British conventions and recognizes the following types of companies:

- Statutory corporations incorporated under a specific statute.
- Companies incorporated under the Companies Ordinance:
  1 limited by guarantee;
  2 limited by shares:
    (a) private;
    (b) public;
  3 unlimited.

Almost all companies are incorporated under the Companies Ordinance and are limited by shares. Because of the reporting and supervisory advantages of private companies, most companies retain that status unless compelled to re-incorporate as public by legislation (e.g. the Banking Ordinance) or prior to seeking a listing on the SEHK. By definition, private companies limit their membership to fifty, restrict the transfer of their shares and prohibit any invitation to the public to subscribe to shares or debentures. All other companies are, by corollary, public. Public companies may be listed by the SEHK under its Listing Rules and the statutory Listing Rules issued under the Securities Ordinance. The Companies Ordinance does not address itself to whether or not a company is listed, restricting itself in this area to regulations regarding the requirements for and contents of prospectuses for public offers of shares or debentures (bonds).

As regards financial reporting, the key factor is that private companies are all effectively exempt private companies as they used to be called in the UK and are still called in Australia, Singapore and Malaysia. As private companies they are exempt in terms of not being required to file financial statements with the relevant authority, the Companies Registry. The contents of the Annual Return made to the Companies Registry is restricted to details of changes in share capital, details of charges (mortgages) and the names and addresses of shareholders, directors and the company secretary. However, even this minimal information can be made meaningless as private companies are permitted to employ corporate and nominee directors. Shareholdings may also be held by nominees. The companies or nominee organizations employed as directors or shareholders are often registered in Liberia, Panama or other jurisdictions of 'incorporation of convenience' – ostensibly for taxation reasons. This situation makes disclosure of related party transactions in and by any Hong Kong company problem-prone and their audit extremely difficult. For obvious reasons, auditors have tried to tie a proposed prohibition on this feature of local companies to an application to the government for a limitation of their liability or to permit incorporation of auditors.

Statutory disclosure requirements

The main financial reporting requirements are contained in the Tenth Schedule of the Ordinance supplemented by the Section 161 requirements regarding the contents of the Directors' Report and disclosure of loans to officers. The disclosure requirements of the Tenth Schedule, Section 161 and Hong Kong accounting standards (HK SSAPs) apply to all forms of company incorporated under the Companies Ordinance. However, in practice it is probably fair to say that the degree of compliance with the Ordinance and HK SSAPs improves the larger the company and the more public exposure to which its financial statements may be subjected.

This situation is quite understandable, of course. The financial statements of a private company are produced for the limited number of persons (usually a family) who own it, the tax authorities and, to a lesser extent, its creditors. None of these parties is likely to be overly concerned with internationally comparable disclosures provided that their own primary reporting requirements are met. As regards banks and other non-trade creditors it is common for a special set of financial statements to be produced in support of a loan with full recording of assets which would be restated at their market value.

Apart from user expectations, there is a supervision factor in the quality of reporting. The financial statements of private companies are not subject to any supervisory review except in liquidation, receivership or upon some other major calamity. The financial statements may then be reviewed by investigating accountants or referred by the Official Receiver to the HKSA for its review, but normally no independent authority reviews the financial statements of private companies unless they are regulated financial institutions. The tax authorities would only be concerned about the tax effect of non-compliance with the Tenth Schedule or HK SSAPs and are restrained from reporting non-compliances to the HKSA because of the secrecy provisions of the Inland Revenue Ordinance. Having said this, it is probably the case that most non-compliance relates to relatively minor matters.

The quality of reporting in public unlisted companies is generally better than that in private companies if only because of the greater number of owners wanting stewardship reports and because of the generally greater public exposure of the financial statements which would naturally make preparers and auditors more circumspect.

Public companies which are also licensed banks or insurance companies are subject to supervision by the Banking Commission and the Insurance Department respectively. The financial statements of all public companies are accessible to the Professional Standards Monitoring Committee (PSMC) of the HKSA.

The financial statements of public listed companies are actively reviewed by the PSMC and the SEHK as well as by financial analysts, fund managers, etc. Hence these tend to have the largest degree of compliance with the Companies Ordinance and HK SSAPs.

'Part III companies'

The exception to this last statement is banking, insurance and shipping companies which take advantage of privileges granted by Part III of the Tenth Schedule of the Companies Ordinance which allow substantially reduced disclosures. Though the privileges are not compulsory all, but a few companies which qualify take advantage of the exemptions. The privilege is available whether the company is private, public or public listed.

The exemption provisions are essentially the same as those available in the UK regarding banks and relate mainly to disclosures of provisions for diminution in value, asset valuations in general and profit disclosures. It is worth noting that in the UK all commercial banks and an increasing number of merchant (investment) banks do not take advantage of the privilege, largely due to a proper regard for their international character and the practices of their US competitors.

The most important effect of the non-disclosures permitted is that so-called 'hidden' or 'inner' reserves are allowed. Although the HSBC and its important local subsidiary the Hang Seng Bank abandoned inner reserves in their 1992 financial statement, there is no indication that other banks are about to follow their lead.

The accountancy profession

Regulation of the professions by law is relatively new in Hong Kong, dating from the 1970s when a series of Ordinances were passed dealing with each of the major professions: law, accountancy, medicine and dentistry. Prior to this most of the local professions were regulated as offshoots of a UK parent body.

The Hong Kong Society of Accountants came into being in 1973 under the Professional Accountants Ordinance. The primary function is the registration and supervision of accountants both in the profession and outside public practice. In support of this responsibility the HKSA has a full range of services including provision of post-qualifying professional education and technical, examination and disciplinary functions.

Reflecting its late start, the profession did not begin issuing statements on accounting and auditing of any kind until 1976 and did not form a technical unit until 1983, some years after its equivalent bodies in Malaysia and Singapore. Work on standard-setting was stimulated by the fall-out from the property crash of 1983 and the collapse of the Carrian Group, with debts of about US$500 million, and of a number of banks – events which drew heavy criticism for the profession, a series of liability suits against auditors, and criminal fraud prosecution against directors and, in one case, the auditors.

Persons who hold themselves out as accountants are required to register as members of the HKSA under the Professional Accountants Ordinance.

Membership of the HKSA is obtained by:

1 Graduates of its own examination system which is conducted in conjunction with the UK-based Chartered Association of Certified Accountants (CACA).
2 Membership of the following overseas bodies (Professional Accountants Ordinance classifications):
   (a) Approved Bodies Schedule A:
   Institute of Chartered Accountants in England and Wales;
   Institute of Chartered Accountants of Scotland;
   Institute of Chartered Accountants in Ireland;
   Institute of Chartered Accountants in Australia;

Chartered Association of Certified Accountants;
The Australian Society of Certified Practising Accountants.

(b) Approved Bodies Schedule B:
Chartered Institute of Management Accountants (UK);
Chartered Institute of Public Finance and Accountancy (UK);

(c) Accepted Bodies under Section 24(1)(c)(ii):
The Canadian Institute of Chartered Accountants;
The New Zealand Society of Accountants;
The South African Institute of Chartered Accountants;
The American Institute of Certified Public Accountants;
The Institute of Chartered Accountants of Zimbabwe.

In addition, there are experience requirements as follows:

- if an HKSA graduate: three, four or five years approved experience (in industry or public practice) depending on the education level at entry;
- if a member of an approved or accepted body: the experience requirements of these bodies.

Persons with more than 10 years membership of the HKSA or the underlying body are designated 'fellows' (FHKSA), those with less than ten years are termed 'associates' (AHKSA).

In order to practise and hence sign audit reports under the Companies Ordinance, a member of the HKSA is required by the Professional Accountants Ordinance to register as a Certified Public Accountant (CPA). This designation can be obtained on request by a HKSA graduate with four years' total experience, following one year's 'recent' post-qualifying experience in a Hong Kong CPA office. This same experience requirement applies to the foreign qualified with, since 1983, the additional requirement of passing two examinations in local tax and company law. There are a small number of 'public accountants' who are unqualified but

Table 5.2 Hong Kong: major audit firms

	Hong Kong listed companies audited	*Number of staff*
Price Waterhouse	65.0	997
KPMG Peat Marwick	45.0	940
Kwan Wong Tan & Fong (BDO)	43.5	–
Ernst & Young	40.0	840
Deloitte Ross Tohmatsu	36.5	714
Coopers & Lybrand	10.5	534
Arthur Andersen	4.0	288
Others (mainly local)	44.5	–
	289.0	

Sources: The Stock Exchange of Hong Kong Ltd; Deloitte Ross Tohmatsu *Report.*

were admitted under 'grandfather' terms in the Professional Accountants Ordinance by virtue of their substantial experience at the time the Professional Accountants Ordinance came into force.

By law, professional accountancy firms must be unlimited liability partnerships although many firms organize themselves so as to incorporate some of their business assets and non-audit operations.

The HKSA is governed by a 14-person council consisting of at least five elected representatives of CPAs and at least five elected representatives of accountants not in public practice plus a representative of the Financial Secretary (Minister of Finance) and of the Director of Accounting Services.

Professional firms

There are approximately 550 professional firms but the audit of listed companies is concentrated in the 'international Big 6' or more specifically the 'Big 2' (in local terms): Price Waterhouse and KPMG Peat Marwick. To these must be added Kwan Wong Tan & Fong (KWTF), a local firm which is affiliated to BDO. Ernst & Young and Deloitte Ross Tohmatsu (DRT) also have an increasing portfolio of listed clients (Table 5.2).

Coopers & Lybrand and Arthur Andersen also have a substantial presence but a limited number of listed clients. However, in the case of Coopers, the 1989 switch of the Deloitte's UK partnership from the DRT merger to Coopers means that they should acquire a number of listed companies with UK parents.

All of these operations, except Andersen's which has a world-wide partnership, are local partnerships of the particular international firm. Some firms also retain the local firm which preceded their international affiliation either as a Chinese name or style or (less often) as a separate partnership. Reflecting these local origins most firms tend to have a high staff-to-partner ratio. They are also reported to be amongst the most profitable in the world.

Most of the larger and internationally affiliated companies provide a full range of services, including taxation, insolvency, business services, executive recruitment, litigation support, and even, in a few cases, share registration. No income figures are published but it is generally assumed that in most firms the bulk of income is audit based even though there is an extensive range of other work.

Amongst the major internationals the professional staff tend to be largely local but with a substantial expatriate presence, particularly at senior and more particularly at partner level. The expatriates are predominantly British (often Scottish) with a significant proportion of Australians and a growing number of Malaysians and Singaporeans. Most international firms also have units to deal with American and Japanese clients and tax matters.

Table 5.3 Equivalent UK and Hong Kong SSAPs and Accounting Guidelines

	UK standards	*Number*	*HKSA statements*
SSAP 1	Accounting for associated companies. Issued January 1971; amended August 1974; revised April 1982.	10	Accounting for the results of associated companies. Issued January 1985.
SSAP 2	Disclosure of accounting policies. Issued November 1971.	1	Disclosure of accounting policies. Revised March 1984.
SSAP 3	Earnings per share. Issued February 1972; revised August 1974. Amended October 1992 by FRS 3.	5	Earnings per share. Revised March 1984.
SSAP 4	The accounting treatment of government grants. Issued April 1974.	–	No equivalent.
SSAP 5	Accounting for value added tax. Issued April 1974.	–	No equivalent. No value added tax in Hong Kong.
SSAP 6	Extraordinary items and prior year adjustments. Issued June 1974; revised June 1975; replaced October 1992 by FRS 3.	2	Extraordinary items and prior year adjustments. Revised March 1984.
SSAP 7	Withdrawn.	–	–
SSAP 8	The treatment of taxation under the imputation system in the accounts of companies. Issued August 1974; amended December 1977.	–	No equivalent. Dissimilar tax system.
SSAP 9	Stocks and work in progress. Issued May 1975; amended August 1980.	3	Stocks and work in progress. Revised March 1984.
SSAP 10	Statements of source and application of funds. Issued July 1975; replaced September 1991 by FRS 1.	4	Statement of changes in financial position. Revised March 1984; revised July 1986; replaced September 1992 by SSAP 15.
SSAP 11	Superseded.		
SSAP 12	Accounting for depreciation. Issued December 1977.	6	Depreciation accounting. Revised November 1987.

Table 5.3 (continued)

	UK standards	*Number*	*HKSA statements*
SSAP 13	Accounting for research and development. Issued October 1977.	–	No equivalent.
SSAP 14	Group accounts. Issued September 1978. Replaced 1992 by FRS 2 Accounting for subsidiary Undertakings.	7	Group accounts. Revised March 1984.
SSAP 15	Accounting for deferred taxation. Issued October 1978; revised May 1985.	12	Accounting for deferred tax.
SSAP 16	Withdrawn.	–	–
SSAP 17	Accounting for post balance sheet events. Issued August 1980.	9	Accounting for post balance sheet events. Revised March 1984.
SSAP 18	Accounting for contingencies. Issued August 1980.	8	Accounting for contingencies. Revised March 1984.
SSAP 19	Accounting for investment properties. Issued November 1981.	13	Accounting for investment properties. Issued October 1987.
SSAP 20	Foreign currency translation. Issued April 1983.	11	Foreign currency translation. Issued February 1985; revised July 1986.
SSAP 21	Accounting for leases and hire purchase contracts. Issued August 1984.	14	Accounting for leases and hire purchase contracts. Issued October 1987.
SSAP 22	Accounting for goodwill. Issued November 1984.		Accounting Guideline 2.204 'Goodwill'. Issued March 1984; major revisions 1988, 1991.
SSAP 23	Accounting for acquisitions and mergers. Issued April 1985.	–	No equivalent.
SSAP 24	Accounting for pension costs. Issued May 1988.	–	No equivalent.
SSAP 25	Segmental reporting. Issued July 1990.	–	Accounting Guideline 2.206. Issued June 1986.

	No equivalent.	–	Accounting Guideline 2.201 'Incomplete records'. Issued March 1984.
	No equivalent.	–	Accounting Guideline 2.202 'The effect of IAS'. Issued July 1987.
	No equivalent.	–	Accounting Guidcline 2.203 'Accounts of dealers in securities'. Issued November 1986.
	No equivalent.	–	Accounting Guideline 2.205 'Capitalization of borrowing costs'. Issued October 1985.
	No equivalent.	–	Accounting Guideline 2.207 'Accounting for textile quota entitlements'. Issued May 1989.
		–	Accounting Guideline ED 'Accounting for general insurance business'.
FRS 1	Cash flow statements. Issued September 1991.	15	Cash flow statements. Issued September 1992.
FRS 2	Accounting for subsidiary undertakings. Issued July 1992.		
FRS 3	Reporting financial performance. Issued October 1992.		Revised SSAP based on IAS E40. From December 1993.

Influences on the accountancy profession

As might be expected the operational culture of the profession is similar to that of the British profession – although it is that of several years ago and is heavily coloured by local attitudes and sensitivities. In this and other ways, the profession is a microcosm of Hong Kong itself. The most widely cited local cultural influence is a reputed tendency of local clients to be reluctant to disclose what they perceive as private information but which in the Anglo-Saxon view is seen as proper disclosure. This view of local sensitivities is generally accepted but has not been subject to any empirical research.

The standard-setting process

The accounting and auditing standard-setting process in Hong Kong is modelled on the pre-Dearing UK system of the CCAB, except of course that there is only one professional body and that is the standard-setting body. Since 1983, the standard-setting process has consisted of two committees of the HKSA:

- the Accounting Standards Committee (ASC);
- the Auditing Standards Committee (AUSC).

Both committees are sub-committees of the HKSA Council and consist of an unstructured mixture of representatives from big and small audit firms and industry including currently one from the SEHK. Smaller professional firms tend to feature more prominently in the AUSC. The secretary of both committees is the full-time HKSA technical director (since May 1990 there have been two technical directors who split the ASC and AUSC work between them). The chairman of both committees was always, until recently, a partner in one of the 'Big Two' firms.

Until 1986 the ASC was also responsible for enforcing the use of standards through the monitoring of published financial statements. This has now passed to a specialist Professional Standards Monitoring Committee (PSMC).

The committees set their own agenda, priorities and work schedules but take advice from the PSMC and other HKSA committees on problem areas. In addition, the industry representatives on the committees and government supervisory agencies supply input on other areas where they believe a statement is warranted. The committees are also open to suggestions from other interested parties.

The committees produce three types of statements of different levels of compulsion, namely:

1. Standards:
   - Accounting: mandatory – enforced by the PSMC but tacitly subject to a true and fair view override.
   - Auditing: mandatory – enforced in disciplinary situations and in PSMC reviews.
2. Guidelines:
   - Accounting: recommended practice only.
   - Auditing: recommended practice but are expected to be applied in all but rare exceptions.
3. Bulletins:
   - Guidance by the PSMC or a technical director expressed as an opinion on points of immediate interest or clarification of a statement.

The first draft of a statement is usually prepared by the technical director on the basis of a brief provided by the relevant committee which is usually to 'Hongkongize' an IAS (until 1993 a UK SSAP) or a UK auditing standard/guideline. Somewhat naturally the variations produced by this process do not follow a consistent pattern. The strategic policy is to produce totally original statements only if no equivalent IAS/IAG or UK Statement exists. For this reason the local statements have been restricted to 'Industry Guidelines'.

The consultative process uses the well-established exposure draft approach and comments arc sought from HKSA members and likely interested groups. Second exposure drafts are produced if the comments on the first draft warrant substantive amendments. Revisions to statements may also necessitate an exposure draft evaluation if they are substantive. The number of comments received on an exposure draft is generally low and is usually restricted to responses by the 'Big Six' firms. Occasionally a draft touches upon an area of particular local sensitivity (e.g. goodwill) and gives rise to significant comment.

Accounting standards: Hong Kong

Accounting standards were first issued in 1976 as non-mandatory Professional Standards Statements and were essentially re-issues of UK SSAPs with a minimum of localization. Ten such Statements had been produced by 1984 when the HKSA Handbook was re-formatted along the lines of the ICAEW equivalent. The Professional Standards Statements were then revised with more local relevance and re-issued as HK SSAPs. As of January 1993, fourteen of these SSAPs and seven Accounting Guidelines had been issued (see Table 5.3). Both SSAPs and Accounting Guidelines are subject to periodic review and most have been revised at some time; some a number of times. The revisions stem from the Technical Directorate, changes in the equivalent IAS or UK Statement, from the PSMC's financial statements review system, lobbying by members and interested parties, feedback from its seminars and, of course, by changing circumstances.

As at January 1993, the HKSA plans to issue new SSAPs or Accounting Guidelines on pension costs, accounting for general insurance business, accounting for investments in the PRC and accounting for foreign incorporated companies. It will also focus on revision of existing HK SSAPs based on IASs. This concentration on local issues is a reflection of the gap in standards produced in the UK where the mid-1990 spate of Exposure Drafts was the only major activity apart from the belated SSAP 25 on segmental reporting. A further problem for the HKSA is that much of the approach and content of recent and proposed UK SSAPs has little relevance to Hong Kong because of a growing gulf between HK and UK law as the latter adopts EEC Directives. The HKSA ASC switched to IASs at the end of 1992 as models of future HK SSAPs and Accounting Guidelines. This initiative is partially prompted by the drying up of the prime source of HK SSAPs, a realization that standard-setting in the UK is increasingly influenced by EEC considerations, and the increasing importance of PRC-based operations and PRC investment in Hong Kong. An additional factor may be the recent moves by the Jardine Group, which is one of the Territory's largest conglomerates, to adopt IASs to reflect its own increasingly international nature. One existing HK SSAP (SSAP 6) is already based on an IAS (IAS 4) and a discussion paper on related party transactions issued in 1986 was substantially derived from IAS 24 and IAG 17.

Existing HK SSAPs are generally regarded as compatible with IASs and they contain a paragraph to that effect. This will also note any alternatives in the IAS which are not compatible with the HK SSAP. Hence, the converse (i.e. that IASs are compatible with HK SSAPs) is not always true. This is due to the alternatives contained in many IASs and also because HK SSAPs understandably do not recognize the interconnections between many IASs and the systematic building-block nature of the IASs. HK SSAPs tend to be more stand-alone definitions of the primary elements of financial statements, much like their UK counterparts.

Accounting standards compared

UK

The UK SSAP equivalents of HK SSAPs and statements are tabulated in Table 5.4. Generally, the accounting and reporting requirements are very similar although the layout of the two SSAPS is slightly different. The main differences occur in HK SSAP 6 which is based on IAS 4 and HK SSAP 11 which is a hybrid of IAS 21 and US FAS 52.

USA

As HKSA standards are largely based on equivalent UK SSAPs, the differences between UK and US financial statements perceivable by American readers also apply in Hong Kong financial statements. However, as noted above, HK SSAP 11 will be more familiar to readers used to US standards as it has elements imported from FAS 52. Otherwise, the same caveats for American readers which apply to UK standards and to UK financial statements apply to Hong Kong financial statements. The terminology, layout and general format of financial statements are quite similar to those in the UK except that the much-reduced disclosure requirements of the Hong Kong Companies Ordinance take their toll on the general informative quality of Hong Kong financial statements. Particular attention should be paid to the financial statements of banks, insurance and shipping companies ('Part III companies') which with few exceptions take advantage of the heavily reduced disclosures allowed to them by the Companies Ordinance.

Table 5.4 Cross-referencing: IAS, HK SSAP, UK SSAP, USA FAS

		HK SSAP	*UK SSAP*	*USA FAS*
IAS 1	Disclosure of accounting policies	SSAP 1	SSAP 2	APB 22 TB 82-1
IAS 2 E 38	Valuation and presentation of inventories in the context of the historical cost system	SSAP 3	SSAP 9	ARB 43 and 45
IAS 3	Consolidated financial statements (superseded by IAS 27 and 28)	–	–	–
IAS 4	Depreciation accounting	SSAP 6	SSAP 12 and SSAP 19	FAS 93 and 99 APB 1, 6 and 12 ARB 44 revised, 9A and 9C
IAS 5	Information to be disclosed in financial statements	–	Sch. 1 CA 89	All FAS specify
IAS 6	Accounting responses to changing prices (superseded by IAS 15)	–	–	–
IAS 7	Statement of changes in financial position	SSAP 4, SSAP 15	FRS 1	FAS 3, 95 and 102
IAS 8 E 46	Unusual and prior period items and changes in accounting policies	SSAP 2	FRS 3	FAS 3, 16, 32, 44, 56, 73 and 83 APB 20 I(1) and (20)
IAS 9 E 37	Accounting for research and development activities	–	SSAP 13	FAS 2, 7, 68 and 86 I(4), (6) and (7) TB 84-1

Table 5.4 (continued)

		HK SSAP	UK SSAP	USA FAS
IAS 10	Contingencies and events occurring after the balance sheet date	SSAP 8 and 9	SSAP 17 and 18	FAS 5, 11, 16, 38 and 47 I(14) and (34)
IAS 11	Accounting for construction contracts	SSAP 3	SSAP 9	ARB 43 and 45
IAS 12	Accounting for taxes on income	SSAP 12	SSAP 15, SSAP 8	FAS 19, 31, 37, 96 and 100 I(18), (22) and (29) APB 10, 23 and 24 TB 79-9, 83-1, 84-2 and 86-1
IAS 13	Presentation of current assets and current liabilities	–	–	FAS 6, 43 and 78 I(8), ARB-1A, 3A APB6 TB 79-3, 85-4 and 88-2
IAS 14	Reporting financial information by segment	2.206	SSAP 25	FAS 14, 18, 21, 24 and 30 TB 79-4 and 79-5
IAS 15	Information reflecting the effect of changing prices	–	SSAP 16 (now non-mandatory)	FAS 89 TB 79-8 and 79-13
IAS 16 E 43	Accounting for property, plant and equipment	SSAP 13 (partly)	SSAP 19	FAS 61
IAS 17	Accounting for leases	SSAP 14	SSAP 21	FAS 13, 22, 23, 27–29, 91 and 98 I(19), (21), (23),

				(24), (26) and (27) TB 79-10, 79-12, 79-14, 79-15, 79-16, 79-17, 79-18, 85-3, 86-2 and 88-1
IAS 18 E 41	Revenue recognition	–	Sch. 1 CA 89	FAS 48
IAS 19 E 47	Accounting for retirement benefits in the financial statements of employers	–	SSAP 24	FAS 87 and 88 TB 81-3 and 87-1
IAS 20	Accounting for government grants	–	SSAP 4	–
IAS 21 E 44	Accounting for the effects of changes in foreign exchange rates	SSAP 11	SSAP 20	FAS 52 I(37)
IAS 22 E 45	Accounting for business combinations – mergers goodwill	– 2.204	SSAP 23 ED 48	FAS 10, 38, 72 and 79 I(9) TB 84-1 and 85-5 APB 16
IAS 23 E 39	Capitalization of borrowing costs	2.205	–	FAS 34, 42, 58 and 62
IAS 24	Disclosure of related party transactions	–	ED 46	FAS 57
IAS 25 E 40	Accounting for investments	SSAP 13	ED 55	–
IAS 26	Accounting and reporting by retirement benefit plans	ED	SORP 1	FAS 35 and 75
IAS 27	Consolidated financial statements and accounting for investments in subsidiaries	SSAP 7	SSAP 14 FRS 2	FAS-94 ARB-51 ARB-1A, 2A

Table 5.4 (continued)

		HK SSAP	*UK SSAP*	*USA FAS*
IAS 28	Accounting for investments in associates	SSAP 10	SSAP 1, plus Interim Statement	–
IAS 29	Financial reporting in hyperinflationary economics	–	–	–
IAS 30	Disclosure in financial statements of banks and similar financial institutions	–	–	FAS 65, 72, 91 TB 85-2 and 87-3
IAS 31	Financial reporting of interests in joint ventures	SSAP 10 Project	SSAP 1 plus Interim Statement	–

Note:
FAS – are issued by the FASB which also issues interpretations (I) of its FAS plus Technical Bulletins (TB).
I represents the FASB Interpretation no.
TB represents the Technical Bulletin no.
ARB represents AICPA Accounting Research Bulletins.
APB represents opinions issued by the Accounting Principles Board of the AICPA.
CA refers to UK Companies Acts.
ED represents exposure draft.
2.xxx = Accounting Guidelines of HKSA.

IAS

The general caveats about the financial statements of private companies, banks, insurance and shipping companies also apply for readers of financial statements based on IAS, particularly since the issue of IAS 30 on disclosures by banks and similar financial institutions.

Auditing standards

There are no significant differences between HK and UK auditing statements and by extension between HK auditing statements and International Auditing Guidelines.

The actual quality of auditing is varied and tends to depend on the size and nature of the client, the size of the audit firm and whether it has international affiliation. Following the series of scandals in the early 1980s referred to earlier, the international and larger local firms improved their quality control and uniformly conduct audits comparable to those in metropolitan countries.

At the other end of the scale, it is unfortunately still the case that the audit of private family companies is driven more by tax and audit fee considerations than by auditing standards. Cultural attitudes to audit and resistance to audit fees coupled with an almost total absence of external review or supervision mean that audits of private companies may be perfunctory. One piece of indicative evidence in this regard is that one of the Territory's largest banks routinely re-audits the financial statements of loan applicants if they do not engage an international or bank-approved firm of auditors. Having said that, it must also be said that there are a significant number of small audit firms whose standards equal those of the internationals.

In addition, the HKSA is pushing ahead with a peer-review system which came into operation in mid-1992. Although not as extensive as the US version, the scheme is a remarkable achievement for a profession in the Western Pacific. This project is partially a response to pressure from other regulators, notably the Official Receiver, the Banking Commission and the SEHK, who all have similar concerns regarding the quality of the audits of private companies within their supervisory ambit.

At the heart of the 'private company problem' is that all but a few hundred companies are classified as private and unless they are in the regulated industries (banking, securities or insurance) there is no supervision, little public information filed and no publicly available financial statements. As noted earlier, all private companies are effectively exempt from legal reporting requirements. In addition, corporate and nominee directorships are permitted and it is not uncommon for shareholders and directors of these companies to be companies registered in unregulated jurisdictions such as Liberia, Panama and the British Virgin Islands. This gives the auditor of the private company obvious problems but also poses risks to the auditor of public companies. One of the more contentious aspects of the Carrian case was the nature and origin of large transfers of funds across year-end by and to apparently unconnected private companies. It was later discovered in criminal investigations that the substantial shareholders and directors of Carrian were involved in the lender. Had the auditors been able to establish this relationship, it is to be expected that their audit and opinion would have been significantly re-oriented.

The problems created by the prevalence of private companies and in their audit have occasionally given rise to discussions in the profession and the business community of whether the audit requirement should be removed for private companies as in most other countries. However, this has received little widespread support and is contested vigorously by the smaller accounting practitioners as private companies provide the bulk of their fee income.

The alternative three-tier approach of public, private and exempt private companies which exists in Australia, Singapore and Malaysia has not been adequately examined in Hong Kong. The additional third tier allows the private family company to take advantage of reduced reporting and audit requirements. These concessions are generally not available to private companies which wish to have holdings in public companies.

Comparative standards

Table 5.4 provides cross-references of IAS with HK SSAPs, UK SSAPs and the gamut of American statements.

The Stock Exchange

The Stock Exchange is operated by The Stock Exchange of Hong Kong Ltd (SEHK), a company organized under the Companies Ordinance and authorized by the government as the sole market for share trading in Hong Kong. The total market capitalization of the SEHK is approximately HKD1,760 billion (US$225 billion) as at 31 July 1993. The SEHK was formed in 1986 from the amalgamation of four pre-existing exchanges and has 928 'seats' (shares) held by 586 member firms. About 830 of these seats are active and held by approximately 490 broking firms. Most of the major UK, American and Japanese broking houses are members but overall the membership is predominantly local sole traders. Seats are freely marketable subject to approval of the buyer as a registered dealer by the supervisory Securities and Futures Commission and as a member by the SEHK. The market price of a seat runs at about US$500 as at July 1993, a rather low figure compared with other exchanges in the region, but this probably reflects the potentially large supply of seats.

Following the 1987 October crash and the SEHK's closure for four days, it was reorganized and the government set up the Securities Review Committee (SRC) headed by UK accountant Ian Hay Davison. The primary brief of the SRC was to investigate the causes and effects of the crash, the SEHK closure and the collapse of the Hong Kong Futures Exchange, which at the time was the third largest in the world. Amongst the SRC's many recommendations was the reorganization of the Securities Commission as an independent body outside of the civil service. On 1 May 1989 the Securities and Futures Commission (SFC) came into being with full powers over all aspects of the securities, futures and commodities industries. To many observers the SRC intended something similar to the SIB arrangement in the UK which supervises by monitoring and audit of the operations of the underlying primary self-regulating organizations. Although it has strong elements of this approach, the SFC also has a hands-on SEC-type involvement in certain areas of the markets which inevitably leads to some duplication of effort. The SEHK's reorganization included a recruitment of professional staff, the restructuring of the governing council and the listing function, and the formation of a compliance unit. There followed a complete revision of the Listing Rules modelled on the UK 'Yellow Book' and of the compliance rules, a process which continues.

The SEHK has a computerized trading and price information system which operates on an order-driven, auction basis through broker-dealers (i.e. there are no jobbers/specialists/market makers). During 1993 the SEHK intends to open a traded options market, encourage a list of about 9 PRC incorporated companies and to institute a fully automated matching trading system. A centralized clearing company began operation of a book-entry settlement system in July 1992.

Stock Exchange reporting requirements

The SEHK's reporting requirements are set out in the standard listing agreement of Appendix 7 of the Listing Rules. These are summarized in Table 5.5, and the current practice in annual financial statements is indicated in Table 5.6. They include somewhat limited segmental reporting, details of directors' shareholdings, and balances of substantial (10 per cent or more) shareholdings. The Listing Rules also set standards for Interim Reports as shown in Table 5.7. Interim statements need not be audited but if they are they must carry a suitably worded auditor's report.

Foreign incorporated companies

A feature of Hong Kong businesses, particularly listed companies, is that a significant number are moving their place of incorporation out of Hong Kong. The favoured jurisdictions are Bermuda and the Cayman Islands.

Table 5.5 SEHK Listing Rules: disclosures in financial statements

Contained in Appendix 7A + B, paras 9 and 10.

- All financial Statements must be in English and Chinese.
- All information is required on a group basis unless indicated or obvious.

1 The information may be provided in the directors' report or the financial statements
2 Principal activities
3 Turnover and contribution per activity
4 Geographic analysis for:
All turnover; and 'abnormal' contribution
• the required degree of analysis is defined
5 Subsidiary companies
Name, principal country of operation
Country of incorporation of all subsidiaries
• unless non-material and inclusion will make details excessive in length
6 Convertible securities, options, warrants issued in year, plus consideration received
7 Conversions of securities in year
8 Redemptions of capital in year
9 Directors' interests in shares and debentures of group companies
• statutory definitions of Securities (Disclosure of Interests) Ordinance (SDI);
• qualifying shares are exempted;
• beneficial and non-beneficial interests to be shown separately
10 Substantial shareholders
Full disclosure of statutory SDI balances
11 Reconciliation of actual results to forecast results
12 Reasons for any non-compliance with HK SSAP
• HKSA accounting statements are specifically endorsed
13 Borrowings in year
14 Capitalized interest
15 Investment, development or trading properties
• specific details of address, area, etc.
16 Unexpired periods of directors' service contracts
17 Directors' interests in significant contracts
• 'significant' is defined
18 Controller's interests in contracts
19 Same as points 11 and 18 for contracts for services
20 Waivers of directors' emoluments
21 Waivers of dividends
22 Unauthorized disproportion all cash issues
• full details
23 Five-year summary
24 Part III 10th Schedule exemptions are permitted

The trend began in 1983 with the announcement that the main companies of the Jardine group were to restructure by moving their place of incorporation to Bermuda. Following that lead, all the Jardine listed companies have reincorporated in Bermuda and about eighty other companies in total have reincorporated there plus eight in the Cayman Islands.

The usual reasons given for the move centred on the archaic prohibitions in the Hong Kong Companies Ordinance on a company's purchase of its own shares (treasury stock), merger accounting (pooling of interests) and a company providing assistance for the purchase of its own shares (e.g. leveraged buy-outs). The other commonly cited reason is 'for tax purposes', although given Hong Kong's 17.5 per cent profits tax rate and territorial (non-World income) basis of taxation, the justification for this reason is not always obvious. It is widely believed that an unspoken reason for reincorporating outside Hong Kong is fear of interference in business by the PRC authorities after 1997. Presumably, by moving incorporation offshore it is hoped that non-Hong Kong assets and income will be protected from any adverse attention by PRC authorities.

The SEHK makes a distinction between primary and secondary listings. What constitutes a primary listing is not spelt out and the final decision on the classification as primary is the prerogative of the SEHK. The general working concept is best illustrated by an example: if a Delaware, USA company listed its shares on the SEHK that would be a secondary listing of a class of stock listed elsewhere in a greater proportion. However, if that company's local or regional subsidiary listed its shares on the SEHK, it would almost certainly be a primary listing. The significance of the distinction is that foreign incorporated companies with a primary listing are for all intents and purposes treated as Hong Kong incorporated companies. This policy is in pursuit of the level-playing-field principle and also a recognition of the special situation in the SEHK where about 30 per cent of its companies are foreign incorporated.

In the same vein, the Listing Rules place restrictions upon Bermuda-type companies regarding their access to the more permissive and enlightened provisions of the Companies Acts of the countries of incorporation. Hence, these companies have the same restrictions on leveraged buy-outs, treasury stock and capital reductions as apply to Hong Kong companies through the Hong Kong Companies Ordinance. The only exception is that merger accounting (pooling) is permitted in foreign incorporated companies, basically because merger accounting is invariably applied in the reconstruction (reincorporation) in the foreign jurisdiction of a Hong Kong company. This is to preserve its distributable reserves which would disappear as pre-acquisition reserves in purchase (acquisition) accounting.

As can be seen from Table 5.6, the reporting standards of Hong Kong-incorporated and foreign primary listed companies are for all intents and purposes identical. Both are normally required to apply HK accounting standards and effectively to use HK CPAs as auditors. However, in both cases a form of true and fair view override is permitted and foreign incorporated companies can apply for a waiver on both accounting standards and auditors. One such waiver has been granted to elements of the Jardine group, allowing it to use IAS in the light of the increasingly international nature of those companies.

Table 5.6 General format of financial statements

Title	*Comments*	*Contents and layout*
1 Corporate data	Non-statutory.	Names of directors, company secretaries, auditors, legal advisers, and bankers and registered office address.
2 Chairman's Report	Non-statutory, not audited.	Usually a review of the year's operations plus a narrative outline of the coming year. Prospective figures are effectively disallowed by SEHK Listing Rules.
3 Directors' Report	Statutory, not required to be audited but usually 'reviewed' by auditors.	– Principal activities (10 per cent or more of group profit) – SEHK.
	Comparative figures must be provided. Contents are usually limited to statutory and SEHK requirements.	– Outline of turnover and contribution to results analysed into geographical and principal activities segments – SEHK.
		– Details of equity issues (inc. reason, price, use of proceeds) – SEHK.
	The disclosures required by the SEHK indicated here may be shown in the Directors' Report or elsewhere in the 'accounts' (i.e. the Notes to the financial statements). The items shown here are those that are usually shown in the Directors' Report.	– From 1991 details of statutory disclosures of interest of directors (beneficial and non-beneficial), chief executive and their families in shares and debentures of group – SEHK.
		– Directors' emoluments waived – SEHK.
		– Details of loans to directors.
		– Unexpired period of directors' service contracts.
		– Details (or nil statement) of directors' interests in significant contracts at any time in year – SEHK.

		– Details of significant contracts (inc. services) between group and a controlling shareholder or its subsidiaries – SEHK. – Details of convertible securities issued in year – SEHK. – Detail of any exercise of rights on convertible securities –SEHK. – Details of any redemption etc. of redeemable securities – SEHK. – Explanation of differences between results forecast in period and actual results – SEHK. – Amount of interest capitalized in year – SEHK. – Statement concerning retirement and re-election at AGM of auditors.
4 Group balance sheet	Statutory (Tenth Schedule). Audited. Usually provided in outline with analysis carried in Notes to financial statements. British format and terminology. Comparative figures are required for all elements of the financial statements.	
5 Holding company balance sheet	Often shown as separate columns in Group Balance Sheet.	As above.
6 Group profit and loss account	Format can incorporate holding company data.	Statutory (Tenth Schedule).

Table 5.6 (continued)

Title	*Comments*	*Contents and layout*
	Audited.	
	Sparse British-style content and format.	
	Details carried in Notes to financial statements.	
7 Group source and application of funds statement	Turnover exceeds $1 million.	
	Audited.	
	Often referred to as 'Consolidated Statement of Changes in Financial Position'.	
	Holding company version not required.	
8 Notes to the financial statements	Audited.	Required by various HK SSAPs.
9 Audit report	Statutory and Hong Kong Auditing Standards and Guidelines.	
10 Five-year summary	Required by SEHK.	
	'Reviewed' not reported upon in audit opinion.	
Foreign Incorporated – Primary listing		
1 Financial statements	Same as Hong Kong incorporated.	
2 Audit report		
Foreign Incorporated – Secondary listing		
1 Financial statements	Can use IAS or other 'acceptable' standards.	May (i.e. will) require reconciliation statement.
2 Audit report	By HKSA CPA or IFAC equivalent.	Use IAG 13 approach which equates 'true and fair' and 'fairly presents'.
	Use HKSA auditing standards or IAG.	

There is no standard audit report for foreign primary listings and most seem to follow the original Jardine model (see Table 5.6). This is a peculiar hybrid, which reports that Hong Kong Auditing Standards are used (because the auditors are HKSA CPAs) and that the financial statements are in accordance with the disclosure requirements of the Hong Kong Companies Ordinance. There are two points to note here. First, that the company applied Hong Kong law rather than that of its country of incorporation. Second, that they have complied with the disclosure requirements of that Hong Kong law rather than the accounting requirements. This statement is necessary because the merger accounting (pooling) applied on their restructuring overseas means they are not in compliance with the accounting requirements of the Hong Kong Companies Ordinance.

The auditors of primary listings may be allowed to apply International Auditing Guidelines (IAG) rather than HK Auditing Standards but this has not happened to date. In any event the source of auditing standards used must be reported along with the title or a description of the underlying law which applies to the financial statements. Secondary listings are required to produce financial statements conforming with accounting standards acceptable to the SEHK which would normally be 'at least' IAS. A reconciliation statement showing the effect of not using IAS or HK SSAP may be required. As regards the auditor, he must be a professional accountant with the same degree of independence as required by Hong Kong law and the International Federation of Accountants (IFAC). The standards applied by the auditor must be in accordance with HKSA auditing statements or IAG. If a true and fair view requirement does not apply to the company's financial statements, subject to SEHK approval, an alternative basis may be allowed. However, given the equivalency granted to 'true and fair' and 'fairly presents' by the revised version of IAG 13 this waiver may be of little significance.

The main effect of this variety of reporting requirements and sources of reporting and auditing requirements is a potential loss of comparability. At the moment, with the exception of Jardine (from June 1991 year-end) there is no problem, because all Hong Kong listed companies apply HK auditing and accounting standards, use HKSA members as auditors and apply the Hong Kong Companies Ordinance except in regard to merger accounting. However, care may have to be taken in the future regarding the accounting and auditing standards used, the contents of the auditor's report and where the audit opinion was signed-off.

SUMMARY

Hong Kong, although a British colony until 1997, is a major global financial centre with a thriving economy and relatively little government intervention in economic affairs. Taxation is low and has little effect on corporate financial reporting. As in the UK, accounting rules are contained

Table 5.7 SEHK Listing Rules: disclosures – interim results

1	Appendix 7A + B, para. 11.1–11.3; these are the minimum requirements
2	Accounting policies must be consistent with those of annual financial statements
3	Turnover
4	Pre-tax profit • exceptional items should be described fully
5	HK profits tax Overseas taxation • basis of charge • includes share of associated companies taxation
6	Minority interests in year's profits
7	Attributable post-tax profit
8	Extraordinary items
9	Attributable profit after extraordinary items
10	Dividends paid and proposed
11	Transfers into and out of reserves
12	Earnings per share on a HK SSAP 6 basis
13	Comparative figures
14	Director's interests • same details as in annual financial statements
15	Substantial shareholdings • same details as in annual financial statements
16	Explanatory statement
17	Supplementary information permitted subject to approval
18	If audited then the Audit Report must be published If not audited the Interim Report should say so

mainly in company law, accounting standards and stock exchange requirements. The Companies Ordinance, based on the UK Companies Acts 1929 and 1948, is rather out-dated and has not been influenced, as has UK company law, by EC Directives.

Statements of Standard Accounting Practice (SSAPs) are issued by the Accounting Standards Committee of the Hong Kong Society of Accountants (HKSA). In the main they are local adaptations of the SSAPs prepared by the former UK Accounting Standards Committee and are compatible with International Accounting Standards. Auditing Guidelines are issued by the Auditing Standards Committee of the HKSA.

The Stock Exchange of Hong Kong is supervised by the Securities and Futures Commission (SFC). The SEHK's reporting requirements are set out in Appendix 7 of its Listing Rules.

Private companies are exempt from filing financial statements with the Registrar of Companies. Internationally comparable disclosures are made by public and listed companies as their financial statements are actively reviewed by the Professional Standards Monitoring Committee (PSMC) of the HKSA and by the SEHK.

APPENDIX

Extracts from the accounts of Hong Kong Telecommunications

HONG KONG TELECOM ANNUAL REPORT 1991

CONSOLIDATED PROFIT AND LOSS ACCOUNT

FOR THE YEAR ENDED 31 MARCH 1991

	Note	1991 $M	1990 $M
Turnover	3	**16,266.1**	14,134.3
Operating costs	4	**11,120.5**	9,693.1
Operating profit		**5,145.6**	4,441.2
Net interest and other income	5	**226.8**	201.9
Profit before taxation		**5,372.4**	4,643.1
Taxation	6	**420.0**	351.5
Profit after taxation		**4,952.4**	4,291.6
Minority interests		**(5.7)**	(2.0)
Profit after taxation and minority interests		**4,958.1**	4,293.6
Development Fund transfer	7	**110.4**	66.5
Profit before extraordinary item		**5,068.5**	4,360.1
Extraordinary item	8	**(729.9)**	—
Profit attributable to shareholders	9	**4,338.6**	4,360.1
Appropriations			
Dividends	10	**3,680.4**	3,122.0
Retained profit for the year	18	**658.2**	1,238.1
Earnings per share	11	**45.4¢**	39.1¢

HONG KONG TELECOM ANNUAL REPORT 1991

BALANCE SHEETS

AT 31 MARCH 1991

	Note	Group		Company	
		1991 $M	1990 $M	**1991 $M**	1990 $M
Employment of Capital					
Fixed assets	12	**12,341.2**	10,360.9	**0.8**	1.3
Interest in subsidiaries	13	**–**	—	**7,159.7**	6,614.7
Other investments	14	**332.5**	290.1	**2.2**	1.6
Current assets	15	**4,529.9**	4,381.3	**1,083.0**	1,573.9
		17,203.6	15,032.3	**8,245.7**	8,191.5
Current liabilities	16	**5,441.5**	4,556.8	**2,120.4**	1,707.6
		11,762.1	10,475.5	**6,125.3**	6,483.9
Financed by					
Share capital	17	**5,576.4**	5,576.4	**5,576.4**	5,576.4
Reserves	18	**5,162.0**	4,503.8	**548.9**	907.5
Shareholders' funds		**10,738.4**	10,080.2	**6,125.3**	6,483.9
Minority interests		**–**	2.6	**–**	—
Deferred taxation	19	**731.8**	5.4	**–**	—
Development Fund	7	**–**	106.1	**–**	—
Long-term liabilities	20	**291.9**	281.2	**–**	—
		11,762.1	10,475.5	**6,125.3**	6,483.9

The financial statements on pages 28 to 48 were approved by the Board of Directors on 21 May 1991 and were signed on their behalf by:

M G Gale
Director

J G Tonroe
Director

HONG KONG TELECOM ANNUAL REPORT 1991

CONSOLIDATED STATEMENT OF CHANGES IN FINANCIAL POSITION

FOR THE YEAR ENDED 31 MARCH 1991

	1991 $M	1990 $M
Source of funds		
Profit before taxation	**5,372.4**	4,643.1
Adjustment for items not involving the movement of funds:		
Depreciation and amortisation	**961.4**	779.0
(Gain) loss on disposal of fixed assets	**(107.8)**	58.6
Interest on Development Fund	**4.3**	10.6
Loss of minority shareholders absorbed by the Group	**3.1**	—
Funds generated from operations	**6,233.4**	5,491.3
Funds from other sources		
Proceeds on disposal of fixed assets	**183.7**	19.7
Increase in long-term liabilities	**10.7**	247.1
Decrease in other investments	**–**	25.8
Proceeds from shares issued to minority shareholders of a subsidiary	**–**	4.0
Increase in deferred taxation on acquisition of a subsidiary company	**–**	0.8
Total source of funds	**6,427.8**	5,788.7
Application of funds		
Purchase of fixed assets	**3,017.6**	2,675.5
Dividends paid	**3,368.1**	2,673.3
Profits tax paid	**458.8**	30.8
Increase in other investments	**42.4**	—
Purchase of goodwill on acquisition of subsidiaries	**–**	55.0
Dividends to minority shareholders in a subsidiary company	**–**	2.9
Decrease in minority interests on acquisition of subsidiaries	**–**	0.3
Total application of funds	**6,886.9**	5,437.8
(Decrease) increase in working capital	**(459.1)**	350.9

	1991 $M	1990 $M
(Decrease) increase in working capital		
Stocks and work in progress	**(50.2)**	60.7
Debtors and prepayments	**746.4**	208.2
Staff housing loans	**14.5**	9.5
Amounts due from holding company and fellow subsidiaries	**(27.4)**	28.1
Interest in partnerships	**(92.1)**	302.8
Creditors, accrued charges and prepaid revenue	**(492.6)**	(166.0)
Amounts due to holding company and fellow subsidiaries	**(29.5)**	(12.5)
Net liquid funds:		
Term deposits	**(516.0)**	(59.1)
Bank and cash balances	**73.4**	7.8
Current portion of long-term liabilities	**(22.8)**	(15.9)
Bank loans and overdrafts	**(62.8)**	(12.7)
(Decrease) increase in working capital	**(459.1)**	350.9

HONG KONG TELECOM ANNUAL REPORT 1991

NOTES TO THE FINANCIAL STATEMENTS

FOR THE YEAR ENDED 31 MARCH 1991

1. General

The Company is a public limited company incorporated in Hong Kong. The ultimate holding company is Cable and Wireless plc, incorporated in England.

2. Principal accounting policies

(a) *Basis of accounting*
The financial statements have been prepared in Hong Kong dollars using the historical cost basis of accounting, modified to include the revaluation of a property and to recognise the Group's share of post-acquisition results of its associated companies.

(b) *Basis of consolidation*
The Group financial statements comprise a consolidation of the financial statements of the Company and all its subsidiary companies made up to 31 March each year. All material intragroup transactions and balances are eliminated on consolidation.

Where subsidiary companies are acquired during the year, on consolidation, the surplus of cost over fair values attributed to the net assets acquired is charged directly to reserves.

(c) *Subsidiary companies*
Subsidiary companies are companies in which the Company has a beneficial interest of more than 50 percent of the issued equity. Investments in subsidiary companies are stated at cost, less amounts written off. Dividends from subsidiary companies are accounted for when declared.

(d) *Associated companies*
An associated company is a company, not being a subsidiary company, where the Group is in a position to exercise significant influence and owns not less than 20 percent but not more than 50 percent of the issued equity. The results of associated companies are accounted for by the Group using the equity method of accounting.

(e) *Depreciation and amortisation of fixed assets*
The Scheme of Control Agreement between Hong Kong Telephone Company Limited (Hong Kong Telephone) and Hong Kong Government requires that the cost of leasehold land held by Hong Kong Telephone is not amortised. The cost of other leasehold land is amortised over periods between 40 and 50 years or the term of the lease, if less.

Depreciation is provided to write off the cost of other fixed assets over their estimated useful lives in equal annual instalments as follows :

Buildings	40 to 50 years or term of lease, if less
Exchange equipment	2 to 15 years
International transmission plant	5 to 40 years
Local transmission plant	8 to 33 years
Other plant and equipment	2 to 20 years

Capital projects under construction are not depreciated until they are ready for service. Certain costs relating to these projects are capitalised and included in the cost of fixed assets; these costs include staff costs, materials, interest and overheads.

(*f*) *Investments in limited partnerships*
Where a company is a partner in a partnership which acts as a lessor under a leasing arrangement, the cost of participating in the partnership is recorded as an interest in partnerships.

(*g*) *Consumable stores, trading stocks and work in progress*
Consumable stores are stated at cost less provision for slow-moving and obsolete items. Trading stocks are stated at the lower of cost and net realisable value. In both cases, cost comprises materials, freight and insurance and is calculated on a first-in first-out basis. Work in progress is stated at cost, which comprises labour, materials and overheads where appropriate.

(*h*) *Taxation*
Profits tax is provided on the estimated assessable profits at the tax rate ruling during the year. Deferred tax is provided at the anticipated tax rate using the liability method, to the extent that there is a reasonable probability that a liability will crystallise in the foreseeable future.

(*i*) *Foreign currencies*
Foreign currencies purchased as a hedge against foreign currency commitments and liabilities are translated into Hong Kong dollars at cost. Liabilities which are covered by forward foreign exchange contracts are translated at the contractual rates of exchange. Other assets and liabilities in foreign currencies are translated at the rates ruling on the balance sheet date. Transactions in foreign currencies are translated into Hong Kong dollars at the spot or forward exchange rates, as appropriate, ruling on the dates of the transactions. Exchange gains and losses resulting from these policies are included in the profit and loss account.

(*j*) *Operating leases*
Annual rental income and expenses under operating leases are respectively credited or charged to the profit and loss account on a straight line basis over the lease term.

HONG KONG TELECOM ANNUAL REPORT 1991

REPORT OF THE AUDITORS

To the members of
Hong Kong Telecommunications Limited
香港電訊有限公司

We have audited the financial statements set out on pages 28 to 48 in accordance with approved Auditing Standards.

In our opinion, the financial statements give a true and fair view of the state of affairs of the Company and of the Group at 31 March, 1991 and of the profit and changes in financial position of the Group for the year ended on that date and have been properly prepared in accordance with the Companies Ordinance.

KPMG Peat Marwick
Certified Public Accountants

Hong Kong
21 May 1991

BIBLIOGRAPHY

—— , Pak-Kuen Au-Yeung, Kwok, Maurice C.M. and Lau, Lawrence W.C. (1990) 'Non-compliance with disclosure requirements in financial statements: the case of Hong Kong companies', *International Journal of Accounting*, 25(2).

Flux, D. (annually updated) *Hong Kong Taxation*, Hong Kong: Chinese University Press.

Government Information Service (annually) *Hong Kong*, Hong Kong: Hong Kong Government.

HKSA, *Handbook* (3 vols), Hong Kong Society of Accountants, Wanchai, Hong Kong.

—— *Annual Reports. The Hong Kong Accountant*, bi-monthly journal.

Stott, V. (1990) *Hong Kong Company Law* (3rd edn), Hong Kong: Pitman.

Tai, Benjamin Y. (1988) 'The accounting profession in Hong Kong: problems and challenges', in V.K. Zimmerman (ed.), *Recent Developments in the Far East*, Champaign, Illinois: Center for International Education and Research in Accounting, University of Illinois.

Wallace, P. (1986) *Company Law in Hong Kong* (2nd edn), Hong Kong: Butterworths.

Yuen, Susanna (1988) *The Institutional Framework of Accounting for Hong Kong*, Goodman Publisher.

6 Thailand

J.S.W. Tay

INTRODUCTION

Until the late 1980s, Thailand was probably best known for its lengthy (though passive) involvement in the US–Vietnam War, and its regular (and largely bloodless) military coups. The country was not the subject of much western observation of, or comment on, Third World development, possibly because, having escaped formal colonization in the nineteenth century, it is not as familiar as, for example, Singapore is to the British, as Indonesia is to the Dutch, and as the Philippines is to the Americans.

This lack of world attention has now changed dramatically, fuelled by Thailand's emergence in 1987 as the sudden, unexpected star performer of Asian tourism, and even more recently as the next growth centre of South-East Asia, and Asia's most obvious candidate for NIE (newly industrializing economy – this term is used in preference to 'newly industrializing country', as it is more politically neutral) status. The increasing comment on its economy and export performance, however, has not been matched by information on the Thai financial reporting environment. The country was included in two international surveys on financial reporting (Gray *et al.* 1984, SGV 1984), and aspects of the Thai profession have been described (Whittle 1980, Needles 1988, Ninsuvannakul 1988). But academic research focused first on the development of the equity market in Thailand (Sareewiwatthana and Malone 1985, Phutrakul 1986), and only more recently on financial reporting requirements and practices (Tay 1989: 279–308).

THE BUSINESS ENVIRONMENT

A brief historical note

Thailand's more recent history helps to explain the nature of its present economic and social systems, and also highlights important aspects of the Thai national character. Both of these have implications for, and effects on, the nature of the financial reporting system in Thailand.

Thailand was the only one of the South-East Asian states to escape formal western political control in the nineteenth century, and remained an absolute monarchy until the 1920s. The maintenance of Thai independence was due to two main factors. First, Thailand was a strategic geographical and political buffer state between the British in India, Burma and Malaya, and the French in Indo-China. Second, the Thai rulers never followed the isolationist foreign policy which had such disastrous results for the Burmese and the Chinese. Instead, their combination of timely territorial sacrifices and selective modernization averted formal colonization, with the important consequence that modern Thais deal with foreigners as equals.

Ordinary Thais were never politicized. There were no food shortage problems, even during the depression of the 1930s, and no formal colonial presence to raise nationalistic fervour. The fifteen military coups that occurred from 1932 were struggles between elite minority factions, with no popular base. Since 1980, however, the internal political climate has been relatively stable, and a limited form of democracy has been introduced. Economic and social recovery from the riots of 1991 is almost complete.

Economic development

The Thai economy has traditionally been self-sufficient. Even at the height of western commercial and territorial dominance, the government maintained a policy of mild tariff protection which helped to preserve the domestic market for household industries. The wisdom of this policy may be more fully appreciated today, when the skills of Thai workers and/or their products are in large demand.

Industrialization was emphasized after the end of the Second World War. At the same time, agricultural production was increased to ensure a sufficient surplus for export in order to earn foreign exchange. For many years Thailand's exports were based on rice, rubber, sugar and other commodities.

While exports have been the main engine of economic growth over the years, their nature, and that of the underlying economy, has changed radically over the past thirty years. This has been a deliberate policy of the National Economic Social Development (NESD) plans. Agriculture has shrunk from 28 per cent of Gross Domestic Product (GDP) and 52 per cent of exports in 1977, to 16 per cent and 34 per cent respectively in 1989. Manufactures now represent about 65 per cent of exports. The growth of this sector contributed to Thailand's growth rate of over 10 per cent for both 1988 and 1989, and the Thai economy continued to grow at about 9 per cent for the next three years.

Factors which have contributed to this success story include the underlying stability of Thai society and the quality of its work-force, and a combination of liberal policies towards foreign investment, conservative fiscal and monetary policies which resulted in a realistic exchange rate for the Thai *baht* (currently about 40 *baht* = £1) and development policies which emphasized free-market economics and private sector orientation. Thailand has a small public sector (about 19 per cent of GDP) compared with other developing countries, and the persistent budget deficit (brought about by extremely poor tax collection practices) has been financed by bonds.

Although such financial conservatism has preserved Thailand's international credit rating, it has also resulted in problems which may affect the country's long-term economic performance. Limited previous investment in infrastructure has led to severe deficiencies in road transportation, port facilities and telecommunications. Another problem area is education: most immediately the country has an acute shortage of scientific and technological workers which has not aided technology transfer, even though investment promotion policies have been geared towards high value-added industries. In the longer term, there are the twin worries of a high primary school dropout rate, and the lowest secondary school enrolment figures in South-East Asia.

The private sector

Private-sector companies are either locally owned, or have international connections. The characteristics of these two broad types of companies differ quite markedly. The majority of locally owned businesses, even very substantial businesses, are still family-owned or controlled by a relatively small number of shareholders. Many of these are led by individuals of Chinese descent, who have shown a marked preference for maintaining close control. Corporate financing has thus been mainly through borrowing, and, in the main, borrowing from banks. Long-term corporate growth has thus been subjected to the vagaries of short-term interest rates. Some of this has begun to change in connection with the concerted effort over the past fifteen years to develop the Thai capital market in general, and the equity market in particular.

The dependence on internally generated or borrowed funds may also have affected the growth of Thai companies. Although some of the largest institutions in South-East Asia are found in Thailand (for example, the Bangkok Bank), in general, Thai listed companies are not as large as similar listed companies in Malaysia and Singapore in terms of assets and turnover.

A possible long-term problem for the private sector relates to the extent and nature of Japanese direct investment in Thailand. Japan is now the largest foreign investor in Thailand (accounting for 53 per cent of total foreign investment as at mid-1990) and also the country's main trading partner (see Appendix C). Thai officials admit that Thailand is virtually a Japanese economic colony, and this may be a source of friction as well as stagnation, in view of the traditional Japanese unwillingness to appoint locals to top-level management positions.

The equity market

The first stock exchange in Thailand, the Bangkok Stock Exchange (BSE), was formed in 1962 by a group of private individuals. It failed due to the lack of knowledge about, and internal and external support for, equity investment. First, as noted above, Thai companies are mainly outgrowths of family businesses and many have private sources of borrowed capital and very limited needs for public funds. Company managements were largely ignorant about the other advantages of being publicly quoted. The disclosure of audited financial information (to provide a modest degree of protection for investors) was also regarded as a distinct disadvantage as it reduced the ability of company management or owners to manipulate profit figures for tax purposes. Thus the BSE was never able to offer a large enough choice of good securities to the investing public, and the maximum number of companies quoted was thirty-six.

There was a dearth of institutional investors, and the general public was largely ignorant about equity investment which was widely regarded as a pastime for millionaires. Individuals also tended to view shareholdings as a source of fixed dividend income. Unfortunately, the members of the BSE did not have a sufficiently serious interest in and commitment to the exchange to seek to educate the public. Moreover, dividends were subject to tax, while interest earned on commercial bank deposits was tax-exempt. The BSE did not have sufficient influence to seek changes in the tax system in order to obtain a better climate for equity investment.

The BSE ceased operations in 1974. Its failure demonstrated the need for the Thai government to direct and accelerate the development of the capital market. This became especially urgent during the late 1960s when large numbers of investment banks and finance and securities companies were established in the country. Professor S.M. Robbins of Columbia University, a former Chief Economist of the US Securities and Exchange Commission (SEC), was engaged as a government consultant. His report was used as the basis for government policy in this area.

The Securities Exchange of Thailand (SET) began operations in 1975 with thirty member firms and fifteen securities issued by eleven quoted companies. Market capitalization at the end of that year was 5.4 billion *baht.* Its objectives were to provide a centre for the purchase and sale of securities, to promote savings and the mobilization of capital funds, and to encourage diversification of share ownership. These objectives have become an important part of the NESD plans to reduce corporate overdraft financing and debt–equity ratios to no more than two. SET is both a stock exchange and a regulatory body. In essence, its trading operations are based on practices in Hong Kong and Australia, while its regulations are based on that of the SEC. It has begun to computerize its transactions, and is currently almost fully on line; it has moved towards scripless trading.

A great deal of effort has been channelled into SET's 'public relations' activities, which are aimed at increasing the awareness of the public, Thai companies and foreign investors of the benefits of investing funds in, or seeking funds through, the Thai equity market. SET actively seeks to increase the supply of listed securities by reviewing and contacting potential candidates. Research is also carried out on the feasibility of introducing new financial instruments.

In mid-1987, a second trading board was inaugurated to accommodate companies which are not yet qualified for the main board, mainly because they do not meet the criterion of having operated profitably for at least three years. The second board is targeted at new shares, shares of companies with good prospects, and state enterprises. There has been much discussion of privatization of state enterprises, in particular of Thai Airways. To date, however, only the Krung Thai Bank has been floated.

SET has been of particular interest to foreign institutional investors. These have been welcomed, as they lend the market a degree of stability. Foreign individuals may, and do, invest in Thai securities either directly or through one or more of twelve country funds, such as the Bangkok Fund, established in 1985 by Merril Lynch, and the Thailand Fund, set up in 1987.

By the end of 1989, 165 companies were listed on the main board, with a market capitalization of 470 billion *baht*. This represented an annual growth of 85 per cent in capitalized value, putting SET among the top ten fastest growing bourses in the world. Its medium-term target is to have 400 listed companies by 1995.

INFLUENCES ON ACCOUNTING

There are three direct influences on Thai financial reporting practices: a Ministerial Regulation relating to financial reporting disclosures, reporting regulations imposed on companies quoted on SET, and accounting standards promulgated by the Institute of Certified Accountants and Auditors of Thailand (ICAAT).

The influence of the law

Ministerial Regulation No. 2 BE 2519 (1976) contains the minimum disclosures to be made in the balance sheet and profit and loss account of various enterprises, including limited liability companies. It came into effect on 1 January 1977, and was the first Thai legislation to have a direct impact on financial reporting. Its requirements remain unchanged, even today.

The disclosure requirements, which may be likened to a (very simple) chart of accounts, vary according to the type of business in which an enterprise is engaged, as well as the legal form of the enterprise. The Regulation distinguishes among registered partnerships, companies engaged in commercial banking, insurance, *crédit foncier* (hire purchase), financing, securities, warehousing and other types of business, branches of foreign banks and insurance companies, and juristic persons established under foreign laws.

The objective of the Regulation is to ensure that the financial statements issued by different entities conform to similar standards. Conformity was sought in order to raise the standard of accounting, to help both in the development of the equity market and in tax and duty collection. Standardization of disclosure was thus equated with improvement in financial reporting. However, the Regulation only deals with disclosure, and not with the valuation of items disclosed. Moreover, the disclosures required (see 'Content of accounts', p. 212) are quite basic, and have never been increased. This is because the majority of Thai companies are still family businesses, with little or no need for external capital.

Tax law requires conformity between book and tax reporting, if companies wish to claim the full amount of allowances. This inevitably has an impact on the valuation of depreciating or depleting assets. In combination with the basic disclosure requirements of Ministerial Regulation No. 2, and a company law requirement that legal reserves be set up and maintained (see p. 206), Thai law appears to have been influenced by Franco-Germanic practices, with the result that the accounts produced, especially by non-quoted companies, are sometimes of more use for tax purposes than for financial analysis.

The influence of the capital market

The development of the equity market has probably been the most important factor in the development of financial reporting in Thailand. In the main, however, SET has not sought to regulate accounting practices under the powers granted by the SET Act, but has acted through the Ministry of Commerce, which monitors compliance by *all* companies with legal and professional reporting requirements, and ICAAT, which has developed a number of accounting and auditing standards. This is because it has not wanted to discourage companies from seeking quoted status through the imposition of significantly heavier reporting requirements for quoted companies. However, in its efforts to promote more widespread ownership and foreign investment, SET has encouraged the development of financial reporting along investor-oriented lines, in particular in the provision of consolidated accounts and more detailed information in the notes.

SET has also organized an annual award for outstanding financial statements, in conjunction with the Ministry of Finance, ICAAT and six associations – the Thailand Management Association, the Board of Trade of Thailand, the Association of Thai Industries, the Thai Bankers' Association, the Association of Members of the Securities Exchange and the Thai Life Assurance Association. The stated aim of these awards is to raise the standards of data disclosure and reporting.

The influence of the profession

As at April 1990, ICAAT has adopted fifteen Statements of Financial Accounting Standards (SFAS) – the first five in 1979, one each in 1986, 1987 and 1988, five in 1989 and two more in 1990. There are currently also twenty-one exposure drafts in issue. These thirty-six statements are listed in Appendix D. There are no official English translations, but summaries of the first five SFASs are available. A review of the subject matter of these statements indicates a surprisingly sophisticated approach to financial reporting in the context of a developing country, especially in relation to company financing. This is perhaps an indication of the influence of the capital market on external financial accounting standards.

Thailand is unique among the Association of South-East Asian Nations (ASEAN) countries in that there has been no wholesale adoption of the accounting standards promulgated by other professional bodies, whether national or international. Gray *et al.* indicated 'significant' IASC influence, and 'moderate' UK influence on Thai financial reporting practice (Gray *et al.* 1984: 23–4). This is apparent from the list of pronouncements, which includes topics not presently covered by UK accounting standards. ICAAT also considers FASB and AICPA pronouncements and, perhaps tellingly, audit reports are couched in terms of 'fair presentation', 'generally accepted accounting principles' and 'generally accepted auditing standards'. These signs indicate that Thai accounting *standards*, at least, are firmly within the Anglo-American tradition of accounting, in contrast to the more Franco-Germanic disposition of Thai law.

THE REGULATORY FRAMEWORK

The legal framework

Company law

The Public Companies Limited Act BE 2521 (1978) was part of the government's efforts to develop the Thai equity market. It came into force at the end of March 1979. In order to encourage share ownership, each public company must have at least 100 shareholders. Furthermore, individuals holding not more than 0.6 per cent of the total number of shares each must form a group holding at least 50 per cent of the total number of shares. The remaining shareholders cannot each hold more than 10 per cent of the total number of shares (sect. 15).

Public company names have to begin with the word '*Borisat*' (company), and end with '*Chamkat* (*Mahachon*)' (public). This can be abbreviated (rather inexplicably) to Bor Mor Jor (sect. 11(1)).

The Act does not impose significantly more legal reporting requirements on public companies compared to private companies. It requires audit of the company's balance sheet and profit and loss account (sect. 122), but no financial statement disclosures beyond those contained in Ministerial Regulation No. 2 (see 'Content of accounts', p. 212) are stipulated. However, an annual report must be produced, containing information about the company, its holdings of shares in subsidiaries and private companies, details of contracts between the company and its directors, and details of directors' holdings of shares or debentures of the company and its subsidiaries (sect. 124).

The Act also stipulates that a public company must create and maintain a legal reserve, consisting of transfers of at least 5 per cent of the annual net profit, until the reserve forms at least 25 per cent of registered capital (sect. 126). However, a company may prescribe a higher amount.

Finally, the annual report and the audited balance sheet and profit and loss account (in Thai) must be filed with the Registrar within one month of their approval at the annual general meeting. The balance sheet must be published in a national newspaper for at least one day within that period (sect. 140).

Audit and supervision of financial reporting

Although ICAAT was established in 1948, there were no legal requirements for the qualifications and experience required of company auditors until 1962. At the same time, increasing numbers of accountants were being produced by the universities and other educational institutes. Auditing was considered essential to development, perhaps chiefly because it instils the notion that accountability is part of the process of operating a business. The Auditor Act BE 2505 (1962) was thus passed in order to establish standards for the educational qualifications and background knowledge required of authorized auditors (i.e. those who could certify company accounts).

The Act set up the Board of Supervision of Auditing Practices (BSAP), which comprises representatives of the government, the universities and the profession. Each member is appointed for a two-year term, and none can serve for more than two consecutive terms.

The BSAP regulates the application for, and issue of, licences to authorized auditors, and maintains a Register of Authorised Auditors. Auditor licences are valid for five years. The BSAP may suspend a licence, though not for more than one year at a time. Licences may also be revoked, but auditors may apply to re-register after three years. The certification of accounts may only be carried out by authorized auditors, and unauthorized certification will involve imprisonment of up to one year, and/or fines of up to 10,000 *baht.*

The Board has fifteen members, of whom eight are officials from government departments and seven are certified public accountants (authorized auditors in public practice). It functions as part of the Ministry of Commerce, with a staff of about seventy-five persons. Of these, only about fifteen are trained accountants.

The Board has two main activities. The first, the setting of licensing examinations for accountants, follows directly from the Auditor Act. The other is the monitoring of annual financial statements produced by *all* Thai companies, of which there are about 50,000. It also advises universities and other educational institutes on auditing practices.

The licensing examinations are held every six months, in June and December. A candidate must have had at least a four-year university education and 2,000 hours in public practice within at least two years. The examination comprises four papers – company law, accounting, auditing, and problems of practice (which includes tax). Accounting graduates, however, need only sit for one paper, which combines company law with problems of practice. Candidates may take the examination three times, after which they are not allowed to sit it again for one year. At each sitting, about 400 individuals register, and only between six and ten pass.

The Board also monitors accounting and auditing compliance with legal and professional requirements. BSAP staff review a sample of financial statements each year. This review process is a lengthy one, involving examination of the working papers from which the financial statements are drawn up, and, should any problems arise, interviews with the company auditors and executives. It is thus probable that only a very small proportion of the accounts published each year are subject to the BSAP's scrutiny. Penalties, however, may be severe for the auditor involved. The BSAP issues warnings when it is not satisfied with the financial statements, and may suspend or even revoke the auditor's licence, depending on the seriousness of the matter involved.

Tax law

The tax year for a company is its accounting period, which must be of twelve months' duration. Corporate income tax is paid semi-annually – within two months of the end of the first half of the accounting period, and within 150 days of the accounting period end. Tax is charged on company net profits at 30 per cent for SET quoted companies and at 35 per cent for other companies and juristic partnerships. Inter-company dividends between Thai-incorporated companies are subject to a 10 per cent withholding tax, unless the recipient company is SET-quoted, and may be excluded from taxable profits. Capital gains are taxed as part of ordinary income. Net operating losses may be carried forward for five years, but may not be carried back. Group taxation is not permitted.

Branches of foreign corporations pay corporate income tax on locally earned profits only, but branch profits credited (even if not remitted) to the foreign head office are subject to an additional 20 per cent tax on the net remittance. While the Revenue Code does not explicitly allow any credit for foreign taxes in the absence of a tax treaty, in practice such credits are usually allowed.

A business tax was until recently levied on gross receipts, the rate varying between 0.1 and 50 per cent depending on the type of activity engaged in and the type and origin of the goods sold. However, this has now been replaced by a value-added tax, in the hope of increasing the effectiveness of tax collection.

Ownership restrictions and tax incentives

Decree No. 281 BE 2515 (1972), also known as the Alien Business Law, classified specified industries into three categories which included basic agricultural industries, some manufacturing industries (cement, beverages, pharmaceuticals), transportation, retailing (except machinery, equipment and tools), advertising, building construction, newspaper publishing and most professions. Such companies either had a restriction on the maximum foreign ownership allowed (49 per cent), or had to operate with restrictions on the rate of growth.

While the original conditions imposed by the Law were certainly anti-foreign, many have since been amended to encourage foreign investment, in particular those relating to land ownership, employment of foreign experts and technicians, and, very recently, restrictions on foreign exchange transactions. Foreign-owned companies are also eligible for many of the subsidies and tax incentives offered to local companies, including exemption from corporate income tax for periods between three to eight years, exemption from or reduction in import duty on imported machinery, tariff protection on raw and/or essential materials and guarantees against price controls. Even more incentives are available to companies located in investment promotion zones.

Securities law

SET was established by the Securities Exchange of Thailand (SET) Act BE 2521 (1978). It is a non-profit-making juristic person governed by a board of directors, under the overall supervision of the Minister of Finance, who is assisted by an advisory board.

SET's board consists of four persons nominated by the government (of whom not more than one can be a government official), four persons nominated by SET members, and a president who looks after the day-today running of the Exchange. The board issues regulations which must be approved both by its members and by the Minister of Finance. These pertain to the way in which member firms (which may only be securities companies) are admitted and monitored, business is transacted, and information about quoted companies is made available and monitored. The SET Act was amended in 1984, but mainly to enable companies quoted or under consideration for quotation on SET to issue new shares and debentures to the public, and to tighten control over insider trading.

The operations and trading activities of member firms and the performance of quoted companies are monitored very closely in order to control any sign of speculative trading. Member firms' activities are screened by the Member Supervision Department, while those of quoted companies are dealt with by the Listing Department and the Listed Company Supervision Department. Information concerning and/or issued by listed and authorized companies are monitored by the fifteen members of staff of the Listed Company Supervision Department, most of whom are accountants, who ensure that all SET rules and regulations regarding information disclosure are strictly observed and that reports are submitted as required. In addition, they screen a sample of the published accounts of quoted companies. This sample is based on their knowledge of companies which are experiencing operating difficulties, as well as the reputation of the auditors of the companies.

SET-quoted companies may only be audited by approved auditors, who are authorized auditors included in the SET Register of Approved Auditors. There are currently only about ninety such individuals. Any observation of infringements of regulations will result in the issue of an oral or written warning to the company and its auditor. More serious cases would lead to the company being de-listed, and the auditor being removed from the Register.

The professional environment

The accountancy profession

The accountancy profession was only formally recognized in 1962, when the Auditor Act was passed. However, it has a relatively high standing in Thailand, especially as the important role of accounting and auditing in the development process has been acknowledged.

ICAAT is the only professional body of accountants and auditors in Thailand. Established in 1948, it was originally called 'The Institute of Certified Accountants of Thailand'. The name was changed in 1975 in order to reflect the two main occupations of its members.

The Institute's objectives, set out in Article 1 of its Regulations, are to promote fellowship and to upgrade the dignity of its members; to propagate, disseminate and exchange expertise in various areas of accounting and other fields of knowledge; to upgrade the standards of the accounting profession; to aid and assist its members; and to co-operate in the upgrading of public welfare (though specifically not in relation to politics). It is governed by a board consisting of a maximum of twenty-one members, elected for two-year terms. Although the Institute has been in existence for forty years, it still does not have a permanent office or full-time staff. This is due primarily to lack of funds. The offices of the Institute have been relocated several times, usually for the sake of convenience for the board's operations. Its present address is that of the new Ministry of Finance complex in Bangkok.

Membership of ICAAT is open to those who possess either a degree in accountancy or some other diploma or certificate which the Institute recognizes as being equal in status to a bachelor degree in accountancy; or a BSAP licence to practise as an auditor in Thailand (which is only available to university-educated accountants).

The Institute presently has about 900 members, who work in both the public and private sectors. About 50 per cent are authorized auditors licensed by the BSAP. This group is only a minority of the 1,500 authorized auditors in public practice, and an even smaller proportion of the total of about 2,800 authorized auditors in Thailand. This is because membership of ICAAT is not a requirement for practice in Thailand. The lack of incentive for qualified persons to join ICAAT, or remain members, is reflected in the remarkably low membership fees (current membership registration fee is 50 *baht*, and annual fees are 100 *baht*), which compound the Institute's funding problems.

Accountancy education consists of a four-year university education, or diploma and certificate courses at vocational schools, technical schools and private colleges. The curricula are more or less interdisciplinary, depending upon the institution. University courses may include up to 30 per cent of 'general education' courses, while the other establishments put more emphasis on the 'procedural aspects of accounting education' (Indaravijaya 1981: 301).

Accounting standard-setting

ICAAT has six sub-committees, dealing with accounting, auditing, ethics, member relations, professional development and management accounting. The first two of these are the largest, with about eighteen members each. The members of the Accounting sub-committee are drawn from the Institute itself, from practice, from academia and from the Ministry of Finance.

The Accounting sub-committee formulates proposals for new standards, and undertakes research into the technical aspects surrounding the topic. First drafts are exposed to ICAAT members and interested parties through seminars and hearings. Questionnaires are also sent to selected individuals in order to elicit more comprehensive responses. An executive committee collates all the amendments or additions suggested in the course of the exposure process, and redrafts the standard. It is then sent to the ICAAT board for approval. Once approved, it is forwarded to the BSAP for official agreement. This is necessary since it is the board which is responsible for monitoring compliance with the standard.

The standard-setting process in Thailand follows that of most other countries in which accounting standards are formulated by professional bodies. The current situation, where there are a very large number of exposure drafts in relation to adopted standards, is somewhat similar to that of the Netherlands. However, it is probably due as much to a lack of resources of finance and manpower, in both setting and enforcing standards, as to a cautious and conservative approach to standard-setting.

Compliance with SFASs is required by both the BSAP and SET. Penalties for non-compliance have been described above. ICAAT drafts are also not without any authority, representing as they do the opinion of the professional accounting body on various important financial reporting issues. Warnings are issued by the BSAP to companies which do not comply with the requirements of the drafts.

GENERALLY ACCEPTED ACCOUNTING PRINCIPLES

The baseline for disclosure in the annual accounts is set by Ministerial Regulation No. 2, which applies to the various types of enterprises listed in Table 6.1. These requirements are supplemented by the Public Companies Act, SET regulation, and ICAAT pronouncements. The enterprises which face the most onerous disclosure requirements are thus the public companies which are SET-listed. SET requires these companies to disclose

Table 6.1 Enterprises specified in Ministerial Regulation No. 2

List 1	Registered partnerships
List 2	Companies engaged in commercial banking
List 3	Companies engaged in insurance
List 4	Companies engaged in the *crédit foncier* business
List 5	Companies engaged in financing
List 6	Companies engaged in the securities business
List 7	Companies engaged in financing and the securities business
List 8	Companies engaged in warehousing
List 9	Companies engaged in any business not specified above
List 10	Branches of foreign banks
List 11	Branches of foreign insurance companies
List 12	Juristic persons established under foreign law engaged in any other business

information about their financial status and operational achievements in accordance with the Regulation and ICAAT standards, and where no ICAAT pronouncements exist, companies must follow the methods prescribed by the IASs and the AICPA, in that order.

General requirements

Until 1979, when ICAAT adopted the first five SFASs, there was no explicit enunciation of the fundamental accounting assumptions underlying the preparation of Thai financial statements. These are now contained in SFAS 1: the going concern and accrual concepts, consistency in the application of accounting principles, and adequate disclosure. The last assumption is defined in relation to the objective of financial reporting, which is to 'present *fairly* the financial position, changes in financial position and results of operations in accordance with *generally accepted accounting principles*' (SFAS 2, emphasis added).

The selection and application of accounting policies are to be governed by considerations of prudence, substance over form and materiality, and non-compliance with any of the basic assumptions must be disclosed (SFAS 1). Accounting policies selected must be explicitly disclosed (SFAS 2).

Formats are not prescribed by law, SET or ICAAT, and the financial statements may be presented in vertical or horizontal form. Regulation No. 2 sets out two types of balance sheets. The first distinguishes between current assets and liabilities and other assets and liabilities (Lists 1, 3, 9, 11 and 12), while the second does not. There are also two types of profit and loss accounts. The first applies only to insurance companies (Lists 3 and 11), and the other encompasses all other enterprises.

SET requires the provision of comparatives for all figures shown in the financial statements.

Content of accounts

Fixed assets

Regulation No. 2 requires separate disclosure of property, plant and equipment by all types of enterprises. Occupancy costs, or costs of maintaining premises, must be shown in the profit and loss account. For tax purposes, the lower of accounting and established tax depreciation rates (5 per cent for durable buildings, 100 per cent for temporary buildings and 20 per cent for other types of property) is allowed in the computation of taxable net profit.

SET regulations require the notes on the accounts to contain details of any restrictions with respect to the ownership or use of property. Disclosure is also required where obligations for the purchase of factories or machinery which involve substantial sums of capital exist, and where assets have been deposited as loan collateral.

There was no specific ICAAT pronouncement on accounting for fixed assets until 1989, when SFASs 9 and 10 were adopted. These contain requirements which are in line with the relevant IASs on accounting for depreciation and property, plant and equipment. Disclosure must be made of the valuation basis of fixed assets, the method used for computing depreciation, and the estimated useful lives of assets or depreciation rates used. SFAS 15, adopted in January 1990, allows for the capitalization of interest costs.

Loans, leases and hire purchase agreements

Regulation No. 2 requires all companies to disclose the amounts of bank overdrafts and loans separately, and enterprises included in Lists 1, 3, 9, 11 and 12 must also indicate the current portion of their long-term debt. Interest and discounts paid on borrowed money must be disclosed in the profit and loss account. Loans made to or from directors and employees must also be disclosed by all enterprises, except banks, finance companies and securities companies (Lists 3, 7 and 10).

SET-listed companies must include details of long-term contracts in the notes, together with the terms and conditions of long-term loans.

SFAS 2 requires the disclosure of the accounting policy used for leases. SFAS 7, adopted in 1987, deals with disclosure requirements for short-term leases, while Exposure Draft (ED) 31 states that leases which transfer substantially all the benefits and risks of ownership may be either capitalized or treated as a sales-type lease by the lessee. Disclosure is required of future commitments and payments expensed.

Intangible assets

For tax purposes, intangibles such as copyrights and licences must be written off over the shorter of useful life and ten years. There are no SET requirements for this type of item, but SFAS 2 requires that the costs of such assets be amortized, and the accounting policy disclosed. SFAS 14, on R&D expenditure, was adopted at the beginning of 1990 and essentially contains the same requirements as the IAS on this subject.

Stocks

Surprisingly, the only accounting pronouncement on stocks is ED 6, which stipulates that stocks must be valued at the lower of cost or market value. This concurs with what is allowed for tax purposes. Cost must include fixed as well as variable production overheads, while market value should be the lower of current replacement cost and net realizable value. Various valuation methods – FIFO, weighted average, LIFO and base stock – are allowed.

Disclosure is required of the principal categories of stocks, the valuation basis and the valuation method.

Pension costs

Regulation No. 2 requires separate disclosure of provident and pension fund liabilities on the balance sheet, and the cost of employee benefits (salaries, wages and other benefits) in the profit and loss account.

SFAS 2 requires disclosure of the accounting policy for pension scheme liabilities, together with the charge made against the profit and loss account for such liabilities. ED 10 also requires that the costs of funding pension schemes be systematically charged against income.

Taxation

Regulation No. 2 requires the separate disclosure in the profit and loss account of all enterprises of the amounts charged for taxes, duties and income tax. ED 18 requires a provision for deferred taxation, using either the deferral or liability methods, with either partial or comprehensive allocation. Deferred tax assets should not be recorded unless there is reasonable expectation of realization.

Group accounts

There are no legal requirements for group accounts. A SET-listed company is required to produce consolidated accounts when it owns, directly or indirectly, more than 50 per cent of the voting shares of another company. If no consolidation is produced, the company must explain why this is so, and attach the financial statements of the subsidiary companies to its own statements.

ED 22 defines a subsidiary as a company in which more than half of the voting shares are owned by the investing company. Consolidation of such subsidiaries is not required if control is temporary or impaired, or if the businesses of the holding and subsidiary companies are very dissimilar.

Uniform accounting policies must be used in the preparation of accounts used in the group consolidation. The accounts of subsidiaries should be consolidated in full, and inter-company transactions and balances eliminated.

Disclosure is required of the consolidation policy, the reasons for non-consolidation of any subsidiary, and the cost of investment in such non-consolidated subsidiaries.

Per ED 22, *associated* companies are defined in terms of 'significant control', which is generally interpreted as a shareholding of between 20 and

50 per cent of *voting* stock. SET regulations define *affiliated* companies as those in which between 20 and 50 per cent of the *registered* capital is held. These should be accounted for using the equity method.

Foreign exchange translation

ED 13 deals with the translation of both transactions and subsidiary accounts denominated in foreign currencies. The former should be translated at the rate ruling at the time of the transactions, with year-end balances re-translated at the year-end rate. Differences on re-translation must be charged to the profit and loss account, but may be deferred under certain circumstances.

The accounts of subsidiaries must be translated using the current rate method. The accounting method used, and the treatment of exchange differences, must be disclosed.

Funds statements

All SET-quoted companies are required to produce funds statements as part of the annual report. However, such statements need not be audited.

ED 23 allows various formats for the funds statements – sources of funds equal to applications, or changes in financial position in terms of cash or working capital.

EPS

Regulation No. 2 requires that the EPS for all companies be shown in the same way: EPS before extraordinary item; extraordinary item per share; and net profit per share. EPS does not have to reflect the effect of any potential share dilution, unless the company is a public company. The Public Companies Act requires the disclosure of a fully diluted EPS. All SET-quoted companies must disclose fully diluted EPS, even if they are not public companies.

SFAS 2 requires disclosure of the basis of computation of EPS. SFAS 5 indicates how companies may compute basic as well as fully diluted EPS figures. The latter is defined as the maximum potential dilution of the basic EPS if there is conversion or exercise of rights of all issued securities equivalent to common stocks. Companies may use other methods to calculate their EPS, but only *in addition* to the methods set out in SFAS 5. Where such different methods are used, all EPS figures calculated must be shown.

Other disclosures

Besides the specific disclosure requirements cited above, Regulation No. 2

also requires all enterprises to make separate balance sheet disclosure of cash in hand and at bank, and short-term investments. Investments in securities must be classified into government or government-guaranteed securities, securities of listed or authorized companies and other types of securities. Any bad debt allowance must be shown, except by domestic and foreign banks and finance and securities companies which are allowed to disclose net loans receivable.

Equity, whether provided by shareholders, partners or a head office, must always be analysed into authorized, issued and paid-up capital, share premium and appropriated and unappropriated retained earnings. Appropriated earnings must be further classified into legal and other reserves. Domestic banks are required to produce a statement of changes in shareholders' interest during the year, showing the opening balance, additions or reductions, and closing balance for each category.

In the profit and loss account, other common disclosure requirements are of interest and discounts received, interest and dividends received on investments, bad debt expense, and expense for fees and services.

Other disclosures required of SET companies which must be made in the notes on the accounts are obligations to maintain a revolving capital ratio or shareholder ratio; restrictions on dividend payments; any obligations to reduce long-term loans; details of directors' loans and any other changes during the year; and any obligations which affect shareholders' benefits.

Other reports

Annual report

The Public Companies Act requires the production of an annual or directors' report, which need not be audited. Information to be disclosed in the report consists of the name, location of head office and category of business of the company, and the number and types of all its shares. The report must also include the number and types of shares of subsidiaries held by the company, and the same information about private or other companies in which the company holds at least 10 per cent of the total number of shares. Details of contracts involving directors; any agreement by which any director receives debentures, shares or other interests in the company; the number of shares and debentures held by the company's directors, either in the company or in its subsidiaries; and changes in such holdings during the accounting period, must all be disclosed.

SET-quoted companies are required to produce annual reports consisting of the full financial statements, certified by an approved auditor, the Chairman's Statement, and information about the company. The minimum information to be included comprises the name of the company and the address of its headquarters, information about its activities and executive directors, a brief analytical report of its operational results and any changes, comparative statistical data for at least the past five years, and information about group companies.

Quarterly reports

Quoted companies must submit quarterly statements to SET within forty-five days of the end of each quarter, consisting of the profit and loss account and balance sheet, with disclosures as prescribed by Regulation No. 2. The statements must be certified by an approved auditor.

Audit and publication

The law requires only that the balance sheet and profit and loss account need be audited. These statements, together with the directors' report, must be filed with the Registrar of Companies within one month of approval by the shareholders at the annual general meeting. During this one-month period, the balance sheet must also be published in a national newspaper for at least one day.

Quoted companies are required to publish their annual accounts and submit them to the annual meeting of shareholders within three months of the end of their financial year. These accounts must be certified by approved auditors.

The Thai auditors' report is worded in the same way as US reports. However, Thai authorized auditors sign the reports in a variety of ways: with their personal names and/or the names of their firms, sometimes giving their registration numbers (i.e. from the BSAP Register of Authorized Auditors) and describing themselves as certified public accountants or chartered accountants.

FINANCIAL ANALYSIS

The previous section outlined financial accounting and reporting requirements prescribed by various internal Thai sources. However, in common with most other countries, actual reporting practice in Thailand does not conform completely with these requirements. This is immediately obvious by simply looking at the size of published annual reports, which are, by any standards, fairly slender volumes, even when containing both Thai- and English-language versions of the statements, notes, reports and various statistics.

The following comments on Thai practice are based on a study of financial information disclosure and accounting measurement methods of nineteen Thai listed companies in the commerce, service and industrial sectors (Tay 1989). Extracts from the financial statements (balance sheet, profit and loss account, funds statement and notes) of The Siam Cement

Company Ltd., a SET-listed limited liability company not engaged in banking, insurance, financing, securities, *crédit foncier* or warehousing activities – basically a 'typical' industrial/commercial company included in List 9 – are included as Appendix A.

General

Thai accounts incorporate a large amount of detail on the face of the balance sheet and profit and loss account. Very few notes on the accounts are provided, and the information contained in them is not comprehensive.

Fixed assets

Fixed assets are usually stated at historical cost. Very little revaluation of assets has taken place. Depreciation is calculated mainly by the straight-line method, but other methods (unit-of-production, sum-of-digits, declining balance) are also used. The depreciation expense for the period is usually disclosed, together with details of important commitments for additions to property.

Loans, leases and hire purchase agreements

The bulk of loans shown on company balance sheets are short-term bank loans, and not all the required detail – interest rates and other terms – are disclosed in the notes. There is *very* little information about leased assets, and costs are generally expensed rather than capitalized.

Intangible assets

Intangible assets are most usually capitalized. Little is spent on research and development, and expenditure is mainly charged to income.

Stocks

A variety of valuation bases and methods are used for stocks, but absorption costing is generally followed. FIFO and weighted average values are most popular, and replacement cost is used to represent market value.

Pension costs

The profit and loss charge for the year and the accounting policy are generally disclosed, but there is little disclosure of how the pension scheme liability is valued. Costs are usually charged when paid.

Taxation

Disclosure of the basis of the tax charge shown in the accounts is very poor. There is some provision for deferred taxation, mostly using the deferral method with comprehensive allocation. However, the majority practice is to charge to the profit and loss account the amount of tax immediately payable.

Group accounts

Very few consolidated accounts are produced, although the number is increasing, especially among SET-listed companies. These take the form of balance sheets and profit and loss accounts for both the holding company and the group, and are based on acquisition rather than merger accounting. Associated companies and non-consolidated subsidiaries are usually valued at cost.

There is little disclosure of definitions of subsidiary and associated/affiliated companies, and reasons for the exclusion of subsidiaries from the consolidated accounts are usually not given.

Goodwill is defined as the excess of cost over the fair value of assets required, and is amortized against income.

Foreign exchange translation

The dearth of consolidated accounts means that translation usually relates to transactions. These are accounted for in accordance with ED 13, although there is little disclosure of the method used, and the accounting treatment of exchange differences.

Funds statements

The most commonly used format for funds statements relates changes in financial position to changes in working capital. The information shown in the statement often cannot be connected to information from the balance sheet, profit and loss account or the notes.

EPS

There is uniformity in the presentation of EPS on the face of the profit and loss account and in the definition of earnings used in the computation. The number of shares is calculated as at the year-end.

SUMMARY

The legal reporting requirements imposed on all Thai public limited liability companies are clearly specified by the law, but are fairly basic. Listed companies are subject to further disclosure requirements imposed by the Securities Exchange of Thailand, including the preparation of consolidated accounts or the provision of information about subsidiary companies. However, the policy has been to include the bulk of financial reporting requirements in the accounting standards developed by ICAAT, the professional accountancy body. A large number of such standards have been exposed, but only fifteen have been adopted as firm standards, with which compliance is required by the monitoring authorities. Of these, the latest nine standards have only been in operation for the last four years at the most.

The main factor which has influenced financial reporting in Thailand has been the development of the equity market. This has been an important part of the government's overall economic strategy, and disclosure of accounting information by listed companies appears to be closely monitored. However, the phenomenal growth in the equity market has not been matched by improvements in the amount and quality of financial information made available through companies' published annual reports. Though there has been progress in recent years, these changes have occurred relatively slowly. The result is that Thai reporting practice lags behind that of Malaysia and Singapore (which represent obvious benchmarks for comparison) in many respects, particularly in the preparation of group accounts.

These reporting deficiencies may not be considered very important while the Thai economy continues to perform strongly in all sectors. They have certainly not acted as a visible brake on the growth of foreign investment in SET securities over the past few years. However, they cannot remain unchanged in the context of the long-term development of the Thai equity market as a major capital market in the Asia–Pacific region.

APPENDIX A

Extracts from the accounts of Siam Cement

BALANCE SHEETS

December 31, 1990 and 1989

Assets	In Baht 1990	1989
Current Assets		
Cash in hand and at banks	**197,473,090**	104,059,417
Accounts and notes receivable-trade (net of allowance for doubtful accounts of Baht 13,000,000 in 1990 and Baht 17,600,000 in 1989)		
Accounts receivable-net	**647,714,172**	463,177,351
Notes receivable-net	**625,875,240**	555,331,209
Receivables from and loans to subsidiaries, associated and other companies-net (Note 3)	**3,691,089,998**	1,907,342,337
Inventories		
Finished goods	**327,722,474**	264,700,347
Goods in process	**127,729,223**	112,708,852
Raw materials	**212,972,039**	133,381,816
Spare parts	**416,807,409**	351,291,866
Stores, supplies and others	**574,632,156**	429,960,959
Raw materials and spare parts in transit	**359,687,245**	145,135,668
Other current assets	**126,782,783**	48,381,842
Total Current Assets	**7,308,485,829**	4,515,471,664
Investments in Subsidiaries, Associated and Other Companies-Net (Note 3)	**6,145,211,426**	4,237,923,732
Property, Plant and Equipment-Net (Note 4)	**12,790,786,090**	8,784,236,802
Other Assets (Note 5)	**563,787,674**	466,112,557
Total Assets	**26,808,271,019**	18,003,744,755

Liabilities and Shareholders' Equity	In Baht	
	1990	1989
Current Liabilities		
Bank overdrafts and loans from banks (Note 6)	**1,806,604,383**	477,025,067
Notes payable	**301,360,000**	302,960,000
Accounts payable-trade	**521,052,342**	333,103,988
Current portion of long-term debt (Note 8)	**820,245,632**	635,680,832
Accrued expenses	**767,022,869**	665,895,884
Income tax payable	**831,189,510**	593,722,988
Other current liabilities	**463,019,740**	256,046,268
Total Current Liabilities	**5,510,494,476**	3,264,435,027
Provident Fund (Note 7)	**1,036,751,841**	895,142,825
Long-Term Debt-Net of portion shown under current liabilities (Note 8)	**9,761,422,071**	6,029,910,136
Other Liability	**106,761,888**	87,696,230
Total Liabilities	**16,415,430,276**	10,277,184,218
Shareholders' Equity		
Share capital-common stock Baht 10 par value in 1990 and Baht 100 in 1989		
Authorized share capital-120,000,000 shares in 1990 and 12,000,000 shares in 1989		
Issued and fully paid-up share capital-120,000,000 shares in 1990 and 12,000,000 shares in 1989 (Note 9)	**1,200,000,000**	1,200,000,000
Premium on share capital (Note 10)	**46,597,200**	46,597,200
Retained earnings		
Appropriated		
Legal reserve (Note 10)	**73,402,800**	73,402,800
General reserve	**2,100,000,000**	2,100,000,000
Unappropriated	**6,972,840,743**	4,306,560,537
Total Shareholders' Equity	**10,392,840,743**	7,726,560,537
Total Liabilities and Shareholders' Equity	**26,808,271,019**	18,003,744,755

For and on behalf of the Board of Directors

Sanya Dharmasakti	Paron Israsena
Chairman	**Director and President**

STATEMENTS OF INCOME

For the years ended December 31,1990 and 1989

	In Baht	
	1990	1989
Revenues		
Net sales	**28,999,149,009**	22,413,424,029
Other income	**2,057,593,407**	1,086,706,816
Total Revenues	**31,056,742,416**	23,500,130,845
Costs and Expenses		
Cost of sales	**21,159,080,543**	15,777,869,944
Selling and administrative expenses	**2,654,494,986**	2,298,108,181
Interest expense and financial charges	**853,644,569**	601,358,780
Income tax (Note 11)	**1,683,242,112**	1,278,128,435
Total Costs and Expenses	**26,350,462,210**	19,955,465,340
Net Income	**4,706,280,206**	3,544,665,505
Earnings per Share	**39.22**	* 29.54

* Adjusted for stock split-up

STATEMENTS OF UNAPPROPRIATED RETAINED EARNINGS

For the years ended December 31,1990 and 1989

	In Baht	
	1990	1989
Unappropriated Retained Earnings at Beginning of Year	**4,306,560,537**	2,201,895,032
Net income	**4,706,280,206**	3,544,665,505
Dividends (Note 12)	**(2,040,000,000)**	(1,440,000,000)
Unappropriated Retained Earnings at End of Year	**6,972,840,743**	4,306,560,537

STATEMENTS OF CHANGES IN FINANCIAL POSITION

For the years ended December 31,1990 and 1989

	In Baht	
	1990	1989
Working Capital was Provided From:		
Operations		
Net income	**4,706,280,206**	3,544,665,505
Add (Deduct) items not involving working capital		
Depreciation and amortization	**1,671,673,717**	1,437,056,599
Company's contributions to provident fund-net	**141,609,016**	139,023,979
Loss on sales of investments	**1,035,291**	-
Deferred income tax-net	**(44,742,257)**	(57,478,069)
Gain on sales of fixed assets	**(8,448,800)**	(16,378,345)
Total Working Capital Provided from Operations	**6,467,407,173**	5,046,889,669
Increase in long-term debt	**4,551,757,567**	2,921,300,290
Proceeds from sales of investments	**123,991,772**	-
Increase in other liability	**19,065,658**	65,838,762
Proceeds from sales of fixed assets	**18,294,325**	19,784,093
Total Working Capital Provided	**11,180,516,495**	8,053,812,814
Working Capital was Used For:		
Additions to property, plant and equipment	**5,687,687,661**	2,179,407,203
Additions to investments in subsidiaries, associated and other companies	**2,032,314,757**	689,174,003
Dividends	**2,040,000,000**	1,440,000,000
Long-term debt classified as current	**820,245,632**	635,680,832
Increase in other assets	**53,313,729**	22,191,806
Total Working Capital Used	**10,633,561,779**	4,966,453,844
Increase In Working Capital	**546,954,716**	3,087,358,970
Changes in Working Capital		
Increase in current assets:		
Cash in hand and at banks	**93,413,673**	19,514,268
Accounts receivable-trade-net	**184,536,821**	105,894,547
Notes receivable-net	**70,544,031**	68,819,012
Receivables from and loans to subsidiaries, associated and other companies-net	**1,783,747,661**	1,907,342,337
Inventories	**582,371,038**	181,421,335
Other current assets	**78,400,941**	17,747,028
Total	**2,793,014,165**	2,300,738,527
Increase (Decrease) in current liabilities:		
Short-term borrowings	**1,327,979,316**	(320,987,355)
Accounts payable and accrued expenses	**289,075,339**	(33,816,876)
Current portion of long-term debt	**184,564,800**	(326,184,982)
Payables to and loans from subsidiaries, associated and other companies-net	-	(361,012,867)
Income tax payable	**237,466,522**	193,902,107
Other current liabilities	**206,973,472**	61,479,530
Total	**2,246,059,449**	(786,620,443)
Increase In Working Capital	**546,954,716**	3,087,358,970

AUDITORS' REPORT

The Shareholders
The Siam Cement Company Limited

We have examined the balance sheets of The Siam Cement Company Limited as at December 31,1990 and 1989, and the related statements of income, unappropriated retained earnings and changes in financial position for the years then ended. Our examinations were made in accordance with generally accepted auditing standards and, accordingly, included such tests of the accounting records and such other auditing procedures as we considered necessary in the circumstances.

In our opinion, the financial statements referred to above present fairly, on the basis described in Note 1, the financial position of The Siam Cement Company Limited at December 31,1990 and 1989, and the results of its operations and the changes in its financial position for the years then ended, in conformity with generally accepted accounting principles applied on a consistent basis.

Y na Thalang.

YUKTA NA THALANG
C.P.A. (THAILAND)
Registration No. 1

SGV-Na Thalang & Co.,Ltd.
514/1 Larnluang Road, Dusit, Bangkok, Thailand
January 31,1991

NOTES TO FINANCIAL STATEMENTS

December 31, 1990 and 1989

1. Basis for Financial Statements

The Company owns substantial portion of the capital shares of the subsidiaries. A substantial portion of the Company's business is represented by transactions with its subsidiaries and related companies and the financial statements reflect the effects of these transactions on the basis determined by the companies concerned.

Significant transactions with certain related companies during 1990 were as follows:

	In Million Baht
Purchases	9,736
Sales	3,857
Service fees and others	694
Interest income-net	454

2. Significant Accounting Policies

Allowance for Doubtful Accounts

The Company provides allowance for doubtful accounts equal to the estimated collection losses that may be incurred in the collection of all receivables. The estimated losses are based on historical collection experience coupled with a review of the current status of existing receivables.

Investments in Shares

The Company accounts for its investments in shares by the cost method. Gains or losses are taken up in the accounts when the investments are disposed of.

Inventory Valuation

It is the policy of the Company to value its inventories as follows:

Finished goods - at standard cost which approximates current production cost or market, whichever is lower.

Goods in process - at standard cost which includes raw materials and variable labor and manufacturing overhead costs.

Raw materials, spare parts, stores, supplies and others-at average cost, except for some major raw materials and certain fast moving stores and supplies which are at first-in, first-out cost.

Depreciation and Amortization

Depreciation of property, plant and equipment has been computed by the straight-line method at the rates ranging from 5% to 20% which represent the maximum rates allowed by the Revenue Code or the rates which approximate the economic useful lives of the assets.

Deferred charges are amortized by the straight-line method over periods of five (5) to twenty (20) years.

Income Tax

The Company provides for deferred income tax resulting from timing differences in reporting expenses for financial reporting purposes compared to income tax reporting purposes. The deferred income tax is amortized as the timing differences later reverse.

Foreign Currency Transactions

All foreign currency transactions are recorded at the rates prevailing on the dates of the transactions. Liabilities denominated in foreign currencies at year-end are translated to Baht at the prevailing rate at that date.

Earnings per Share

Earnings per share is determined by dividing the net income by the number of shares outstanding at the end of the year.

APPENDIX B

Major economic indicators

	1984	*1985*	*1986*	*1987*	*1988**
1 *Gross Domestic Product (GDP)*					
Current prices	973	1,014	1,100	1,223	1,466
Constant prices (1985)	984	1,014	1,062	1,101	n/a
Percentage real change	7.1	3.5	4.7	3.7	n/a
(Thai *baht* billion)					
2 *GDP per head*					
Percentage real change	5.1	5.0	(0.4)	1.8	n/a
3 *Exchange rate*					
Thai *baht* to US$ (year-end)	23.53	27.19	26.36	25.80	25.35
4 *Trend in prices*					
Consumer prices	189.5	194.1	197.7	202.6	210.4
Producer prices	169.1	169.0	168.4	178.4	193.0
(1976 = 100)					
5 *Balance of payments*					
Net exports/(imports)	(1,898)	(1,332)	388	(424)	n/a
Current account	(2,109)	(1,537)	247	(365)	n/a
Overall balance	439	216	952	1,279	n/a
(US$ million)					
6 *Gross external debt*					
Percentage of Gross National Product	36.8	47.8	45.3	44.2	n/a

Source: Economist Intelligence Unit, *Country Profile: Thailand and Burma, Annual Survey 1989–90.*

Notes: *Estimated; n/a = not available.

APPENDIX C

Major trading partners

	Percentage
Exports	
USA	20
Japan	16
Singapore	8
Netherlands	5
West Germany	5
Hong Kong	4
Imports	
Japan	29
USA	14
Singapore	7
West Germany	5
Taiwan	4
Total value	
Japan	23
USA	16
Singapore	8
West Germany	4

Source: Economist Intelligence Unit, *Country Profile: Thailand and Burma, Annual Survey 1989–90.*

Note: Apart from the countries listed above, other important trading partners are the United Kingdom, the People's Republic of China, Malaysia, France, Saudi Arabia and South Korea.

APPENDIX D

Technical pronouncements issued by ICAAT

1 *Statements on Financial Accounting Standards (SFAS)*

		Adopted
SFAS 1	Fundamental Accounting Assumptions	1/9/79
SFAS 2	Disclosures of Accounting Policies	1/9/79
SFAS 3	Extraordinary Items	1/9/79
SFAS 4	Accounting Changes	1/9/79
SFAS 5	Earnings per Share	1/9/79
SFAS 6	Method of Income Recognition	1/1/86
SFAS 7	Accounting for Leases	28/2/87
SFAS 8	Accounting for Construction Contracts	1/1/88
SFAS 9	Accounting for Property, Plant and Equipment	1/1/89
SFAS 10	Accounting for Depreciation	1/7/89
SFAS 11	Accounting for Doubtful Receivables	1/7/89
SFAS 12	Accounting for Marketable Securities	1/7/89
SFAS 13	Disclosure of Related Parties	1/7/89
SFAS 14	Accounting for Research and Development	1/1/90
SFAS 15	Capitalization of Interest Cost	1/1/90

2 *Exposure Drafts*

No. 6	Inventory Accounting
No. 9	Accounting for Development State Enterprises
No. 10	Accounting for Provident Funds and Retirement Benefits
No. 11	Contingencies and Events Occurring after the Balance Sheet Date
No. 12	Accounting for the Appropriation of Income
No. 13	Accounting for the Translation of Foreign Currency
No. 14	Interim Financial Statements
No. 17	Restructuring for Troubled Debt
No. 18	Accounting for Taxes on Income
No. 22	Consolidated Financial Statements
No. 23	Statement of Changes in Financial Position
No. 24	Liabilities Reacquisition Prior to Maturity
No. 25	Classification of Short-term Liabilities Expected to be Converted to Long Term
No. 26	Accounting for Non-monetary Items
No. 27	Current Assets and Current Liabilities
No. 28	Presentation of Effects of Changing Prices in Financial Reporting
No. 30	Accounting for Government Grants and Subsidies
No. 31	Accounting for Long-term Leasing
No. 32	Accounting for Disclosure of Long-term Contingent Liabilities
No. 33	Accounting for Product Financing Arrangements
No. 34	Statement of Cash Flow

BIBLIOGRAPHY

Much of the information in this chapter was derived from personal interviews with officials of the Securities Exchange of Thailand, the Board of Supervision of Auditing Practices and the Institute of Certified Accountants and Auditors of Thailand. Other more immediately accessible sources are as follows:

Economist Intelligence Unit, *Country Profile: Thailand and Burma, Annual Survey 1989–90.*

Gray, S.J., Campbell, S.G. and Shaw, J.C. (1984) *International Financial Reporting: A Comparative Survey of Accounting Requirements and Practices in 30 Countries*, Basingstoke: Macmillan.

Price Waterhouse (1989) *Corporate Taxes, Individual Taxes, Foreign Exchange, Investment Regulations: An Asia Pacific Region Summary*, London: Price Waterhouse.

SGV (1984) *Comparative Accounting Practices in ASEAN*, London: Sycip, Gorres, Velayo and Co.

Securities Exchange of Thailand, *Securities Market in Thailand* (an occasional publication).

Regulation

Auditor Act BE 2505 (1962).

Ministerial Regulation No. 2 BE 2519 (1976).

Ministerial Regulation No. 5 (1986) issued under the Limited Public Company Act 1978.

Regulations Governing the Securities Exchange of Thailand.

Other references

Indaravijaya, S. (1981) 'Accounting education in Thailand', in A.J.H. Enthoven (ed.), *Accounting Education in Economic Development Management*, North-Holland.

Needles, B.E. (1988) 'Auditing standards in the Far East: an overview', in V.K. Zimmerman (ed.), *Recent Accounting and Economic Developments in the Far East*, Champaign, Illinois: Centre for International Education and Research in Accounting, University of Illinois.

Ninsuvannakul, P. (1988) 'The development of the accounting profession of the ASEAN countries: past, present and future', in V.K. Zimmerman (ed.), *Recent Accounting and Economic Developments in the Far East*, Center for International Education and Research in Accounting, University of Illinois.

Phutrakul, T. (1986) 'Securities markets and portfolio investment in East Asia', M.Sc. Dissertation, University of Exeter.

Sareewiwatthana, P. and Malone, R.P. (1985) 'Market behaviour and the capital asset pricing model in the Securities Exchange of Thailand: an empirical application', *Journal of Business Finance and Accounting* 12(3), 439–52.

Tay, J.S.W. (1989) 'Financial reporting requirements and practice in Thailand', in 'Corporate financial reporting: regulatory systems and comparability', Ph.D. Thesis, University of Exeter.

Whittle, J.D. (1980) 'The accountancy profession in Thailand', *Accountants' Magazine*, March, pp. 112–13.

7 Malaysia

J.S.W. Tay

INTRODUCTION

Malaysia, a multi-racial Muslim country, is simultaneously a member of the British Commonwealth, the Association of South-East Asian Nations (ASEAN), and the Organization of Islamic Countries. There are two physical parts to the country, separated by over 500 miles of the South China Sea: West Malaysia, formerly known as Malaya or the Malay Peninsula, is part of the South-East Asian land mass; East Malaysia comprises Sarawak and Sabah on the island of Borneo.

Malaysia has one of the highest living standards among developing countries in Asia, but its past economic performance has been adversely affected to some degree by the political and social implications of its New Economic Policy (NEP). This development plan, drawn up in 1970, sought to unite the country's various ethnic factions through the eradication of poverty and the restructuring of a society which traditionally identified different races with specific economic functions – a legacy of Malaysia's colonial past. The emphasis on social objectives has meant that the Malaysian economy has been consistently overshadowed by that of its fellow ASEAN members, Singapore and, more recently, Thailand.

THE BUSINESS ENVIRONMENT

A historical perspective

The Malay Peninsula, in common with the rest of South-East Asia, has been likened to a 'frontier' area between India and China. It was subject to influences from both these major civilizations, as well as pressures from Thailand to the north and from Indonesia to the south. As a result, indigenous institutions and culture were never highly developed.

The sources of foreign influences widened when the Portuguese arrived in the early sixteenth century, seeking to participate in the spice trade carried on between Europe and South-East Asia via India. This was also the objective of the Dutch in the seventeenth century. Ironically, Malaya was only of incidental interest to the British, whose presence was to have the strongest long-term effects on the country.

By the mid-eighteenth century, the British had established themselves in India, and were trading with China. Malaya became important to them basically because the India–China sea-route passed through South-East Asia, because a naval base in the region could command the Bay of Bengal, and because the Peninsula had produce – tin, marine and jungle products – which could be used in the China trade.

In 1786, the first British base was established in Penang, an island off the west coast of the northern state of Perak. Within forty years, two other 'Straits Settlements', Malacca and Singapore, had been acquired. By the end of the nineteenth century, economic and political interests had combined to extend British influence throughout the Peninsula. World demand for tin and rubber (introduced from South America by the British), made Malaya of real importance to Great Britain. The political consequence of this was the formation of a federation of four Malay states, each with a British Resident and Federal Council, and the appointment of British advisers to each of the unfederated Malay states. The booming economy also attracted substantial numbers of Chinese and Indian labourers to the mines and plantations, and unlike their trading predecessors, this second wave of foreigners usually settled in the Peninsula.

Decolonization was also due to economic and political factors. Lower rubber prices after the Second World War coincided with higher costs of colonial administration, and local nationalism increased, at least partly as a result of the Japanese Occupation during the war. These factors combined to convince the British government to grant Malaya its independence in 1957. Malaysia was formed in 1963 as a means whereby Great Britain could also decolonize Sabah, Sarawak and Singapore. The first two of these countries had relatively undeveloped economies and administrative systems, and did not appear viable as independent national entities. Singapore had an overwhelmingly Chinese population, and appeared most susceptible to Communist influence from China. The new enlarged federation was formed in the hope that it would bring some measure of economic and political stability to South-East Asia.

The Malaysian economy

Malacca was already a busy entrepôt port when the Portuguese captured it in 1511, indicating the traditional importance of trade in the Malaysian economy. Presently, exports form about 50–60 per cent of the gross national product. The biggest foreign exchange earners are manufactures (machinery and transport equipment, electronic components, textiles), commodities (crude petroleum, tin, rubber, palm oil) and tourism.

Agriculture was until recently the largest sector of the economy, and the country is more or less self-sufficient in food. Rubber and palm oil were both introduced to the country by the British in the twentieth century, and, together with tin, have been traditional commodity exports. Timber is also an important export of East Malaysia. However, after the Second World War, efforts were made to diversify the economy and to promote industrialization in order to stabilize export earnings and provide employment for the country's growing population.

These efforts have been increasingly successful. Manufacturing has developed at a rapid pace, especially in export-oriented industries – for example, Malaysia is now the world's third largest manufacturer of electronic components after the US and Japan. It became the largest sector in 1987 – 22.4 per cent, compared with 21.5 per cent for agriculture. But the economy is still significantly dependent on commodity exports – low commodity prices in 1985 led to a recession, just as higher commodity prices from 1987 started a remarkable turnaround which was augmented by growth in manufactured exports. Gross domestic product (GDP) grew by 8.7 per cent in 1988 and by 8.5 per cent in 1989, supported by increases in private consumption and investment. The sources of such investment have been both foreign and domestic, and the rate of growth of investment has been quite spectacular. Investments approved in the first four months of 1990 were almost as large as those approved for the whole of 1989 (M$19 billion in total), reflecting Malaysia's increasing attractiveness, due at least in part to uncertainties in the Philippines and bottlenecks in Thailand. Although there are problems in the shape of inflation (forecast at 4 per cent for 1990), a skilled labour shortage combined with 7–8 per cent unemployment, relatively high costs and the possible withdrawal of trading privileges in the US market, no one is currently disputing the Malaysian government's prediction that the country will be an NIE by the turn of the century.

Company ownership and management

Malaysian companies are fairly substantial relative to other companies in the region. The Malaysian International Shipping Corporation is one of the top 500 listed companies in the world (excluding the US) in terms of earnings, the only other ASEAN company ranked being Singapore Airlines. However, the general optimism over economic growth must be tempered by the public acknowledgement of a dearth of local managers with business skills and risk-taking habits. This has been attributed to two, possibly related, causes: the size of the public sector, and the objectives of the NEP, which resulted in the creation of a favoured *bumiputra* (indigenous racial group) business class. While the government has declared its intention to privatize as many of its activities and agencies as possible, radical changes in the NEP are unlikely to be as forthcoming.

The NEP has been one of Malaysia's most contentious policies, accused of institutionalizing racial discrimination. The planned redistribution of wealth and opportunities was intended to ensure that, by 1990, Malays and other indigenous groups would own and manage at least 30 per cent of the country's total commercial and industrial activities. Its practical effect has been to discourage or even prevent the immigrant groups within the country, which have traditionally been more enterprising, from engaging in useful economic activities. And although foreigners are encouraged to set up joint ventures with residents which utilize local resources or transfer high-level technology, foreign investment is closely monitored to ensure that overall foreign ownership of the economy is no more than 30 per cent.

Actual ownership of the economy as at the end of 1989 was estimated at 23 per cent held by Malays, 35 per cent by non-Malays (mainly Chinese), 24 per cent by foreigners and 18 per cent by nominees (race of beneficial owners unknown). However, political leaders have indicated that, while lowering the target for *bumiputra* ownership is politically unacceptable, neither will it be raised to reflect the actual size of the *bumiputra* group (currently slightly over 50 per cent of the total population).

The equity market

The Kuala Lumpur Stock Exchange (KLSE) is the only exchange in Malaysia. It was formed in 1960 with two trading rooms, one in Kuala Lumpur and the other in Singapore. Singapore's secession from Malaysia eventually led, in 1973, to the separate formation of the KLSE and the Stock Exchange of Singapore (SES), which have become the most active and developed exchanges in South-East Asia.

The KLSE has a main and a second board. The former lists 262 Malaysian companies and three UK-based companies; the latter has between 10–15 local companies. Market capitalization at the end of 1989 was about M$140 billion. In common with capital markets in other developing countries, trading volume on the KLSE is quite low; but there are an increasing number and amount of cash calls and new or special issues (M$3 billion was raised through the market in 1989, and M$8 billion in the first six months of 1990) and some evidence of market efficiency (Barnes 1986). Revisions in the Listing Manual and Takeover Code, together with a real-time information system, have also given the KLSE one of the most advanced regulatory frameworks in the Far East.

The increasing divergence of the KLSE and SES culminated at the beginning of 1990 with the delisting of Malaysian stocks from the SES and Singapore stocks from the KLSE. Prior to this mutual delisting, Malaysian stocks formed between 30–60 per cent of SES trading, while Singapore stocks formed only about 4 per cent of KLSE trading. The delisting has had no apparent effect on volumes traded, and in fact the level of activity on the KLSE in January increased so significantly that brokers had much-publicized problems dealing with delivery of scrip and settlement of transactions.

These problems have now been overcome by computerization, but others will inevitably accompany the KLSE's emergence from the SES's shadow, as it develops and generates a distinct international identity of its own. The prospects are promising, given the buoyant Malaysian economy and the establishment of foreign country and mutual funds worth over US$500 million targeted specifically at Malaysia. KLSE members are aware of the need to increase the level of research and investment in manpower and technology, as well as reducing their dependence on Singapore brokers for marketing of their products and information processing. Various developments are in the pipeline relating to operational and institutional arrangements which will increase investor confidence in the KLSE, as well as deal with the continued trading of 133 Malaysian stocks in Singapore's over-the-counter market.

INFLUENCES ON ACCOUNTING

Malaysia's colonial past is reflected in many ways in the current reporting environment, which is very similar, though not identical, to the UK environment. Gray *et al.* (1984: 23) reported three international influences on Malaysian financial reporting: the UK (very strong), Australia (strong) and the US (moderate). The two most important influences on financial reporting are the 1965 Companies Act and the standard-setting activities of the Malaysian Association of Certified Public Accountants (MACPA). These two sources have changed the reporting requirements imposed on Malaysian companies quite radically within the last decade, so that it is no longer true that 'the absence of adequate legal or professional disclosure standards has resulted in many unacceptable disclosure practices' (Mitchell 1981: 234–5).

The influence of the law

Malaysia is a federation with a constitutional monarchy. Its entire Constitution is based on that of Great Britain, together with substantial Australian influence in the area of company law (Walton 1986: 353). The Companies Act 1965 drew on several sources, principally the UK Companies Act 1929 and the Victoria Companies Act 1961. The latter was in turn adapted from the UK Companies Acts 1907, 1929 and 1948 (Walton 1986: 353). The Malaysian Act adopted the UK 1948 Act's preference for consolidated accounts, and the Victorian 1961 Act's more detailed disclosure requirements for the balance sheet and profit and loss account. However, it goes beyond these pieces of legislation in relation to the scope of the directors' report, with directors being required to take responsibility for asset valuation, unusual items and contingent liabilities. The law also requires the provision of a funds statement.

The financial statements (balance sheet, profit and loss account, funds statement and associated notes) must be prepared in accordance with the 'true and fair view' criterion. In addition, the director or officer responsible for the company's financial management must also provide a statutory declaration on the *correctness* of the statements. All limited liability companies are subject to a statutory audit requirement, regardless of size. The auditor must be approved by the Minister of Finance, usually on the condition that he is a member of the Malaysian Institute of Accountants (MIA) (see pp. 240–3), and has his principal or only residence in Malaysia. The auditor is required to report on the *truth and fairness* of the financial statements, and the auditor's report and financial statements must be filed together.

The influence of the profession

The Malaysian profession is regulated by the Accountants Act 1967, which set up the Malaysian Institute of Accountants (Institut Akauntan Malaysia). However, the Institute was dormant for many years, and the main influence on financial reporting practices came from the standard-setting activities of the Malaysian Association of Certified Public Accountants (Institut Akauntan Umum Malaysia – MACPA).

Before 1978, Malaysian professional accounting standards did not exist. Financial reporting practice was based on a small number of statements issued by the MACPA, together with the recommendations of the various foreign bodies of which practising Malaysian accountants were members, mainly the ICAEW and the CACA.

The MACPA became a member of the IASC in 1975. There are currently four types of financial reporting standards or statements in Malaysia – IASs issued by the IASC, which have been specifically adopted by the MACPA; and Malaysian Accounting Standards (MASs), Technical Bulletins (TBs) and Statements (MS) promulgated by the MACPA. The IASs and MASs constitute approved Malaysian accounting standards, while the other two statements may be regarded as opinions on best current practice, thus forming part of local GAAP. Appendix D summarizes these various standards and pronouncements as at July 1990.

Apart from the direct influence of accounting standards, both the MACPA and the MIA have sought to influence financial reporting practices by organizing competitions for the 'best' annual reports. The MACPA established the Malaysian Annual Corporate Reports Award in 1986, in conjunction with the Malaysian Institute of Management. The award aims to encourage higher reporting standards, and has three categories (accounting information, corporate information and graphic presentation), together with an overall award. In 1989, the MIA and the KLSE organized a National Annual Report Award as part of an effort to improve the quality and timeliness of financial reporting by listed companies. From

1990, these two separate awards have been combined as the National Annual Corporate Reports Award.

Other influences on financial reporting

The KLSE

The KLSE Listing Manual contains various regulations with which member firms and quoted companies must comply. This was revised in 1987, when a new Takeover Code was also issued. However, the only financial reporting requirement which the Manual imposes on listed companies is compliance with MACPA accounting standards and pronouncements and the Ninth Schedule of the Companies Act. As such, the KLSE's influence on financial reporting is indirect, through the implied threat of de-listing of companies which do not comply with legal and professional requirements.

The Capital Issues Committee (CIC)

The CIC is an agency of the Ministry of Finance, established to supervise the securities industry and administer the KLSE. It operates together with the Foreign Investment Committee to control public share issues, transactions involving more than M$1 million, and the racial and national composition of the ownership of Malaysian companies.

Although the CIC has been described as 'the Malaysian SEC' (Phenix 1986: 11), it does not impose additional reporting requirements on listed companies, nor does it have the direct power to delist companies. It has endorsed both IASC and MACPA standards, but its main concerns are reconstructions and transfers of assets involving foreign companies. These situations are now governed by sect. 60 of the Companies Act (which effectively legalizes merger accounting in Malaysia), although the CIC accepts methods set out in standards of the MACPA and 'any other recognized accounting body'.

Bank Negara Malaysia *(BNM)*

The BNM is the Malaysian central bank. Under sect. 169(9) of the Companies Act, it is empowered to modify or grant exceptions from the Act's requirements. Furthermore, the system of professional standards recognizes that the law can, and should, overrule professional pronouncements of accounting requirements. However, in its review and approval of financial statements of banks and finance companies, the BNM has clearly given IASs implicit recognition.

Ministry of Finance

Since March 1985, the Ministry has required that statutory bodies and corporations under its control should apply MACPA standards or recognized standards of other established accountancy bodies, or, failing that, the standards of the IASC. It does not issue any standards of its own.

THE REGULATORY FRAMEWORK

The legal framework

Company law

The 1965 Companies Act established limited companies which may be either public or private. The former must include the word *Berhad* (limited) in its name, while the latter must also include the word *Sendirian* (private). A private company is one in which share transfers are restricted by the articles of association; where there are less than fifty shareholders; and in which public offers of shares or debentures and invitations for the public to place deposits of any nature are prohibited. A public company is any company which is not private.

The financial statements which must be filed under the Act consist of the balance sheet, profit and loss account, statement of changes in financial position (funds statement) and the notes to these three documents; the directors' report; a statement signed by two directors, that in their opinion the financial statements present a *true and fair view* of the company's financial position and results for the period; and a statutory declaration by the director or officer responsible for the company's financial management on the *correctness* of the financial statements.

These documents must be presented to the shareholders within six months of the accounting period end, and filed no more than one month after approval at the Annual General Meeting. Thus there is a maximum period of seven months between the accounting period end and the filing date.

The bulk of the reporting requirements imposed by the Act are contained in the Ninth Schedule, which also contains some valuation rules. The Schedule was substantially revised in 1985, effective from 1 February 1986, to include many of the disclosures previously required only by professional standards, including the provision of the funds statement.

Tax law

The rate of income tax for companies is 35 per cent. Other taxes include a 45 per cent tax on profits from petroleum operations, a tax on real property gains ranging from 5 to 20 per cent, and a sales tax of 5–15 per cent on non-exempt goods imported into or manufactured in Malaysia. Operating losses can be offset against all other sources of income in the year of loss. They may be carried forward indefinitely, but only used against business income in subsequent years. Group taxation is not permitted.

Tax rates on branch profits are the same as on corporate profits, and no tax is withheld when profits are transferred to a foreign head office. Foreign branch income and investment income is taxed on receipt, except for income from banking and air or sea transport which is assessed on a world-wide basis. Inter-company dividends from Malaysian subsidiaries are taxable on the recipient corporation, with a credit for the 35 per cent tax paid by the subsidiary.

The Malaysian tax system does not require conformity between tax and financial accounting. Thus the cost of inventory may be based on unit cost, average cost, FIFO, LIFO, etc., although LIFO is not allowed for tax purposes. Depreciation allowances are also available on machinery, equipment and industrial buildings at rates ranging between 8 and 20 per cent.

Tax assessments are based on income earned in the preceding calendar year, but companies are required to pay tax on a monthly instalment basis. These amounts are based on estimates until the actual assessment is raised.

Investment incentives and ownership and other restrictions

Over the years, the Malaysian government has devised a wide array of incentives for both domestic and foreign direct investment in targeted industries, activities and areas, including tax holidays for up to 10 years, tariff protection and import restriction on competing goods, capital investment tax allowances of up to 100 per cent, double deductions for approved research and development expenditures or approved training expenditure, and a 5 per cent abatement of profit for at least five years for companies located in promoted industrial areas. Exports of manufactures are also encouraged by provisions for abatement of 50 per cent of export income, doubling of allowable expenditure for export promotion, and export credit refinancing facilities.

However, such incentives have been offered in tandem with certain restrictions on foreign equity participation and foreign acquisition of assets, set up in line with the objectives of the NEP. In particular, foreign acquisition of assets or interests exceeding M$5 million or 15 per cent or more of the voting power in a Malaysian company must be approved by the Foreign Investment Committee, as must the foreign acquisition of substantial fixed assets. However, this last restriction has very recently been relaxed in relation to acquisitions of real property.

Foreign exchange movements and loans are also restricted in a number of ways. For example, official approval is required for any foreign borrowings of Malaysian currency, and foreign borrowings of foreign currency which exceed M$1 million; and a non-resident-controlled company operating in Malaysia may only borrow up to M$10 million from local sources. However, payments for dividends, profits and repatriation of capital are freely remittable, although exchange control formalities are required for amounts exceeding M$10,000.

The overall 30 per cent limit specified by the NEP may be waived under specific conditions, particularly when the ventures proposed are aimed at export markets, involve high technology, or provide employment for substantial numbers of locals.

The professional environment

The 1985 revision of the Companies Act required that all firms of public accountants, and individual partners of such firms, register with the Registrar of Companies. Each partner is allocated a number, which must be cited in all audit reports. However, public accountants are not exclusively confined to their traditional role as statutory auditors. Thus the larger partnerships frequently offer many other services, such as acting as company directors, trustees, and management and financial advisers.

The professional bodies

The MIA's sole activity for twenty years was registering practising accountants, thus determining who was qualified to provide audit and accountancy services in Malaysia. Such registration was necessary because Malaysian accountants had (and still have) varied educational backgrounds and qualifications. Membership in the MIA has usually been obtained through membership of other accountancy bodies, principally the MACPA. At the end of 1989 the MIA had approximately 5,500 members of whom one-third were public accountants.

More recently, the Institute has been actively prosecuting non-registered individuals who have been holding themselves out as accountants. It has also instigated a review of by-laws on professional conduct and ethics in order to minimize government intervention in the self-regulation of the profession.

The MACPA was incorporated in 1958. At the end of 1989 it had about 1,700 members of whom about one-third were in public practice. The Association is an active one, with a relatively high profile. Its technical activities are not restricted to the setting of accounting and auditing standards but include consultations on the implementation of amendments to the Companies Act and revision of its schedules, the revision of the KLSE Listing Manual, and Guidelines issued by the BNM and the CIC. It also represents the interests of its members *and* taxpayers in talks with the Inland Revenue.

The MACPA provides for qualification of its members through a combination of a series of examinations and approved practical experience. This system is almost identical to the one operated by the ICAEW, although certain modifications have been introduced in order to make good the chronic shortage of qualified accountants in Malaysia. Registered students may qualify either by entering a training contract with a firm of certified public accountants (CPAs) or with a MACPA member working in commerce, industry or government service, and passing examinations set by the Association. Alternatively, students may study at approved universities or colleges and obtain practical experience by working for a CPA firm. Finally, members of foreign accountancy bodies may also become MACPA members by passing its examinations in Malaysian law and taxation.

Since 1973, the MIA and the MACPA have been negotiating to integrate. However, an Amendment Bill to the Accountants Act to effect their merger was rejected by the Malaysian Cabinet in 1985. Instead, a co-operation agreement was signed in 1987 to provide for a joint secretariat and collaboration in numerous activities, including research and development of technical and ethical standards, education and training of members and students, and conduct of professional accountancy examinations.

A second-tier professional body, the Malaysian Association of Accounting Technicians (MAAT), has also been formed. This body was organized with two objectives: to help meet Malaysia's acute shortage of accountants while circumventing the lengthy process of gaining full professional qualification; and to provide an alternative, legitimate qualification for accountants (usually part-qualified, with many years in practice) not registered with the MIA. MAAT is administered by the MIA and keeps a fairly low profile.

Professional accounting standards

Although the MACPA has developed and issued its own accounting standards, statements and technical bulletins, and has a significant number more in draft form awaiting approval and adoption, it is expected that IASs will continue to form 'the backbone of standard-setting in Malaysia' (Phenix 1986: 11). Since their introduction in 1978 they have become 'an accepted part of accounting and financial reporting in Malaysia, even amongst non-members of the MACPA' (Phenix 1986: 11).

The MACPA Accounting and Auditing Standards Committee reviews *all* issued IASs, and recommends statements to the Council for adoption. Where amendments are considered necessary in order to adapt the statement to Malaysian circumstances, the statement is exposed as a potential Malaysian Accounting Standard (MAS). Otherwise it is exposed as an IAS, with a local foreword or introduction. The exposure period generally lasts for six months, after which the statement is amended to incorporate any comments received. It is then issued with effect from six months of the issue date.

The requirements of IASs 1 to 4 became operative in Malaysia from the beginning of 1978. The others have been gradually adopted by the Association, although some are still at the exposure stage (see Appendix D). The exceptions are IAS 15 (Information Reflecting the Effects of Changing Prices) and IAS 22 (Accounting for Business Combinations). The former has been deferred pending a larger degree of international consensus on appropriate ways to account for changes in price levels. The topics dealt with by the latter – accounting for acquisitions and mergers and the treatment of goodwill – are, or will be, dealt with by local standards. IASC Exposure Drafts are noted, but not exposed until their adoption as IASs.

Two Malaysian Accounting Standards (MASs) have been issued to date, and there are five other MASs in draft form, generally dealing with topics not covered by IASs or topics of local importance. Technical Bulletins (TBs) represent the opinion of the Association's Technical Committee in situations where no standards or guidelines have been issued, or where an existing statement requires amplification. Seven TBs have been issued to date, with a further eight in draft form.

MACPA Statements (MSs) were issued in the early 1970s, prior to the MACPA's membership in the IASC. They deal with financial reporting disclosures and the forms of various reports such as the auditor's report and the accountant's report for prospectuses, but some have been superseded by auditing standards and guidelines. As such, they are of diminishing importance in the regulation of financial reporting in Malaysia.

The co-operation agreement between the MACPA and the MIA provided that all technical standards for the accountancy profession in Malaysia be developed and issued as joint statements to members of the profession. This has not affected the standard-setting process in the country, as various MIA working committees have reviewed and adopted the IASs and other technical pronouncements issued by the MACPA.

Enforcement of accounting standards

As IASC members, both the MIA and the MACPA expect their members, in their roles as officers or directors of companies or as reporting accountants or auditors, to ensure that IAS and MAS requirements are complied with in published financial statements. Non-compliance must be disclosed, and explained by way of note. Failing this, non-compliance must be disclosed in the auditor's report. However, where IAS requirements differ from, or conflict with, legal requirements, companies are expected to obey the latter, while disclosing non-compliance with the former.

Observance of TBs is not mandatory, but the MACPA stresses that they are to be regarded as authoritative opinions as to best current practice, thus forming part of local GAAP.

Both the MIA and the MACPA have established separate Financial Statements Review Committees, with the objective of raising professional standards by undertaking reviews of published statements. These reviews are carried out to ensure that statements conform with legal and professional requirements, with the MACPA focusing on public listed companies and the MIA on unlisted companies. Where a set of statements falls short of requirements, the attention of the company and its auditors is drawn to the areas of non-compliance.

The Committees' work is unquestionably very limited – no more than about twenty-five annual reports are reviewed by each in any year. The results of these reviews are not made public, and pressure for improvement can only be exerted by the professional bodies on their members, with no support from the law, the financial press or public opinion. The fact that there have been no cases to date of MIA or MACPA members who have been disciplined for failing to ensure that requirements have been met suggests either that non-compliance is not significant, or that the procedure may be relatively ineffective. Whichever is the case, neither the legal nor professional framework in Malaysia provides for formal and regular checks on the vast majority of Malaysian companies outside the scope of the statutory audit.

GENERALLY ACCEPTED ACCOUNTING PRINCIPLES

The Malaysian financial reporting environment is very similar to the UK environment in many respects. The objective of financial statements is, as in the UK, to present a 'true and fair view' of the company's results and financial position. More detailed reporting requirements, both legal and professional, also show few differences, as Malaysian company law is based on UK and UK-derived statutes and Malaysian standards are to a large degree IASs, which have often been branded as Anglo-Saxon in tenor. There has been some development of pronouncements specific to local conditions, such as accounting for plantations, but these have not yet been adopted as formal standards. Thus Malaysian GAAP is very similar, though not identical, to UK GAAP.

The bulk of statutory reporting requirements are found in Part 6 of the Companies Act, which deals with Accounts and Audit and contains the disclosure requirements for the directors' report; and in the Ninth Schedule, which contains the requirements governing the balance sheet, profit and loss account, statement of changes in financial position, and notes. The Act does not specify the language in which records and accounts must be produced, but, significantly, is itself produced in both English and Malay.

Professional accounting standards issued by the MACPA to July 1990 are listed in Appendix D. These standards are published in English.

Accounting records

Records may be kept in any form which will 'sufficiently explain the transactions and financial position of the company, and enable true and fair profit and loss accounts and balance sheets and any documents required to be attached thereto to be prepared ... [and] be conveniently and properly audited' (sect. 167(1)). They must thus take the form of books, computer print-outs or microfiche.

Form and content of accounts

The law stipulates that every profit and loss account and balance sheet must be accompanied by a statement of accounting policies. Certain items must be disclosed in the notes, rather than in other parts of the accounts. These items are specified below (see 'Fixed assets').

The balance sheet must contain appropriate headings for fixed and current assets, liabilities and provisions. The method of classifying items under these headings must be stated. Items from different classifications may be combined if they are immaterial or inseparable.

Comparative figures for the previous year must be provided. Where amounts shown in the financial statements of previous years are not comparable with amounts shown in the current financial statements, adjustments must be made to the prior years' figures, and reasons for the adjustments disclosed.

Fixed assets

The Companies Act requires separate disclosure of land and buildings and plant and machinery. Other categories depend upon the nature of the business. Land must be further classified according to whether it is freehold, long leasehold (i.e. with at least fifty years unexpired) or short leasehold. Any restrictions to title must be disclosed. Material amounts of fixed assets not used, but held for disposal, must also be disclosed.

All provisions for depreciation, amortization or diminution in the value of fixed assets, shown in separate categories, must be separately disclosed in the profit and loss account. The effect of any changes in accounting methods or bases of classification for any of these changes must be given, together with reasons for the changes.

Where fixed assets are shown at valuation, disclosure must be made of the year(s) of valuation, the several values, whether the items were externally valued, and the bases of valuation.

The notes must contain information on depreciation methods, rates used, or the number of years over which cost is expensed, for each category of asset.

Any material profit or loss from the sale of fixed assets must be separately disclosed.

IAS 4 (Depreciation Accounting) has been in operation since 1978, and IAS 5 (Information to be Disclosed in Financial Statements) since 1979. The former requires disclosure of the major categories of property, plant and equipment, and the basis of valuation of fixed assets. Depreciation must be charged on a systematic basis on all depreciable assets, and the method of computing depreciation, the estimated useful lives of assets, and the depreciation expense for the period must all be disclosed. IAS 5 requires the disclosure of important commitments for additions to property.

TB 2, issued in 1982, distinguishes between land held for development and resale, and land held for long-term investment. Auditors are advised to obtain written representation from the board of directors as to which category of land is held, and to ensure that the former type is included in inventories and valued at the lower of cost and net realizable value, while the latter is shown as a long-term asset and valued on the existing use basis. Any net surplus arising from the latter may be distributed in the form of a bonus issue.

Leases and hire purchase agreements

Material amounts of fixed assets acquired on instalment purchase plans, and amounts expended on the hire of plant and machinery, are legally required items of disclosure. Where the company is a borrowing corporation the notes must classify payables into items with at least two years, between two and five years, and more than five years to maturity.

IAS 1 (Disclosure of Accounting Policies), in operation since 1978, requires disclosure of the accounting policy for leases. IAS 17 (Accounting for Leases) distinguishes between finance and operating leases, and requires capitalization of the former. It was implemented with transitional requirements between 1987 and 1991, since which date its requirements must be fully met.

Intangible assets and research and development expenditure

The law allows a company to either capitalize or write off its preliminary expenses, issue expenses, commission paid on shares or debentures, discounts on debentures and shares; goodwill and other intangible assets; and development expenditure. The notes must describe the bases on which expenditure is carried forward rather than expensed, for each item so capitalized. Movements in deferred development expenditure during the accounting period must also be shown.

Amortization of goodwill and other intangibles, including the amortization of development costs previously deferred, must be separately disclosed in the profit and loss account. The effect of any changes in accounting methods or bases of classification for any of these charges must be given, together with reasons for the changes.

Any material profit or loss from the sale of intangible assets must be disclosed.

IAS 1 requires disclosure of the amortization policy for intangible assets which have been capitalized. IAS 9 (Accounting for Research and Development Activities) has been in effect since 1980. It requires that all R&D expenditure be charged to the profit and loss account as incurred, except where deferral is considered appropriate. However, all deferred expenditure must be reviewed at the end of each period, and the unamortized balance charged immediately if deferral is no longer appropriate. The accounting policy, total R&D costs, and the balance of unamortized costs must be disclosed.

Stock

The law requires that stock be shown in 'the main categories appropriate to the business of the company', and valued at the lower of cost and net realizable value. Cost is defined to include all expenses necessary to bring items to their present condition and location.

IAS 2 (Valuation and Presentation of Inventories in the Context of the Historical Cost System), effective since 1978, also requires that stocks be valued at the lower of cost and market value. Cost includes all fixed and variable production overheads, and may be calculated by using the FIFO, LIFO, weighted average or base stock methods. Market value is realizable value, less predictable costs of completion and disposal.

Pension costs

The Companies Act requires separate disclosure of the provision for pension or retirement benefits, and IAS 1 requires disclosure of the accounting policy for such costs. IAS 19 (Accounting for Retirement Benefits in the Financial Statements of Employers) was adopted by the MACPA in 1991. The valuation method used must be disclosed, and current service costs charged against income.

Taxation

The law indicates an expectation for deferred tax accounting by requiring that the tax provision disclosed be classified into tax payable and deferred taxation. The profit and loss account tax charge must also disclose the tax payable in Malaysia before double taxation relief, tax payable outside Malaysia, relief granted for double taxation, and deferred taxation.

Where material tax losses exist, separate disclosure is required of the amount of tax saving due to credit taken in the period of loss, the amount due to loss brought forward, and the amount and future availability of tax losses not used.

IAS 12 (Accounting for Taxes on Income) became effective in Malaysia in 1983. It stipulates that companies must provide for deferred taxation, using either the deferral or liability methods, with either partial or comprehensive allocation. Deferred tax assets should not be recorded unless there is reasonable expectation of their realization.

Group accounts

The law allows group accounts to be drawn up using the purchase/acquisition method or the merger method, depending on the surrounding circumstances.

Acquisition accounting

Sect. 5 defines a holding company as one which controls the composition of the board of directors, controls more than 50 per cent of the voting capital, or holds more than 50 per cent of the issued share capital (excluding preference shares) of another company. A related company is either the holding company, subsidiary, or fellow subsidiary of another company (sect. 6). The Act makes no mention of associated or related companies.

The accounts of a company must disclose separately the amounts owed to the holding company, subsidiaries and other related companies, and significant transactions with related corporations.

A holding company is required to publish its own profit and loss account and balance sheet, as well as the consolidated accounts. Sub-holding companies need not produce consolidated accounts if they are wholly owned subsidiaries of Malaysian companies.

All group companies must use the holding company's accounting policies. Where the use of different policies has material effects, the consolidated accounts must be adjusted.

For each subsidiary included in the consolidated accounts, the notes must state the name, place of incorporation, principal activities and the percentage of issued share capital held by the holding company.

Subsidiaries may be excluded from the consolidated accounts if the directors believe that inclusion would be impractical, or of no value, or involve disproportionate expense or delay; if control of the subsidiary is only temporary; if the holding company's control over a foreign subsidiary is impaired; if inclusion would be misleading, or harmful to business; or if the businesses are so dissimilar that the subsidiary and holding company cannot reasonably be treated as a single undertaking. Where subsidiaries are not consolidated, the notes must state the reasons for the exclusion, and contain the balance sheet, profit and loss account and auditor's report on the excluded subsidiaries.

The consolidated accounts must exclude all inter-company transactions and balances. The minority interest in the results of subsidiaries, and the net assets of the group, must be shown clearly.

Where a subsidiary's accounts are qualified, the consolidated balance sheet must contain particulars of the qualification if the holding company's own accounts do not deal with the matter, and if it is material to the shareholders of the holding company.

IAS 3 (Consolidated Financial Statements) was adopted in 1978. It defines a subsidiary in line with the Companies Act, as well as a company in which more than half the equity capital (though less than half the voting power) is held; and also as a company whose financial and operating policies can be controlled by another, either by statute or by agreement.

Subsidiaries need not be consolidated when control is temporary or impaired, or when their businesses are too dissimilar from the rest of the group. The reasons for non-consolidation must be disclosed, and such subsidiaries included in the consolidated accounts using the equity method. The holding company's equity in excluded subsidiaries must also be disclosed.

Associated companies must be included in group accounts using the equity method.

Goodwill is defined in IAS 3 as the excess of cost over the fair value of assets acquired.

Merger accounting

Merger accounting is allowed by the Act, under circumstances similar to those stipulated in the UK. MAS 2, operational from 1989, details these conditions and the recommended accounting method. It is substantially similar to IAS 22, but was issued as a separate standard because of the perceived importance of the topic.

MAS 2 stipulates that merger accounting is allowed, but not required, when certain conditions are all met – that is, when an offer is made for all the equity and other voting shares not held by the offeror; when the offer secures at least 90 per cent of the equity and 90 per cent of all voting shares; where the offeror did not previously hold 20 per cent or more of the equity and total voting shares in the offeree; and where at least 90 per cent of the fair value of the consideration given for the equity share capital and non-equity voting capital is in the form of similar capital.

Whether the acquisition or merger method is used, MAS 2 requires disclosure of the names of the combining companies, details of the securities issued and other consideration given, the accounting method used, and the nature and amount of significant accounting adjustments made to achieve consistency of accounting policies.

In addition, where the merger method is used, disclosure is required in the accounts of the issuing company of the fair value of the consideration given; the profit before unusual items relating to the period before and after the effective date of the merger; the same profit for the period up to the effective date of the merger and of the previous year, analysed between the issuing company and the subsidiary; and unusual items relating to the pre- and post-merger periods, analysed between issuing company and subsidiary.

Foreign exchange translation

The Companies Act stipulates that all amounts in the accounts must be shown in Malaysian dollars. Where translations of amounts and balances have occurred, this fact, and the basis on which translations have been carried out, must be disclosed.

IAS 21 (Accounting for the Effects of Changes in Foreign Exchange Rates), was adopted in 1987. It differentiates between subsidiaries which are integral parts of their parent company's operations, and those which are independent, and recommends the use of the temporal method for the former, and the closing rate method for the latter.

Funds statements

The inclusion of the funds statement as part of the accounts was effected by the 1985 amendment to the Companies Act. Separate disclosure must be made of the funds provided from, and used in, the company's operations, and other sources and uses of funds. If a consolidated statement is produced then there is no need for a holding company funds statement.

IAS 7 (Statement of Changes in Financial Position) has been in effect since 1979.

Earnings per share (EPS)

There are no legal requirements for disclosure of earnings per share, but all listed companies are required to disclose EPS on the face of the profit and loss account, and the method used in calculating the ratio. In MAS 1, issued in 1984, profit is defined as after adjustments for associated companies, minority interests, tax and preference dividends, but before extraordinary items. The number of shares are those ranking for dividends in the accounting period.

Diluted EPS must be disclosed when there are issued shares which did not rank for dividends during the accounting period, but will do so in future periods; or when there are any convertible preference shares, debentures or loan stock, or options and warrants on shares. The dilution must be material (i.e. more than 5 per cent of the basic EPS).

Valuation rules

The Companies Act contains only two valuation rules. The first relates to fixed assets and investments, which must be stated at either cost or valuation, less provisions for depreciation or any diminution in value. This rule does not apply in circumstances where the cost of assets cannot be ascertained without undue expense or delay, where asset replacement is either wholly or partially provided for, or where investments are shown at market value, either in the accounts or in the notes.

The second valuation rule applies to stock, which must be shown in the accounts at the lower of cost and net realizable value, with cost defined to include all expenses necessary to bring items to their present condition and location.

Directors' report

The 1985 revision of the Act greatly expanded the scope of the directors' report. In addition to various disclosure requirements described below, the directors are also required to take responsibility for asset valuations, unusual items, contingent liabilities and the true and fair view presented by the accounts.

The report must state the principal activities of the company, and any significant changes in activities during the year. The post-tax result for the year must be disclosed, as must the amounts of paid and proposed dividends. Disclosure must also be made of amounts and particulars of any material transfers to or from reserves, or provisions made during the year. Details are required of shares or debentures issued during the year, including the purpose of the issue, the number or amount issued, and the terms.

The report must describe changes in accounting policies and stock valuation methods, and state whether the directors are aware of any circumstances which would affect any amount shown in the accounts, in particular the bad debt provision and the valuation of assets and liabilities. Items appearing in, or excluded from the accounts for the first time must be described.

The report must disclose whether the enforcement of any liability could affect the ability of the company to meet its obligations as they fall due. It must state whether charges on assets or contingent liabilities have arisen since the period-end, and particulars, amounts and effects of extraordinary items and post-balance sheet events must be given.

The report must include the names of the directors in office since the date of the last report, and details of arrangements to help directors to buy shares or debentures in the company or in any other company. For each director at the year-end, interests in shares or debentures of the company, or any other group company, at the beginning and end of the year, and changes during the year, must be disclosed.

The report does not have to be audited, but auditors are required, under certain circumstances to report non-compliance with legal requirements to the Registrar of Companies.

Other reports

Directors' statement

Two directors, on behalf of all the others, must sign a statement that the profit and loss account and balance sheet are true and fair representations of the company's result for the period, and financial position at the period-end (sect. 169(15)).

Statutory declaration

The officer responsible for the accounts and the company's financial management must sign a statutory declaration 'setting forth his opinion as to the correctness or otherwise of the balance sheet and the profit and loss account' (sect. 169(16)).

FINANCIAL ANALYSIS

Given the similarity of Malaysian and UK GAAP, financial analysis of Malaysian published financial statements would not present UK or US analysts with the same problems as would be encountered in examining the statements of, say, continental European companies. Instead, a possible problem would be lack of information through the failure of companies to comply with legal and professional requirements. The following comments are based on a study of financial information disclosure and accounting measurement methods of about 30 smaller and larger KLSE-listed companies in the commerce, service and industrial sectors (Tay 1989). The extracts from the financial statements of DMIB Berhad are included as Appendix A, as a fairly typical example of reporting by a medium-to-large listed Malaysian company.

Fixed assets

Accounting practice in this area is very much in compliance with legal and professional requirements. Historical cost combined with revaluation of property is the most common basis of valuation. However, there is low disclosure of the type of revaluation basis employed, and directors' valuation is often used. The most common method of computing depreciation is the straight-line method, although all other methods are also used.

Leases and hire purchase agreements

Lease financing is still relatively little used in Malaysia, even though the transitional grace period is over. Companies are fairly divided between capitalizing finance leases and treating them as revenue leases.

Intangible assets and R&D expenditure

Intangible assets are most commonly capitalized and amortized over a number of years. There is relatively little expenditure on R&D, but practice seems to be in accordance with IAS 9 requirements.

Stocks

Practice accords with legal and professional requirements. FIFO and weighted average are the most popular valuation methods.

Pension costs

These are most usually recognized by systematic charges in the profit and loss account, although some companies only charge pension costs as they are paid to employees. Disclosure is usually made of the accounting policy and the cost for the period, but no descriptions of the scheme are given.

Taxation

Practice is in accordance with legal and professional requirements.

Group accounts

Group accounts are prepared very much in compliance with legal requirements. Only a few companies treat as subsidiaries companies in which they do not hold more than 50 per cent of voting power.

In 1986, the year reviewed by Tay (1989), the most common form of group accounts involved full consolidation of subsidiaries under the acquisition method. The Companies Act amendment allowing merger accounting only came into force at the beginning of that year, and MAS 2 (Accounting for Acquisitions and Mergers) had not yet been issued. Since that period, the relevant circumstances have not arisen very frequently, so that merger accounting is still relatively rare in Malaysia.

Subsidiaries are most commonly excluded from group accounts on the grounds that their business is too unlike that of the rest of the group, and valued by the equity method. Goodwill is most commonly retained indefinitely in the balance sheet.

Foreign exchange translation

Foreign currency transactions are recorded at the rates ruling during the transaction period, and re-translated at year-end rates as necessary. Differences are usually charged to the profit and loss account.

The accounts of foreign subsidiaries are most commonly translated using the current rate method, though some companies use the temporal method.

Funds statements

Funds statements are most usually provided in the form of expressing changes in financial position in terms of working capital.

EPS

EPS data are not always disclosed in the accounts of non-listed companies, but disclosure is usually accompanied by a description of the computation method used.

SUMMARY

The similarity between Malaysian and UK GAAP is striking, but not complete. There are two important differences in legal requirements: Malaysian companies must include a funds statement with the financial statements, and also declarations from directors and company officers on, respectively, the truth and fairness and correctness of the accounts.

Procedures for monitoring compliance of financial statements with requirements are also similar. There is no formal mechanism for ensuring compliance in Malaysia, and much reliance is placed on the statutory auditors. Although reporting practice by listed companies complies to a high degree with regulation, practice in areas not covered by formal requirements is often unsatisfactory – for example, the indefinite maintenance of goodwill in group accounts and the use of directors' valuation for fixed assets. However, an MAS on goodwill accounting is currently in the pipeline, and there is some prospect of improvement in accounting practice in this area.

APPENDIX A

Extracts from the accounts of DMIB

ACCOUNTING POLICIES

The accounts are prepared under the historical cost convention modified by the revaluation of certain fixed assets and investments and comply with approved Accounting Standards.

The following notes describe the main accounting policies of the Group which are consistent with those adopted in the previous year:

(a) **Basis of consolidation**

The consolidated accounts include the accounts of the Company and all its subsidiary companies made up to 30th June 1992. The results of subsidiary companies acquired or disposed during the year are included in the consolidated profit and loss account from the date of their acquisition or up to the date of their disposal.

(b) **Associated companies**

A company in which the Group has a long term equity investment of from 20% to 50% and where the Group has representation on the board and is in a position to exercise significant influence is accounted for as an associated company.

The consolidated profit and loss account includes the Group's share of the profits less losses of associated companies based on the latest audited accounts of the companies concerned. In the consolidated balance sheet, the Group's interest in associated companies is stated at cost plus the Group's share of the post acquisition reserves.

(c) **Inventories**

Inventories are stated at the lower of cost and net realisable value. Cost includes, where relevant, appropriate proportions of overheads and is determined on a first-in, first-out basis.

(d) **Depreciation**

Freehold land is not amortised. Leasehold land is amortised over the period of the lease except for those leases which have an unexpired term in excess of 50 years, in which case no amortisation is provided. Depreciation of other fixed assets is provided on the straight line basis to write off the cost or valuation of each asset over its estimated useful life. The principal annual depreciation rates are:

Buildings	– 2½%
Plant, machinery, equipment and vehicles	– 5% to 33⅓%

Gains, less losses, on disposal of land and buildings held as fixed assets are included in extraordinary items.

(e) **Foreign currencies**

The accounts are stated in Malaysian ringgit.

Transactions in foreign currencies are translated into Malaysian ringgit at the exchange rates prevailing at the transaction dates or, where settlement has not yet taken place at the balance sheet date, at the approximate exchange rate prevailing on that date. All exchange gains or losses, including those arising from translation of assets and liabilities at balance sheet date, are taken up in the profit and loss account. Assets and liabilities of overseas subsidiaries at the balance sheet date are also translated at the prevailing rate and exchange differences arising from the restatement of the opening net assets are dealt with through reserves.

(f) **Retirement benefits**

The Group contributes to approved provident funds for its employees and the Company maintains a provision for unfunded retirement benefits payable to employees in accordance with the terms of the Collective Agreement between the Company and the Staff Union.

(g) **Taxation**

The taxation charge in the profit and loss account is calculated at current rates based on the estimated chargeable income for the year.

Provision is made, on the liability method, for taxation deferred by capital allowances and other timing differences, except where the tax effects of such timing differences are expected to be deferred indefinitely.

PROFIT AND LOSS ACCOUNTS

For The Year Ended 30th June 1992

Amounts in M$'000	Note	**Group 1992**	Group 1991	**Company 1992**	Company 1991
Turnover	1	**307,257**	302,179	**223,007**	220,054
Operating profit	2	**40,166**	39,887	**32,431**	31,755
Share of loss of associated company		**(828)**	(531)	–	–
Profit before taxation		**39,338**	39,356	**32,431**	31,755
Taxation	3	**(13,593)**	(14,209)	**(11,258)**	(11,832)
Profit after taxation		**25,745**	25,147	**21,173**	19,923
Extraordinary items	4	**(422)**	(1,582)	**(422)**	(3,180)
Profit after taxation and extraordinary items		**25,323**	23,565	**20,751**	16,743
Retained profits brought forward		**51,907**	47,885	**26,624**	29,381
Profit attributable to shareholders		**77,230**	71,450	**47,375**	46,124
Dividends – net	5	**(19,500)**	(19,500)	**(19,500)**	(19,500)
Retained profits carried forward		**57,730**	51,950	**27,875**	26,624
		Sen	Sen		
Earnings per stock unit	6	**8.6**	8.4		

The accounting policies set out on page 26 and the notes on pages 30 to 39 are to be read as part of the accounts.

BALANCE SHEETS
At 30th June 1992

Amounts in M$'000	Note	Group 1992	Group 1991	Company 1992	Company 1991
SOURCES OF CAPITAL					
Issued share capital	7	**150,000**	150,000	**150,000**	150,000
Retained profits	8	**57,730**	51,950	**27,875**	26,624
Shareholders' funds		**207,730**	201,950	**177,875**	176,624
Deferred taxation	9	**10,253**	11,904	**7,827**	9,187
Retirement benefits		**2,559**	2,663	**2,559**	2,663
		220,542	216,517	**188,261**	188,474
EMPLOYMENT OF CAPITAL					
Current assets					
Inventories	10	**48,857**	52,495	**32,987**	37,873
Debtors	11	**68,828**	69,176	**48,698**	53,882
Bank balances and deposits	12	**58,737**	52,684	**55,586**	49,708
		176,422	174,355	**137,271**	141,463
Current liabilities					
Creditors	13	**51,817**	49,742	**49,996**	47,130
Current taxation		**26,721**	27,836	**19,842**	22,441
Proposed dividends		**13,650**	13,650	**13,650**	13,650
		92,188	91,228	**83,488**	83,221
Net current assets		**84,234**	83,127	**53,783**	58,242
Investments	14	**17**	16	**11**	10
Associated company	15	**8,130**	6,544	**12,386**	9,973
Subsidiary companies	16	**–**	–	**17,709**	18,645
Fixed assets	17	**128,161**	126,830	**104,372**	101,604
		220,542	216,517	**188,261**	188,474
		Sen	Sen		
Net tangible assets per stock unit		**69**	67		

The accounting policies set out on page 26 and the notes on pages 30 to 39 are to be read as part of the accounts.

GROUP SOURCE AND APPLICATION OF FUNDS STATEMENT
For The Year Ended 30th June 1992

Amounts in M$'000	Note	1992	1991
SOURCE OF FUNDS			
Profit before taxation		39,338	39,356
Extraordinary items		(422)	(1,582)
		38,916	37,774
Adjustments for items not involving the movement of funds :			
Depreciation		12,194	11,394
Exchange differences		(48)	109
Extraordinary items		–	(246)
Fixed assets written off		484	269
Profit on sale of fixed assets		(537)	(376)
Share of loss of associated company		828	531
Funds generated from operations		51,837	49,455
Funds from other sources:			
Proceeds from disposal of fixed assets		623	3,907
Proceeds from disposal of subsidiary companies	18	–	30,579
		52,460	83,941
APPLICATION OF FUNDS			
Retirement benefit payments		(103)	(430)
Dividend payments		(19,500)	(19,500)
Taxation payments		(16,355)	(16,194)
Purchases of fixed assets		(14,095)	(14,463)
Purchase of investment		(1)	(10)
Investment in associated company		(2,700)	–
		(294)	33,344
CHANGES IN WORKING CAPITAL			
Decrease/(increase) in inventories		3,638	(12,597)
Decrease/(increase) in debtors		634	(6,566)
Increase in creditors		2,075	21,520
NET FUNDS INFLOW		6,053	35,701
Represented by:			
Increase in bank balances and deposits		6,053	35,701
INCREASE IN LIQUID FUNDS		6,053	35,701

The accounting policies set out on page 26 and the notes on pages 30 to 39 are to be read as part of the accounts.

STATEMENT BY DIRECTORS, STATUTORY DECLARATION AND AUDITORS' REPORT

Statement by Directors

We, Dato' Seri Syed Nahar bin Tun Syed Sheh Shahabuddin and Yip Jon Khiam, two of the Directors of DMIB Berhad, do hereby state that, in the opinion of the Directors, the accounts set out on pages 26 to 39 are drawn up so as to give a true and fair view of the state of affairs of the Group and of the Company at 30th June 1992 and of the results of the operations of the Group and of the Company and the source and application of funds of the Group for the year then ended.

On behalf of the Board

DATO' SERI SYED NAHAR BIN TUN SYED SHEH SHAHABUDDIN

YIP JON KHIAM

Petaling Jaya
8th September 1992

Statutory Declaration

I, Faridah bte Yassin, the Director primarily responsible for the financial management of DMIB Berhad, do solemnly and sincerely declare that the accounts set out on pages 26 to 39 are, to the best of my knowledge and belief, correct and I make this solemn declaration conscientiously believing the same to be true, and by virtue of the provisions of the Statutory Declarations Act, 1960.

SUBSCRIBED AND SOLEMNLY DECLARED by the abovenamed FARIDAH BTE YASSIN at Petaling Jaya, Selangor Darul Ehsan, Malaysia on 8th September 1992.

G. VIJAYAN
Commissioner for Oaths (No. 637)
Petaling Jaya

FARIDAH BTE YASSIN
Finance Director

Auditors' Report to The Members of DMIB Berhad

We have audited the accounts set out on pages 26 to 39 in accordance with approved Auditing Standards.

In our opinion:

(a) the accounts give a true and fair view of the state of affairs of the Group and the Company as at 30th June 1992 and of the results of the Group and the Company and the source and application of funds of the Group for the year ended on that date and comply with the Companies Act, 1965; and

(b) the accounting and other records and the registers required by the Act to be kept by the Company and by the subsidiaries of which we have acted as auditors have been properly kept in accordance with the provisions of the Act.

The names of the subsidiaries of which we have not acted as auditors are indicated in Note 16 on the accounts. We have considered the accounts of these subsidiaries and the auditors' reports thereon.

We are satisfied that the accounts of the subsidiaries that have been consolidated with the Company's accounts are in form and content appropriate and proper for the purposes of the preparation of the consolidated accounts and we have received satisfactory information and explanations required by us for these purposes.

The auditors' reports on the accounts of the subsidiaries were not subject to any qualification and did not include any comment made under subsection (3) of section 174 of the Act.

PRICE WATERHOUSE
(No. AF-0052)
Public Accountants
Certified Public Accountants

TENGKU YUNUS KAMARUDDIN
(No. 585/3/94(J/PH))
Partner of the firm

Kuala Lumpur
8th September 1992

APPENDIX B

Major economic indicators

	1984	*1985*	*1986*	*1987*	*1988*
1 *Gross National Product (GNP)*					
Current prices	74,182	72,039	66,953	74,729	85,798
Constant prices (1978)	53,315	52,895	54,266	57,203	62,609
% real change	6.7	(1.2)	2.6	5.4	9.5
(M$ million)					
2 *GNP per head*					
% change (current prices)	n/a	(5.7)	(10.8)	10.8	12
3 *Exchange rate*					
M$ to US$1	2.42	2.42	2.60	2.49	2.71
(year-end)					
4 *Trend in prices*					
% change					
Consumer prices	3.5*	0.4	0.6	0.8	2.5
(1980 = 100)					
Producer prices	3.5	(2.1)	(6.2)	3.7	7.4
(1978 = 100)					
5 *Balance of payments*					
Net exports/(imports)	5,721	7,579	7,800	13,921	11,967
Current account	(3,917)	(1,522)	(316)	6,454	4,720
Overall balance	312	3,209	4,345	2,893	(1,104)
(M$ million)					
6 *Gross external debt*					
% of GNP*	50.5	62.7	78.4	74.3	n/a

Source: Malaysian Ministry of Finance, *Economic Report.* *Economist Intelligence Unit, *Country Profile: Malaysia and Brunei, Annual Survey 1989–90.*

Note: n/a = not available.

APPENDIX C

Major trading partners

Malaysia's three major trading partners are the USA, Japan and Singapore, a situation which has remained unchanged for many years.

	1988 (%)	*1989* (%)*
Exports		
Singapore	19	19
USA	17	18
Japan	17	16
Imports		
Japan	23	24
USA	18	16
Singapore	13	14
Total value		
Japan	20	20
USA	18	17
Singapore	17	17

Source: Malaysian Ministry of Finance, *Economic Report 1989–90*.

Note: *Figures in this column are estimates.

APPENDIX D

Approved accounting standards and other pronouncements issued by the MACPA

I	*Approved Accounting Standards*		*Operational date*
	Statement of Approved Accounting Standards		1988
1	*International Accounting Standards (IAS)*		
	Preface to IAS		1978 (revised 1983)
(a)	Adopted		
	IAS 1	Disclosure of Accounting Policies	1978
	IAS 2	Valuation and Presentation of Inventories in the Context of the Historical Cost System	1978
	IAS 3	Consolidated Financial Statements	1978
	IAS 4	Depreciation Accounting	1978
	IAS 5	Information to be Disclosed in Financial Statements	1979
	IAS 7	Statement of Changes in Financial Position	1979
	IAS 8	Unusual and Prior Period Items and Changes in Accounting Policies	1979
	IAS 9	Accounting for Research and Development Activities	1980
	IAS 10	Contingencies and Events Occurring after the Balance Sheet Date	1980
	IAS 11	Accounting for Construction Contracts	1982
	IAS 12	Accounting for Taxes on Income	1983
	IAS 13	Presentation of Current Assets and Current Liabilities	1982
	IAS 14	Reporting Financial Information by Segment	1983
	IAS 16	Accounting for Property, Plant and Equipment	1983
	IAS 17	Accounting for Leases	1987–91
	IAS 18	Revenue Recognition	1985
	IAS 21	Accounting for the Effects of Changes in Foreign Exchange Rates	1987
	IAS 23	Capitalization of Borrowing Costs	1986
(b)	Exposed by the MACPA		
	IAS 19	Accounting for Retirement Benefits in the Financial Statements of Employers	
	IAS 27	Consolidated Financial Statements and Accounting for Investments in Subsidiaries	
(c)	Informational only		
	IAS 20	Accounting for Government Grants and Disclosure of Government Assistance	

2	*Malaysian Accounting Standards (MAS)*		
(a)	Issued		*Operational date*
	MAS 1	Earnings per Share	1984
	MAS 2	Accounting for Acquisitions and Mergers	1989
(b)	Exposed		
	MAS B	Accounting for Property and Planting Costs in Plantation Operations	
	MAS C	Equity Accounting	
	MAS D	Accounting for Investments	
	MAS G	Accounting for Goodwill	
	MAS H	Accounting for Investments in Associates and Joint Ventures	
II	*Technical Bulletins (TB)*		
(a)	Issued		*Operational date*
	TB 1	Accounting for Investments	March 1982
	TB 2	Accounting for Land Held for Development and Resale	March 1982
	TB 4	Reporting in Connection with the Capital Adequacy Ratio of Banks	April 1983
	TB 5	Accounting for the Acquisition Costs of Assets in a Subsidiary	September 1984
	TB 6	Auditor's Reports on Financial Statements Published in the Print Media by Financial Institutions	April 1988
	TB 7	Accounting for Bankers' Acceptances	January 1989
(b)	Draft form		
	DTB F	Merger Accounting	
	DTB J	Turnover Disclosure for Financial Institutions	
	DTB K	Accountant's Report in Connection with Profit Forecasts	
	DTB L	Reports on Audits Involving the Use of Work of Another Auditor	
	DTB M	Banking Commitments and Contingent Liabilities	
	DTB N	Accounting for Investment Properties	
	DTB O	Presentation of Loss Situation in Statements of Changes in Financial Position	
	DTB R	Accounting for Fee-based Income in Financial Institutions	
III	*MACPA Statements*		*Date issued*
	No. 4	Specimen Accounts: The Blank Co. Berhad	November 1983
		Directors' Report	November 1985
	No. 5	Statement of Source and Application of Funds	May 1981

IV *Status of other IASs*

(a) Being considered for exposure

IAS 24	Related Party Disclosures
IAS 25	Accounting for Investments
IAS 26	Accounting and Reporting by Retirement Benefit Plans
IAS 28	Accounting for Investments in Associates
IAS 29	Financial Reporting in Hyperinflationary Economies
	Framework for the Preparation and Presentation of Financial Statements

(b) Deferred by the MACPA

IAS 15	Information Reflecting the Effects of Changing Prices
IAS 22	Accounting for Business Combinations

BIBLIOGRAPHY

Much of the descriptive material in this chapter is based on information drawn from the annual reports of the MIA and the MACPA. Other sources include:

Economist Intelligence Unit, *Country Profile: Malaysia and Brunei Annual Survey 1989–90.*

Malaysian Ministry of Finance, *Economic Report* (published annually).

Price Waterhouse (1989) *Corporate Taxes, Individual Taxes, Foreign Exchange, Investment Regulations: An Asia Pacific Region Summary,* London: Price Waterhouse.

SGV (1984) *Comparative Accounting Practices in ASEAN,* Sycip, Gorres, Velayo and Co.

Regulation

Malaysian Companies Act 1965.

Other references

Barnes, P. (1986) 'Thin trading and stock market efficiency: the case of the Kuala Lumpur Stock Exchange', *Journal of Business Finance and Accounting* 13(4), 609–17.

Gray, S.J., Campbell, S.G. and Shaw, J.C. (1984) *International Financial Reporting: A Comparative Survey of Accounting Requirements and Practices in 30 Countries,* London: Macmillan.

Mitchell, C.M. (1981) 'Accounting education in Malaysia', in A.J.H. Enthoven (ed.), *Accounting Education in Economic Development Management,* North-Holland.

Phenix, P. (1986) 'International Accounting Standards and the regulation of corporate business', *The Malaysian Accountant,* July, pp. 11–15.

Tay, J.S.W. (1989) 'Financial reporting requirements and practice in Malaysia', in 'Corporate financial reporting: regulatory systems and comparability', Ph.D. Thesis, University of Exeter.

Walton, P. (1986) 'The export of British accounting legislation to Commonwealth countries, *Accounting and Business Research* 16(64), 353–7.

8 Singapore

Foo See Liang and Ng Shwn Yng

BACKGROUND: POLITICAL AND SOCIAL PERSPECTIVES

Singapore is situated at the tip of the Malay Peninsula. The island of Singapore and 57 adjacent islets constitute the Republic of Singapore and encompass a total land area of 622 square kilometres. The main island is 42 kilometres in length and 23 kilometres in breadth, and 570 square kilometres in area. Singapore is a multiracial society. It has a population of about 2.6 million consisting of 77 per cent Chinese, 15 per cent Malay, 6 per cent Indian and Pakistani and 2 per cent others. It has one of the highest average per capita incomes in Asia, second only to Japan (see Appendix B). Owing to her strategic location, Singapore is the world's busiest port (PSA 1989).

In late 1818, Lord Hastings, Governor-General of India, gave approval to Sir Stamford Raffles to establish a trading station at the southern tip of the Malay Peninsula. The British, whose trade with China was expanding, saw the need of a half-way house to refit, revitalize and protect their merchant fleet as well as to forestall any advance by the Dutch in the East Indies. On 29 January 1819, Raffles landed on Singapore island. In 1824, Singapore's status as a British possession was formalized by two treaties, one the Anglo-Dutch Treaty of March 1824, by which the Dutch withdrew all objections to British occupation of Singapore, and the other with Sultan Hussein of Johor and Temenggong Abdu'r Rahman in August, by which the island was ceded outright to the British in return for increased cash payments and pensions. Singapore, together with Malacca and Penang became the Straits Settlements in 1826, under the control of British India. In 1832, Singapore became the centre of government of the settlements. On 1 April 1867, the settlements became a Crown Colony under the Colonial Office in London.

With the opening of the Suez Canal in 1869, Singapore became a major port of call for ships plying between Europe and East Asia. The development of rubber planting in Malaya after 1870 made Singapore the world's main sorting and exporting centre for that product. As trade expanded eightfold between 1873 and 1913, Singapore attracted many migrants from around the region. With this influx of migrants, whose intention was to make a better living for themselves, free enterprise flourished.

On 15 February 1942, Singapore fell to the Japanese and was occupied until their surrender in 1945. Between September 1945 and March 1946, Singapore came under the British Military Administration. The Straits Settlements was dissolved when the British Military Administration ended. On 1 April 1946, Singapore became a separate Crown Colony. In June 1948, a state of emergency was declared when the Communist Party of Malaya tried to take over Malaya and Singapore by force. The Rendell Commission, appointed by the British government in 1953 to review Singapore's Constitution, recommended measures to give Singapore a greater degree of self-government. The 1955 election resulted in the formation of a coalition government of the Labour Front, the United Malays National Organization and the Malayan Chinese Association. David Marshall of the Labour Front became Singapore's first chief minister on 6 April 1955.

Following the breakdown of constitutional talks in London for full internal self-government, Marshall resigned on 6 June 1956 and he was succeeded by his deputy, Lim Yew Hock. An agreement on the main terms of a new Singapore Constitution was reached after further negotiation, and the signing was held on 28 May 1958. Singapore's first general elections were held in May 1959 and the People's Action Party (PAP) formed the first government with Lee Kuan Yew as prime minister. In June 1959, the new Constitution confirming Singapore as a self-governing state was brought into force by the proclamation of the Governor as the Head of State. The British were responsible for the external affairs, defence and security of Singapore.

In 1963, to promote closer political and economic co-operation, Singapore joined Malaysia, which consisted of the Federation of Malaya, Sarawak and Sabah. The merger was endorsed by the people of Singapore in a referendum held on 1 September 1962. President Sukarno of Indonesia, who opposed the merger, embarked on a confrontation against Malaysia which lasted for three years. The merger was short-lived and Singapore was separated from the rest of Malaysia on 9 August 1965 and became a sovereign, democratic and independent nation. In August 1967, Singapore joined Indonesia, Thailand, the Philippines and Malaysia to form the Association of South-East Asia Nations (ASEAN).

To diversify her economy away from over-dependence on entrepôt trade, a massive industrialization programme was launched in the early 1960s. Foreign investments were encouraged, and private enterprises took the leading role in the development of commerce and industry. Government activities concentrated on the development of the infrastructure, an efficient administrative framework, and an array of public and social services.

THE SINGAPORE ECONOMY

The small population in Singapore poses a limit on the domestic market for her produce. The only natural resource is the strategic geographical location. Owing to this advantage, Singapore used to thrive on entrepôt trade. The trade sector, which historically had been the mainstay of the economy in Singapore, is still important, although its share of GDP has declined. When Singapore gained self-government in 1959, unemployment was high, and the priority of the government then was job creation. A programme of industrialization was instituted as it was realized that Singapore's traditional entrepôt trade faced limited growth. Initially, the growth of the manufacturing sector in the 1960s was stimulated by labour-intensive industries (such as textiles, garments, foods, paper and wood products) to absorb the unemployed. In the 1970s, as a result of the policy of upgrading the manufacturing sector, industrial expansion shifted to higher value-added and export-oriented industries. The 1970s was a period of high economic growth averaging 8.5 per cent per annum. By the 1980s, emphasis was also placed on making Singapore an important financial centre in the region with the manufacturing sector upgraded to concentrate on high technology products.

Singapore has an active stock exchange. The Stock Exchange of Singapore (SES) has a main and secondary board. As at June 1991, the main board had about 170 companies with about 14 companies on the secondary board. Due to the advent of modern communication technology and Singapore's open economy, the market trend of the SES is particularly sensitive to developments in major exchanges such as London, New York, Hong Kong and Tokyo. The capital market has grown in sophistication over the years, this being facilitated by the growing presence of major international stock broking and securities firms in Singapore.

Singapore has implemented successful economic plans by seeking a manufacturing sector geared to export markets, to provide suitable infrastructure, to attract foreign and domestic investors to industry, to develop managerial and marketing expertise, and to foster a disciplined labour force. The manufacturing sector continues to grow and remained the prime mover of the economy in the 1980s. Foreign investments, which constitute a significant proportion of total investments in Singapore, have been vital to Singapore's economic growth and survival. The key players in this area are Japan and the United States. They replaced the British who were previously key investors for historical reasons.

THE REGULATORY FRAMEWORK

An outline of the regulatory system in respect of financial reporting in Singapore is illustrated in Figure 8.1. The system comprises regulatory bodies in both the public and private sectors. The main difference is that the public sector regulatory bodies are government agencies with legal power to enforce compliance with the statutes. On the other hand the private bodies are mainly professional bodies and advisory committees set up to maintain a certain standard of financial reporting by their members. These private regulatory bodies do not have any legal power to enforce compliance with their standards and rules, but they usually act as advisers to the public regulators in matters such as violation of statutory requirements and incorporation of accounting standards into mandatory requirements. The various public and private regulatory bodies governing financial reporting in Singapore are discussed below.

Public sector regulators

The public sector regulatory bodies are dominated by Parliament which has the power to pass legislation. Based on recommendations from the Minister of Finance, bills on financial reporting are passed into statutes and made legally enforceable. The administration of these statutes is the duty of different government agencies. These government agencies include ministerial organizations (i.e. departments within a ministry) and non-ministerial organizations (i.e. statutory boards or corporations set up by a specific Act of the Parliament).

The Registry of Companies and Businesses (RCB) is under the Ministry of Finance which is responsible for the administration of the Companies Act and the Business Registration Act. These Acts are established to regulate the setting up and operation of companies and businesses. The Companies Act originated from the Indian Joint-Stock Companies Act of 1857. The Indian law was applied to Singapore because from 1826 to 1867 Singapore was part of the Straits Settlements and came under British India rule from 1830. The 1857 Act provided for the establishment of joint-stock companies with or without limited liability. It required a company to produce a balance sheet and file it with the Registrar of Joint-Stock Companies. The balance sheet and the auditors' report could be inspected at the company's registered office, and the auditors had to certify that the balance sheet contained a true account of the capital and liabilities, and of the property and assets of the company, or make such special report as they thought necessary. The current Companies Act, which was enacted in 1990, incorporates a substantial portion on financial reporting requirements in its Ninth Schedule in addition to other accounts keeping requirements in Part V of the Act. The Registrar of Companies and Businesses is vested with the legal power to charge anyone found guilty of non-compliance with the requirements of the Act.

Besides the Registrar of Companies and Businesses, the Monetary Authority of Singapore (MAS) is another government agency responsible for regulating financial reporting in Singapore. The MAS is a statutory board established as a non-ministerial organization under the Ministry of

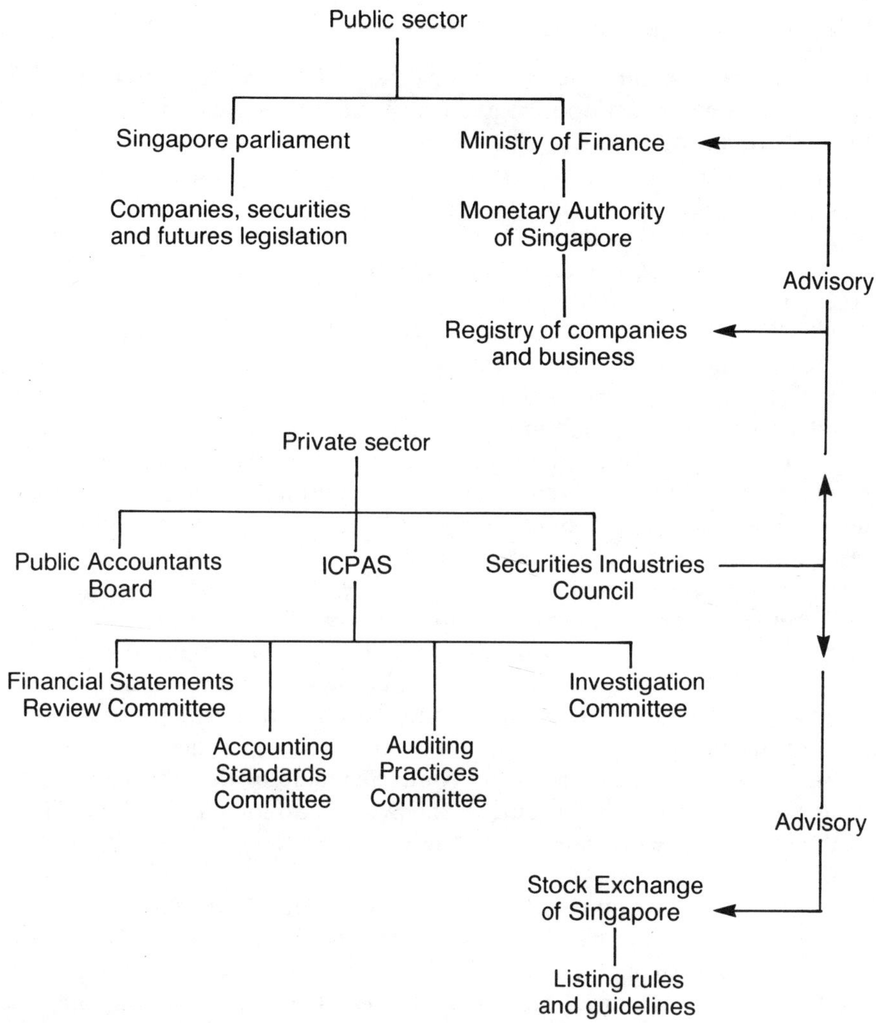

Figure 8.1 The regulatory framework in Singapore

Finance. Among its other regulatory functions is the administration of the Securities Industry Act 1986 and The Futures Trading Act. These Acts aim to provide more effective control and supervision of the SES and the securities and futures industries. The MAS has the authority and legal power to control and supervise the activities of the capital market. The RCB and MAS are two key regulatory bodies in the public sector with legal powers to enforce compliance with financial reporting requirements in the respective Acts.

Private sector regulators

In the private sector, there is a professional accounting body and an advisory committee set up to regulate and maintain a minimum standard of financial reporting practice. The Singapore Society of Accountants was the only professional accounting body in Singapore. It was established on 13 December 1963 under the Singapore Society Accountants Act. The Society was subsequently replaced by two organizations, the Institute of Certified Public Accountants of Singapore (ICPAS) and the Public Accountants Board (PAB), following the enactment of the Accountants Act 1987. The Public Accountants Board is set up to strengthen the control on public accountants practising in Singapore.

The ICPAS continues to perform its role as the only accounting standard-setting body in Singapore. This is done through a committee appointed by the Council of the Institute. The Accounting Standards Committee examines all International Accounting Standards (IASs) and determines the propriety of adopting the IASs in the Singapore context. So far twenty-six IASs have been adopted and issued as Statements of Accounting Standards (SASs) by the Institute. A list of the SASs with their IAS equivalents is shown in Appendix C. These standards are not mandatory but members of the Institute are strongly urged to adhere to them in preparing financial statements. As a result of the emphasis placed on incorporating good accounting standards and practices into the statute, most of the accounting standards and recommended practices issued by the ICPAS have been included in the Ninth Schedule of the Companies Act. Thus non-compliance with some of the SASs is no longer a mere violation of the Institute's regulation, but may also amount to an act liable to conviction.

In its bid to maintain a certain standard of financial reporting practice by its members, the ICPAS also conducts regular reviews of financial statements prepared by its members. This is done by another committee under the Council, the Financial Statements Review Committee. This committee reviews published financial statements of listed, gazetted and private companies for compliance with statutory requirements, SASs and ICPAS' recommendations. For the year 1990, 155 sets of accounts were selected for review. The composition of these accounts is shown in Table 8.1.

The Financial Statements Review Committee refers errant members to

Table 8.1 Composition of accounts reviewed

Type	*Number*
Public listed companies	78
Prospectuses and private limited	60
Gazetted and other accounts	17
Total	155

either the Public Accounting Practice Committee (PAPC) or the Investigation Committee. Members who have committed a series of serious defaults are referred to PAPC for counselling. Follow-up actions are taken by FSRC (Financial Statements Review Committee) in these cases to ensure that attempts are made to improve professional standards. In 1990, only one member was referred by the Committee to PAPC and there was one case reported to the Investigation Committee. Members who are suspected of gross negligence are referred to the Investigation Committee. If found guilty by the Committee, the Disciplinary Committee is informed and the member may be sanctioned as follows:

- removal of names from the register;
- suspension of membership for a certain period of time;
- fine of a sum not exceeding S$5,000;
- censure by the ICPAS.

Complaints against any practising CPAs are directed to the Public Accountants Board's Inquiry Committee. As compliance with the SASs is not mandatory, the disciplinary action taken by the ICPAS Council will only be effective if the person found violating the standards is a member of the ICPAS. Unless the relevant standards are also part of the statutory requirements in the Companies Act, non-members are not bound by the standards issued by the ICPAS.

Within the private sector, an advisory committee known as the Securities Industry Council (SIC) was set up in January 1973 under the Securities Industry Act to act as a consultative body to the Minister of Finance, the Stock Exchange and the Registrar of Companies. The terms of reference of the SIC include:

- advising the Minister on all matters concerning the securities industry, including the administration of legislation, particularly on the protection of investors;
- advising the Committee of the Stock Exchange on matters referred to it and considering recommendations submitted by the Committee, including listing requirements and the suspension and delisting of companies;
- advising the Committee of the Stock Exchange on actions to be taken to prevent or expose unlawful or dishonest forms of trading;
- advising the Committee of the Stock Exchange on applications by companies wishing to raise money by a public issue in any form;
- advising the Registrar of Companies on matters referred to it and on the activities of any company which in the opinion of the Council are suspect;
- administering and enforcing the Singapore Code on Takeovers and Mergers.

The setting up of the SIC appears to be a half-way house between an

SEC type of control and total self-regulation. The advice of the SIC legally binds neither the government nor the Stock Exchange nor the Registrar of Companies, and it operates by way of consultation and the moral weight of its opinion. Even under the Takeover Code, its sanctions against breaches consist of a recommendation to the Stock Exchange for the withdrawal of market facilities or public reprimand in the case of an individual offender. The duty of the Council is the enforcement of good business standards and not the enforcement of law, and its ruling is final. Besides the SIC, the SES also monitors and regulates its members by issuing Listing Manual and Disclosure Policy Guidelines with additional financial reporting requirements. Again, these rules and regulations are only applicable to members of the SES.

The Companies Act

The Companies Act has always been an important influence on corporate reporting in Singapore. At present, sect. 199 of the Act requires every company and directors and managers to be responsible for accounting, and other records to be properly kept. The records should not only be able to explain sufficiently the transactions and financial position of the company but also should enable a true and fair profit and loss account and balance sheet and any documents required to be attached thereto to be prepared from time to time. They ought to be kept so as to be audited conveniently and properly and retained for at least seven years. The accounts (i.e. the balance sheet and profit and loss account) should be audited and laid before the company in the Annual General Meeting. Sect. 201(15) requires directors of holding companies to prepare and lay consolidated accounts before the annual general meeting. The audited accounts have to be filed with the Registrar of Companies and Businesses.

No standard reporting format of the accounts is required by law, although considerable details must be disclosed as prescribed in the Ninth Schedule of the Companies Act. Notwithstanding the requirements of the Ninth Schedule of the Companies Act, sect. 201(14) provides for departure from these requirements if adherence would affect the true and fair view of the accounts. In such circumstances, the directors of the company shall add such information and explanations as will give a true and fair view of such matters. The Act provides that the accounts must present a true and fair view of the company's results and financial position, and additional information must be given in the directors' report.

Some of the important requirements of the Ninth Schedule are as follows:

- The profit and loss account (income statement) must disclose details of investment income, profits and losses on sale of fixed assets, depreciation charges, debt write-offs and provisions, directors' and auditors'

remuneration, taxation charges, movements in reserves and provisions, and dividends payable for the year.
- the balance sheet must disclose details of share capital, reserves and provisions, current and non-current liabilities, contingent liabilities, fixed and current assets, intangibles, and liabilities secured on assets of the company. Assets and liabilities must be analysed in some detail, the basis of valuation of assets must be stated and foreign currency conversion bases must be disclosed.

In line with the trend in other countries (e.g. the UK), the emphasis is to incorporate into statute those elements that are regarded as best accounting standards and practices. The Companies Act made extensive changes to the previous Ninth Schedule, which brings the provisions on the form and content of annual accounts substantially into line with the accounting standards and recommended practices adopted by the Institute of Certified Public Accountants of Singapore. The main amendments are in relation to the profit and loss account, the profit and loss appropriation account and the balance sheet.

The above requirements apply to all companies registered with the RCB with the exception of exempt private companies. Exempt private companies do not have to comply with the requirement to file their annual financial statements. An exempt private company is a private company with no more than 20 members, none of which are corporate bodies or nominees of corporate bodies (even if they are exempt private companies themselves). The Singapore subsidiary of a foreign corporate body could not qualify as an exempt private company.

The Act also requires all limited companies to appoint independent auditors, who must be registered with the Public Accountants Board and the Institute of Certified Public Accountants of Singapore.

Taxation

Singapore's principal taxes are income tax, estate duty and property tax. The Inland Revenue Department is the central body charged with the administration of tax laws. A company with a financial year ending on or before 30 September is required to furnish an estimate of its chargeable income within three months of the end of its financial year. This requirement does not extend to companies with financial years ending between 1 October and 31 December. Every company is required to submit a return within 21 days of being requested and notified in writing.

Financial statements are not influenced by the requirements of tax law. For tax purposes, the financial statements prepared for information of proprietors are supplemented by a tax computation schedule that reconciles commercial and taxable results (Touche Ross 1988).

The Securities Industry Act 1986 and Stock Exchange Requirements.

The Securities Industry Act 1986 came into effect on 15 August 1986. It repeals the Securities Industries Act 1973. The Act covers the following areas:

- Establishment, etc. of stock markets.
- Licensing of dealers, dealers' representatives, investment advisers and investment representatives.
- Reports to be kept by dealers, dealers' representatives, investment advisers and investment representatives, financial analysts, etc.
- Conduct of securities business.
- Accounts to be kept by dealers and to be audited.
- Investment of stockbrokers' Trust Funds.
- Fidelity Fund.
- Trading in securities.

The Stock Exchange Listing Manual requires a company to submit a semi-annual/interim report to the SES not later than three months after the end of the first six months in the fiscal year. In addition, a company should also submit preliminary financial statements as soon as the figures are available, and in any event not later than three months after the end of the fiscal year. The maximum interval between the end of the fiscal year of the company and the issue of the printed annual report to the company's shareholders and the SES should not exceed six months (Stock Exchange of Singapore 1987).

The SES's Corporate Policy was issued on 26 May 1973 in recognition of the need by the management of publicly held corporations for more specific guidance in making decisions involving full and timely disclosure of significant corporate developments. By means of a question-and-answer format, policies on six areas of corporate disclosure are given as follows:

1 *Immediate public disclosure of material information.* A listed company is required to make immediate public disclosure of all material information concerning its affairs, except in exceptional circumstances.
2 *Thorough public dissemination.* A listed company is required to release material information to the public in a manner designed to obtain its fullest possible public dissemination.
3 *Clarification or confirmation of rumours and reports.* A listed company should publicly clarify as promptly as possible rumours or reports that contain information that is likely to have or has had an effect on trading in the company's securities or would have a bearing on investment decisions.
4 *Response to unusual market action.* Whenever unusual market action takes place in a listed company's securities, the company should make inquiries to determine whether rumours or other conditions requiring

corrective action exist and, if so, to take whatever action is deemed appropriate.

5 *Unwarranted promotional disclosure.* A listed company should refrain from promotional disclosure activity which exceeds that necessary to enable the public to make informed investment decisions.

6 *Insider trading.* Insiders should be prohibited from trading on the basis of material information which is not known to the investing public. Insiders should be restricted from trading, even after material information has been released, for a period sufficient to permit thorough public dissemination and evaluation of the information.

A set of SES Guidelines was issued to help management of listed companies and to facilitate the application of the SES's disclosure policies. These guidelines set out various criteria and situations which give rise to questions in respect of full and timely disclosure. The new guidelines reflect the views of the SES in the light of their experience with disclosure problems of listed companies as well as with problems occurring in recent court decisions relating to disclosure. They also describe in detail the contents and preparation of public announcements by listed members and set out the new SES Exchange Surveillance Procedures which are carried out by the Listing Department. The important disclosures that are above the normal requirements of accounting standards and the Ninth Schedule of the Companies Act are:

- Provision of a statement showing the sales turnover figures or gross trading income during the preceding five financial years.
  Statement giving
  (a) the financial and trading prospects;
  (b) analysis of the financial conditions and operations of the company or group;
  (c) particulars of the directors, proposed directors and executives, such as the name, address, other directorships, bankruptcy suits and criminal convictions (if any) of such persons;
  (d) statements by experts and a valid written consent from the expert to have the statements included in the prospectus;
  (e) history of the company;
  (f) profit forecast and dividend and an accountant's report on these.

Accounting standards and recommended practices

To date, the ICPAS has issued twenty-seven accounting standards out of which twenty-six are adapted from International Accounting Standards. The list in Appendix C illustrates the SASs and their IAS equivalents. Some of the IASs have been modified and adapted to local circumstances. These are:

SAS 1 Disclosure of Accounting Policies

IAS 1 was modified by way of an appendix on the concept of substance over form. This appendix was added to elaborate on the application of the stated concept in special cases. Examples of these special cases include:

- Finance leases. Although finance leases are classified as leases, their accounting treatment should be different from that of operating leases and a finance lease asset should be shown as an asset in the lessee's financial statements.
- Sale of securities under repurchase agreement. Repurchase and reverse repurchase agreements are in substance not sales and purchases of securities but financing transactions and the accounting treatment should therefore reflect their economic substance rather than their legal form. To treat such transactions as dealings in securities in the financial statements may therefore be misleading.
- Imputation of interest. Certain long-term receivables and payables which are contractual rights to receive or pay money at a fixed or determinable future date should be recorded at their present value, if either the interest rate is not stated or the stated interest rate is unreasonable.

SAS 4 Depreciation Accounting

IAS 4 was modified by way of an appendix on depreciation accounting for investment properties. As a result of this appendix, investment properties are exempted from the requirements of SAS 4 and SAS 14. An option is given to accounting for such properties: the investment property can either be treated as property in accordance with SAS 14 and depreciated according to SAS 4, or accounted as an investment in the balance sheet at open market value, taking into consideration increases and decreases in its carrying amount. The application of this appendix must be disclosed in the notes to the financial statements.

SAS 5 Information to be Disclosed in Financial Statements

IAS 5 was modified by way of a foreword as follows:

- banks, insurance and discount companies are exempted from the requirements of this statement;
- companies with total assets or other operating revenues of less than S$1 million per annum need not disclose the amount of sales or other operating revenues.

Extra guidelines on certain items in SAS 5 are also given to assist members in deciding what is regarded as best practice.

SAS 6 Earnings Per Share

This statement is not adopted from the IAS, but is taken from *Statement of Standard Accounting Practice No. 3* issued by the Institute of Chartered Accountants in England and Wales.

SAS 7 Statement of Changes in Financial Position

IAS 7 was modified by way of a foreword exempting enterprises other than public companies with sales and other operating revenues of S$1 million or less and exempt private companies from the requirements of this statement. However, all companies whose financial statements are required to be published under regulatory requirements (e.g. in the government gazette) must comply with this statement.

SAS 11 Accounting for Construction Contracts

Additional guidelines on definition of terms and examples of special circumstances are given in the foreword to assist members in applying the statement.

SAS 12 Accounting for Taxes on Income

Additional guidelines on the interpretation of terms and the accounting treatment for companies granted tax incentives are given in the foreword.

SAS 14 Accounting for Property, Plant and Equipment

IAS 16 was modified by way of a foreword on the accounting treatment for transactions such as exchange of assets and trade-ins. In exchange transactions whereby non-monetary assets are exchanged between entities, the fair value of the asset surrendered or the asset received (whichever is more clearly evident) should be used to record the transaction. For trade-ins, the cost of the new asset is commonly recorded at the amount of the monetary consideration paid plus the lower of the unexpired cost or the fair value of the trade-in surrendered.

SAS 20 Accounting for the Effects of Changes in Foreign Exchange Rates

Additional guidelines are given by way of a foreword on the definitions of terms and a hypothetical example to illustrate the calculation of unrealized gains and losses.

SAS 21 Related Parties Disclosures

The Singapore standard adheres closely to the International Accounting Standard equivalent (IAS 24).

SAS 23 Reporting Financial Information by Segment

In Singapore the standard is not mandatory for banks, insurance and discount companies.

SAS 24 Accounting and Reporting by Retirement Benefits Plans

The statement is modified to exclude retirement benefits provided under the Central Provident Fund Scheme.

SAS 25 Accounting for Investments

This statement is modified by way of a foreword which supersedes the appendix to SAS 4 on accounting for investment properties.

SAS 27 Accounting for Investments in Associates

IAS 28 was modified by way of a foreword as follows:

- In Singapore, in addition to the consolidated financial statements, separate financial statements for the holding company are also required. In the separate financial statements of a holding company, where the equity method is used for associates, the same method should be used for subsidiaries, or vice versa.
- A wholly owned subsidiary which is exempt from issuing consolidated financial statements is also exempt from applying the equity method to account for investments in associates.
- An investor which has no subsidiaries or which does not otherwise prepare consolidated financial statements should equity-account its share of the results of associates according to paragraph 27(b) and its share of the post-acquisition retained profits and reserves as follows:
    (a) Balance sheet items – the investor's share of post-acquisition retained profits and reserves in associates should be shown in the balance sheet or by way of a note.
    (b) Profit and loss items – in addition to the investor's own profit and loss account, a profit and loss account should be prepared for the investor which incorporates the results of its associates. Such a profit and loss account may be shown by way of a note or presented as a separate profit and loss account.

GENERALLY ACCEPTED ACCOUNTING PRINCIPLES

Fundamental assumptions

The fundamental accounting concepts underlying the preparation of financial statements are: going concern, consistency and the matching concept. In applying these concepts, management take into account the following considerations: prudence, substance over form and materiality. The accounting policies should be disclosed, and if changes occur, the reasons and the effects on the accounts should be disclosed. The accounts are generally prepared on the historical cost convention as modified by revaluations of some items in the accounts. The Singapore Companies Act does not specify the accounting conventions to adopt in preparing the accounts; all the above are recommended by SAS 1.

Fixed assets

Fixed assets must be disclosed by major categories such as land, buildings, plant, machinery, etc. Further breakdowns are also required for items such as land and buildings. Under general practice, all assets with limited useful lives must be depreciated. The straight-line method is the most widely used method of depreciation. Intangibles must be amortized. SAS 14 allows fixed assets such as properties, plant and equipment to be stated at revalued amount instead of historical cost. The valuation is subject to the condition that an entire class of assets should be revalued or the selection of assets for revaluation should be made on a systematic basis. The policy on the frequency of revaluation, the method adopted to compute the revalued amounts, the year of appraisal and whether an external valuer was involved must be disclosed. SAS 15 requires the methods of accounting for leases and the amount of assets which are the subject of finance leases to be disclosed.

Stocks

Stocks have to be classified by major categories (e.g. materials, work-in-progress, and finished goods), and valued at the lower of cost and net realizable value. Cost includes all fixed and variable production overheads. Inventories are generally accounted for using FIFO or weighted-average cost. SAS 2 permits the use of specific identification, LIFO and base-stock formulas for inventory accounting only under special circumstances. If inventories are not ordinarily interchangeable or are goods manufactured and segregated for specific projects, they should be accounted for by specific identification of their individual costs. The LIFO or base-stock formula may be used if there is disclosure of the difference between the amount of the inventory as shown in the balance sheet and (a) the lower of

FIFO or weighted average and net realizable value, or (b) the lower of current cost at balance sheet date and the net realizable value.

Pensions

Essentially, separate disclosure of pension or retirement benefits is required. In Singapore, all employees must contribute to the Central Provident Fund which can be withdrawn at the age of 55. Unlike the UK, pensions are not a widely accepted corporate practice in Singapore.

Taxation

With respect to deferred taxation, companies can either use the deferral or liability methods, with partial or comprehensive allocation. Deferred tax assets should not be recorded unless there is reasonable expectation of their realization. Tax effect accounting is recommended in SAS 12. All timing differences should be accounted for by this method except where there is reasonable evidence that these timing differences will not reverse for at least three years ahead and there should be no indication that after this period those timing differences are likely to reverse. The amount of timing difference not accounted for must be disclosed. Deferred tax balances should be presented in the balance sheet of the company separately from shareholders' interest.

Foreign exchange translation

Translation differences and the basis of translation must be disclosed. Each asset, liability, revenue, or expense resulting from the foreign currency transaction must be translated at the rate at the transaction date, while at balance sheet date, foreign currency monetary items resulting from foreign currency transactions are translated at the rate at that date. Exchange gains and losses on unsettled and settled transactions should be recognized as income in the period that they occur. Where the foreign subsidiary is an integral part of the parent company's operations, SAS 21 recommends the use of the temporal method. Otherwise the closing rate method should be used.

Funds statements

Under SAS 7, funds statement should form part of the accounts. Separate disclosure must be made of the funds provided from, and used in the company's operations, and other sources and uses of funds. Where consolidated accounts are prepared, a consolidated funds statement is also required.

Business combinations

SAS 22 allows for both the purchase and the pooling of interest methods to be used in accounting for business combinations. The latter method is used when a business combination meets specified conditions (e.g. the offer secures at least 90 per cent of equity and 90 per cent of all voting shares, the offeror does not previously hold 29 per cent or more of the equity and total voting shares in the offeree, etc.). Pooling of interest or merging accounting is allowed only if it is deemed to be a uniting of interest, which rarely happens. A business combination is deemed to be a uniting of interest only if the shareholders of the combining enterprises achieve a continuing mutual sharing in risks and benefits attached to the combined enterprise and:

- the basis of the transaction is principally an exchange of voting common shares of the enterprise involved;
- the whole, or effectively the whole, of the net assets and operations of the combining enterprises are combined in one entity.

Investments

The market values of quoted securities have to be disclosed if they are different from their carrying amount. Associated companies, or subsidiaries where control is temporary or impaired, or when their businesses are too dissimilar from those of the rest of the group, must be accounted for using the equity method. A holding company is required to publish its own profit and loss account and balance sheet, as well as the consolidated accounts. All group companies must use the holding company's accounting policies. Where different policies are adopted and have material effects the consolidated accounts must be adjusted.

Receivables

A company is required to disclose amounts due from affiliated companies, its directors and employees. Where possible losses on different accounts are envisaged, provisions have to be made to the related receivable accounts.

Liabilities

In addition to disclosing the nature of the liabilities, a company's liabilities to its affiliated companies, contingent liabilities and also liabilities to employees have to be included. Assets and liabilities can be offset if a legal right of set-off exists.

Profit and loss account

Revenue from operations has to be distinguished from other sources of income. Extraordinary items are to be separately disclosed. Apart from taxation, other items of expenditure that have to be disclosed are: directors' remuneration, audit fees, depreciation, interest expense. For listed companies, the earnings per share, fully diluted earnings per share, and the basis of earnings per share calculations must be disclosed.

Directors' report and directors' statement

The contents of the directors' report are prescribed in the Companies Act. *Inter alia*, they include names of the directors, principal activities of the company, details of acquisition and disposal of subsidiaries, results for the financial year, transfers to/from reserves or provisions, issues of shares and debentures, directors' contractual benefits, usual items, etc. The directors have to issue a directors' statement which must be signed by two directors which states that the profit and loss account and the balance sheet are a true and correct representation of the company's financial affairs.

AUDIT

Under sect. 203(1) of the Companies Act, all companies incorporated under the Act are required to be audited. According to sect. 205(1) of the Act, within 3 months of incorporation, the directors of a company must appoint an auditor who shall hold office until the conclusion of the first Annual General Meeting (AGM). Sect. 205(2) provides for subsequent appointments of auditors at each AGM.

The powers and duties of the auditors are stated in sect. 207 of the Act. Of significant importance is sect. 207(9A) which requires an auditor of a public company or a subsidiary of a public company who has reason to believe that a serious offence of fraud or other dishonesty has been committed against the company by officers or employees of the company to report immediately to the Minister of Finance. A serious offence is one where:

- the offence is punishable by imprisonment for a term not less than two years;
- the value of the amount involved is not less than S$20,000.

The Standards of Auditing Guidelines (SAGs) promulgated by the ICPAS are based on the International Auditing Guidelines (IAGs) issued by the International Auditing Practices Committee (IAPC) of the International Federation of Accountants (IFAC), but modified to suit local requirements. The Accounting Standards Committee and the Auditing Practices Committee consider the standards/guidelines issued by IASC and IFAC respectively, and if suitable, they are adopted with such modifications as are necessary. These standards/guidelines must be approved by the Council of the ICPAS before they are officially adopted and issued.

According to SAG 1, the objective of an audit of financial statements, prepared within a framework of recognized accounting policies, is to enable an auditor to express an opinion. The auditor's opinion helps establish the credibility of the financial statements but is not an assurance as to the future viability of the entity nor to the effectiveness and efficiency with which the entity is managed.

COMPARISON WITH UNITED KINGDOM COMPANIES LAW

Some of the important differences between the Singapore and the UK Companies Acts are as follows:

Format of financial statements

The Ninth Schedule of the Singapore Act prescribes details to be disclosed in financial statements but does not lay down any formats for the financial statements. The UK Act, on the other hand, prescribes formats for both the balance sheet and the profit and loss account.

Contents of profit and loss account

Unlike the UK Act the Singapore Companies Act does not require the disclosure of cost of sales and gross profit. Income from investments need only be split into quoted/unquoted and subsidiary/non-subsidiary categories. Depreciation expenses for fixed assets, investments and intangibles must be disclosed separately. Interest on loans, debentures, deposit, or advances must be split into those paid to:

- holding company;
- subsidiaries;
- other related corporations; other persons.

Filing exemptions for certain companies

The UK Companies Act exempts 'small' and 'medium-sized' companies from full filing requirements that meet certain conditions. These exemptions do not include public companies or banking, insurance or shipping companies. These conditions must be satisfied for at least two consecutive years. However, the company may then miss a year and still qualify. In contrast, if a company is an exempt private company, which the Singapore Act defines as a private company with no more than twenty members and whose shares are not held directly or indirectly by any corporation, the company is not required to submit financial statements to the Registrar of Companies and Businesses. In lieu of the financial statements, the Eighth Schedule of the Act requires a certificate to be signed by a director, the secretary and the auditor of the company, and filed with the Registrar of Companies. The certificate states, *inter alia*, that the company appears able to meet its liabilities as and when they fall due.

SUMMARY

For historical reasons, corporate reporting practices in Singapore are to a large extent quite similar to the UK and Commonwealth countries such as Malaysia and Australia. Singapore has adopted International Accounting Standards as generally accepted practice. This, it hopes, will narrow the differences in practice between Singapore and the international community. As an open economy, investments flow into Singapore from many countries. Hence, there are economic as well as administrative advantages for Singapore to have internationally acceptable accounting standards. The participation of ICPAS as a member of IFAC and adoption of IFAC's promulgations, subject to adaptation to suit local environment, symbolizes Singapore's commitment to the cause of international harmonization.

APPENDIX A

Extracts from the accounts of Straits Steamship Land

Profit and Loss Account

	Note	Group 1990 $'000	Group 1989 $'000	Company 1990 $'000	Company 1989 $'000
SALES	*1*	**130,022**	115,246	**1,661**	1,732
OPERATING PROFIT/(LOSS)	*2*	**25,195**	14,916	**(1,874)**	(1,545)
Investment and interest income	*3*	**16,352**	12,666	**27,490**	19,502
Interest expense	*4*	**(4,851)**	(3,426)	**(2,926)**	(2,196)
Share of profits less losses of associated companies	*18*	**7,823**	7,574	—	—
PROFIT BEFORE TAXATION		**44,519**	31,730	**22,690**	15,761
Taxation	5	**(11,649)**	(5,933)	**(7,487)**	(4,516)
PROFIT AFTER TAXATION		**32,870**	25,797	**15,203**	11,245
Minority interests		**(7,431)**	(3,200)	—	—
PROFIT BEFORE EXTRAORDINARY ITEMS		**25,439**	22,597	**15,203**	11,245
Extraordinary items	*6*	**4,081**	67,356	**163**	41,507
PROFIT ATTRIBUTABLE TO STOCKHOLDERS		**29,520**	89,953	**15,366**	52,752

	Note	Group 1990 $'000	Group 1989 $'000	Company 1990 $'000	Company 1989 $'000
STATEMENT OF RETAINED REVENUE RESERVES					
At 1st January:					
As reported		**106,734**	31,557	**97,140**	55,267
Prior year adjustment (See paragraph (f) of Accounting Policies)		**17,667**	16,515	**193**	157
As restated		**124,401**	48,072	**97,333**	55,424
Profit for the year		**29,520**	89,953	**15,366**	52,752
Exchange differences arising on consolidation		**(3,660)**	(2,429)	—	—
Adjustment arising from change in Group structure		**(596)**	(352)	—	—
Dividends	*7*	**(6,671)**	(10,843)	**(6,671)**	(10,843)
At 31st December		**142,994**	124,401	**106,028**	97,333
Retained in:					
Company		**106,028**	97,333	**106,028**	97,333
Subsidiaries		**28,251**	(8,944)	—	—
Associated companies	*18*	**8,715**	36,012	—	—
		142,994	124,401	**106,028**	97,333

	Note	Group 1990	Group 1989
Profit per stock unit (cents):	*8*		
Before tax and extraordinary items		**10.6**	8.6
After tax but before extraordinary items		**7.9**	7.2
After tax and extraordinary items		**9.1**	28.6

The notes shown on pages 54 to 76 form part of these accounts

Balance Sheet

	Note	Group 1990 $'000	Group 1989 $'000	Company 1990 $'000	Company 1989 $'000
SHARE CAPITAL	9	**160,831**	157,142	**160,831**	157,142
SHARE PREMIUM	10	**92,315**	69,948	**92,315**	69,948
CAPITAL RESERVES	11	**507,924**	491,229	**544,890**	518,297
REVENUE RESERVES	12	**142,994**	124,401	**106,028**	97,333
SHARE CAPITAL AND RESERVES		**904,064**	842,720	**904,064**	842,720
MINORITY INTERESTS		**315,913**	270,379	—	—
DEFERRED TAXATION		**2,350**	2,951	—	—
LONG TERM BORROWINGS	14	**149,966**	154,498	**149,966**	149,998
		1,372,293	1,270,548	**1,054,030**	992,718
Represented by:					
FIXED ASSETS	15	**902,655**	894,859	**9,873**	10,418
PROPERTIES HELD FOR DEVELOPMENT	16	**435,605**	382,947	—	—
INVESTMENTS					
Subsidiary companies	17 & 35	—	—	**759,395**	838,039
Associated companies	18 & 35	**197,147**	52,330	**184,046**	38,115
Other	19	**5,308**	1,776	**1**	1
		202,455	54,106	**943,442**	876,155
DEFERRED ASSETS	20	**1,545**	2,182	**1,522**	1,933
CURRENT ASSETS					
Completed properties held for sale		**23,535**	21,871	—	—
Stocks	21	**1,611**	5,023	—	—
Trade debtors	22	**8,481**	16,480	—	—
Other debtors	23	**10,588**	8,307	**1,966**	615
Fixed deposits, bank balances and cash		**25,392**	17,276	**214**	264
		69,607	68,957	**2,180**	879
Less:					
CURRENT LIABILITIES					
Trade creditors		**29,317**	19,814	—	—
Other creditors and provisions	24	**86,300**	150,998	**2,910**	3,025
Net tax provision/(refund receivable)	25	**1,810**	(12,498)	**4,843**	(5,763)
Amounts owing to/(by) holding and related companies	26	**87,415**	(36,692)	**(111,424)**	(111,438)
Short-term borrowings	27	**3,902**	38	—	—
Bank overdrafts	28	**24,172**	—	—	—
Proposed final dividends	7	**6,658**	10,843	**6,658**	10,843
		239,574	132,503	**(97,013)**	(103,333)
NET CURRENT ASSETS/(LIABILITIES)		**(169,967)**	(63,546)	**99,193**	104,212
		1,372,293	1,270,548	**1,054,030**	992,718

The notes shown on pages 54 to 76 form part of these accounts

Group Statement of Changes in Financial Position

		1990 $'000		1989 $'000
OPERATIONS				
Profit before taxation		**44,519**		31,730
Non-cash items:				
Depreciation of fixed assets	**2,727**		3,883	
Share of results of associates	**(7,823)**		(7,574)	
		(5,096)		(3,691)
(Increase)/Decrease in:				
Stocks and completed properties held for sale	**1,931**		(164)	
Debtors	**(446)**		(6,750)	
	1,485		(6,914)	
Increase in creditors	**8,867**		13,212	
		10,352		6,298
FUNDS FROM OPERATIONS		**49,775**		34,337
Sales of fixed assets and investment property		**39,064**		1,612
Purchases of fixed assets		**(1,922)**		(4,311)
Net tax refund received/(taxes paid)		**661**		(2,459)
Development expenditure incurred	**(87,134)**		(288,828)	
Progress payments received	**7,686**		6,473	
		(79,448)		(282,355)
Other items		**(560)**		(134)
NET FUNDS FROM/(APPLIED IN) OPERATIONS		**7,570**		(253,310)
FINANCIAL AND OTHER TRANSACTIONS				
Proceeds from share issue		**26,056**		890
Sale of shares in subsidiaries and other investments		**3,580**		63,684
Acquisition of additional shares in subsidiaries and other investments		**(9,375)**		(1,885)
Net advances (to)/from and dividends from, less investments in, associates		**(133,321)**		29,475
(Repayment of advances to)/advances from minority shareholders of certain subsidiaries		**(57,522)**		119,512
Net proceeds from issue of Loan Stock 89/94		—		149,998
Net loan (repayment)/drawdown		**(3,248)**		958
Contribution by, less dividends to, minority shareholders of subsidiaries		**36,320**		9,847
Dividends to stockholders		**(10,856)**		(6,278)
NET FUNDS (APPLIED IN)/DERIVED FROM FINANCIAL AND OTHER TRANSACTIONS		**(148,366)**		366,201
NET (DECREASE)/INCREASE IN LIQUID FUNDS		**(140,796)**		112,891
Represented by:				
(Increase)/Decrease in short term borrowings from:				
Banks		**(26,752)**		(178)
Related companies		**(118,959)**		25,146
Increase/(Decrease) in short term deposits and cash from:				
Banks		**9,634**		5,760
Related companies		**(4,719)**		82,163
		(140,796)		112,891

The acquisition and disposal of shares in subsidiaries have been shown as separate items, and their effect on the individual assets and liabilities of the Group is not reflected in the above statement. The net assets of subsidiaries acquired and sold during the year may be analysed as follows:

	1990 $'000	1989 $'000		**1990 $'000**	1989 $'000
Fixed assets	**974**	7,562	Purchase consideration paid for in cash	—	(111)
Stocks, debtors and creditors	**1,292**	(2,003)	Sales proceeds	**3,580**	61,742
Taxation	—	(1,873)			
Advances from associates	—	(1,200)			
Net bank balances, cash and deposits with related companies	**1,602**	17,378			
Minority interests	**66**	—			
Net assets reclassified as investment in associates	—	(6,919)			
	3,934	12,945			
Goodwill on acquisition	—	(64)			
(Loss)/Profit on sale of subsidiaries	**(354)**	48,750			
	3,580	61,631		**3,580**	61,631

Summary of Significant Accounting Policies

In order to assist in the understanding of the figures presented in these accounts, the following summary explains the Group's significant accounting policies which have been consistently applied except where otherwise indicated:

(a) **Basis of Accounting**
The accounts are prepared in accordance with the historical cost convention modified by revaluation of certain fixed assets and investments in subsidiary and associated companies.

(b) **Basis of Consolidation**
The Group accounts consolidate the accounts of the Company and its subsidiary companies, all of which prepare audited accounts at 31st December. Subsidiary companies are those in which more than 50% of the issued share capital is held or in which the Group has management control.

The accounts of subsidiary companies acquired or disposed of during the year are included in or excluded from Group figures from the effective date of acquisition or disposal. Any excess or deficit of the cost of investments over net assets acquired is shown as a direct movement in capital reserves. On realisation, this excess or deficit is transferred direct to revenue reserves.

(c) **Subsidiary Companies**
Investments in subsidiary companies are stated in the accounts of the Company at the attributable share of their combined net asset value. Any revaluation surplus or deficit arising each year is transferred direct to capital reserves.

(d) **Associated Companies**
Associated companies are those in which the Group has a long-term substantial equity interest and in whose commercial and financial policy decisions the Group actively participates. The Group's share of profits less losses of associated companies, as shown in their audited accounts for the year ended 31st December (except for certain associated companies), is included in the Group's results.

The results of certain associated companies which do not prepare audited accounts at 31st December are based on their latest audited accounts and unaudited management accounts for the ensuing months up to 31st December.

Investments in associated companies are stated in the Company's and Group's accounts at the attributable share of their combined net asset value as shown in their accounts. Any revaluation surplus or deficit arising each year is taken direct to capital reserves.

(e) **Other investments**
Investments held on a long-term basis are stated at average cost. Provision is made for any diminution in value which is considered to be permanent.

Dividend income is recognised in the accounts when it is received from the investee companies.

(f) **Fixed Assets**

All fixed assets, except for freehold and long leasehold (i.e. over 50 years) land and investment buildings, are depreciated evenly over their expected useful lives and residual values have also been taken into account where appropriate. The estimated useful lives of the Group's fixed assets have been taken as follows:

Buildings	30 to 50 years
Short leasehold land and buildings	Over period of lease (ranging from 2 to 30 years)
Plant and equipment:	
Lifts, escalators and electrical installation	20 to 28 years
Computers	8 years
Other	3 to 7 years
Motor vehicles	4 to 5 years

Profits or losses on disposal of all fixed assets, except major asset items presently defined as investment properties, are included in the profit before tax for the year. Profits or losses on disposal of major assets so defined are treated as extraordinary items in the profit and loss account. Any surpluses held in capital reserves in respect of previous revaluations of fixed assets disposed of during the year are regarded as having become realised and are transferred to the profit and loss account.

Revaluation surpluses arising on valuations of the Group's properties are credited direct to capital reserves. Revaluation deficits are taken to the profit and loss account as extraordinary items in the absence of or to the extent that they exceed any surpluses held in reserves relating to previous revaluations of the same class of assets.

Since 1984, the Group had been providing depreciation on its investment properties. In order to bring the Group's accounting policy on these properties in line with the general practice in the industry and to better reflect their underlying values, Directors have decided to adopt Statement of Accounting Standard 25 under which investment properties will be stated at their market values. The change in this policy has resulted in an increase in Group profit after taxation and minority interests of $3,000,000 for the current year. The comparative figures for the full year in 1989 have been restated, and the corresponding increase in Group profit is $3,200,000. The effect of this change in accounting policy on the Company's results is not material.

Arising from the abovementioned change in accounting policy, the Group's completed investment properties have been restated to their market values. Based on valuations as at 31st December 1990 by Colliers Jardine (Singapore) Pte Ltd, an independent firm of professional valuers, the market value of the Group's investment properties amounted to $896,000,000 (1989: $883,750,000). The capital reserves of the Group have been restated to reflect this change in accounting policy. The Group's share of the net revaluation surplus for the year amounting to $9,339,000 (1989: $222,493,000) is taken direct to capital reserves.

The Group's net tangible asset per stock unit has increased by $0.80 to $2.81 (1989: by $0.78 to $2.68) as a result of this change in accounting policy.

The net asset value of subsidiaries as at 31st December 1989 has been adjusted in the Company's accounts to reflect the change in accounting policy, and its effect is shown as a prior year adjustment to capital reserves.

(g) **Properties Held for Development**
Properties held for development are stated at cost, which includes cost of land and construction, related overhead expenditure and financing charges incurred during the period of construction. Developments are considered complete upon the issue of temporary occupation permits. When completed, properties held for investment are reclassified as fixed assets and properties for sale are transferred to current assets as completed properties held for sale.

Profit recognised on partly completed projects is based on the percentage of completion method. The amount brought into the accounts is the direct proportion of total expected project profit attributable to the actual sales contracts signed, but only to the extent that it relates to the stage of physical completion at the end of the year and after making provision for contingencies. When losses are expected, full provision is made in the accounts after adequate allowance has been made for estimated costs to completion. Any expenditure incurred on abortive projects is written off in the profit and loss account for the year.

Profit on partly completed projects less any provision to reduce cost to estimated realisable value as well as the profit or loss on sale of completed properties are included in the operating results for the year.

(h) **Lease of Fixed Assets**
Lease rentals are charged to the profit and loss account in the year in which they are incurred.

(i) **Completed Properties Held for Sale**
Completed properties held for sale are stated at the lower of cost and net realisable value. Cost includes cost of land and construction, and interest incurred during the period of construction.

(j) **Stocks**
Stocks are valued at the lower of weighted average cost and net realisable value after adequate provision is made for damaged, obsolete or slow-moving stocks on an item by item basis. For finished goods and work-in-progress, cost comprises materials, direct labour and an appropriate proportion of fixed and variable factory overheads.

Profits are not recognised on short-term contracts until the contracts are completed. In the case of partly completed long-term contracts, profits recognised are based on the percentage of completion method. When losses are expected, full provision is established in the accounts after adequate allowance has been made for estimated costs to completion.

Progress claims made against work-in-progress are offset against the cost of work-in-progress and the profits recognised on partly completed long-term contracts less any provision required to reduce cost to estimated realisable value.

(k) **Debtors**
Known bad debts are written off and specific provisions are made for any debts which are considered doubtful.

(l) **Expenditure Carried Forward**
This is stated at cost less amounts amortised. Amortisation is over a period not exceeding five years.

(m) **Deferred Taxation**
Deferred taxation has been provided for under the liability method at current rates of taxation on the excess of book values of fixed assets over their tax written down values, and timing differences on certain provisions or charges in the accounts for which tax relief is not immediately available.

Future tax benefits arising from unutilised tax losses and capital allowances are recognised in the accounts only if there is reasonable assurance that they will be utilised against future taxable profits. These future tax benefits are offset against deferred tax liability in the Group's accounts.

(n) **Foreign Currencies**
Foreign currency assets and liabilities are converted into Singapore dollars, the currency in which these accounts are stated, at the exchange rates ruling at the end of the year. All exchange differences arising from the conversion are dealt with through the profit and loss account.

Transactions arising in foreign currencies during the year are converted at rates closely approximating those ruling on the transaction dates. Profits or losses arising from completed transactions are taken to the profit and loss account.

For inclusion in Group accounts, all assets and liabilities of foreign subsidiaries and associated companies are translated into Singapore dollars at the exchange rates ruling at the end of the year. Exchange differences due to such currency translations are dealt with through retained revenue reserves. The trading results of foreign subsidiaries and associated companies are translated into Singapore dollars at the average exchange rates for the year.

Auditors' Report

We have audited the accounts set out on pages 50 to 76 in accordance with Statements of Auditing Guideline and Statements of Auditing Practice and, accordingly, included such tests of accounting records and such other auditing procedures as we considered appropriate in the circumstances.

In our opinion:

(a) the accompanying accounts are properly drawn up in accordance with the provisions of the Companies Act, Cap. 50 and Statements of Accounting Standard and so as to give a true and fair view of:

   (i) the state of affairs of the Company and of the Group as at 31st December 1990 and of the results of the Company and of the Group and the changes in financial position of the Group for the year ended on that date; and

   (ii) the other matters required by Section 201 of the Act to be dealt with in the accounts and consolidated accounts;

(b) the accounting and other records and the registers required by the Act to be kept by the Company and by the subsidiaries incorporated in Singapore, have been properly kept in accordance with the provisions of the Act.

We have considered the accounts and auditors' reports of all the subsidiary companies for which we have not acted as auditors, and whose accounts have been included in the consolidated accounts. The subsidiary companies audited by our associated firms are indicated in Note 35.

We are satisfied that the accounts of the subsidiary companies that are consolidated with the accounts of the Holding Company are in form and content appropriate and proper for the preparation of the consolidated accounts, and we have received satisfactory information and explanations as required by us for those purposes.

The auditors' reports on the accounts of the subsidiary companies were not subject to any qualification, and in the case of subsidiaries incorporated in Singapore, did not include any comment made under sub-section (3) of Section 207 of the Act.

Ernst & Young

ERNST & YOUNG
Certified Public Accountants,
Singapore, 12th March 1991

APPENDIX B

Trade and Economic Indicators

Exhibit 1 Trade performance

	1987 ($bn)	*1988 ($bn)*	*Percentage increase*
Domestic exports			
By MNCs	33.5	42.4	27
By locals	5.5	7.2	31
Entrepôt trade	42.4	59.0	39
Retained imports			
Industrial inputs	40.8	50.8	25
Consumer products	6.4	8.0	25

Source: Singapore Trade Development Board, *Annual Report 1988/89.*

Exhibit 2 Economic indicators

	1989 (S$m)	*1988 (S$m)*	*1987 (S$m)*
Trade			
Exports	183,980.2	167,279.0	128,680.9
Imports	96,863.7	88,226.7	68,415.2
National income (at current market price)			
Gross national product	56,347.4	50,359.3	43,191.6
Per capita indigenous gross national product	17,910	16,483	14,510
Gross national saving	24,128.3	20,831.7	17,108.4
Gross capital formation	19,568.6	18,204.1	16,636.6
GDP (at 1985 market prices)	52,687.7	48,223.7	43,387.4

Source: *Yearbook of Statistics*, Singapore 1989, Department of Statistics.

Exhibit 3 Imports and exports by country of origin and destination

	Import CIF		*Export FOB*	
	1989 (S$'000)	*1990 (S$'000)*	*1989 (S$'000)*	*1990 (S$'000)*
United States	16,605,261	17,579,142	20,090,817	20,245,526
Japan	20,669,351	22,146,176	7,447,683	8,301,528
Malaysia	12,783,982	14,963,464	11,914,794	12,447,770

Source: *Singapore Trade Statistics, Imports and Exports*, December 1990, Singapore Trade Development Board.

APPENDIX C

Technical Pronouncements issued by the Institute of Certified Public Accountants of Singapore at March 1991

Statement of Accounting Standard (SAS)

SAS	*IAS*	*Standard*	*Effective date*
1	1	Disclosure of Accounting Policies	1 January 1977
2	2	Valuation and Presentation of Inventories in the Context of the Historical Cost System	1 January 1977
3	3	Consolidated Financial Statements (superseded by SASs 26 and 27)	1 January 1977
4	4	Depreciation Accounting	1 January 1977
5	5	Information to be Disclosed in Financial Statements	1 January 1982
6	–	Earnings per Share	1 January 1983
7	7	Statement of Changes in Financial Position	1 January 1979
8	8	Unusual and Prior Period Items and Changes in Accounting Policies	1 January 1981
9	9	Accounting for Research and Development Activities	1 January 1981
10	10	Contingencies and Events Occurring after the Balance Sheet Date	1 January 1981
11	11	Accounting for Construction Contracts	1 January 1983
12	12	Accounting for Taxes on Income	1 January 1984
13	13	Presentation of Current Assets and Current Liabilities	1 January 1983
14	16	Accounting for Property, Plant and Equipment	1 January 1984
15	17	Accounting for Leases	1 January 1985
16	18	Revenue Recognition	1 January 1985
17	19	Accounting for Retirement Benefits in the Financial Statements of Employers	1 January 1985
18	20	Accounting for Government Grants and Disclosure of Government Assistance	1 January 1985
19	23	Capitalization of Borrowing Costs	1 January 1986
20	21	Accounting for the Effects of Changes in Foreign Exchange Rates	1 January 1986
21	24	Related Party Disclosures	1 January 1987
22	22	Accounting for Business Combinations	1 January 1987
23	14	Reporting Financial Information by Segment	1 January 1987

24	26	Accounting and Reporting by Retirement Benefit Plans	1 January 1988
25	25	Accounting for Investments	1 January 1988
26	27	Consolidated Financial Statements and Accounting for Investments in Subsidiaries	1 January 1990
27	28	Accounting for Investments in Associates	1 January 1991

REFERENCES

Briston, R.J. and Foo, S.L. (1990) 'The evolution of corporate reporting in Singapore', *Research in Third World Accounting*, vol. 1, pp. 263–280.

Companies Act (Cap. 50).

Department of Statistics, *Yearbook of Statistics*, Singapore, 1989.

The Securities Industries Act 1986.

Stock Exchange of Singapore, *Listing Manual*, 1987.

Touche Ross, Singapore: *Tax & Investment Profile*, 1988.

Singapore Trade Development Board, *Annual Report 1988/89.*

Yearbook of Statistics, Singapore 1989, Department of Statistics.

Monthly Digest of Statistics, March 1991, Department of Statistics, Singapore.

PSA (Port of Singapore Authority) *1989 Annual Report.*

Singapore Trade Statistics, Imports and Exports, December 1990, Singapore Trade Development Board.

9 The Philippines

P. Tan

INTRODUCTION

The accounting profession and the practice of financial reporting have had a relatively long history in the Philippines in comparison with other East Asian countries. Financial reporting practices in the Philippines are largely influenced by the United States through close ties that date back to the period of US colonial rule in the Philippines. Although this period was less than 50 years, the Americans had a greater impact on financial reporting in the Philippines than the Spanish who governed the country for 300 years. During the American period, accounting education was introduced and the accounting profession was formally organized. Even after the end of US colonial rule in 1946, ties continued between the two countries through trade and investment. The regulatory framework in the Philippines is similar to that of the United States, in spite of significant differences in their socio-economic backgrounds and capital market structures.

This chapter aims to provide information on financial reporting in the Philippines as well as an analysis of financial reporting within the country's socio-economic framework. The experience in financial reporting in the Philippines is typical of many developing countries where exogenous influences have greater impact on the country's reporting practices than endogenous factors.

THE BUSINESS ENVIRONMENT

The political and socio-economic environment: an overview

Political system

The political system in the Philippines is basically that of a democratic republican state within which free enterprise is allowed to flourish. This system is provided for under the new Constitution of 1987 and is fundamentally different from its predecessor, which prevailed from 1972 to 1986. During the earlier period, martial law under Ferdinand Marcos provided legitimacy to authoritarianism and one-man rule.

Cultural influences

The Philippines has a rich cultural heritage because of the influence of different groups of people that came to its shores. The plurality of cultures inevitably had an influence upon the managerial styles of Philippine businessmen. An eclectic management style emerges that brings to bear the richness of the oriental and occidental heritage.

Industrial organization, which is founded in western management philosophies, is a relatively recent phenomenon in the Philippines. While western management styles are grounded in the concepts of objectivity, organizational goals and impersonality, the indigenous Philippine culture is dominantly subjective and familial and emphasizes the importance of the person *vis-à-vis* the organization (Andres 1985). The *barangay* or family unit was of paramount importance in Philippine culture because it preceded the notion of government, organization or even society. In fact, the *barangay* was so self-contained that the functions of these other societal units were internalized within it. Thus the familial values of small-group centredness and respect for authority and power are ingrained in the fabric of Philippine business culture.

The original peoples of the Philippines were of Malay ancestry. However, 'international' trade in the pre-Spanish era brought to the country both Indian and Chinese influences. The Chinese influence in business is evidenced today by the presence of many large conglomerates which are owned by Philippine–Chinese families.

The Spanish period of 300 years to 1898 left many indelible marks on Philippine life, particularly on religion. However, the Spanish influence on commercial practices and accounting is minimal. One of the major legacies of the Spanish rule was the emergence and consolidation of well-defined social and economic classes. The hierarchy that evolved separated the land owners from the rest of society. Thus began the consolidation of economic wealth and power for some Philippine families (Burley 1973: 237). While time may have diminished the intensity of the class structures, the patterns of concentration are discernible in present-day business. In a sense, Ferdinand Marcos continued this legacy through his practice of 'crony capitalism' which saw the granting of massive privileges (such as control of specific commodity markets) to favoured individuals. The unequal distribution of wealth still remains a critical problem in the economy.

The US colonial period that followed from 1898–1946, while comparatively shorter than the Spanish period, was significant in terms of its influence on the major institutions of the country which included the educational system and the professions. The US influence continued even after the end of the colonial period through close economic links.

Gray (1988) hypothesized that relationships exist between identified cultural characteristics and the development of accounting systems. Applying his hypotheses and using the Hofstede (1980) classification of 'culture areas', Gray proposed two maps which show the positions of accounting systems of various cultural groups against the axes of 'statutory control versus professionalism', 'flexibility versus uniformity', 'secrecy versus transparency' and 'optimism versus conservatism'. The Philippines is included under the 'less developed Asian' cultural classification. On these hypothetical maps, 'less developed Asian' is shown to be more subject to statutory control than it is to professionalism and has a greater element of secrecy than transparency. On both maps, the position of the accounting systems of the 'less developed Asian' group is closer to the 'more developed Latin' group (which includes Spain) than it is to the 'Anglo' group (which includes the USA and the UK).

Gray's hypotheses does not bear out well in the case of the Philippines. It is shown later in this chapter that the country's financial reporting framework bears a closer resemblance to the framework in 'Anglo' countries than it does to the 'Latin' framework. In the Philippines, non-cultural factors play a more important role in the development of financial reporting than cultural characteristics.

Economic environment

The Philippines is well-endowed naturally, with its large reserves of arable land, fishing grounds, minerals and forestry. It is therefore not surprising that the agricultural and mining sectors contribute to about a third of GNP. Another asset of the country is found in its large, highly literate work force. Many skilled Filipinos work abroad in the Middle East, Hong Kong and South East Asia. Their remittances have helped to mitigate the economic situation in the country. However, economic observers feel that the potential of the country's natural resources has not been fully realized. The country suffers from economic problems of severe dimensions which include deterioration of the trade balance, volatile inflation, declining value of the peso, widespread poverty and a large foreign debt (see Appendix B for economic indicators). The country's infrastructure is underdeveloped and power shortages affect economic growth and productivity.

These problems may be attributable to poor economic management by past regimes as well as the country's vulnerability to world market conditions and natural disasters. One controversial economic policy was the ambitious industrialization programme launched during the Marcos era which made the country dependent on foreign sources for materials and industrial goods. The dependence on oil imports precipitated major debt problems during the oil crisis. On the export side, the agricultural and mining sectors were exposed to volatility in world commodity markets. Structural economic problems were aggravated by the country's turbulent political history. For example, soon after the assassination of Benigno Aquino in 1983, the country experienced capital flight and hyperinflation.

Analysis of financial statements of companies must take into account the vulnerability of these entities to their economic environment. In this respect, generally accepted accounting principles (GAAP) in a country have to be evaluated for the degree to which they have specifically dealt with economic risk factors. Other than a few accounting principles which arose in response to environmental demands (e.g. allowing for revaluation of property, plant and equipment and the valuation of certain products at market prices), most of GAAP in the Philippines do not differ significantly from GAAP in the US or the UK which operate in very different economic settings (see 'Comparison with the UK and USA', p. 320). For example, the accounting standards in the Philippines are posited on the assumption that the income statement is pre-eminent in the meeting of user needs (SFAS 1, 1983). This raises a question of whether the balance sheet should not be given more emphasis than the income statement since financial condition, liquidity and long-term solvency of entities may be critical issues in such an economic environment.

Government policy on business

The role of the Philippine government in business has changed rather dramatically over time. Prior to the installation of martial law by Marcos, the economic role of the state had been largely non-interventionist. The situation changed significantly during the martial law period when state enterprises became bigger and more dominant in the life of the economy. Expenditures by government corporations rose from P8 billion in 1970 to P122 billion in 1984, an increase of 1425 per cent (Robledo 1989). In the corporate sector alone, the number of government-owned or controlled corporations rose from 35 in 1970 to 290 in 1985. The Aquino government, on assuming power, was committed to reversing this trend of bureaucratization of business and declared the private sector as the 'motor of economic recovery'. The privatization programme was started in 1986 with the divestment of government interests in various economic sectors such as agriculture, banking, transportation and tourism. A special agency, the Asset Privatization Trust, was established to oversee the programme.

In its programme to promote private enterprise, the government encourages both domestic and foreign investments in those sectors of the economy which will provide significant employment opportunities to the populace and which will help improve the productivity of the natural resources of the country and the technical skills of the labour force. The government agency that administers the scheme of investment incentives and regulates foreign investment is the Board of Investments (BOI). It executes the various incentive acts that are in operation, of which the Omnibus Incentives Code and the Investment Priorities Plan are of pertinence to foreign investors.

Capital market

The stock market in the Philippines is relatively unimportant as a source of finance. An analysis of the top 1,000 business corporations shows that only about 60 of such corporations are listed on the Philippine stock exchanges (Business Day 1987). Of the balance of these firms, about 900 are privately held corporations and 40 are government owned. During the last decade, market capitalization as a percentage of GNP ranged between 3 to 10 per cent. This is relatively low when compared to Japan (100 per cent), USA (50 per cent) and the UK (80 per cent) (Rowley 1987). Given the fact that the GNP of the Philippines is much smaller than the GNP of these other countries, the stock market in the Philippines is small in both absolute and relative terms.

The Philippine stock market is characterized by a low supply of and low demand for publicly traded equities. There is a general reluctance of top corporations to go public because many are family-vested and closely held interests where owners prefer to raise finance through debt rather than public issues of equity (Robledo 1989). On the demand side, the stock market is generally considered speculative since oil and mining shares predominate. Thus equity investments are less appealing to the investor than 'safer' alternatives such as money market instruments and government securities.

The dominance of oil and mining equities pervades the history of the Philippine stock market where such equities first gave rise to the need for a stock exchange. Commercial and industrial equities listed on the stock exchanges are comparatively few and do not reflect the overall importance of this sector in the economy. While oil and mining have a wider equity base and make frequent calls upon the public to provide capital, commercial and industrial firms tend to rely on debt financing to preserve private ownership (Rowley 1987).

Tan (1981) is a study on the pattern of financing by corporations in the Philippines. In the 1950s and 1960s, internally generated savings were a very important source of finance. With the advent of industrialization and the growth of company size and financial requirements, external sources of funds had to be sought. It was found that a larger and expanding proportion of external corporate fund requirements came from trade credit. This reliance on internal financing through savings and established credit relationships helped to preserve family control over businesses. Thus, both primary and secondary markets for corporate equity and long-term debt instruments have remained underdeveloped.

The dependence on external debt by Philippine companies is borne out by an analysis of the financing patterns of the top 1,000 corporations in the Philippines. During the period 1970–84, the debt–equity ratio (total liabilities to total stockholders' equity) averaged 2.9 (Robledo 1989). Furthermore, the dependence on external debt was on the increase during this period. In 1987, this ratio rose to 3.73.

The indebtedness of corporations reflects a wider macroeconomic problem. At the end of 1990, the country's foreign borrowings totalled US$30 billion which was more than ten times the borrowings at the start of the previous decade. The economy's foreign indebtedness had its origins in the 1970s when the country experienced a persistent savings–investment gap. Domestic savings failed to match the rise in investments, creating a vacuum that needed to be filled by non-domestic sources. During the second half of the 1970s, low interest rates in foreign financial markets encouraged increasing reliance on foreign borrowings to fill the gap. The deterioration of the country's net terms of trade, following the oil crises and the commodity slumps, aggravated the indebtedness.

Another factor that may explain the private sector's dependence on debt may be found in the governmental policy on credit and interest rates. It was only in 1984 that interest rates were liberalized to reflect market forces. Prior to this, ceilings for interest rates were set by the government. At the same time, credits from the Central Bank and other government banks were made available to priority sectors at concessional rates. The availability of cheap funds in the banking system may have led to the corporate preference for debt over equity and may have dampened the development of the stock market as an alternative source of finance.

Another noteworthy feature of the Philippine stock market is that active trading is limited to only a fraction of the listed securities. For example, at the end of 1987, the top four (of about 150) companies accounted for 51.9 per cent of total market capitalization. The largest corporation alone accounted for 22.5 per cent of the total market capitalization (de Caires 1988). Ten of the most actively traded shares accounted for 78 per cent of total market turnover on the Manila Stock Exchange during that year.

Table 9.1 Profile of the top 1,000 corporations in the Philippines

Ranked corporations	*Gross revenue (%)*	*Total assets (%)*	*Equity (%)*
1 - 100	63.60	68.27	74.20
101- 200	10.79	15.41	7.19
201- 300	6.96	5.19	5.68
301- 400	5.04	3.61	4.78
401- 500	3.61	2.71	2.31
501- 600	2.80	1.55	1.86
601- 700	2.28	1.05	0.81
701- 800	1.92	0.77	0.86
801- 900	1.61	0.81	1.61
901–1000	1.39	0.63	0.70
Total	100.00	100.00	100.00

Source: *Top 1000 Corporations*, 1988 edn.

Mega-sized firms are predominant in Philippine business. Many if not most Philippine industries are relatively concentrated – that is, a few companies account for a large share of total industry assets, sales and employment (Saldana 1985). Table 9.1 depicts this pattern.

Although the Philippine market shows signs of underdevelopment, it is by no means a young market. The establishment of the Philippine stock exchanges preceded most of the other Asian stock exchanges. There are two active stock exchanges in the Philippines – the Manila and Makati stock exchanges. The Manila Stock Exchange was founded as early as 1927 during the period of American colonial rule, while the Makati Stock Exchange started operations in 1965 to compete with the Manila Stock Exchange. (There are current plans to merge the two exchanges.)

For a long time, the Philippine stock exchanges were fairly important in the region. It was not until the 1970s that the Hong Kong stock exchanges overtook the Philippines in terms of capitalization and turnover (Rowley 1987). Unfortunately, political and economic problems in the 1970s and 1980s prevented the Philippine stock exchanges from maturing further to realize their full potential. The growth of the stock exchanges were disrupted by a series of crises that included the near collapse of the financial system in 1979, the political assassination of Benigno Aquino and the massive capital flight from the country during 1979–84.

Something has to be said for the optimism and positiveness of the Philippine market. A less resilient stock market would have been demolished by the magnitude of the problems faced by the country. However, the Philippine experience has shown that, in spite of the numerous set-backs, it was able to sustain recovery after each crisis. In fact the market showed signs of revival recently with market capitalization growing by about 95 per cent per annum for 1988 and 1989. The government also realized the need for a comprehensive policy to develop and promote the equities market. It proposed that a commission be set up to monitor and assess the changing conditions in the capital markets and to recommend the necessary measures which will accelerate domestic capital formation and economic recovery through capital markets.

Some observations can be made of the study of the capital market and financial reporting in the Philippines. In spite of the underdeveloped capital market, the disclosure requirements for financial information are rigorous and match those of countries with more active capital markets (see 'A summary of GAAP', pp. 311–20). This suggests that the state of capital markets does not always determine the disclosure demands on financial reporting. Another observation is that the financial reporting framework in the Philippines does not provide for a greater orientation towards the creditor group or an emphasis on the balance sheet despite the heavy reliance on debt financing by most corporate entities.

INFLUENCES ON ACCOUNTING

The preceding analysis shows that the socio-economic environmental factors and the capital market patterns in the Philippines did not lead to a unique form of financial reporting. In the Philippines, financial reporting did not evolve to respond to indigenous factors. As is the case in many other developing countries, these practices were largely imported from an accounting 'sphere of influence' through historical colonization and international trade (AAA 1977).

Financial reporting in the Philippines is primarily influenced by US financial reporting practices and pronouncements. The Spanish influence is negligible in spite of the 300-year colonial rule. Financial reporting as practised in the Philippines today bears little resemblance to the Spanish mode of accounting which is characterized by a more legalistic approach with significant influences from tax laws and governmental regulation.

The US influence can be traced to the period of American rule of the Philippines from 1898 to 1946. It was during this period that two major processes were set in motion. One was the institutional learning of accounting and the other was the founding of the accounting profession.

One of the legacies of American rule was the provision of education to the masses. The school house became the symbol of American colonization in the same way that the church was the symbol of Spanish colonization. The influence of the American schoolmaster was important in the dissemination of American culture and traditions (Burley 1973: 243).

During the first few years of the American colonial period, the government established business schools in different parts of the country to train bookkeepers, typists, and clerks needed by government and business firms. One of these was the Manila Business School founded in 1904. The orientation gradually shifted from vocational training to formal academic study at university level. In 1916, the University of the Philippines began to offer accounting courses. Other pioneering institutions which launched accounting courses included the José Rizal College in 1919, the De La Salle College in 1919, the National University in 1921 and the Far Eastern University in 1928 (Casino 1981: 273).

In 1923, accounting practice had become sufficiently important to lead to governmental recognition of the formal accounting profession. An act of the Philippine legislature created a Board of Accountancy vested with the power to conduct CPA exams and to confer the CPA title. In 1929, the Philippine Institute of Certified Public Accountants was formally established to regulate members.

Another channel for the assimilation of US accounting was through the medium of international trade. Foreign trade and investment indirectly created the need for an accounting that was compatible to that of foreign parent companies. It is not surprising that Philippine accounting is so akin to that of the US. The roots of the close US–Philippine economic ties began in the colonial period when the Payne–Aldrich Act of 1909 and the Underwood–Simons Act of 1913 placed the commercial relationship of the US and the Philippines on the basis of reciprocal free trade. The duty-free status of imported American products had the effect of driving out other foreign competitors. Even after the country gained independence in 1946, the pre-war link continued through a parity clause in the Philippine Constitution which granted American firms the same rights as Philippine-owned businesses. Although these arrangements are no longer in force, the US remains a major trade partner of the Philippines (see Appendix C). The US also has a major presence in the form of its MNCs. In 1987, the number of US MNCs exceeded the combined total of all other MNCs.

REGULATORY FRAMEWORK OF PHILIPPINE FINANCIAL REPORTING

The regulation of financial reporting operates largely within the arena of the private sector through the auspices of the professional group, the Philippine Institute of Certified Public Accountants (PICPA) and the Accounting Standards Council (ASC), an independent group representing the profession, governmental agencies and financial executives. Governmental regulation of financial reporting operates within a co-operative framework with the private sector through the agency of the ASC. While government is not overly interventionist in its regulation of financial reporting, it has indirect influence through its oversight of the profession through the Professional Regulation Commission, and its surveillance over business entities through its agencies such as the SEC and the Central Bank.

Regulation through statute is confined to very broad issues and is not involved with the detailed aspects of financial reporting. Thus state regulation of accounting in the Philippines is not in the legalistic tradition of Franco-Germanic countries but is more akin to the US framework, where standard-setting is vested in an independent body over which both the private sector and the governmental agencies have oversight.

The major statutory provisions governing financial reporting are found in the Corporation Code and the Revised Securities Act of the Philippines. While statute does not mandate detailed requirements of financial reporting, the Code and the Act give substantial powers to the Securities Exchange Commission (SEC), a quasi-judicial agency, to promulgate rules and regulations governing corporations registered with it. Accounting regulations and opinions of the SEC are authoritative over reports issued by corporations whose shares are traded in stock exchanges or over-the-counter markets and those with twenty or more stockholders. However, given the SEC's representation on the Accounting Standards Council, its requirements of financial reports would be largely reflected through the pronouncements of the ASC.

COMPANY LAW

The Corporation Code of the Philippines had its origins in laws enacted in the early 1900s that authorized the creation of corporations. Prior to the American period, there was no entity in Spanish law exactly corresponding to the notion of the corporation found in English and American law. The main business entities then were partnerships and associations which were created by agreements (De Leon 1983).

The Corporation Code is an Act which:

- provides for the incorporation, organization and regulation of private corporations, both stock and non-stock, including educational and religious corporations (the term 'private corporations' refers to those corporations that are not public – that is, not organized by state for public welfare);
- defines their powers and provides for their dissolution;
- fixes the duties and liabilities of directors or trustees and other officers thereof;
- declares the rights and liabilities of stockholders and members;
- prescribes the conditions under which corporations, including foreign corporations, may transact business;
- provides penalties for violations of the Code;
- repeals all laws and parts of laws in conflict and inconsistent with the Code.

The code mandates the requirements for financial reporting in very broad terms. Sect. 74 of the Corporation Code requires proper records to be kept of business transactions and minutes of shareholders' and directors' meetings. Sect. 75 and sect. 141 of the Code require corporations to submit annual financial statements, which are duly audited, to shareholders and the Securities and Exchange Commission respectively. Sect. 75 allows for exemptions from audit requirements if the paid-up capital sum is below P50,000.

TAX LAWS

The main tax laws in the Philippines are the National Internal Revenue Code (NIRC) and the Tariff and Customs Code. The Bureau of Internal Revenue (BIR) and the Bureau of Customs (BC) are the authoritative agencies that interpret the statutes in accordance with the intent of the legislature and enforce the statutes.

Tax laws do not dictate how audited financial statements should be prepared. As in the UK and the US, business income for financial reporting purposes in the Philippines is determined on the basis of generally accepted accounting principles rather than on tax laws. The reported income from the profit and loss account is normally used for tax computations and adjusted, where necessary, to comply with tax statutes. It can be said that the tax authorities exercise some form of persuasive authority over financial reporting in that any change of accounting policies or methods by corporations must receive prior approval from the Commissioner of Inland Revenue. But there is no compulsion for only one set of financial statements to be issued for both financial reporting and tax purposes.

Generally, the revenue authorities will accept an accounting method that clearly reflects the taxpayer's income and conforms to the best accounting practice of the industry. For example, the depreciation and amortization methods and rates used for financial reporting are generally allowed for tax purposes (Price Waterhouse 1989).

The Bureau of Internal Revenue indirectly lends impetus to audit services by requiring corporations, partnerships or persons with gross quarterly earnings of greater than P25,000 to file audited financial statements with the tax returns.

SECURITIES LAWS AND THE SECURITIES EXCHANGE COMMISSION

The legislation that regulates the issue and trading of securities in the Philippines is the Revised Securities Act. The basic purposes of the Revised Securities Act are stated in the explanatory note of the related Parliamentary Bill and are as follows:

- to require full and fair disclosure of the character of the securities to be offered to the investing public;
- to provide for the regulation of securities exchanges and of over-the-counter markets and to prevent inequitable and unfair practices and transactions;
- to co-ordinate the securities industry with the monetary and credit policies of the government.

The Act does not define the term 'securities' but merely enumerates all possible papers that can be included in the word. It may be said however that 'securities' within the meaning of the Act are evidences of obligation to pay money, or the right to participate in earnings or distribution of property.

Several features are incorporated into the Revised Securities Act to protect the interests of the investing public. De Leon (1983) discusses them in detail and a summary of the main features of the Act is provided below:

- the granting of powers to the SEC as the enforcement agency of the Act;
- the mandating of prerequisites that must be observed before a sale or offer for sale of a security can be made to the public;

- the mandating of disclosure requirements in the registration of securities and a continuous system of disclosure thereafter;
- the regulation of persons involved in the selling or dealing of securities and the specification of rules concerning trading in securities;
- the placement of the operations of the stock exchanges under the jurisdiction of the SEC.

Within its general powers to regulate the securities industry, the SEC has specific powers that pertain to the sphere of financial reporting. However, as in the Corporation Code, these powers are broadly defined. Specifications concerning the form and content of financial information are not themselves written into the statute but are incorporated in directives issued by the SEC.

In particular, sect. 48 of the Act grants authority to the SEC, subject to the approval of the Minister of Finance, to

- make, amend, and rescind such accounting rules and regulations as may be necessary to carry out the provisions of this Act, including rules and regulations governing registration statements and prospectuses for various classes of securities and issuers;
- define accounting terms used in this Act;
- prescribe the form(s) in which required information shall be set forth, the items or details to be shown in the balance sheet and earnings statement, and the methods to be followed in the preparation of accounts, appraisal or valuation of assets and liabilities, determination of depreciation and depletion, differentiation of recurring and non-recurring income, differentiation of investment and operating income, and the preparation of consolidated accounts where deemed necessary.

In addition to powers granted by the Revised Securities Act, the SEC also derives its authority from the Corporation Code. Sect. 143 of the Code gives the SEC the power and authority to implement the provisions of the Code.

In its capacity to regulate financial reporting, the SEC issues rules and regulations covering the form and content of financial statements. The regulations affect those corporations with twenty or more shareholders and those whose securities are offered for sale to the public (the term 'public' is defined as twenty or more natural or juridical persons). The rules and regulations issued by the SEC are primarily an authoritative reinforcement of the accounting standards issued by the ASC.

However, special requirements are also mandated that are not included in the standards. The more significant of these include the following:

- management's responsibility for the financial statements must be expressedly acknowledged through the filing of a statement of management's responsibility;

- earnings per share data are required in the financial statements of issuers of securities traded on securities exchanges or over-the-counter markets.

ACCOUNTANCY PROFESSION

The accountancy profession in the Philippines is a well-established one and plays an important role in the country's business community. There are presently some 23,000 CPAs in the Philippines. There is a heavy demand for accounting-related services in the country. As was discussed earlier, audit of financial statements is required in most cases by the SEC and the Bureau of Internal Revenue. Other agencies, such as the Board of Investment, the Central Bank and the Board of Transportation, also require audited financial statements for those companies under their jurisdiction.

The first public accounting firms were set up at the turn of the century by British chartered accountants. These were followed by American CPAs and some Filipinos who obtained CPA certificates in the US (Casino 1981: 269–70). Formal recognition was given to the profession as early as 1923 with the enactment of the Accountancy Law. This early founding of the profession makes the Philippine accounting body the oldest in the ASEAN region.

The accredited professional organization in the country is the Philippine Institute of Certified Public Accountants (PICPA). The PICPA does not, however, have the right to license accountants. The licensing authority is the Professional Regulation Commission which is a governmental agency, created in 1973 to supervise and regulate all professions in the Philippines. To be a CPA, a person must have completed the degree of Bachelor of Science in Commerce or Business Administration (with a major in accounting) and must have passed the examinations conducted by the Board of Accountancy, a regulatory board of the Professional Regulation Commission. Subjects examined include theory of accounts, business law and taxation, management services, auditing theory and practice and practical accounting.

Although the PICPA does not have the power to license accountants, it performs several important regulatory functions. The PICPA, together with the Association of Certified Public Accountants in Public Practice, jointly sponsors the creation of the Auditing Standards and Practices Council which promulgates auditing standards that govern the practice of auditing in the Philippines. The auditing standards are approved by the Professional Regulation Commission before implementation. The Code of Ethics is enforced by the Ethics Board of the PICPA and the Board of Accountancy. The Board of Accountancy also requires each CPA to earn a stipulated minimum credit hours of continuous professional education (CPE) before he can renew his professional licence. The PICPA is the national professional organization accredited by the Professional Regulation Commission to oversee the CPE programme.

ACCOUNTING STANDARDS

The present machinery for standard-setting was created in November 1981 when the PICPA formally established the Accounting Standards Council (ASC). The creation of the ASC received formal support from the SEC, Central Bank and the Professional Regulation Commission as well as the largest organization representing the preparers of financial statements, the Financial Executives Institute of the Philippines (FINEX). The independent constitution of the ASC, and the representation of the various interest groups on its board, lends considerable authority to its pronouncements. Representatives from each interest group are nominated to the ASC to achieve the following mix:

PICPA	4 members
SEC	1 member
Central Bank	1 member
Professional Regulation Commission	1 member
FINEX	1 member

The main function of the ASC is to establish and improve accounting principles that will be generally accepted in the Philippines (ASC 1983). The principles are codified and issued in the form of Statements of Financial Accounting Standards (SFASs). The authority of the standards is founded not only on grounds of the independence of the standard-setting mechanism but also by the fact that all approved standards must be submitted to the Professional Regulation Commission for their final concurrence. Since the latter is a government watchdog body which has oversight over all regulated professions, its stamp of approval lends formal authority to the standards.

The SFASs have mandatory application to all financial statements of any commercial, industrial, or business enterprises which purport to be prepared in accordance with generally accepted accounting principles for issuance to other persons, such as stockholders, creditors, employees and the public at large (ASC 1983). Other pronouncements, including those issued by the PICPA Committee on Accounting Principles, the International Accounting Standards Committee and the Financial Accounting Standards Board of the United States, have persuasive authority over financial reporting in the Philippines.

A SUMMARY OF GAAP

As mentioned earlier, the SFASs are the official embodiment of generally accepted accounting principles (GAAP) in the Philippines. A synopsis of the main statements is provided below. (To further illustrate disclosure requirements an extract from the audited financial statements of a major Philippine company is included in Appendix A.)

SFAS 1 Basic Concepts and Accounting Principles (July 1983)

The primary objective of financial reporting has been identified as the provision of financial information that is useful to statement users, particularly owners and creditors, in the making of economic decisions.

The financial statements that are deemed necessary to reflect economic activities are the balance sheet, the income statement, the statement of changes in financial position, the statement of retained earnings, disclosures of other changes in owners' equity, description of accounting policies and related notes. SFAS 1 upholds the income statement as being the most important because 'profitability is a paramount concern to those interested in the economic activities of the enterprise'.

Financial statements should be prepared on the going concern and accrual basis, with due regard for the principles of substance over form and materiality. Conservatism is a 'modifying convention' to be used by accountants under limited circumstances.

SFAS 2 Summary of GAAP on Cash (July 1983)

Cash is usually presented as the first item under 'current assets'. Credit balances can only be set-off against demand deposit balances of the same bank where there is a legal right of set-off.

SFAS 3 Summary of GAAP on Receivables (July 1983)

Receivables may be classified as trade or non-trade, current or non-current. Trade receivables arise from the sale of goods or services to customers. Non-trade receivables include all others. Receivables from subsidiaries and affiliates, if significant in amount, should be stated separately. Credit balances, if significant, should be reclassified as liabilities unless these can be properly set-off against debit balances. Allowance for doubtful debt should be disclosed if net receivables are shown. Receivables discounted without recourse should be excluded from receivables and the gain or loss on sale recognized.

SFAS 4 Summary of GAAP on Inventories (July 1983)

Inventories should be stated at the lower of cost or market. Cost refers to direct and indirect expenditures incurred in bringing inventory items to their existing condition and location and should include production overheads. In cases where foreign currency liabilities are incurred to import inventories, a proportion of the foreign exchange adjustment (i.e. the additional amount required to liquidate the liability) may be added to or deducted from the cost of such inventories. Cost may be determined on the basis of any one of the cost flow assumptions: average cost, FIFO, LIFO and the specific identification method. Standard costs are acceptable if, at balance sheet date, they approximate those computed under one of the recognized bases. The major objective in selecting a method should be to choose one which clearly reflects periodic income. Thus LIFO is justified on the grounds that the resultant costs of sales reflect current prices although the balance sheet valuation may be far removed from them (SFAS 1).

Market is determined on the basis of replacement cost, except that market should not be more than net realizable value and not less than net realizable value reduced by a normal profit margin. The lower of cost or market rule can be applied to inventory items, in total, sub-total or individually, whichever method best reflects periodic income.

Valuation above cost is allowed for inventories which have immediate marketability at quoted prices and for which appropriate costs are difficult to obtain. Examples include agricultural, mineral and forestry products.

SFAS 5 Summary of GAAP on Liabilities (July 1983)

Current liabilities should be segregated according to the source of credit (e.g. accounts payable, notes payable, income tax payable and accrued expenses). Similarly, material items of long-term debt should be shown separately. Additional disclosures required in respect of long-term debt include interest rates, maturity dates, number of periodic instalments, nature and extent of restrictive covenants and security provided, the amount payable in foreign currency, default on loan agreements and any other significant information.

Certain short-term obligations may be included under long-term liabilities if there is intent and ability to consummate the refinancing on a long-term basis. Major commitments that will result in liabilities in succeeding periods (e.g. long-term leases or purchase commitments of merchandise) must be disclosed.

SFAS 6 Summary of GAAP on Property, Plant and Equipment (Carried at Historical Cost) (December 1983)

Property, plant and equipment (PPE) are normally carried at cost, less allowance for depreciation. However, revaluation is permitted in periods of inflation, whereby SFAS 12 will apply. Costs of PPE include all expenditures necessary to put the asset in condition and location for use. These may include the costs of interest of mortgages on land accrued at the date of purchase and financing costs incurred up to the completion of a construction project.

All PPE, excepting non-exhaustible assets, must be depreciated on a rational and systematic basis over the life of the asset. Acceptable methods include straight-line, units of production, sum-of-digits and the declining balance method.

The required disclosures include the major classes of PPE, basis of valuation, depreciation expense for the period, method used, accumulated depreciation at year-end, mortgages or lien on property, and important commitments for future additions.

SFAS 7 Contingencies and Subsequent Events (December 1983)

A loss from a contingency should be accrued by a charge to income if information available prior to the issuance of the financial statements indicates that the loss is probable and that the amount of the loss can be reasonably estimated. If no accrual is made, disclosure of the contingency should be made when there is at least a reasonable possibility that a loss may have been incurred.

A common practice in financial reporting is the disclosure of contingencies even when there is only a remote possibility of loss. These contingencies are normally in the nature of guarantees. The disclosure of these loss contingencies should continue. However, the accrual of so-called 'reserves for general contingencies' for general or unspecified business risks should not be made.

Contingencies that might result in gains are usually not reflected in the accounts since to do so might be to recognize revenue prior to realization. However, disclosure shall be made of them but care should be taken not to mislead as to the likelihood of realization. Subsequent events should be distinguished between adjusting and non-adjusting events and treated accordingly.

SFAS 8 Accounting for Foreign Exchange (March 1984)

A transaction in a foreign currency is to be recorded in the financial records using the exchange rate prevailing on the date of the transaction. At each balance sheet date, foreign currency monetary items should be reported at the closing rate or at forward rate, where applicable. Exchange differences between spot rates and settlement or closing rates must be taken to income except in instances when the exchange difference is in respect of (a) an intercompany monetary item that is in effect in the nature of a parent's net investment, in which case the difference can be taken directly to equity; (b) a foreign currency loan or transaction designated as an economic hedge of a net investment in a foreign entity, whereby differences are similarly treated as in (a); and (c) devaluation of a currency against which there is no practical means of hedging, and which is incurred in the acquisition of assets, whereby differences may be included in the carrying costs of assets.

As concerning translation of financial statements of a foreign entity, all assets and liabilities of that entity shall be translated at the closing rate and the exchange difference between the closing and opening rate of the opening net investment shall be taken to equity. Income statement may be translated at either closing rate or rates at transaction dates. However, when the foreign entity is an integral component of the parent's operations, the temporal method of translation shall be used.

SFAS 9 Summary of GAAP on Intangible Assets (March 1984)

SFAS 9 allows for the capitalization of costs of intangible assets. In particular, externally acquired intangibles should be capitalized. Costs of internally developed intangibles may also be capitalized except where measurement problems arise. The latter include practical difficulties in estimating the useful life of the intangible or where it lacks specific identification. Intangibles should be amortized over their useful life using a straight-line method in the absence of a more appropriate method. The period of amortization should not exceed forty years.

SFAS 10 Summary of GAAP on Investments (June 1984)

Marketable securities which are held for working capital purposes should be valued at the lower of its aggregate cost or market value at balance sheet date. Both realized and unrealized gains or losses shall be accounted for in the determination of net income. Significant gains or losses after balance sheet date should be disclosed but should not be adjusted for.

Long-term marketable securities should be similarly valued as current securities. However, unrealized losses are to be taken to equity unless a decline in market value is of a permanent nature, in which case the difference is treated as a realized loss and charged to the income statement. Other long-term investments should be accounted for under the equity method or the cost method, depending on the circumstances. The equity method of accounting should be used in respect of investments where the investor has control or the ability to exercise significant influence over operating and financial policies of the investee (dealt with in SFAS 11). Other investments are to be carried at cost after allowing for permanent declines in values. Investments of certain institutions (e.g. insurance companies, retirement plans, etc.) may be carried at their market values in accordance with industry practices.

SFAS 11 Equity Method of Accounting (October 1984)

The equity method should be used for accounting for investment of (a) all unconsolidated subsidiaries; (b) subsidiaries in parent company financial statements; (c) corporate joint venture; and (d) investees where the holding of voting shares is less than 50 per cent but where the investor has the ability to exercise significant influence over policies of the investee.

Usual procedures involved in the equity method apply. However, SFAS 11 requires any excess of cost of an investment over the net asset value of the underlying equity to be amortized over the life of the under-valued asset(s) of the investee where identifiable, or over a maximum period of forty years where non-identifiable.

SFAS 12 Revaluation of Property, Plant and Equipment through Appraisal (October 1985)

Revaluation of PPE is permitted but the following requirements must be observed: (a) appraisal should be made by recognized and independent specialists; (b) depreciation charges should be based on appraised values; (c) revaluation increment should be shown separately under shareholders' equity; and (d) adequate disclosures of the revaluation basis as well as of the original costs and depreciation of the asset must be made.

SFAS 13 Disposal of a Segment of a Business, Extraordinary Items and Prior Period Adjustments (December 1985)

Extraordinary items should be segregated from the results of ordinary operations and shown separately in the income statement. Extraordinary items arise from events or transactions of material effect that are distinguished by their unusual nature and by the infrequency of their occurrence.

Prior period adjustments should be presented in financial statements to reflect the retroactive application of the adjustments (i.e. against comparative figures) where these are present.

The results of continuing operations should be reported separately from discontinued operations and any gain or loss from disposal of a segment of a business should be reported in conjunction with the related results of discontinued operations and not as an extraordinary item.

SFAS 14 Changes in Financial Position (September 1986)

This standard reinforces the requirement of SFAS 1 that a statement of changes in financial position is needed to present the financial position and the results of an enterprise fairly. Funds may be presumed to be either cash or working capital but the ASC believes that the cash concept is the more informative form of presentation. The normal procedures of preparation and presentation apply.

SFAS 15 Disclosure of Accounting Policies (September 1986)

A description of all significant accounting policies of the reporting enterprise shall be included as an integral part of the financial statements. Changes in accounting policy are dealt with in SFAS 17.

SFAS 16 Related Party Disclosures (September 1986)

Financial statements shall include disclosure of material-related party transactions, other than compensation arrangements, expense allowances and other similar items in the ordinary course of business. The disclosure shall include: (a) the nature of the relationship(s); (b) a description of the transactions and such other information necessary to an understanding of the effects on the financial statements; (c) the peso amount of the transactions; and (d) amounts due from or to related parties at balance sheet date, and terms of settlement.

SFAS 16 does not define the meaning of 'related parties' but describes the possible entities that may be described as 'related parties'. There is also no explicit requirement to disclose the arm's-length equivalent of these transactions.

SFAS 17 Accounting Changes (May 1987)

Accounting changes refer to changes in accounting principle, estimate or reporting entity. The nature of and justification for a change in accounting principle and its effect on income should be disclosed in the financial statements. The cumulative effect of changing to a new accounting principle on the retained earnings at the start of the period should be included in net income of the period of change and reported in the same manner as an extraordinary item. Pro forma effects of retroactive application should be shown on the face of the income statement for income before extraordinary item, net income and earnings per share. Exceptions are allowed for those situations where pro forma accounts or determination of cumulative effect may be 'impossible'. Disclosure will be limited to showing the effect of the change on the results of the period of change and to explaining the reason for omitting the required information.

SFAS 18 Summary of GAAP on Stockholders' Equity (May 1987)

The standard prescribes the accounting and disclosure requirements on equity-related matters and takes into account the legal requirements of the Corporation Code.

One important requirement of SFAS 18 is that retained earnings must be distinguished between 'appropriated' and 'unappropriated'. Appropriated retained earnings are those required by law or contractual arrangements. However, the board of directors may also voluntarily designate a portion of retained earnings for future expenses, contingencies or other purposes. The distinction between appropriated and unappropriated retained earnings is important because sect. 43 of the Corporation Code prohibits stock corporations from 'retaining surplus profits in excess of 100% of their paid-in capital stock', except when justified by circumstances. Unappropriated surplus profits must be distributed as dividends.

SFAS 19 Summary of Generally Accepted Accounting Principles for the Banking Industry (February 1988)

This statement is the first of a series of statements of Generally Accepted Accounting Principles (GAAP) for specialized industries to be issued by the ASC. The statement prescribes requirements as to valuation and financial statement presentation of specific assets and liabilities of banks and other financial intermediaries.

SFAS 20 Accounting for Business Combinations (April 1991)

This statement deals with accounting for business combinations and the treatment of any resultant goodwill. A business combination is the result of the acquiring of control of one or more enterprises by another enterprise or the uniting of interests of two or more enterprises. Control is ownership, directly or indirectly through subsidiaries, of more than half of the voting power of an enterprise.

The purchase method and the pooling of interests method are not alternatives in accounting for the same business combination. A single method should be applied to an entire combination. Pooling of interests accounting is applied to combinations where each of the combining interests are autonomous and independent of the other and the manner of exchange are effected in a way to merge separate stockholder interests.

Under the purchase method of accounting, all identifiable assets acquired, either individually or by type, and liabilities assumed in a business combination, whether or not shown in the financial statements of the acquired company, should be assigned a portion of the cost of the acquired company normally equal to their fair values at date of acquisition. The excess of the cost of the acquired company over the sum of the amounts assigned to identifiable assets acquired, less liabilities assumed, should be recorded as goodwill. Goodwill recorded in a business combination accounted for by the purchase method should be amortized in accordance with the provisions of SFAS 9.

SFAS 21 Summary of Generally Accepted Accounting Principles on the Consolidation of Financial Statements (April 1991)

The statement defines a subsidiary as a company which is controlled by another company (known as the parent company). Control is ownership, directly or indirectly through subsidiaries, of more than one-half of the outstanding voting stock of a company.

A parent should present consolidated financial statements:

1 when the total liabilities of any one entity in the group is more than P50 million, or when total liabilities of the group is more than P150 million as shown in the balance sheets at the beginning of the most recently completed fiscal year;
2 when it falls under one of the following categories whether or not it meets the condition set forth in 1 above:
   (a) companies whose securities are traded on securities exchanges or over-the-counter markets;
   (b) the following financial intermediaries: banks, financing companies, investment houses, investment companies;
   (c) companies issuing commercial papers or other securities registered with the Securities and Exchange Commission.

A parent company that is itself a subsidiary is not required to present consolidated financial statements unless it falls under one of the categories in 2 above. However a parent company that is a subsidiary of a foreign entity is required to present consolidated financial statements.

A subsidiary should be excluded from consolidation if control is likely to be temporary or when control does not rest with the majority owners or operates under government imposed conditions so severe that they cast significant doubt on the parent's ability to control the subsidiary.

SFAS 21 describes the necessary procedures for consolidation and the disclosure requirements. The statement is based on sect. C51 of the Accounting Standards Current Text of the Financial Accounting Standards Board and on IAS 3 issued by the International Accounting Standards Committee.

SFAS 22 Statement of Cash Flows (July 1992)

This statement supersedes SFAS 14, 'Changes in Financial Position' and requires a business enterprise to provide a statement of cash flows in place of changes in financial position. It also requires that specified information about non-cash investing and financing transactions and other events be provided separately. The statement of cash flows shall use descriptive terms such as cash or cash equivalents rather than ambiguous terms such as funds. For the purposes of this statement, cash equivalents are short-term, highly liquid investments that are both readily convertible to known amounts of cash and so near their maturity that they present insignificant risk of changes in value because of changes in interest rates. The statement is largely based on Statement No. 95, 'Statement of Cash Flows' issued by the Financial Accounting Statements Board.

COMPARISON WITH THE UK AND USA: PITFALLS FOR THE ANALYST

The following characteristics account for major differences between financial reporting in the Philippines and those in the United States and the United Kingdom:

1 Several of the differences arise in the area of inventory valuation (see preceding discussion on SFAS 4).

   In the first instance, valuation at market prices is allowed under certain circumstances. The technical interpretation of the lower of cost or market principle differs in some respects from that in the UK. For example, comparison of cost and market can be made on a total basis whereas in the UK a separate comparison for each item is necessary. 'Market' is determined on the basis of replacement cost insofar that it does not exceed or fall below ceilings determined on the basis of net realizable value. Replacement costs are generally not used in the UK to determine 'market'.

   Costs may include an element of foreign exchange gain or loss arising from the settlement of liabilities. The additional amount required to liquidate a liability relating to the purchase of inventories may be apportioned to the costs of the inventories still on hand at balance sheet date. The same applies to the determination of costs of fixed assets.

2 A form of price-level adjustment is permitted, although it applies only to fixed assets and depreciation (SFAS 12). This practice is consistent with that of the UK, except that revaluation in the Philippines must be supported by appraisals from independent third parties. It differs from the US where no revaluation is permitted.

3 Deferred taxation is recommended by PICPA Bulletin No. 2 but no statement of financial accounting standard has yet been issued on it. However SEC regulations require that an explanation be made for significant variations in the customary relationship between income tax expense and net income before tax, if the reasons are not apparent.

SOME TRENDS IN PHILIPPINE FINANCIAL REPORTING PRACTICES

A review was carried out by the author on a sample of thirty audited Philippine financial statements from 1989/1990. The accounting policies and financial disclosures were reviewed for their compliance with Statements of Financial Accounting Standards. The review was a limited one because it was based on information provided in the financial statements. It was not possible to ascertain whether accounting policies were in fact complied with. Given this limitation, the compliance rate with respect to acceptability of accounting policies and adequacy of disclosures was high (approximately 94 per cent). Some observations pertaining to general trends in financial reporting are as follows:

1 Accounting policy on consolidation differed among companies. Full consolidation of group companies was not widely practised. This was probably due to the absence of an accounting standard on consolidation during the period under review. Most of the companies practised equity accounting for investments which exceeded 20 per cent of outstanding voting shares of the investee companies.
2 Retained earnings of all the companies reviewed had partially been appropriated for various reasons including contingencies, plant expansion and self-insurance. In all cases, the appropriations were voluntary (i.e. not required by law or contractual requirements). No disclosure was made of the specific circumstances (e.g. the actual expansion plans) that warrant the setting aside of reserves. In one company, a charge was made to the Income Statement for a reserve for contingencies. No information was provided as to whether the contingencies were specific or general in nature. It would appear that Philippine companies are generally cautious about retained earnings that are available for distribution as dividends. A company is legally prohibited from retaining surplus profits in excess of 100 per cent of its paid-in capital stock, unless justified by circumstances.
3 The companies under review also preferred to defer exchange differences (mostly losses) arising from long-term foreign currency borrowings and to amortize the differences over the period of the borrowings. This accounting treatment is allowed by the Philippine SFAS 8 and is an alternative to the charging of exchange losses to the Income Statement.
4 The practice of a modified historical cost accounting was prevalent. Most of the property, plant and equipment were carried at appraisal values.

SUMMARY

Financial reporting in the Philippines is well supported by a regulatory framework which includes an independent and authoritative standard-setting body, a reasonably well-documented GAAP, a long-established professional body and the mandatory requirement for audits of most entities. The standard-setting body is represented by both private sector and government and its pronouncements have mandatory status. Company and securities laws do not regulate financial reporting through detailed legislation of reporting requirements but vest broad powers on the SEC to carry out such regulation. Tax laws do not have significant influence on financial reporting practices.

The Philippines, with its early start in the sphere of financial reporting, is well positioned to take an active role in research efforts among developing countries on financial reporting and other accounting-related matters. In particular, it can take up the challenge to spearhead research into modes of accounting which are sensitive to the socio-economic contexts of developing nations and which are directly responsive (as far as accounting can be) to indigenous needs.

APPENDIX A

Extracts from the accounts of San Miguel Corporation

Consolidated Balance Sheets

December 31, 1989 and 1988
(Amounts in Thousands)

ASSETS

	1989	1988
CURRENT ASSETS		
Cash and short-term securities	₱ **3,679,914**	₱ 3,718,807
Receivables (Note 2)	**3,694,735**	3,202,771
Finished goods and in process	**1,526,524**	1,254,415
Materials, supplies and containers (including in transit) — net of allowance for losses and obsolescence	**6,100,980**	4,929,301
Deferred income tax	**111,030**	115,733
Prepaid expenses and other current assets	**410,733**	351,945
Total Current Assets	**15,523,916**	13,572,972
INVESTMENTS — Net of Allowance for Decline in Value (Note 3)	**1,433,370**	1,527,412
PROPERTY, PLANT AND EQUIPMENT — Net of Accumulated Depreciation (Notes 4 and 16)	**12,286,958**	8,766,189
OTHER ASSETS (Notes 5 and 6)	**809,290**	526,858
	₱ **30,053,534**	₱ 24,393,431

LIABILITIES AND STOCKHOLDERS' EQUITY

	1989	1988
CURRENT LIABILITIES		
Loans payable	₱ **4,101,790**	₱ 3,553,033
Accounts payable and accrued expenses	**4,639,993**	3,393,421
Drafts and acceptances payable	**932,822**	1,118,913
Income and other taxes payable	**622,229**	803,901
Dividends payable	**599,422**	488,907
Current maturities of long-term debt (Note 5)	**615,808**	789,919
Total Current Liabilities	**11,512,064**	10,148,094
LONG-TERM DEBT — Net of Current Maturities (Note 5)	**5,596,950**	4,244,391
DEFERRED INCOME TAX	**330,332**	201,779
MINORITY INTEREST IN CONSOLIDATED SUBSIDIARIES	**1,305,965**	935,078
STOCKHOLDERS' EQUITY		
Capital stock (Note 6)	**2,829,583**	1,398,927
Capital in excess of par value	**434,047**	167,483
Revaluation increment in property (Notes 4 and 7)	**1,235,749**	1,123,621
Cumulative translation adjustment (Note 8)	**297,278**	242,866
Retained earnings:		
Appropriated for expansion projects	**1,482,880**	2,882,880
Unappropriated (Note 9)	**5,028,686**	3,048,312
	11,308,223	8,864,089
	₱ **30,053,534**	₱ 24,393,431

Consolidated Statements of Income and Unappropriated Retained Earnings

For the Years Ended December 31, 1989 and 1988
(Amounts in Thousands, Except Per Share Data)

	1989	1988
NET SALES	**₱ 36,713,759**	₱ 30,866,414
COST OF SALES AND OPERATING EXPENSES	**32,853,277**	27,255,240
INCOME FROM OPERATIONS	**3,860,482**	3,611,174
OTHER INCOME (CHARGES)		
Equity in earnings of affiliates (Note 3)	**242,960**	229,425
Interest — net	**(1,360,102)**	(877,607)
Minority interest in earnings of consolidated subsidiaries	**(297,670)**	(155,032)
Others (Note 10)	**925,408**	250,913
	(489,404)	(552,301)
INCOME BEFORE INCOME TAX	**3,371,078**	3,058,873
PROVISION FOR INCOME TAX (Note 11)	**940,267**	1,006,736
NET INCOME	**2,430,811**	2,052,137
UNAPPROPRIATED RETAINED EARNINGS, AT BEGINNING OF YEAR	**3,048,312**	3,570,952
Appropriated for expansion projects	—	(2,000,000)
Reversal of appropriation for expansion projects	**1,400,000**	—
Cash dividends (Note 13)	**(437,922)**	(392,308)
Stock dividends — 100% in 1989 and 15% in 1988	**(1,412,515)**	(182,469)
UNAPPROPRIATED RETAINED EARNINGS, AT END OF YEAR	**₱ 5,028,686**	₱ 3,048,312
EARNINGS PER SHARE	**₱ 4.31**	₱ 3.67

Consolidated Statements of Changes in Financial Position

For the Years Ended December 31, 1989 and 1988
(Amounts in Thousands)

	1989	1988
WORKING CAPITAL WAS PROVIDED FROM		
Net Income	**₱ 2,430,811**	₱ 2,052,137
Items not affecting working capital:		
Equity in earnings of affiliates	**(242,960)**	(229,425)
Depreciation	**1,038,262**	764,074
Increase in deferred income tax — noncurrent	**128,553**	71,271
Gain on disposal of property, equipment and investments	**(679,527)**	(2,786)
Total from operations	**2,675,139**	2,655,271
Dividends received from affiliates	**189,000**	119,179
Proceeds from sale of property, equipment and investments	**974,159**	331,363
Proceeds of long-term debt	**1,988,939**	1,651,000
Issuance of capital stock	**284,705**	—
Increase in minority interest — net	**352,028**	74,637
Others	**10,675**	6,307
	6,474,645	4,837,757
WORKING CAPITAL WAS USED FOR		
Additions to property, plant and equipment	**4,500,240**	3,079,982
Additions to investments	**30,697**	3,418
Reduction of long-term debt	**636,380**	888,941
Cash dividends	**437,922**	392,308
Increase in other assets	**282,432**	9,890
	5,887,671	4,374,539
INCREASE IN WORKING CAPITAL	**₱ 586,974**	₱ 463,218
WORKING CAPITAL INCREASED (DECREASED) BY		
Cash and short-term securities	**(₱ 38,893)**	₱ 705,680
Receivables	**491,964**	301,285
Finished goods and in process	**272,109**	211,144
Materials, supplies and containers	**1,171,679**	1,122,871
Deferred income tax	**(4,703)**	(30,443)
Prepaid expenses and other current assets	**58,788**	10,796
Loans payable	**(548,757)**	(780,217)
Accounts payable and accrued expenses	**(1,246,572)**	(375,118)
Drafts and acceptances payable	**186,091**	(509,098)
Income and other taxes payable	**181,672**	(352,947)
Dividends payable	**(110,515)**	(213,536)
Current maturities of long-term debt	**174,111**	372,801
INCREASE IN WORKING CAPITAL	**₱ 586,974**	₱ 463,218

Notes to Financial Statements

(Amounts in Thousands, Unless Otherwise Specified)

1. SUMMARY OF SIGNIFICANT ACCOUNTING AND FINANCIAL REPORTING POLICIES

The accounting and financial reporting policies of San Miguel Corporation and Subsidiaries (the Group) conform to generally accepted accounting principles and reflect practices common to the Group and are set forth to facilitate the understanding of data presented in the consolidated and Parent Company's financial statements.

Principles of Consolidation

The consolidated financial statements include the audited accounts of the Parent Company and the following majority owned subsidiaries:

	Percentage of Ownership
San Miguel International Limited and its subsidiaries, principally Neptunia Corporation Limited	100
Premium Packaging International, Inc.	100
Tagbita Silica Industries Corporation	100
San Miguel Metal Works, Inc.	100
Pacific Warehouse Company	100
Packaging Products Corporation	100
Philippine Breweries Corporation	99
Monterey Farms Corporation	92
Coca-Cola Bottlers Philippines, Inc.	70
Philippine Dairy Products Corporation	70
La Tondeña Distillers, Inc.	70
Rizalag Land Company, Inc.	60
Anchor Insurance Brokerage Corporation	58

Investments in 20% to 50% owned companies are accounted for by the equity method, i.e. at cost, increased or decreased by the Parent Company's share of earnings or losses, less dividends. The affiliates accounted for by the equity method include the following:

	Percentage of Ownership
Ramie Textiles, Inc.	49
Nestlé Philippines, Inc.	45
SMC Shipping and Lighterage Corporation	40

All significant intercompany transactions have been eliminated.

The Company adopted the practice of full consolidation in 1989 and restated the 1988 financial statements accordingly. In the Parent Company financial statements, investments in both the subsidiaries and affiliates are accounted for by the equity method.

The financial statements of subsidiaries and affiliates were examined by independent auditors other than the Parent Company's independent auditors.

Inventories

Inventories are stated at cost (computed principally on the moving average method) which is not in excess of net realizable value.

Containers in circulation (bottles and shells) are amortized over their estimated useful lives.

Investments

Other investments are carried at cost less allowance for decline in value.

Property, Plant and Equipment

Property, plant and equipment are carried at cost and at appraised values established by independent firms of appraisers in 1979 for the Parent Company and at various dates for certain subsidiaries and affiliates.

Depreciation is computed on the straight-line method over the estimated useful lives of the assets ranging from 3 to 50 years.

Maintenance and repairs are charged to income as incurred; significant renewals and betterments are capitalized.

Retirement Plans

Pension cost is computed based on an accepted actuarial method and includes normal cost and amortization of past service cost. It is the policy of the Company and certain subsidiaries and affiliates to fund accrued pension costs.

Income Tax

Deferred income taxes are provided to reflect the timing differences between financial and tax reporting, principally related to provisions for doubtful accounts, provisions for inventory obsolescence and other losses, duties paid in the importation of property and equipment, and equity in undistributed net earnings of foreign subsidiaries.

Foreign Currency Transactions

Foreign exchange gains or losses arising from foreign currency transactions are reflected in income.

The Parent Company and a foreign subsidiary translate the financial statements of their foreign subsidiaries substantially in accordance with Statement of Financial Accounting Standards No. 8, entitled "Accounting for the Effects of Changes in Foreign Exchange Rates." All assets and liabilities are translated at year-end exchange rates and the results of operations at average exchange rates prevailing during the year. The resulting translation adjustment is reported in the "Cumulative Translation Adjustment" account under stockholders' equity.

Earnings Per Share

Earnings per share is computed based on the weighted average number of shares outstanding during each year, with retroactive adjustments for the two-for-one stock split and the 100% stock dividend declared in 1989.

Auditors' Report

Member Firm of
Price Waterhouse
Worldwide Organization

8th Floor, BA-Lepanto Building
8747 Paseo de Roxas,
Makati, Metro Manila

Postal Address:
P.O. Box 2288
Manila Philippines

Telephones 818 76 22
Telex 22370 (RCA), 66546 (ETP)
45087 (ITT)
Telecopier (632) 8153514

Joaquin Cunanan & Co.

Report of Independent Certified Public Accountants

To the Board of Directors and Stockholders of San Miguel Corporation

We have examined the balance sheets of San Miguel Corporation, and the consolidated balance sheets of the Company and its subsidiaries, as at December 31, 1989 and 1988, and the related statements of income and unappropriated retained earnings and of changes in financial position for the years then ended. Our examinations were made in accordance with generally accepted auditing standards and accordingly included such tests of the accounting records and such other auditing procedures as we considered necessary in the circumstances.

As described in Note 15 to the financial statements, the Board of Directors of the Company has approved a modified compromise agreement and amicable settlement among the terms of which is the manner of disposing the ₱500 million initial payment made under the stock purchase agreement. The compromise agreement is subject to approval by the Presidential Commission on Good Government and the Sandiganbayan, as may be required.

In our opinion, subject to the effects, if any, of the resolution of the matter referred to in the preceding paragraph, the financial statements examined by us and appearing on pages 30 through 43 present fairly the financial position of San Miguel Corporation, and of the Company and its subsidiaries, as at December 31, 1989 and 1988, and the results of their operations and the changes in their financial position for the years then ended, in conformity with generally accepted accounting principles consistently applied.

Joaquin Cunanan & Co.

Makati, Metro Manila
February 28, 1990

APPENDIX B

Major economic indicators

	1987	*1988*	*1989*	*1990*	*1991*
1 GNP (peso billions)					
Current prices	674	796	911	1,077	1,254
Constant (1985) prices	609	653	690	717	717
Real change (%)	5.2	7.2	5.7	3.9	–
2 GNP per head (pesos)					
Current prices	11,749	13,551	15,161	17,510	19,936*
Constant (1985) prices	10,614	11,114	11,476	11,659	11,393*
Real change (%)	2.7	4.7	3.3	1.6	−2.3
3 Exchange rate					
Peso to US dollar annual average	20.57	21.09	21.74	24.31	27.48
4 Trend in prices (% change)					
Consumer prices	3.8	8.7	10.6	12.7	17.7
Wholesale prices	9.1	13.4	10.7	10.2	13.5
5 Trend of foreign trade (pesos million)					
Net exports/(imports)	(31,638)	(36,095)	(74,085)	(106,925)	(86,443)†
6 External debt‡					
To nearest US$ bill	30	29	28	30	n/a

Source: IMF, *International Financial Statistics.*

Notes: *Estimate by Economist Intelligence Unit, London; †January to September; ‡information from World Bank, *World Debt Tables.*

APPENDIX C

Main trading partners

	1985	*1986*	*1987*	*1988*	*1989*	*1990*
			(% of total value)			
Exports to:						
USA	35.7	35.5	36.1	35.6	35.7	37.8
Japan	18.9	17.6	17.2	20.1	20.3	19.7
ASEAN nations	11.5	7.3	8.8	7.0	6.8	8.5
West Germany	3.8	5.0	5.1	4.2	4.3	4.8
Netherlands	3.1	5.1	5.4	4.5	4.2	4.4
United Kingdom	3.6	4.8	4.3	4.6	4.2	4.3
Imports (fob) from:						
USA	25.1	24.9	22.1	21.0	19.0	19.4
Japan	14.4	17.2	16.6	17.4	19.6	18.3
Taiwan	3.5	5.6	5.5	6.3	6.7	6.6
Hong Kong	3.9	5.1	4.6	4.6	4.6	4.5
Saudi Arabia	5.2	4.3	3.2	1.4	2.4	4.5

Source: National Statistical Coordination Board, *Philippine Statistical Yearbook*.

BIBLIOGRAPHY

Regulations

Accounting Standards Council of the Philippines (ASC) (1983) *Preface to Statements of Financial Accounting Standards of the Accounting Standards Council*, Manila: ASC.

Accounting Standards Council of the Philippines *Statements of Financial Accounting Standards*, ASC.

The Corporation Code of the Philippines (B.P. Blg. 68).

The Revised Securities Act (B.P. Blg. 178).

Other references

American Accounting Association (AAA) (1977) *Accounting Review*, Supplement to vol. 52, pp. 105, 129–30.

Andres, T.D. (1985) *Management by Filipino Values*, Quezon City: New Day, pp. 12–14.

Burley, T.M. (1973) *The Philippines: An Economic and Social Geography*, London: Bell.

Business Day (1987) *Top Corporations in the Philippines*, Quezon City: Business Day Corporation.

Caires, B. de (ed.) (1988) *The GT Guide to World Equity Markets 1988*, London: Euromoney Publications, pp. 345–54.

Casino, J.A. (1981) 'Accounting education in the Philippines', in A.J.H. Enthoven (ed.), *Accounting Education in Economic Development Management*, Amsterdam: North-Holland.

De Leon, H.S. (1983) *The Corporation Code of the Philippines* (annotated), Manila: Rex Book Store.

Economist Intelligence Unit (1992) *Philippines: Country Profile 1992–1993: Annual Survey of Political and Economic Background*, London: Economist Intelligence Unit.

Gray, S.J. (1988) 'Towards a theory of cultural influence on the development of accounting systems internationally', *Abacus*, March, pp. 1–15.

Hofstede, G. (1980) *Culture's Consequences*, Beverly Hills, California: Sage Publications.

International Monetary Fund (1992) *International Financial Statistics*, June, Washington, DC.

Mahal Kong Pilipinas Foundation Inc. (1988) *Top 1000 (1988) Edition: Philippines Best 1000 Corporations*, Manila: Mahal Kong Pilipinas Foundation.

Price Waterhouse (1989) *Doing Business in the Philippines*, Price Waterhouse.

Robledo, C.T. (1989) 'Development of the capital market in the Philippines', in B.K. Ng (ed.), *The Development of Capital Markets in the SEACEN Countries*, Kuala Lumpur: South-East Asian Central Banks Research & Training Centre.

Rowley, A. (1987) 'Asian stockmarkets: the inside story', *Far Eastern Economic Review*, Hong Kong, pp. 219–35.

Saldana, C.G. (1985) *Financial Management in the Philippine Setting*, Quezon City: AFA Publications, pp. 19–29.

Tan, E.A. (1981) *The Structure and Growth of the Philippine Financial Market and the Behaviour of its Major Components*, Working Paper 81-06, Philippine Institute of Development Studies.

10 Australia

M.C. Miller

This chapter examines financial reporting in Australia. First, there is a brief introduction covering salient features of Australia's history, geography, demography, government and legal system. Important aspects of the business environment are then surveyed. Next, the influences on accounting are discussed. The regulatory framework is outlined prior to a closer look at company law, tax law, stock exchange requirements and accounting standards. A summary of generally accepted accounting principles in Australia is provided. This body of principles is compared with those in place in the UK and the USA and pitfalls for analysts are identified. Extracts from a sample set of financial statements are included as an appendix.

Unless otherwise specified, references to dollar amounts are to Australian dollars. The foreign currency equivalents for one Australian dollar at 30 June 1993 were 0.4418 pounds sterling and 0.6667 US dollars. The corresponding average rates for the year ended 30 June 1993 were 0.4158 pounds sterling and 0.7052 US dollars.

THE LAND, THE POPULATION AND GOVERNMENT

Australia is an ancient land that has been inhabited by the Aboriginal races for thousands of years. In 1788 a fleet of settlers arrived to establish a British penal colony. By the end of the nineteenth century, there existed a set of substantially self-governing colonies, which in 1900 formed a federal system of government with the creation of the Commonwealth of Australia on 1 January 1901. The ties with Britain remained strong for many decades after the granting of independence and to this day Australia has remained a member of the British Commonwealth.

The mainland of Australia is a self-contained continent lying in a relatively isolated section of the southern hemisphere. Including the island of Tasmania its area is 7,682,300 square kilometres, 32 times the area of the UK and about the same size as the USA, excluding Alaska. But Australia's estimated population of 17.5 million at 30 June 1992 is less than 29 and 7 per cent of the corresponding UK and US populations.

The low average population density does not indicate the uneven pattern of population distribution. A third of the country is so arid that its commercial use is limited to mining and another third is only able to support a sparse population of pastoralists and miners. The majority of the population is concentrated in two widely separated coastal areas. The much larger and more populous region stretches along the south-east coast spanning the state capital cities of Adelaide, Melbourne, Sydney and Brisbane. The other coastal region, with substantially fewer people, is a short strip in the south-west which includes the capital city of Western Australia, Perth. Contrary to the rural image arising from Australia's exports of agricultural and mineral products, Australia is one of the world's most urbanized countries with in excess of 70 per cent of the population residing in cities with over 100,000 inhabitants. Two in every five Australians live in the two largest state capital cities, Sydney and Melbourne, and almost three in every five live in one of the five mainland state capitals. Approximately 90 per cent of the work-force is occupied in the secondary and tertiary industries as distinct from the primary industries.

Australia's political and legal institutions follow the western democratic tradition. Australia is a federation of six states and two mainland territories. There are three tiers of government: federal (or Commonwealth), state and local. The Australian Constitution confers specific powers on the federal parliament and residual powers on the states. Despite this similarity to the US Constitution, the Australian Constitution does not adopt the American separation of executive and legislative powers but provides for a parliamentary system that operates on a similar basis to the Westminster system of the UK.

The federal government comprises the elected Australian parliament with legislative power and the Cabinet of about half the full ministry presided over by the Prime Minister (the leader of the majority party in the lower house) with the main policy-making power. The federal parliament has the power to legislate in areas such as defence, taxation, interstate and overseas commerce, customs, banking, currency, foreign affairs and social services.

The state parliaments have the power to legislate on all the matters not exclusively assigned by the Constitution to the Australian parliament. As at the federal level, the main policy-making power is in the hands of the Cabinet comprising certain ministers and presided over by the Premier (the leader of the majority party in the lower state house).

The third tier is local government in the form of councils, municipalities, shires or local authorities. These bodies normally derive their power from statutes passed by state parliaments and their responsibilities are in such areas as town planning, garbage collection and the maintenance of local roads, streets and parks.

Australia has a strong independent judiciary. The primacy of parliament is recognized although the courts will rule on the legal status of legislation passed in parliament. Australian law consists of federal statutes, state statutes and the common law as developed from the original English base by the Australian courts. There is a hierarchical system of courts with the nation's final court of appeal being the High Court of Australia.

THE BUSINESS ENVIRONMENT

Australia has a capitalist economy where there is considerable reliance on the market and private enterprise. However, it is far from being a pure capitalist system as the functioning of the private sector is modified significantly by the public sector which employs about 30 per cent of the total wage and salary earners at the three tiers of government – federal (25 per cent), state (66 per cent) and local (9 per cent). Public sector outlays were around 40 per cent of gross domestic product in 1988/89 with about half the outlays being made at the federal level and the other half being made at the state and local government levels (Clark 1990: 154).

Government business enterprises contribute approximately 10 per cent of gross domestic product and are most conspicuous in the public utility sector and in the transport and communications industries. State governments often spend about 5 per cent of their outlays on subsidizing government business enterprises such as railways. Both the labour and capital productivity levels of the public utilities (electricity, gas and water) appear to be less than 55 per cent of the OECD average levels (OECD 1990: 50). At both federal and state levels action has been taken to 'privatize' some of the government undertakings by transferring ownership of their assets to the private sector or, at least, to 'corporatize' them by imposing policies and disciplines similar to those applying to private enterprise units.

A survey of the top 1,000 business enterprises operating in Australia in 1992 by *Business Review Weekly* (21 October 1992: 72–3) revealed that the range in revenue stretched from $72.5 million to over $15,000 million. An analysis of the top 100 within the 1,000 indicated the breakdown, by type of enterprise, shown in Table 10.1. Table 10.2 shows pertinent data

Table 10.1 Australia's top 100 companies by type

	Number in top 100	*Percentage of total*
Publicly listed companies	40	55.1
Foreign-owned companies	21	13.6
Government business enterprises	24	14.2
Private and other entities	15	17.1
Total	100	100.0

Table 10.2 Australia's largest companies, by sector

	Net revenue ($m)	*Profit (loss) after tax ($m)*	*Number of employees*	*Total assets ($m)*
Publicly listed companies				
Coles Myer (7/92)	15,178	371	132,543	5,728
BHP (5/92)	14,961	507	49,000	23,588
Adsteam (6/92)	12,746	(357)	n/a	6,210
Westpac (9/91)	12,351	476	42,431	106,019
Foreign-owned companies				
Mitsui & Co. (Aust) (3/92)	5,284	7	144	996
Shell Australia (12/91)	4,602	204	6,965	6,140
Government business enterprises				
Telecom Australia (1/92)	6,346	(205)	78,000	22,500
Qantas (6/92)	4,036	137	18,000	6,488

(compiled from the BRW survey with a ranking on the basis of revenue) for the four largest publicly listed companies, the two largest foreign-owned companies and the two largest government business enterprises.

Although there is an abundance of sole poprietorships and partnerships in Australia, it has been estimated that companies produce almost two-thirds of the nation's business output (Jackson and McConnell 1988: 96). Many industries in Australia, such as manufacturing, mining and chemicals, are dominated by large companies. It is widely recognized that the Australian economy is highly concentrated. There are a significant number of industries where a high percentage of the industry output is produced by the four largest firms, e.g., tobacco products, biscuits, cable and wire, pulp and paper products, and motor vehicles. In addition to concentration, certain industries are characterized by a high degree of foreign ownership and control.

The sources of finance for Australian companies may be divided into internal equity, external equity and external debt. Of these the largest source has been internal equity (funds from operations after tax and dividend payments). Historically, this source contributes about 50 per cent of total sources each year. Since the introduction of a dividend imputation scheme affecting dividend payments in 1988 and subsequent years, the pattern has been undergoing change as explained in a later section (see 'Tax Law', pp. 354–7). When raising capital from external sources, companies in the 1980s favoured debt over equity. Private sector debt increased by $279,000 million from $54,000 million in 1979/80 to $333,000 million in 1989/90. In contrast, new equity capital raised on the Australian Stock Exchange (ASX) amounted to $72,200 million over the same ten-year period (Heffernan 1992: 18). The 1991/92 figures on capital raisings indicate a swing back in the direction of equity as companies seek to reduce their debt levels and reconstruct their operations.

Company gearing in 1991, as measured by the debt–equity ratio (calculated by dividing all interest bearing debt, excluding convertible securities, by ordinary equity), varied greatly across industry groups (e.g., 0.34 for gold, 0.50 for developers and contractors, 0.83 for food and household goods and 11.52 for banks and finance). The average debt–equity ratios for all listed resource companies and for the 251 companies which comprised the All Ordinaries Index were 0.58 and 2.16 respectively (ASX 1992: 46).

Australia's relatively small population and economy cannot support capital markets of the breadth and depth of those in the UK and the USA. Corporate finance executives do not always find the optimum long-term type of financing easy to arrange. There is, however, a well-organized stock exchange as well as four nation-wide major commercial banks and a variety of merchant and investment banks (both local and foreign-owned). The banks and other financial institutions have the capacity alone or in syndication to structure financing packages to suit the requirements of creditworthy clients. A broad-ranging deregulation of financial markets started in 1983. This led to considerable lender competition in the last half of the 1980s. The consequence was some bold lending decisions followed by bad debt losses. As a result lenders are now exhibiting a more cautious approach in appraising corporate borrowers.

In 1987 the six state stock exchanges united under a new name and structure: the Australian Stock Exchange Limited (ASX). This created a strong single body to govern stock market trading in Australia, while business is conducted in each state capital city through the state subsidiaries of the ASX. Although most of the state exchanges had existed for over a hundred years, one national exchange was necessary to compete with overseas exchanges and to retain the major market for Australian securities within Australia.

To become a listed company an enterprise must comply with the ASX Listing Rules. Public companies, public trusts, no-liability companies, and overseas companies may list if they are of sufficient size to maintain a public market in their securities. Listing rules vary for mining and industrial companies but in both cases it is necessary to have at least 300 shareholders. In addition to the main board, a second board was established in the mid-1980s to give smaller and newer companies the opportunity to list

Table 10.3 Company listings, 1988–92

Year ended 30 June	*1992*	*1991*	*1990*	*1989*	*1988*
Main board listings	1,168	1,151	1,318	1,446	1,510
Main board equity raisings ($m)	12,289	6,596	9,147	10,952	13,395

and gain access to new capital. While it succeeded in this objective for a period, an unsustainable low level of liquidity led to the closure of the Second Board on 30 June 1992. Pertinent data from the ASX *Annual Report* (1992: 42) is set out in Table 10.3. The main board equities capitalization at 30 June 1992 was $276,822 million. The equities market is heavily concentrated. The top fifty listed companies represented approximately 80 per cent of both the market capitalization and the value of the equity turnover for the six months to 30 June 1992.

Finally, comment should be made on a striking feature of Australia's business environment – the industrial relations system. In conjunction with other factors, the system has had a retarding influence for decades on management and employee attitudes. Australia has a highly unionized labour force and a highly centralized system at both federal and state levels for determining wages and conditions of employment and for the settlement of disputes. The proportion of the work-force that is unionized is about 42 per cent and the proportion of the work-force covered by awards (legally binding agreements made by an industrial tribunal) is over double that proportion at 85 per cent (Hilmer 1990: 105).

The origins of the system can be traced back to developments early in the twentieth century when the interests of the infant manufacturing industry seeking protective tariff barriers and the interests of organized labour seeking regulated wages were linked. Subsequently, most unions developed on the basis of craft, skill or occupation and employers did not have the incentive to fight against restrictive work practices and other labour rigidities as long as their local competitors were subject to the same disadvantages.

The historical combination of tariff protection and rigid labour awards has had an adverse effect on Australian productivity levels particularly in manufacturing. Furthermore, it stunted the vision of management and labour:

> In such an environment, Australian management may have remained less flexible, and more paternalistic and autocratic in style than elsewhere, while some parts of the union movement have had very conservative attitudes towards change, focusing most of their attention on wage-related matters.
>
> (OECD 1990: 87)

Fortunately for Australia, a concerted effort by the government, with support from employer groups and certain enlightened sections of the union movement, is underway to reform the industrial relations system. A major shift in attitude seems to be occurring in Australian society. The old industrial relations system reflected a widespread view held for decades by many groups in Australia that the country was a resource-rich continent that could afford its own idiosyncratic systems and be remote from international competitive forces. Given Australia's rising international debt and other negative economic signals, the federal government in the 1980s decisively rejected this view and made an attempt to integrate Australia more fully into the world economy by the deregulation of the financial markets and the lowering of trade barriers. Moving into the 1990s, more and more Australians appear to be aware that competition for markets is now global and that there is a need to be open to and responsive to international forces.

INFLUENCES ON ACCOUNTING

The influences on external financial reporting in Australia are not unlike those operating in the UK and the USA and the outcome has been no radical differences in their broad approaches. All three countries are democracies with stable political systems, market-oriented economies, the same forms of business organization, and legal systems that rely on a limited amount of statute law which is supplemented by court decisions (a common law system rather than a Roman or code law system). Each country has a strong well-established accountancy profession that has sought to avoid 'excessive' government interference by accepting a degree of responsibility for accounting and auditing standards although the aim is never an absolute national uniformity in accounting classification and measurement.

As the sources of equity and debt finance are not limited to private or government sources, and as the stock exchange is charged with a fundamental role to provide facilities for the maintenance of a fair and fully informed stock market, there is an emphasis in general purpose financial reporting on satisfying the information needs of existing and potential shareholders along with the information needs of lenders and other creditors. Satisfying the information needs of the taxation authorities is viewed as a separate issue related to special purpose financial reporting.

Despite the common environmental and other variables, there are important differences in generally accepted accounting principles, disclosure requirements, and the mechanisms for the regulation of financial reporting in the three countries. These differences reflect not only variations in economic and business conditions but also a range of additional factors related to the country's history, politics and culture.

In Australia the most direct influence on corporate financial reporting has been company law and the government bodies associated with the operation of that law. However, the framework put in place by government has been bolstered by a concept of co-regulation. Under the co-regulation philosophy self-regulatory professional bodies and industry organizations develop rules and guidelines and monitor or enforce compliance subject to oversight and control by the responsible government regulatory authority to ensure adequate protection of the public.

The most important body in the private sector exerting an influence on financial reporting has been the accountancy profession through its contributions in preparing accounting and auditing standards and in promoting compliance with those standards. Complementing the statutory and professional requirements are the stock exchange listing rules which call for more timely reporting and widen the scope of reporting for listed companies in particular respects, as described later in this chapter (see pp. 357–8).

Both the public and private sector bodies are aware that income taxes substantially affect the way commercial transactions are structured, and some members of the accountancy profession have been accused of going too far in assisting clients to avoid tax by using artificial schemes. None the less, tax rules relating to classification and calculation are given little weight in specifying rules for reporting to shareholders and creditors. The financial statement impact of taxes is not, of course, ignored. Where the amount provided for income tax in the financial statements differs by more than 15 per cent from the amount prima facie payable on the profit for the year, a reconciliation that explains the difference is required in a note to the financial statements. In addition, comprehensive tax-effect accounting is standard accounting practice.

Company law in Australia was for a long period the result of a series of local adoptions of legislation passed in the UK. Through to the 1960s Australian company law tended to lag and then copy the advances in UK company statutes except for a few pioneering pieces of legislation in the state of Victoria (Gibson 1971, Parker 1982). This pattern has been broken in recent decades. Local committees reviewing the operation of the law in the light of any domestic corporate abuses and taking stock of international developments (normally including the USA, Canada, and New Zealand as well as the UK) now provide the stimuli for changes to company legislation.

Also of British origin is the institution of professional accountancy. In the second half of the nineteenth century Australia imported the idea of self-regulating professional accountancy associations from the UK (Parker 1989). The British model seemed to serve admirably for the first half of the twentieth century. But increasing US investment in Australia after the Second World War, greater exposure to the members of the US accounting profession in international partnership affiliations, and some parallels in reporting problems have tended to move the Australian accounting profession more towards the US vision of the role and duties of a self-regulating accountancy profession.

Moreover, although the most important external influence on accounting and auditing matters is now the USA, it should be recognized that Australia has reached a stage of maturity where it is eclectic in its approach and has taken a strong leadership role in the developmental process of producing certain standards for the International Accounting Standards Committee, of which Australia was a founder member.

Notwithstanding that an independent line has been taken within Australia on some issues (e.g., requiring goodwill to be amortized over a maximum period of twenty years and prohibiting the use of equity accounting in the primary financial statements), there is, with the heightened awareness of the globalization of markets, an increasing reluctance to deviate from what is perceived to be any world-wide norm. For this reason the Australian accounting profession views it as important to stay abreast of overseas developments and to enter into the debate in international forums in the formative stages before final decisions are taken on standards and other regulations that may become the basis for international harmonization.

Puxty *et al.* (1987) have presented a framework for examining the regulation of accounting practices in advanced market-oriented economies. They perceive accounting regulation to be a mix of market, state, and community. At one end of the market-state axis is 'liberalism' (exclusive reliance on market forces), and at the other end is 'legalism' (exclusive reliance on the powers of the state to legislate and coerce). Between the extremes are mixed modes such as 'associationism' (reliance on the principle of community coming into play in professional associations or other private sector groupings) and 'corporatism' (the state acting as an overseer and 'leaning' on the private sector bodies to achieve public interest goals). They applied their framework to four countries to obtain the following results:

- West Germany: approximates legalism;
- UK: principally associationism;
- Sweden: corporatism;
- USA: Elements of legalism and associationism, with the latter subordinated to the former.

Parker (1991) applied the same framework to Australia and Canada. He concluded that it was unclear whether the Australian system is better described as corporatism or associationism (Parker 1991: 64–8). Given the recent shift in the balance of forces which make the federal government the decisive authority (as discussed in the next section of this chapter), it is arguable that the system, while still between the two, has moved closer to corporatism.

Gray (1988) has taken a first step in the formulation of a theory of cultural influence on the development of national systems of corporate financial reporting. He describes culture as a system of collectively held values and identifies four value dimensions at the accounting subculture level:

- professionalism versus statutory control;
- uniformity versus flexibility;
- conservatism versus optimism;
- secrecy versus transparency.

Four hypotheses are framed about how these values may be linked to four underlying societal value dimensions. As the hypotheses are not operationalized and no empirical tests are carried out, Gray acknowledges that the explanatory and predictive power of the theory is limited. None the less, Gray's analysis does provide some insights as demonstrated by the attempt by Wines (1989) to use it to explain the Australian corporate reporting system. Wines draws on the work of Hofstede (1987) who has placed Australia towards the centre of the scale on certain societal value dimensions. This absence of extremes in cultural values is perceived to be at least partially responsible for the emphasis apparent in Australia on obtaining a balance between professionalism (self-regulation) and statutory control, and a balance between absolute uniformity and complete flexibility.

In terms of Gray's hypothesis on conservatism versus optimism, the prediction is that Australia would not have a highly conservative set of accounting principles. This is in fact the case as will become evident when later in this chapter Australian accounting principles and disclosures are outlined (see pp. 361–70). At this stage it is sufficient to note that there are few constraints on non-current asset revaluations, certain market values for quoted investments and land and buildings are required to be disclosed, and excessive liability provisions are discouraged. At the conceptual level Australia's Statement of Accounting Concepts No. 3 (SAC 3) rejects the concept of conservatism where it is understood to mean 'deliberate bias' by the understatement of revenues and assets and the overstatement of expenses and liabilities (para. 26).

Finally, Gray's hypothesis on secrecy versus transparency suggests Australia would be closer to the transparency end of the spectrum. This appears to be in agreement with contemporary Australian practice and thought. For the first half of this century disclosure in Australia was at a token or very basic level often lagging behind the British level. However, whether owing to cultural factors, the greater opening up of the Australian economy to world forces, or public outrage at corporate excesses, Australian authorities are now downplaying any right to secrecy in entities raising capital from the public. Significantly expanded disclosure requirements came into force in both 1986 and 1987. Recent accounting standards on related party transactions and superannuation plans demand an open accountability approach. The three Statements of Accounting Concepts (SAC 1, SAC 2 and SAC 3) issued in 1990 all provide conceptual support for a non-secretive approach in respect of 'reporting entities' defined as entities for 'which it is reasonable to expect the existence of users dependent on general purpose financial reports for information which will be useful to them for making and evaluating decisions about the allocation of scarce resources' (SAC 1, para. 40).

THE REGULATORY FRAMEWORK

The aim of this section is to give an overview of the Australian regulatory system in respect of corporate financial reporting. Figure 10.1 depicts the main elements in the present system. Dominating the system is the national scheme for the regulation of companies and securities in Australia. This system was the result of an agreement reached on 29 June 1990 between the federal and state governments and it replaced, on 1 January 1991, the discredited co-operative scheme that operated during most of the 1980s. A review of the evolution of the system will help readers to understand why corporate and securities regulation in Australia was not very effective in the 1980s.

Over a hundred years ago the first companies acts were passed by the state governments. The federal government was not assigned specific power under the Australian Constitution to create companies. Consequently, this area remained the province of state governments without any serious attempt to obtain uniformity across Australia until 1961 when uniform legislation was agreed to and passed in each jurisdiction. However, this arrangement was less than satisfactory as states varied in the timing and content of subsequent company law amendments and there was no strong central administration. The latter deficiency contributed to the many abuses during the late 1960s' mining boom as the limited jurisdiction of each state severely hampered action in dealing with serious interstate fraud and market manipulation. The inadequacies were highlighted when a senate select committee report (the Rae Report) was released and received extensive publicity in 1974.

In November 1978 the federal government and the six states bound themselves, through what was called the Formal Agreement, to a co-operative scheme for uniform companies and securities law and for (what it was hoped would be) uniform and effective administration. The Northern Territory became a party to the Formal Agreement in 1986. The administrative framework for the scheme was provided by the Ministerial Council for Companies and Securities, the National Companies and Securities Commission (NCSC) and the Corporate Affairs Commissions in each state, the Australian Capital Territory and the Northern Territory. An associated agency, the Accounting Standards Review Board (since renamed, the Australian Accounting Standards Board), was established from January 1984 by the Ministerial Council to consider existing and proposed accounting standards and to approve appropriate standards as company financial statement requirements. Figure 10.1 shows the present national scheme. However, to visualize the more decentralized co-operative system consider the box for the 'Federal Attorney-General' to be the box for the Ministerial Council, the box for the 'Australian Securities Commission' to be the box for the NCSC and the box for 'Business Centres and Regional Offices' to be the box for the State and Territory Corporate

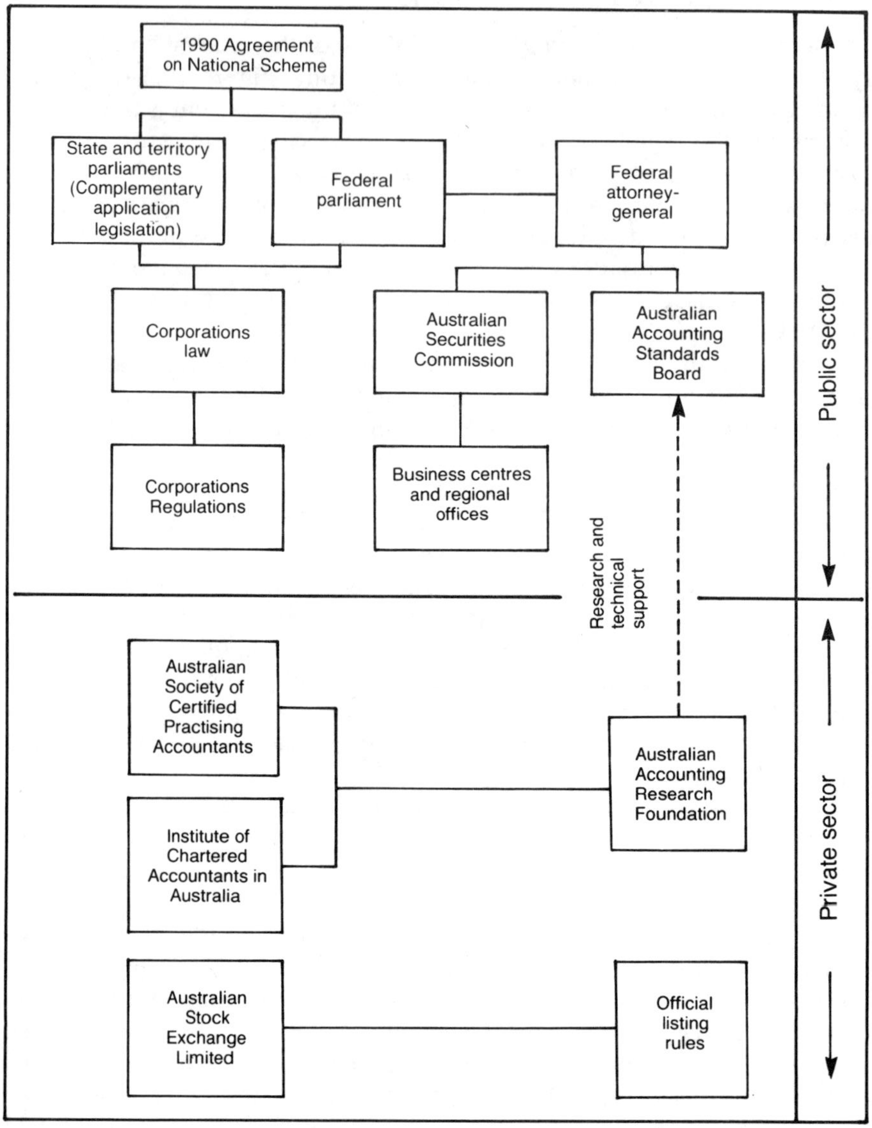

Figure 10.1 The regulatory framework in Australia

Affairs Commissions. As will become evident, the co-operative scheme was deeply flawed with a number of divided responsibilities.

Each member of the co-operative scheme was represented on the Ministerial Council by the relevant Minister administering companies and securities law (usually, the Attorney-General). The responsibilities of the

Ministerial Council were to consider and keep under review the scheme legislation and to exercise general oversight and control over the operation of the scheme. An important role of the Council, which normally met four times a year, was to approve amendments of the scheme legislation. The NCSC, subject only to the direction of the Ministerial Council, was responsible for policy and administration with respect to company law and the regulation of the securities industry and futures industry. However, the NCSC was empowered to delegate to state and territory Corporate Affairs Commissions the functions and powers conferred on it by the legislation. Indeed, the NCSC was required to have regard to the principle of maximum development of a decentralized capacity to administer the scheme. Consequently, most of its administrative responsibilities were delegated to the state and territory Commissions.

In operation the co-operative scheme was beset by problems. It was radical for its time and delegate Commissions, which had been fully autonomous, resisted at times the intrusion of the NCSC. Also, none of the parties to the Formal Agreement seemed prepared to resource the scheme adequately. Under the Agreement the funds for the functioning of the NCSC were to be provided one half by the federal government and one half by the other parties jointly in accordance with their proportion of the Australian population. Given this joint responsibility, no party appeared keen to increase its contribution.

When the system was devised, it was assumed that the constitutional position prevented the federal government from simply legislating for every party to the scheme. Consequently, a legislative device was used. The federal government first enacted companies and securities legislation that applied in the Australian Capital Territory. That legislation was then adopted by each state and later by the Northern Territory when it joined the scheme. In the Australian Capital Territory the legislation was referred to as the Companies Act 1981 and in each state it was referred to as the Companies (Name of State) Code. Accordingly, in the state of New South Wales the applicable companies legislation was the Companies (New South Wales) Code. For the sake of convenience the package of federal and state companies legislation was often called the Companies Code. That practice will be followed in the remainder of this chapter.

Dissatisfaction with the co-operative arrangement and several supportive High Court decisions suggesting it might be constitutional led the federal government to propose a genuine national scheme in the Corporations Bill 1988. The passing by the federal parliament of the Corporations Act 1989 did not see the Act come into operation that year because three states challenged in the High Court the constitutional validity of the Act. The High Court handed down in February 1990 its decision that the federal government did not have the power to legislate for the incorporation of trading and financial corporations. A federal election intervened and for a period the re-elected government needed to consider the options open to it. In the meantime the Companies Code remained in operation. Only in mid-1990 did the federal government reach general agreement with the states about a way of proceeding.

The Australian Securities Commission (ASC) was established as a new national regulatory authority by the Australian Securities Commission Act 1989 which was proclaimed to commence on 1 July 1989. The ASC replaced the NCSC, which ceased operations on 31 December 1990. The two organizations were in operation concurrently in the second half of 1990 with the same chairman, Tony Hartnell. The ASC is solely responsible to the federal minister and through him to federal parliament.The ASC Act gives strengthened inspection and investigation powers to the ASC compared to those of the NCSC. Further, the ASC has taken over the formerly state-run Corporate Affairs Commissions and replaced them with directly controlled business centres (providing over-the-counter service and access to the ASC database for company searches) and regional offices (carrying out the corporate regulation duties of the ASC). The role of the states has been greatly diminished. Their representation on the Ministerial Council counts for less because that body has no control over the ASC and, although it must be consulted on all legislative proposals, its approval is not needed for amendments related to national markets (that is, take-overs, securities, public raising of funds, and futures). In respect of other proposals, the Council has a deliberative function but the federal government has four votes, each state and territory one vote, and the federal government a casting vote. Further, the federal government is not obliged to introduce any proposal with which it does not concur. An incentive for the states to agree to this transfer of power was an offer from the federal government to compensate them generously for the loss of revenue from their Corporate Affairs Commissions. In addition, the federal government is funding the ASC at a level that will not restrict it in the same way as the NCSC was restricted by severe resource constraints.

In November 1990 the Corporations Legislation Amendment Bill was introduced into federal parliament. This bill converted the former Corporations Act into law of the Australian Capital Territory, called the 'Corporations Law'. This 'Corporations Law' was then passed in each state. The law of the new national scheme is similar to the old except that the law operates as if it were federal law. This applied laws regime is aimed at achieving the same effect as references of power by the states to the federal government without those references having actually occurred. Once companies are registered, they need not concern themselves with state boundaries and, for instance, it is unnecessary for companies to reserve names interstate. The law is not enforced by state investigating and prosecuting authorities and federal law prevails in respect of prosecution, arrest, bail, trial, conviction, sentencing, and so on.

It should be made clear that at the time of its commencement the Corporations Law did not radically change the content of company law in

Australia. The accounting and auditing requirements imposed on companies were virtually unaltered. The significant changes in the system related to the administration of the law and the resources available for the task. There have already been improvements in efficiency and effectiveness, particularly in the area of enforcement. Also, as the federal government has virtually sole control over the corporations legislation, faster responses may be made to calls for extensions to or reforms of the Corporations Law.

The former Companies Code and the present Corporations Law require the preparation of 'accounts' – a profit and loss account and a balance sheet to which must be attached or endorsed a statement by directors and an auditors' report. A directors' report covering specified items is required. The accounts in their form and content must comply with the 'prescribed requirements' which were set out in Schedule 7 of the Companies Regulations and are now set out in Schedule 5 of the Corporations Regulations. The statutory reporting requirements will be examined in more detail in a separate section on company law (see pp. 350–4).

Within the public sector is the Australian Accounting Standards Board (AASB), which prior to 1991 was called the Accounting Standards Review Board (ASRB). The establishment of the AASB was largely a response to the problems that the accounting profession was experiencing in obtaining compliance with its accounting standards. As there was no mechanism for enforcing compliance on company directors who were not members of the accounting profession, it seemed desirable to give statutory recognition to the standards. However, several committee reports (the Chambers Report in 1978 and the Campbell Report in 1981) questioned the suitability of the body of accounting standards on issue at the time for immediate statutory recognition.

Although the Australian accounting profession proposed that Australia follow the Canadian precedent of giving statutory recognition to standards developed and approved by the accounting profession, the Ministerial Council decided to set up a government-sponsored committee to approve standards. Legislation passed in 1983 introduced a requirement for accounts to be prepared in accordance with accounting standards so approved.

The legislation did not formally establish a board. This was done by resolution of the Ministerial Council in January 1984. The first AASB comprised seven members – a chairman selected by the Ministerial Council, two nominees of the accounting bodies and the remaining four drawn from panels of names submitted by various organizations with an interest in financial reporting.

The Ministerial Council gave the AASB broad powers and duties including the determination of priorities, sponsoring the development of accounting standards, reviewing accounting standards referred to it, seeking expert advice, conducting public hearings, inviting public submissions, and approving accounting standards. This set the AASB on a collision course with the accounting profession which had invested considerable resources in standards-setting and whose leaders were reluctant to allow the AASB to take over the standards-setting area and dictate priorities and other policy matters.

Before continuing with the recent history of the progress of the AASB, it is desirable to outline the private sector standards-setting arrangements around the time the AASB commenced operations, as those arrangements help explain how the present role and functioning of the AASB evolved. The two main professional accountancy bodies in Australia, the Australian Society of Certified Practising Accountants (ASCPA) and the Institute of Chartered Accountants in Australia (ICAA), established the Australian Accounting Research Foundation (AARF) in 1966. The Foundation became the organizational structure for the standards-setting procedures of the two professional bodies. By 1984 there were two accounting standards-setting boards operating within the AARF: the Accounting Standards Board (AcSB) and the Public Sector Accounting Standards Board (PSASB). The AcSB succeeded the Australian Accounting Standards Committee in 1981 and was established as a board of the AARF with the prime purpose of preparing Statements of Accounting Standards to be issued jointly by the ASCPA and the ICAA. The PSASB was established in 1983 to give explicit recognition to the need to improve financial reporting in the public sector. Shortly after its establishment, the PSASB resolved to co-operate and work concurrently with the AcSB to the fullest possible extent with the idea of producing a common set of standards for the public and private sectors.

The establishment of the AASB in 1984 meant Australia had three standards-setting bodies. Two of them (the AcSB and the AASB) were on the same turf preparing and issuing standards for enterprises operating in the private sector. As the AARF was the main body submitting standards to the AASB for approval and those standards had been through a long due process procedure, many accountants thought the AASB would merely rubber stamp the profession's standards. However, the AASB often re-opened issues and took an independent line on standards. Strains developed in the system as the AASB was meagrely resourced by the government and depended on the AARF which, although it had built up a first-class cluster of technical support staff, had difficulty in coping with all the extra work that the AASB was generating.

The AASB made very little progress in approving standards in its first few years. The Chairman of the NCSC intervened to try to get the parties to co-operate more fully and to speed up the production of approved accounting standards. While there was a spurt in the approval of standards, most of the parties came to the conclusion that the arrangements in place were less than ideal. The accounting bodies came to believe a merger of the AASB and the AcSB was the best way forward. The Ministerial Council approved the merger in 1988 and the AASB became the sole accounting standards-setting body for the private sector when the accounting bodies disbanded the AcSB. It was understood that the AASB would work closely with the AARF in the preparation and promulgation of accounting standards. It was agreed that the AASB would continue to receive public funds from the NCSC and the accounting bodies would maintain their commitment of resources for research and support staff at the AARF to service the AASB activities. The AASB membership was increased from seven to nine with the addition of two further members nominated by the ASCPA and the ICAA. This brought to four the number of AASB members nominated by the professional bodies. The Ministerial Council retained its power at that time to appoint members to the Board and to disallow any accounting standards approved by the AASB within sixty days of them being approved.

The position of the AASB was regularized when the Corporations Law was introduced. The AASB was formally established from 1 January 1991 as a federal statutory board and given the power to 'make' accounting standards for corporate financial reports. Under the law any standard made by the AASB is deemed to be a 'disallowable instrument', which means it is equivalent to a regulation under an Act of Parliament. Accordingly, new standards made by the AASB must be laid before both houses of federal parliament for fifteen sitting days, during which time a motion for disallowance could be moved by a member of parliament. Unless the motion was debated and defeated, the standard would be rejected. Thus a power to veto AASB accounting standards has stayed in the hands of government but it has moved from the Ministerial Council to the federal parliament.

In September 1990 the Board of Management of the Australian Accounting Research Foundation released (simultaneously with a report prepared for it on the subject by Professor Graham Peirson) an invitation to comment on proposals for reform of the institutional arrangements for accounting standards-setting in Australia. The major reforms proposed were the establishment by 1995 of one accounting standards-setting board for the private and public sectors within a foundation (to be called the Australian Accounting Standards Foundation) that to the extent feasible would be independent of the accounting profession, business and government, and whose funding would be broadly based. It was also proposed that there would be a full-time chairman and eight part-time members. In response to the profession's initiative the federal Attorney-General's Department undertook a review in 1991 of the accounting standards-setting arrangements. In early 1992 the federal Attorney-General decided to maintain the existing arrangements except for increasing the number of members of the AASB from nine to eleven to allow for an expansion in the representation of various preparer and user interest groups. The Attorney-General retained his power to appoint board members from panels of names submitted to his department. Also, a senior representative of the

Attorney-General's Department was given observer status at AASB meetings.

The above outline of the regulatory arrangements for standards-setting in Australia is supplemented by a discussion on the form and content of the accounting standards on issue in a later section headed 'The Accountancy Profession and Accounting Standards' (see pp. 358–61).

To complete the picture on the regulatory framework for corporate financial reporting, Figure 10.1 shows the Australian Stock Exchange Limited, which increases the reporting obligations on companies that are listed by issuing official listing rules. If the rules are not observed, a company may be delisted. The more significant rules are discussed in a subsequent section of this chapter (see 'Stock Exchange Requirements', pp. 357–8).

CORPORATIONS LAW

Most Australian companies are formed by incorporation under the Corporations Law and the most usual class of company is the company limited by shares as shown in Table 10.4.

A company limited by shares has the substantial advantage of limiting the liability of shareholders to the unpaid portion of the nominal value of the shares. The no-liability class of company goes even further and relieves shareholders of any obligation to pay calls on their shares. But only a mining company may be incorporated in Australia as a no-liability company. The company limited by guarantee (the members' liability is limited to a fixed amount pledged in the event of a winding up) is widely used for clubs and other not-for-profit entities. The unlimited company is equivalent in effect to an incorporated partnership but the form has certain advantages for mutual fund companies.

Table 10.4 indicates that nearly 98 per cent of the companies limited by shares are proprietary companies. While the number of proprietary

Table 10.4 Australian companies registered as at 30 June 1992

	Number	*Percentage*
Limited by shares		
Public	9,351	1.09
Proprietary	839,946	97.70
Subtotal	849,297	98.79
Limited by guarantee	8,691	1.01
No Liability	958	0.11
Unlimited	732	0.09
Total	859,678	100.00

Source: Australian Securities Commission, *Annual Report*, 1992.

companies includes some very substantial subsidiaries of local and overseas companies, a high proportion relates to small-scale family entities or similar business units. Under the Corporations Law, a proprietary company is one having a share capital that restricts the right to transfer shares, limits its members to not more than fifty persons, and prohibits invitations to the public for equity or debt funds. These constraints must be contained in the company's memorandum or articles of association. A public company is any company other than a proprietary company.

Proprietary companies only require two members (whereas public companies need five), only require two directors (whereas public companies need three), and are relieved of certain incorporation and administration formalities. Given the simpler and less costly procedure, foreign companies that do not intend to raise equity or debt capital from the Australian public most often use a proprietary company as the investment vehicle. If there is a change of mind about a public offering, it is not difficult for a proprietary company to convert to public company status.

The more significant privileges (particularly in the area of financial disclosure) are reserved for exempt proprietary companies. A proprietary company is exempt if, broadly speaking, none of its shares is deemed to be owned by a public company and no member is a public company. In effect, exempt proprietary companies are proprietary companies which are beneficially owned entirely by natural persons. While all companies must prepare financial statements and circulate them to shareholders, exempt proprietary companies are freed from the need to include a range of notes required of other companies. Further, there is no obligation to file those financial statements with corporate authorities to make them available for public inspection. Exempt proprietary companies, if all the members agree, escape from the general rule that every company must have an auditor. However, if an auditor is not appointed, exempt proprietary companies are required to file a summary of key financial data (the totals of certain balance sheet classifications and the amount of profit after tax).

Every company must hold an annual general meeting before which financial statements and related documents must be sent to shareholders and after which copies must be lodged with the Australian Securities Commission as part of its annual return (except in the case of exempt proprietary companies as mentioned above). The documents to be presented to shareholders include:

- a copy of the accounts (defined to include the profit and loss account and balance sheet, notes thereto, and a directors' statement);
- a directors' report;
- an auditor's report (other than an exempt proprietary company whose members have agreed not to appoint an auditor).

The directors' statement differs in content from the directors' report. The former contains the directors' opinion on whether the accounts give a true and fair view and whether there are reasonable grounds to believe that the company will be able to pay its debts as and when they fall due, as well as a declaration on whether the accounts have been prepared in accordance with applicable approved accounting standards. The directors' report, on the other hand, requires disclosures on items such as the names of directors, principal company activities and significant changes therein, net profit after tax, dividends paid and proposed, a review of operations, the significant changes in the state of affairs of the company, post-balance date events, and likely developments in the operations of the company and their impact. While the type of information required to be disclosed in directors' reports is potentially very relevant to shareholders, the full benefit has not always been obtained as some companies have complied in a perfunctory or non-revealing manner, the information on likely developments does not have to be disclosed if it would prejudice the interests of the company, and there has been little enforcement activity to ensure the reports fully comply with the statutory requirements.

Although the reporting package outlined above does not explicitly mention cash flow information, a statement of cash flows is required to be included in company accounts by Accounting Standard AASB 1026.

In the case of a holding or parent company there is a requirement for the presentation of its own accounts along with consolidated accounts for the economic entity comprising the parent entity and subsidiary entities operating under the control of the parent entity.

The accounts are required to give a true and fair view; to comply with the prescribed requirements (set out in Schedule 5 of the Corporations Regulations); and to be made out in accordance with applicable AASB accounting standards. There was an overriding requirement to give a true and fair view that prevailed over the requirement to comply with accounting standards. However, amendments to the Corporations Law in June 1991 turned this around to give primary emphasis to a requirement to comply with accounting standards. After compliance with all applicable AASB standards, the directors must add such information and explanations as will give a true and fair view. Previously, relief from compliance with AASB accounting standards was given by the law where compliance would cause the financial statements not to give a true and fair view. The fall of the true and fair criterion from its paramount status arose, in part, from the lack of any firm consensus on its meaning and from certain companies abusing the former statutory let-out from compliance with accounting standards (McGregor 1992).

The prescribed accounts requirements in the regulations were fundamentally restructured in 1986 with further amendments in 1987. Fixed formats for the profit and loss account and the balance sheet were introduced and a form of differential reporting adopted whereby the level of mandatory financial disclosure varies according to specified company categories. The company categories reflect, in a general way, size and public involvement. Additional substantive amendments were made in 1991 to make the regulations consistent with amendments to the Corporations Law for the consolidation of economic entities in accordance with Accounting Standard AASB 1024.

Table 10.5 shows the main company categories and the associated disclosure requirements. Exempt proprietary companies are only required

Table 10.5 Differential financial reporting requirements

	Exempt proprietary companies	*Non-exempt proprietary and public companies*		*Borrowing companies*	*Listed companies*
		*Large**	*Other*		
Balance sheet	✓	✓	✓	✓	✓
Profit and loss account	✓	✓	✓	✓	✓
Remuneration of auditors	✓	✓	✓	✓	✓
Commitments	✓	✓	✓	✓	✓
Contingencies	✓	✓	✓	✓	✓
Unearned revenue	✓	✓	✓	✓	✓
Profit and loss detail note		✓	✓	✓	✓
Income tax note		✓	✓	✓	✓
Dissections and particulars of assets and liabilities		✓	✓	✓	✓
Share capital detail		✓	✓	✓	✓
Valuations supported by guarantees, warranties or indemnities		✓	✓	✓	✓
Remuneration and pensions of directors		✓	✓	✓	✓
Financing arrangements				✓	
Maturity schedule of debts receivable and debts payable				✓	
Economic dependency		✓		✓	✓
Recent valuations of land and buildings		✓		✓	✓
Superannuation commitments		✓		✓	✓
Interests in business undertakings and corporations		✓		✓	✓
Remuneration of executives					✓

Note: *Where assets exceed $10 million or revenues exceed $20 million.

by Schedule 5 to prepare the standard profit and loss account and balance sheet and four additional notes. As the fixed format accounts are highly condensed, the informativeness of the resulting skimpy accounts is quite limited. Non-exempt proprietary and public companies are required to give further dissections and further particulars of specified line items reported in the financial statements. When those companies reach a specified size threshold (assets exceed $10 million or revenues exceed $20 million), they must provide additional footnotes. Corporations that have borrowed from the public are also required to provide information on financing arrangements (credit standby and loan rollover facilities, etc.) and a schedule of debts receivable and debts payable dissected according to maturity dates. Listed companies must include certain details regarding the number of executives who receive income from the company in excess of $100,000.

Schedule 5 is almost exclusively concerned with disclosure and presentation. Definition, recognition and measurement are left to accounting standards and accepted practice. Further, disclosure of sales revenue, segment information and certain other items are required by AASB accounting standards rather than Schedule 5. As there is no clean line of division between the two, it has been proposed that the requirements of Schedule 5 be incorporated into approved standards so that measurement, disclosure and other aspects of any particular reporting topic are dealt with together.

TAX LAW

The main taxes are imposed by the federal government which distributes a portion of the proceeds through grants to the other levels of government. Over half the tax revenue raised in Australia comes from income tax which is only levied by the federal government. Revenue is also raised by the federal government from indirect taxes (sales tax, customs and excise duties, fringe benefits tax and bank account debits tax) and natural resource levies and taxes (e.g., Petroleum Resource Rent Tax).

After income tax, sales tax has been historically the most important source of tax revenue to the federal government. It is imposed on the sales value of certain goods at the time of the last wholesale sale at rates ranging from 10 to 30 per cent. A wide range of basic commodities (most foodstuffs, clothing, drugs, aids to manufacture, building materials, etc.) are exempt. There continues to be a debate in Australia as to whether more reliance should be placed on an indirect tax such as a value added or a retail tax. The federal Liberal opposition party has adopted a policy commitment to change the tax regime so that less reliance is placed on income tax.

The principal state and territory taxes are payroll tax, stamp duty, financial institutions duty, and land tax. Local government bodies levy annual rates on the owners of property.

Table 10.6 Resident personal tax rates, 1992/93

Taxable income ($)	*Tax ($)*	*Marginal rate on excess ($)*
0– 5,400	Nil	
5,401–20,700	Nil	+20% over 5,400
20,701–36,000	3,060	+38% over 20,700
36,001–50,000	8,874	+46% over 36,000
Over 50,000	15,314	+47% over 50,000

Note: On top of the above, most residents are subject to an additional 1.25 per cent of taxable income for a national health care levy (1.4 per cent from 1 July 1993).

Since 1979 no federal death (estate) duties or gift taxes have been imposed. Also, no such taxes are presently imposed by any state or territory. As mentioned previously, while there is a limited sales tax, there is no retail (turnover) tax or value added tax. There is no wealth tax.

Income tax is imposed on all Australian residents whether they are individuals or companies. The tax applies to income derived both from within and outside Australia subject to minor exceptions and a credit against Australian income tax for foreign income tax. Income tax is also imposed, in general, on nonresidents for income derived from Australian sources.

Resident individual tax rates for the 1992/93 tax year are shown in Table 10.6. Nonresident individuals are liable to tax at a 29 per cent rate from $1 to $20,700, and thereafter at the same marginal rates as residents. The same tax rates applied to residents and nonresidents in the 1991/92 tax year.

The company tax rate has been a flat 39 per cent since the year ended 30 June 1989. Te rate is unaltered for the year ended 30 June 1993. The same rate applies to both public and proprietary companies and to resident and nonresident companies.

Tax is assessed on 'taxable income' which is the excess of gross 'assessable income' over 'allowable deductions'. There is a broad correspondence between these items and accounting revenue and expense. Commonly recurring differences relate to depreciation and provisions. Accelerated depreciation deductions are allowed for certain asset acquisitions and depreciation is only allowed on buildings in specified circumstances. No deductions are allowed for the amounts provided for items such as employee leave, warranties and doubtful debts, while the amounts paid and the amounts written off as bad debts are deductible.

Income tax losses incurred before the 1989/90 year may be carried forward for seven years, and losses incurred in the 1989/90 year and thereafter may be carried forward with no time limit and offset against taxable income subject to certain restrictions. Loss carry-backs are not permitted.

Dividends received by a resident company from other resident companies are included in assessable income but are generally free from tax by a full rebate of the tax otherwise payable on this income. Income tax deductions are not allowed for amortization of goodwill and for most entertainment expenses and for fringe benefits tax paid by employers on non-cash employee benefits provided in such forms as company cars for personal use, low interest loans and holiday travel.

A comprehensive capital gains tax came into effect in 1985. Net capital gains realized from the disposal of assets acquired after 19 September 1985 are required to be included in assessable income and are, therefore, subject to income tax at ordinary rates. However, in calculating the net gain the cost base is indexed by the Australian Consumer Price Index. Consequently, no tax is payable on the sale of a capital asset where the asset increased in value at a rate no more than the general inflation rate. Only that part of the gain which exceeds the inflation rate is taxed. Capital losses are not indexed and may be offset only against capital gains realized in the current year or be carried forward and offset against capital gains in later years.

A major reform to Australia's taxation system has been the introduction of a dividend imputation scheme which became operative on 1 July 1987. Prior to that date there was double taxation of dividends in the sense that tax was imposed at the company level and also at the shareholder level on the same income. This type of system still applies in the USA. The effect of the Australian imputation system is to remove the double taxation by allowing the shareholder credit for tax paid at the company level. In effect, the payment of the company tax is imputed to the shareholder. Dividends attract a 'franking' rebate provided they are paid out of company profits that have borne Australian company tax at the 39 per cent rate. Individual shareholders are assessed on the total amount of the 'franked dividend' and a gross-up to reflect the company tax paid, but are then entitled to a tax rebate (i.e., a reduction in their tax payable) equal to the gross-up. Accordingly, a shareholder would generally only have to pay tax on 'franked' dividend income to the extent that his or her marginal tax was higher than 39 per cent. Inter-company dividends are tax free by virtue of the rebate system that has been in force for many years. But the rebate attached to a 'franked' dividend passes through a chain of companies to benefit the ultimate resident shareholders who are natural persons.

The combination of the net capital gains tax and the dividend imputation system means most shareholders presently prefer dividends to the retention of profits. This is changing company policies on dividend distribution. Since 1988 Australian companies with the capacity to pay 'franked' dividends have been increasing their dividend payout rates and certain companies are letting dividends fluctuate from year to year in accordance with profit movements. Frequently, the dividends are recaptured by the company through dividend reinvestment plans that many shareholders now find attractive. Of the $12,289 million raised by the main board listed companies in the year ended 30 June 1992, $2,200 million or 18 per cent was raised through shareholders opting to reinvest their dividends in the company for extra shares, a slight increase in amount from the previous year but a reduction in relative terms from 33 per cent of the total capital raised in the year ended 30 June 1991.

As mentioned in the section on 'Influences on Accounting', tax rules do not have a direct influence on published financial statements. In this respect Australia is unlike certain West Pacific Rim countries.

STOCK EXCHANGE REQUIREMENTS

Listed companies must comply with the Listing Rules of the Australian Stock Exchange Limited. The rules have statutory backing in the Corporations Law under which a court order may be obtained to enforce compliance with the listing rules.

The emphasis of the Stock Exchange has been on extending the range of financial disclosure and in improving the frequency and timeliness of reporting. Companies are obligated to notify the Exchange immediately of any information necessary to avoid the establishment of a false market in the company's securities or which would be likely to affect materially the price of the company's securities. A half yearly report is required immediately figures are available and in any event no later than 75 days after the end of the first half-yearly period in the financial year. A preliminary final statement is required immediately figures are available and in any event no later than 75 days after the end of the financial year. The annual report needs to be issued to shareholders and the Exchange within four months of year-end. Mining exploration companies are subject to more stringent rules.

The Exchange was the first authority to call for certain disclosures such as the amount of turnover and a funds statement, but many of these disclosures have now been incorporated into accounting standards or Schedule 5. None the less, there are a range of disclosures remaining that are not called for by other authorities such as:

- names of substantial shareholders;
- details of the shareholdings of the twenty largest shareholders;
- a distribution schedule of shareholdings;
- reasons for any material differences between the results in the official year-end financial statements and the preliminary final statement.

A significant revision of the listing rules came into operation on 1 January 1992. The major effect was to subject listed entities to a stricter regime of continuous disclosure of information to the market, together with more detailed disclosure in six-monthly financial reports (including summarized operating data, a statement of cash flows and segment reports for the half year as well as a statement of assets, liabilities and shareholders' equity). Quarterly reporting was not required, pending a review of experience with the tougher continuous and half-yearly reporting arrangements.

THE ACCOUNTANCY PROFESSION AND ACCOUNTING STANDARDS

The main representation of the accountancy profession in Australia is by two national bodies – the Institute of Chartered Accountants in Australia (the 'Institute') and the Australian Society of Certified Practising Accountants (the 'Society'). The Institute has over 22,000 members of whom 55 per cent are principals or employees in public practice; the Society has over 62,000 members of whom 22 per cent are principals or employees in public practice. Approximately 4,200 accountants are members of both bodies. While both organizations have members in the fields of commerce, industry and academia, the Society is particularly strong in the field of government where over 18 per cent of its membership work.

Both bodies regulate the conduct of their members, issue and cancel practice certificates, require graduate entry from accredited institutions supplemented by rigorous professional educational schemes, and issue ethical rulings in an attempt to maintain high standards in such areas as integrity, independence and professional competence.

A company auditor must be registered with the Commission, which requires certain standards as to character, experience and professional education. To qualify for registration, an auditor must be a member of the Institute or Society or have equivalent qualifications. The two bodies, through the Auditing Standards Board of the Australian Accounting Research Foundation, have issued a Statement of Auditing Standards (AUS 1) and over thirty Statements of Auditing Practice (AUPs) as well as various audit guides and auditing guidance releases. The practice of auditing in Australia is very similar to that in the UK and the USA. As overseas, the 'Big Six' internationally known accounting firms are very prominent in carrying out the audits of public companies.

As the two professional accounting bodies overlap considerably in their functions, there have been four major attempts in the last twenty years to integrate the two bodies. The fourth attempt failed in March 1991. Society members voted overwhelmingly in favour of unification but the Institute vote was only 64 per cent (2.7 per cent short of the two-thirds majority required).

In the first half of this century the accountancy profession did not believe it had a major role to play in the preparation and enforcement of accounting standards. However, a spate of corporate collapses and investigators' reports thereon in the 1960s exposed the consequences of not specifying any firm accounting rules. A significant turning point was

Table 10.7 Accounting standards as at 31 December 1992

AASB	*AAS*	*Title*
1001	6	Accounting Policies – Disclosure
1002	8	Events Occurring After Balance Date
1003	–	Superseded (Foreign Currency Translation – Disclosure)
1004	15	Disclosure of Operating Revenue
1005	16	Financial Reporting by Segments
1006	19	Accounting for Interests in Joint Ventures
1007	12	Superseded (Financial Reporting of Sources and Applications of Funds)
1008	17	Accounting for Leases
1009	11	Accounting for Construction Contracts
1010	10	Accounting for the Revaluation of Non-Current Assets
1011	13	Accounting for Research and Development Costs
1012	20	Foreign Currency Translation
1013	18	Accounting for Goodwill
1014	23	Set-Off and Extinguishment of Debt
1015	21	Accounting for the Acquisition of Assets
1016	14	Disclosure of Information about Investments in Associated Companies
1017	22	Related Party Disclosures
1018	1	Profit and Loss Accounts
1019	2	Measurement and Presentation of Inventories in the Context of the Historical Cost System
1020	3	Accounting for Income Tax (Tax-Effect Accounting)
1021	4	Depreciation of Non-Current Assets
1022	7	Accounting for the Extractive Industries
1023	26	Financial Reporting of General Insurance Activities
1024	24	Consolidated Accounts
1025	–	Application of the Reporting Entity Concept and Other Amendments
1026	28	Statement of Cash Flows
1027	–	Earnings per Share
–	5	Materiality in Financial Statements
–	9	Expenditure Carried Forward to Subsequent Accounting Periods
–	25	Financial Reporting by Superannuation Plans
–	27	Financial Reporting by Local Governments

reached in 1973 when the leaders of the Institute and Society resolved to accept joint responsibility for the formulation of accounting standards. They decided to form a single accounting standards-setting committee under the umbrella of the mutually funded Australian Accounting Research Foundation. After their drafting, exposure and polishing, the standards had to be forwarded to the respective National Councils of the two bodies, which both had a final say on their acceptability before they were issued. The standards developed out of this process came to be referred to as 'Australian Accounting Standards' (AASs). Professional Statement APS-1 on conformity with accounting standards, a version of which was first issued by the Institute and subsequently adopted by the Society in 1973, required members of the two bodies to support the AASs, subject to the directors' ultimate responsibility for the accounts, with appropriate disclosure in the financial statements and the auditor's report of departures therefrom.

As mentioned in the section on 'The Regulatory Framework', the inability of the accountancy profession to obtain a high level of compliance with its standards led to the establishment of the Australian Accounting Standards Board and that Board issuing accounting standards (AASBs) which had statutory backing in relation to corporate entities. The first approved standard (AASB 1001) was issued in September 1985. By the end of 1992 the majority of the profession's AASs had been reviewed and issued as AASBs as shown in Table 10.7.

Initially corporate entities were expected to comply with the two sets of accounting standards – the AASs and the AASBs. Before the merger of the profession's Accounting Standards Board and the Australian Accounting Standards Board in 1988, there were often minor differences in the respective standards and companies, and their auditors found it irritating when they were forced to check compliance with two accounting standards on identical subjects. In April 1989 the Institute and the Society announced that members were no longer required to ensure compliance with AASs in the preparation and audit of company financial statements where a corresponding AASB standard had been issued and was operative. As shown in Table 10.7, there are only two of the original series of AAS standards for which an equivalent AASB standard has not been issued. It is expected that AAS 9 will be withdrawn as it has been superseded by the issue of a concepts statement on the elements of financial statements.

In the future it is contemplated that in most cases each AASB will be issued concurrently with an AAS standard on the same topic and both standards will as far as possible have identical rules. The AASBs will apply to corporate entities and the AASs will apply to non-corporate reporting entities.

In addition, all reporting entities will be expected to comply with the Statements of Accounting Concepts (SACs) issued jointly by the Australian Accounting Standards Board and the Australian Accounting Research Foundation. Three concepts statements were issued in August 1990 as follows:

- SAC 1 Definition of the Reporting Entity;
- SAC 2 Objective of General Purpose Financial Reporting;
- SAC 3 Qualitative Characteristics of Financial Information.

In March 1992 SAC 4 on the 'Definition and Recognition of the Elements of Financial Statements' was issued. The concepts statements are component parts of a conceptual framework that it is hoped will define the nature, subject, purpose and broad content of general purpose financial reporting. This commitment to a conceptual framework stretches back to the mid-1970s and the issued concepts statements were preceded by the publication of eight accounting theory monographs. Australia was in a position to and did contribute substantially to the production of the *Framework for the Preparation and Presentation of Financial Statements* issued by the International Accounting Standards Committee in 1989. As reporting requirements are set in Australia on a number of fronts and on specialized topics, it is anticipated they will be more consistent and logical if they are evaluated by reference to an orderly set of general concepts.

Under Professional Statement APS 1 as reissued in November 1990, concepts statements are mandatory requirements for members of the Institute and the Society as are accounting standards (AASs or AASBs, depending on whether it is a corporate entity and whether there are corresponding AAS and AASB standards) except where there is an incompatibility between an accounting standard and a concepts statement, in which case the standard prevails. In addition, the accountancy profession has made it clear in APS 1 that it regards compliance with the concepts statements and the applicable accounting standards as necessary for a true and fair view. Moreover, there appears to be a growing feeling that they might be sufficient for such a view so that eventually that criterion may be dropped in favour of one stressing fair presentation in accordance with concepts statements and accounting standards.

Apart from the AASs, the AASBs and the SACs, one Statement of Accounting Practice (SAP 1) and twelve Accounting Guidance Releases (AAGs) have been issued. SAP 1 is on Current Cost Accounting and, although it was strongly recommended at the time of its reissue in 1983 that all entities publish supplementary current cost financial statements, only certain public sector entities regularly report in current cost terms. The purpose of the AAGs is to give guidance on the application of concepts statements and accounting standards and this scope has been adhered to, except for AAG 10 on the 'Measurement of Monetary Assets and Liabilities', which went further in specifying a present value measurement principle for interest-bearing assets and liabilities.

SUMMARY OF AUSTRALIAN ACCOUNTING PRINCIPLES

Australian accounting principles are only partially codified. As mentioned previously, the most authoritative explicit sources for companies are the Corporations Law requirements, AASB Accounting Standards, AAS Accounting Standards where there is no corresponding AASB, and Statements of Accounting Concepts. Because this body of accounting rules and guidance has been built up slowly over many years, it has a number of inconsistencies. For instance, it will become obvious as specific standards are examined that they embody different criteria for the recognition of assets.

Objectives and general basis of accounting

According to SAC 2, the objective of general purpose reporting is to 'provide information useful to users for making and evaluating decisions about the allocation of scarce resources'. This broad objective is viewed as encompassing the rendering of accountability by reporting entities. SAC 3 requires general purpose financial reports to 'include all financial information which satisfies the concepts of relevance and reliability, and which passes the materiality test' and to 'be presented on a timely basis and in a manner which satisfies the concepts of comparability and understandability'.

SAC 4 rejects the use of deferred debit and deferred credit accounts where those accounts do not possess the essential characteristics of assets and liabilities respectively. While some commentators have claimed that SAC 4 embodies 'a balance sheet bias', others contend that SAC 4 is merely opposing the bias or filtering that occurs when the recognition of revenue or expense is smoothed in accordance with the preparer's feeling for the long-term trend of the entity's performance (Paul 1992: 12).

The measurement side of the conceptual framework project has not been resolved (and may never be neatly resolved). AASB 1001 requires the disclosure of all material accounting policies and, while it exempts the disclosure of the accrual basis and the going concern basis because those bases are so generally adopted in Australia, it does not accept that the historical cost basis can be assumed in the preparation of financial statements. This is a correct approach as very few companies in Australia strictly adhere to the historical cost convention. Apart from writing inventories and other current assets down where necessary to net realizable value, many Australian companies revalue land and buildings. As indicated in Table 10.5, certain companies are required, if current values (defined as the most recent valuations made within the last three years) are not shown in the balance sheet, to disclose in a note the current values of interests in land and buildings. Since Schedule 5 requires the valuations and their disclosure, some companies follow the policy of revaluing land and buildings in their books every three years. In addition, non-current investments as well as plant and equipment may be revalued on a regular or on an *ad hoc* basis.

Revaluations of non-current assets are officially sanctioned in AASB 1010; however, that standard does little to stop a hotchpotch of revaluations arising as it is concerned with the accounting entries for any revaluations rather than the timing and the basis of upwards revaluations. AASB 1010 is strict on downwards revaluations as it requires a write-down whenever the carrying amount of a non-current asset is greater than its recoverable amount, which is defined, in relation to an asset, as 'the net amount that is expected to be recovered through the cash inflows and outflows arising from its continued use and subsequent disposal'. In determining recoverable amount, discounting is encouraged but not mandated so AASB 1010 requires disclosure of whether the expected net cash flows included in determining the recoverable amounts of non-current assets have been discounted to their present value. Downward revaluations to less than recoverable amount are not allowed and upward revaluations to more than recoverable amount are not allowed. When the option to revalue upwards is taken, the standard requires all the non-current assets in a class to be revalued at approximately the same date. A revaluation increment must be credited directly to an asset revaluation reserve (except where the increment reverses a former decrement) and a decrement must be debited to the profit and loss account (except where the decrement reverses a former increment). Reversing entries (or entries that are the flip-flop of the original entry) are made for previous revaluations that are reversed. When previously revalued assets are sold, the gain or loss on sale is required to be determined as the difference between the net proceeds and the carrying amount of the asset (the revalued amount net of any accumulated depreciation) at the time of the sale.

Profit and loss

In Australia the profit and loss standard is based on an all-inclusive concept of profit. Subject to three exceptions, AASB 1018 requires the profit and loss account to include all items of revenue and expense (including gains and losses) arising in a period irrespective of whether they relate to items inside or outside ordinary operations and even though the items may relate to prior financial periods. The three exceptions are gains (and reversals of gains) on the revaluation of non-current assets taken to a revaluation reserve in accordance with AASB 1010, certain items treated as movements in the foreign currency translation reserve in accordance with AASB 1012, and adjustments arising from a change in accounting policy in specified circumstances.

The bottom line profit figure of the period is labelled ‘Operating profit or loss and extraordinary items after income tax’. AASB 1018 requires the separate disclosure of profit items that are abnormal (items ‘considered abnormal by reason of their size and effect on the results for the financial period’) and non-operating items that are extraordinary (items ‘attributable to events or transactions of a type that are outside the ordinary operations of the company . . . and are not of a recurring nature’).

Balance sheet classification

In the basic format balance sheet current assets and current liabilities must be shown separately. Current assets, which are shown in a decreasing order of liquidity, are defined by Schedule 5 as cash or other assets that would be consumed or converted into cash within 12 months after the end of the last financial period. This means that companies with long operating cycles may find it necessary to divide the amount for inventories into a current and a non-current portion. Current liabilities are amounts that would be due and payable within 12 months after the end of the last financial period.

Assets and related expenses

SAC 4 defines assets as 'service potential or future economic benefits controlled by the entity as a result of past transactions or other past events'. This broad definition does not attempt to specify the conditions that must be met before an asset is recognized in the financial statements. The recognition criteria are that (a) it is probable that the service potential or future economic benefits will eventuate, and (b) the asset possesses a cost or other value that can be measured reliably.

Inventories are required by AASB 1019 to be measured at the lower of cost and net realizable value. The cost of manufactured inventories must be ascertained in accordance with the absorption costing method. Only the following methods are allowed in assigning costs to inventories: specific identification, average cost (weighted), FIFO and standard cost. The LIFO method is not permissible. In a separate standard on construction contracts (AASB 1009), the profits on both fixed price and cost plus contracts are required to be recognized in accordance with the percentage of completion method provided certain conditions are met.

AASB 1021 requires non-current assets with a limited useful life to be depreciated. Over 90 per cent of companies use the straight-line method or the fixed-percentage-on-declining-balance method. Explicit mention is made of the need to depreciate buildings although non-current investment properties are excluded from the ambit of the standard. Investment properties are sometimes viewed as similar to investments not requiring write-downs unless the carrying amount is greater than the recoverable amount.

The treatment of leased assets is governed by AASB 1008 which prescribes that finance leases must be capitalized by lessees and treated as receivables by lessors. A finance lease is 'any lease which is not an operating lease and which effectively transfers from the lessor to the lessee substantially all the risks and benefits incident to ownership of the leased property without transferring the legal ownership'. Guidelines are provided for identifying a finance lease: (a) the lease is non-cancellable; and (b) either (i) the lease term is for 75 per cent or more of the useful life of the property, or (ii) the present value of the minimum lease payments equals or exceeds 90 per cent of the fair value of the property.

AASB 1022 on accounting for the extractive industries allows pre-production costs (a) to be written off as incurred; or (b) to be capitalized in accordance with the area of interest method provided (i) there is an expectation of recoupment, or where (ii) if exploration and evaluation activities in the area of interest have not reached a stage that permits a reasonable assessment, active and significant operations are continuing in respect of that area of interest. It will be noticed that the asset recognition criteria in AASB 1022 are less strict than those in SAC 4. Pre-production costs carried forward are required during the production phase to be amortized over the life of the area of interest to which they relate. A production output basis is to be used unless, in the particular circumstances, a time basis is more appropriate.

There is no standard on the capitalization of interest. Practice varies although it is normal to capitalize interest on development and construction projects before they are ready for their intended purpose. Other interest costs are usually written off as incurred.

AASB 1011 requires research and development costs to be charged to the profit and loss account as incurred, except they must be deferred where they are expected beyond any reasonable doubt to be recoverable. This asset recognition criterion is more strict than that in SAC 4.

The goodwill standard AASB 1013 requires purchased goodwill, measured as the excess of the acquisition cost over the fair value of the identifiable net assets acquired, to be recognized as a non-current asset and amortized over a period not exceeding twenty years. Where the fair value exceeds the acquisition cost, the resultant 'discount on acquisition' must be accounted for by reducing proportionately the fair values of the non-monetary assets acquired. If those assets are reduced to a zero value and a discount balance remains, that balance must be recognized in the profit and loss account as a gain.

Coupled with AASB 1015 which prohibits the use of the pooling-of-interests method, Australian companies have protested the severity of the Australian rules. Prior to the approval of AASB 1013 in 1988, it was not uncommon for companies to ignore the AAS standards and write off goodwill either as an extraordinary item or directly against retained profits. Another technique to avoid periodic amortization charges was to be inventive in the recognition of identifiable intangible assets such as brands, newspaper and magazine mastheads, licences and intellectual properties (specialized technical or managerial resources). Once recognized, company representatives argued that such assets required no amortization as they were being maintained or enhanced. To deal with this situation an exposure draft of an accounting standard was issued in 1989 on accounting for identifiable intangible assets. It was proposed to require the amortization of such assets over the period of expected future benefit subject to that period being a finite period. Where the amortization period exceeded twenty years, it was proposed to require disclosure of a detailed explanation of the reasons for the extended period. As the exposure draft contained other more controversial proposals including the option for companies to value and recognize internally generated identifiable intangibles and the responses to the exposure draft revealed considerable division of opinion, finalization of a standard has been postponed until such time as there is an international consensus on the issues.

Liabilities and related expenses

SAC 4 defines liabilities as 'the future sacrifices of service potential or future economic benefits that the entity is presently obliged to make to other entities as a result of past transactions or other past events'. As with assets, this generic definition is accompanied by recognition criteria: a liability should be recognized in the financial statements when (a) it is probable that the future sacrifice will be required and (b) the amount of the liability can be measured reliably.

The liability definition and recognition criteria are in accord with Australian practice in that liabilities are not allowed to be inflated and used in a discretionary way to smooth profits. Provisions for uninsured losses are not, for instance, viewed as liabilities.

AASB 1014 permits debt to be extinguished by either a legal or an in-substance defeasance provided strict conditions are met. Gains and losses on defeasance must be included in the profit and loss as at the date of entering into the defeasance arrangement. In contrast to US rules, AASB 1014 allows an instantaneous in-substance defeasance to be treated as an extinguishment of debt provided all the normal conditions for in-substance defeasances are met.

The offsetting of assets and liabilities is restricted by AASB 1014 which only allows it where there is a 'right of set-off' defined as that right which

(a) exists when each of two entities (including groups of entities) owes the other determinable amounts;
(b) allows the reporting entity to offset the amount owed against the amount owed by the other entity;
(c) the reporting entity intends to exercise; and
(d) is recognised at law or in equity.

(AASB 1014)

As an interim measure prior to the completion of a major project on financial instruments, Accounting Guidance Release 10 stresses the general principle of a present value approach using the effective rate of interest when measuring monetary assets and liabilities. The approach is illustrated with reference to a split defeasance, deep discount and zero coupon bonds. Accounting Guidance Release 11 deals with a debtor's accounting for debt restructuring and reinforces the principle that any gains or losses on extinguishment of debt should be recognized at the time of the extinguishment in the profit and loss account.

A form of comprehensive tax-effect accounting using the liability method is required by AASB 1020. The tax-effect of timing differences (arising from corresponding book and tax items falling in different periods) are treated as either a liability, 'Provision for deferred income tax', or an asset, 'Future income tax benefit'. The balance sheet amounts are adjusted when tax rates change. A future income tax benefit can only be carried forward 'where realisation of the benefit can be regarded as being assured beyond any reasonable doubt'. In the case of a future benefit arising from an operating loss, it may only be carried forward if 'realisation of the benefit is virtually certain'. There is no recognition test to be applied in carrying forward a deferred tax 'liability' other than the mere existence of the relevant timing difference. These divergent recognition criteria are inconsistent with each other and with those in SAC 4. Except in the case of group accounts, the account for the deferred tax provision is required to be offset against the account for future tax benefits to the extent that the amounts in the accounts are expected to reverse in the same periods.

In August 1990 the Australian Accounting Research Foundation issued on behalf of the accounting bodies AAS 25 on financial reporting by superannuation plans (pension funds). While the standard was being developed, there was extensive consultation with fund managers and actuaries. With that standard promulgated, a major project on accounting for employment entitlements is under way. At present there are no standards in Australia on accounting for pension costs in the financial statements of employers. Normally pension funds are managed by an external entity and the pension expense is the amount of contributions made during the year. As shown in Table 10.5, certain companies are required to disclose information on superannuation commitments. The information must include disclosure of the existence of any plan, the principal type of benefit, the basis of contributions, whether the contributions are legally enforceable, date of last actuarial assessment and the name and qualifications of the actuary, position of the fund regarding the availability of funds to satisfy the vested benefits, and the details of any deficiency.

Group structures

In current commercial practice it is not uncommon to have complex business structures involving diversified operations and comprising a parent or holding company, subsidiaries, associated companies, joint arrangements, trusts and other entities connected by varying degrees of ownership and control. Legislators and standard setters have had difficulty keeping up with these developments.

Prior to 31 December 1991 a number of companies exploited a restricted legal definition of 'subsidiary' to remove large amounts of operating liabilities and assets from their balance sheets. Under the prior law a company for accounting and other purposes was deemed to be a subsidiary of a parent company where the parent company:

- controlled the composition of the board of directors;

- controlled more than half the maximum number of votes that might be cast at a general meeting of the company; or
- held more than half of the issued share capital (excluding any part that carried no right to participate beyond a specified amount in a distribution of either profits or capital).

As consolidation was limited to subsidiary companies as defined, parent companies used devices such as unit trusts to remove from the consolidated balance sheet all the underlying assets and liabilities of the trust (or other non-corporate entity) and its subordinate entities. Further, various methods of control were devised (such as attaching to preference share capital control of voting at meetings of directors) so that the statutory definition of subsidiary was avoided.

The proliferation of off-balance sheet financing arrangements caused concern in the accounting profession and an exposure draft (ED 40) was issued in 1987 to deal with some of the abuses along with other matters. A standard, AAS 24 ('Consolidated Financial Statements'), was issued in June 1990. AAS 24 broadened the basis for determining the existence of a 'parent – subsidiary' relationship and included in the 'group' any entity, whether incorporated or not, over which the parent had control. As far as companies were concerned, the Corporations Law required amendment to accommodate the new approach. The amendments were proclaimed in July 1991 and AASB 1024 ('Consolidated Accounts') was issued in September 1991. Both the Corporations Law changes and AASB 1024 apply to financial years ending on or after 31 December 1991.

AASB 1024 prescribes that group accounts must be prepared in the form of one set of consolidated financial statements for the economic entity encompassing the parent company and all the entities controlled by it, regardless of the organizational form of those subsidiaries. Control is defined as 'the capacity of an entity to dominate decision-making, directly or indirectly, in relation to the financial and operating policies of another entity so as to enable that other entity to operate with it in pursuing the objectives of the controlling entity'. Another important aspect of AASB 1024 is that it has adopted the entity concept of consolidation by which the full amounts of the assets and liabilities of the parent and each subsidiary are consolidated and by which the minority interest (called 'outside equity interest' as it may be a majority interest in certain circumstances) is classified as part of the shareholders' equity of the group.

While AASB 1024 requires the consolidation of dissimilar activities and has forced some companies to re-consolidate their finance subsidiaries, AASB 1005 requires the provision of disaggregated information about significant industry and geographical segments.

AASB 1006 requires those entities with joint ventures to account for them using the proportionate consolidation basis – that is, the venturer recognizes in its own financial statements under the respective classification categories its share of assets, liabilities and expenses. A joint venture is defined narrowly as 'an unincorporated contractual association, other than a partnership or trust, between two or more parties to undertake a specific business project in which the venturers meet the costs of the project and receive a share of any resulting output'. The standard does not purport to cover any of the other entity structures through which joint arrangements may be conducted.

Accounting for associated companies (non-subsidiary companies over which the investor exercises significant influence) is governed by AASB 1016. That standard requires the disclosure of information determined in accordance with the principles of the equity method of accounting. In Australia equity accounting is not applied in the books of the investor. Moreover, because of a legal opinion provided about a decade ago that it would be contrary to certain company law definitions to employ the equity method of accounting as a consolidation-type technique, AASB 1016 requires the equity data to be disclosed only by way of note. This has been ruled not to preclude its disclosure in the financial statements in a third column presenting 'equity consolidated' amounts along with the columns for 'parent company' and 'statutory consolidated' amounts. The regulatory authorities have warned, however, that the third column cannot be given undue emphasis (e.g., by heavier type) to give the impression that it is the primary one. While the third column approach is popular with certain companies, it is not the predominant practice in Australia as the required supplementary information on associated companies is most often found in a special note to the financial statements.

Foreign currency translation

AASB 1012 prescribes the accounting for foreign currency transactions and for the translation of the financial statements of foreign operations. Foreign currency transactions are recognized in the domestic currency using the exchange rate in effect at the date of the transaction. At balance date outstanding foreign currency monetary items are translated at the then current spot rate. The exchange differences are required to be recognized as exchange gains and losses in the profit and loss account except in relation to qualifying assets under construction.

Foreign currency financial statements of foreign operations are translated in two different ways depending on the financial and other operational relationships which exist between the reporting entity and its foreign operations. Where the foreign operations are self-sustaining, the current rate method is required to be used. Where the foreign operations are integrated with those of the reporting entity, the temporal method is required to be used.

A self-sustaining operation is an operation that is independent, financially and operationally, of the reporting entity and whose operations do not normally expose the reporting entity to foreign exchange gains and losses. Applying the current rate method will usually give rise to exchange differences; however, the standard requires them to be taken directly to a separate reserve titled 'foreign currency translation reserve' in the shareholders' equity section of the balance sheet.

An integrated foreign operation is an operation that is financially and operationally interdependent, either directly or indirectly, with the reporting entity and whose day-to-day operations normally expose the reporting entity to foreign exchange gains and losses. Applying the temporal method, exchange differences arise mainly from translating monetary items at current rates and under the standard they are reflected in the profit and loss standard.

SAMPLE SET OF FINANCIAL STATEMENTS

In the Appendix are extracts from the 1992 Annual Report of Burns, Philp & Company Limited, a diversified listed public company operating in 22 countries but with over half its sales in Australia. The profit and loss accounts and balance sheets are in accordance with the basic format required by Schedule 5, although the company has opted to supply comparative figures for more than one preceding year.

MAKING COMPARISONS AND THE PITFALLS

In the UK, the USA and Australia there are many commonalities in the underlying philosophy of external financial reporting and the accepted principles to be applied in preparing and presenting financial statements. None the less, it is dangerous to assume that the three systems produce roughly equivalent financial statements. This is dramatically illustrated by the group financial information provided for US investors in the 1992 preliminary final statement of Westpac Banking Corporation. The information is shown in a condensed format in Table 10.8.

Westpac is at the more extreme end of the reconciliation spectrum owing to the particular adjustments required in the past two years for future income tax benefits (affected by a change in the US income tax accounting standard) and for its pension accounting. A more typical set of reconciliation figures is provided by Burns Philp. Included in the Appendix is Note 33 from the company's 1992 Annual Report which provides a reconciliation and an explanation of the adjustments. It is worth while to highlight the major adjustments in a general way as they tend to recur in making comparisons:

- Australian companies are barred from using equity accounting in the primary financial statements although they are required to show the effect of equity accounting in a note to the financial statements.

Table 10.8 Westpac Banking Corporation reconciliation to US Generally Accepted Accounting Principles (GAAP)

	Year to 30 Sept. 1991 ($m)	*Year to 30 Sept. 1992 ($m)*
Net profit (loss) as reported	476	(1,562)
Adjustment for future income tax benefits	(234)	204
Pension accounting adjustment	(303)	189
Other (net)	8	(8)
US GAAP net profit (loss)	(53)	(1,177)
Shareholders' equity as reported	7,223	6,650
Elimination of asset revaluation reserve	(1,153)	(731)
Pension accounting adjustment	(364)	(175)
Adjustment for future income tax benefits	(204)	
Other (net)	152	264
US GAAP shareholders' equity	5,654	6,008

- The revaluation of non-current assets can materially affect the amounts charged for depreciation, the amounts included in the profit or loss account for gains and losses on disposals, and the aggregate reported as shareholders' equity.
- Intangible asset accounting can substantially affect expenses, assets and shareholders' equity. The maximum amortization period for goodwill in Australia is twenty years while it is forty years in the USA. The present UK standards are more flexible and the immediate write-off of goodwill to reserves is common practice. In Australia intangible assets may be specifically identified as items such as trade or brand names and there is no requirement for the amortization of such identifiable intangible assets.
- The treatment of income taxes (especially the criteria applied in recognizing future income tax benefits) can result in significant differences even where accounting standards are based on the general principle of comprehensive tax allocation as in Australia and the US. There is the potential for bigger differences in making comparisons between Australian and UK companies as partial tax allocation is the rule in the UK.
- Superannuation or pension expense may be materially different especially given the complex rules in force in the USA for determining pension expense and the present lack of any firm rules in Australia.

- Proposed dividends can cause a discrepancy as in the USA dividends are only recorded as liabilities if they are formally declared, whereas Australian and UK practice is to raise a provision at year-end before the actual declaration.

In addition to the above adjustments, the following aspects of Australian accounting principles and practice may require attention when adjusting Australian financial statements to either UK or US GAAP for ratio or other analysis:

- the basis of asset classification in the balance sheet;
- the measurement of inventories with 'market' interpreted to mean 'net realizable value';
- the ban on the use of LIFO;
- the requirement to write non-current assets down to recoverable amount;
- in the extractive industries the allowing of the immediate expensing of pre-production costs and the disallowing of the full cost method;
- flexible practice on the capitalization of interest costs;
- requirement to capitalize research and development costs when they are expected beyond any reasonable doubt to be recoverable;
- prohibition on the application of the pooling-of-interests method in accounting for business combinations;
- toleration of instantaneous in-substance defeasances;
- inclusion of certain subsidiaries in the consolidated financial statements owing to a very broad definition of subsidiary and total reliance on control as the basis for consolidation;
- minority interests included as part of the shareholders' equity of the group.

It is evident that there are pitfalls to be avoided by UK and US analysts in relying on Australian company financial statements. Despite similar accounting rules on particular topics, there are significant variations in the GAAP of Australia, the UK and the USA. The differences have the potential to alter reported figures drastically. Consequently, the analyst would need to consider adjusting to a bench-mark set of accounting principles before attempting to draw conclusions on relative performance from the financial statements published in the different countries.

SUMMARY

Australia has a market-oriented economy with political, economic and legal institutions that resemble in many respects those in the UK and the USA. However, a distinctive regulatory framework for financial reporting has developed in which important roles are played by the federal Corporations Law, certain government authorities, the accountancy profession and the Stock Exchange. Furthermore, while much progress has been made in specifying the rules to govern financial reporting, those rules are rarely exact replicas of those on corresponding topics in the UK or the USA. Indeed, particular variations in the rules can create significant illusory differences across the countries in the amounts reported in relation to performance and financial position. Consequently, financial analysts should be aware of the adjustments that may be necessary to Australian company financial statements to make reliable transnational comparisons.

APPENDIX

Extracts from the accounts of Burns, Philp & Company

Statements of Profit and Loss

For the year ended 30 June 1992

		Consolidated			Burns, Philp & Company Limited		
	Note	**1992 $'000**	1991 $'000	1990 $'000	**1992 $'000**	1991 $'000	1990 $'000
Operating profit before abnormal items and income tax	2,3	**132,157**	101,715	107,299	**85,757**	75,884	60,862
Income tax attributable to operating profit before abnormal items	5	**(25,005)**	(12,278)	(6,016)	**(14,700)**	(15,308)	(3,917)
Operating profit before abnormal items		**107,152**	89,437	101,283	**71,057**	60,576	56,945
Profit/(loss) on abnormal items	2,4	**(2,696)**	(22,242)	(38,896)	**(7,124)**	(5,122)	20,940
Income tax attributable to abnormal items	5	**4,191**	1,642	1,425	**2,623**	(260)	(1,206)
Profit/(loss) on abnormal items after income tax	4	**1,495**	(20,600)	(37,471)	**(4,501)**	(5,382)	19,734
Operating profit including abnormal items after income tax		**108,647**	68,837	63,812	**66,556**	55,194	76,679
Outside equity interests in operating profit including abnormal items after income tax	6	**(16,512)**	(15,545)	(9,938)	**-**	-	-
Operating profit including abnormal items after income tax attributable to members of Burns, Philp & Company Limited		**92,135**	53,292	53,874	**66,556**	55,194	76,679
Profit/(loss) on extraordinary items		**-**	128,722	-	**-**	(5,930)	-
Income tax attributable to extraordinary items		**-**	(19,587)	-	**-**	-	-
Profit/(loss) on extraordinary items after income tax	7	**-**	109,135	-	**-**	(5,930)	-
Operating profit including abnormal and extraordinary items after income tax attributable to members of Burns, Philp & Company Limited		**92,135**	162,427	53,874	**66,556**	49,264	76,679
Retained profits at the beginning of the financial year		**337,643**	215,742	189,191	**83,384**	84,587	53,339
Aggregate of amounts transferred from reserves	8	**7,735**	10,701	31,362	**3,735**	-	381
Total available for appropriation		**437,513**	388,870	274,427	**153,675**	133,851	130,399
Net dividends provided for or paid	9	**(49,777)**	(49,168)	(46,179)	**(48,181)**	(48,633)	(45,812)
Aggregate of amounts transferred to reserves	8	**(2,621)**	(2,059)	(12,506)	**-**	(1,834)	-
Retained profits at the end of the financial year		**385,115**	337,643	215,742	**105,494**	83,384	84,587

The attached notes form part of these financial statements.

Balance Sheets

At 30 June 1992

	Note	Consolidated			Burns, Philp & Company Limited		
		1992 $'000	1991 $'000	1990 $'000	**1992 $'000**	1991 $'000	1990 $'000
Current assets							
Cash	11	**280,089**	331,745	98,235	**288,363**	299,626	49,357
Receivables	10	**298,017**	258,200	247,581	**1,197,514**	1,126,758	410,454
Investments	12	**150**	5,517	1,067	**-**	-	-
Inventories	13	**368,342**	371,298	377,240	**738**	733	4,634
Other	14	**20,328**	23,205	18,316	**695**	2,098	7,081
Total current assets		**966,926**	989,965	742,439	**1,487,310**	1,429,215	471,526
Non-current assets							
Receivables	10	**15,051**	16,799	13,977	**-**	-	1,148
Investments	12	**76,059**	61,912	216,097	**109,309**	113,484	909,267
Property, plant and equipment	15	**696,282**	640,616	595,561	**5,916**	7,719	89,961
Intangibles	16	**440,069**	321,444	280,740	**-**	88,700	105,012
Other	14	**80,885**	53,803	54,424	**16,754**	14,580	14,105
Total non-current assets		**1,308,346**	1,094,574	1,160,799	**131,979**	224,483	1,119,493
Total assets		**2,275,272**	2,084,539	1,903,238	**1,619,289**	1,653,698	1,591,019
Current liabilities							
Creditors and borrowings	17	**409,756**	405,515	397,765	**577,632**	600,409	364,697
Provisions	18	**90,900**	85,126	87,735	**34,514**	43,762	29,082
Total current liabilities		**500,656**	490,641	485,500	**612,146**	644,171	393,779
Non-current liabilities							
Creditors and borrowings	17	**497,371**	453,430	487,929	**80,859**	139,255	353,408
Provisions	18	**43,637**	34,819	38,213	**6,591**	2,130	10,975
Total non-current liabilities		**541,008**	488,249	526,142	**87,450**	141,385	364,383
Total liabilities		**1,041,664**	978,890	1,011,642	**699,596**	785,556	758,162
Net assets		**1,233,608**	1,105,649	891,596	**919,693**	868,142	832,857
Shareholders' equity							
Share capital	19	**194,527**	187,063	174,051	**194,527**	187,063	174,051
Reserves	8	**381,714**	332,639	276,514	**462,256**	436,495	389,626
Retained profits		**385,115**	337,643	215,742	**105,494**	83,384	84,587
Shareholders' equity attributable to members of Burns, Philp & Company Limited		**961,356**	857,345	666,307	**762,277**	706,942	648,264
Outside equity interests in controlled entities	6	**114,836**	87,104	40,696	**-**	-	-
Total shareholders' equity		**1,076,192**	944,449	707,003	**762,277**	706,942	648,264
Subordinated perpetual unsecured convertible notes	19	**157,416**	161,200	184,593	**157,416**	161,200	184,593
Total shareholders' equity and convertible notes		**1,233,608**	1,105,649	891,596	**919,693**	868,142	832,857

Commitments and contingent liabilities 20,21,31

The attached notes form part of these financial statements.

Statements of Cash Flows

For the year ended 30 June 1992

	Consolidated			Burns, Philp & Company Limited		
	1992	1991	1990	**1992**	1991	1990
	$'000	$'000	$'000	**$'000**	$'000	$'000
Cash flows from operating activities						
Receipts from customers	**2,247,721**	2,283,439	2,242,424	**4,373**	3,482	579,932
Payments to suppliers and employees	**(2,054,197)**	(2,073,710)	(1,959,066)	**(7,809)**	(29,277)	(427,927)
Interest received	**51,012**	24,880	38,934	**122,265**	109,147	25,021
Interest and other costs of finance paid	**(87,205)**	(101,932)	(101,113)	**(70,026)**	(72,573)	(77,164)
Dividends received	**4,221**	8,806	14,453	**43,690**	40,417	49,638
Income taxes paid	**(26,666)**	(18,945)	(19,011)	**(587)**	–	–
Payments arising from the closure and rationalisation of businesses	**(19,456)**	(22,273)	(38,432)	**(445)**	–	–
Net cash provided by operating activities (refer note 29 b))	**115,430**	100,265	178,189	**91,461**	51,196	149,500
Cash flows from investing activities						
Payment for property, plant and equipment	**(98,388)**	(86,360)	(109,600)	**(681)**	(788)	(19,950)
Proceeds from sale of property, plant and equipment	**23,798**	18,887	13,205	**500**	137	4,565
Payment for investments	**(11,960)**	(14,671)	(44,060)	**–**	(17,350)	(14,838)
Proceeds from sale of investments:						
QBE Insurance	**–**	316,336	–	**–**	–	–
Other	**18,013**	2,162	4,326	**880**	–	3,732
Payment for businesses, net of cash acquired (refer note 29 c))	**(58,952)**	(54,956)	(87,977)	**–**	–	–
Proceeds on sale of businesses, net of cash disposed of (refer note 29 c))	**27,816**	21,718	61,013	**–**	–	30,800
Other payments	**(5,840)**	(7,089)	(671)	**–**	(6,501)	(6,459)
Net cash (used in)/provided by investing activities	**(105,513)**	196,027	(163,764)	**699**	(24,502)	(2,150)
Cash flows from financing activities						
Proceeds from issue of shares and options	**37,339**	34,793	26,477	**37,339**	34,793	26,477
(Repayments of)/proceeds from borrowings	**(20,455)**	11,899	(41,851)	**(113,200)**	(198,597)	(56,914)
Loan repayments by/(loans to) controlled entities	**–**	–	–	**27,724**	447,321	(12,332)
Dividends paid to:						
Burns, Philp & Company Limited shareholders	**(49,250)**	(48,250)	(45,454)	**(47,654)**	(47,715)	(45,087)
Outside equity interests	**(18,005)**	(7,699)	(5,509)	**–**	–	–
Net cash (used in)/provided by financing activities	**(50,371)**	(9,257)	(66,337)	**(95,791)**	235,802	(87,856)
Net (decrease)/increase in cash held	**(40,454)**	287,035	(51,912)	**(3,631)**	262,496	59,494
Cash at the beginning of the financial year	**422,756**	135,734	184,955	**331,227**	68,731	9,237
Effects of exchange rate changes on the balances of cash held in foreign currencies at the beginning of the year	**15,442**	(13)	2,691	**–**	–	–
Cash at the end of the financial year (refer note 29 a))	**397,744**	422,756	135,734	**327,596**	331,227	68,731

Notes to the Financial Statements

Note 1 Accounting Policies

a) Underlying accounting principles
The financial statements of Burns, Philp & Company Limited and the consolidated financial statements of the economic entity, being Burns, Philp & Company Limited (the chief entity) and its controlled entities, have been prepared on the basis of historical costs, or valuations where stated, and comply with the provisions of Schedule 5 of the Corporations Regulations, Statements of Accounting Concepts, applicable Accounting Standards and in all material respects are consistent with International Accounting Standards except that supplementary information reflecting the effects of changing prices is not provided.

The directors review the carrying amounts of all non-current assets at least annually. If the carrying amount of a non-current asset exceeds the recoverable amount, the asset is written down to the lower value. In assessing the recoverable amount of an asset, cash flows have been discounted to their present value, where appropriate.

b) Principles of consolidation
The consolidated financial statements comprise the financial statements of Burns, Philp & Company Limited and its controlled entities.

Where a controlled entity is acquired or disposed of during the year, its results are included in consolidated profit only from the date of acquisition or up until the date of disposal. All inter-entity balances and transactions are eliminated.

c) Segment information
The operating results disclosed in the segment information are based on consolidated & equity results before abnormal items as the directors are of the opinion that this more fairly represents the segmental results and reflects how the operations are managed. A reconciliation of the consolidated & equity operating profit before abnormal items with the consolidated operating profit before abnormal items is set out in note (b) to the segment information.

d) Goodwill
Purchased goodwill, being the excess of purchase consideration over the fair value attributed to net assets acquired, is amortised on a straight line basis over the period of expected benefit, not exceeding 20 years. In addition, the carrying value of goodwill is reviewed annually by the directors and adjusted where necessary.

In determining the value of purchased goodwill on acquisition, appropriate consideration is given to assigning a fair value to trademarks, tradenames, brandnames, fermentation and other technologies acquired.

e) Foreign currency
Transactions in foreign currencies are translated at the rate of exchange ruling on the date of each transaction.

Amounts receivable and payable in foreign currencies at balance date are translated at the rates of exchange ruling on that date except where forward exchange cover has been obtained, the forward exchange rate is used.

Statements of profit and loss for overseas controlled entities are translated to Australian currency at the average rates of exchange ruling during the year (refer note 30). All overseas operations are deemed to be self-sustaining.

On consolidation, exchange differences arising on the translation of financial statements of overseas controlled entities are transferred directly to the foreign currency translation reserve (refer note 8) together with any exchange gains or losses on foreign currency monetary liabilities, after applicable income tax, which hedge the net investment in self-sustaining overseas operations.

Foreign exchange translation gains or losses arising out of current account balances and unhedged foreign currency borrowings are reflected in the results for the year.

f) Trademarks, tradenames and brandnames
Burns Philp develops and acquires products and businesses with registered trademarks, tradenames and brandnames. Acquired trademarks, tradenames and brandnames are included in the financial statements at the lower of cost of acquisition and recoverable amount.

At the present time, no value has been placed on trademarks, tradenames and brandnames developed by Burns Philp from its own resources. The directors have, however, adopted a policy of regular independent review of the value of trademarks, tradenames and brandnames and disclose the independent valuation of these assets in the financial statements (refer note 16). Should any independent review indicate that the recoverable amount of trademarks, tradenames and brandnames falls below cost, then such fall in value will be brought to account in the statement of profit and loss.

No amortisation is provided on trademarks, tradenames and brandnames until an event occurs which results in a loss or limitation of the useful life of the asset.

Expenditure incurred in developing, maintaining or enhancing trademarks, tradenames and brandnames is written off against profits in the year in which it is incurred.

g) Technological assets
Burns Philp develops and acquires fermentation and other technologies. These assets are included in the financial statements at either independent valuation or cost, neither of which exceeds their recoverable amount (refer note 16).

No amortisation is provided on technological assets until an event occurs which results in a loss or limitation of the useful life of the asset.

h) Research and development
Research and development expenditure, including expenditure on developing, maintaining or protecting fermentation and other technologies, is charged against profits in the year in which it is incurred.

i) Property, plant and equipment
i) Depreciation and amortisation
Depreciation is provided on plant and equipment generally on a straight line basis so as to write off the cost of the assets over their expected economic useful lives Depreciation is also provided on all freehold buildings. Leasehold land and buildings are amortised over the economic useful life of the property or the period of the respective lease, whichever is the shorter.

Notes to the Financial Statements

Note 1 Accounting Policies (continued)

ii) Revaluations
Properties are independently valued at least once every three years. Non-Pacific properties are included in the financial statements at the revalued amount. For Pacific properties, being a separate class of asset, revaluations since 1988 have not been included in the financial statements for the reasons set out in note 15. No property is carried at a value in excess of its recoverable amount.

The independent valuations are performed on the basis of open market value and existing use.

All other items of property, plant and equipment are carried at the lower of cost less accumulated depreciation, and recoverable amount. When revaluing a property, potential capital gains tax is not taken to account unless there is an intention to sell that property.

j) Subordinated perpetual unsecured convertible notes
The inclusion of subordinated perpetual unsecured convertible notes in the shareholders' equity section of the balance sheet differs from the prescribed format of Schedule 5 of the Corporations Regulations. In the opinion of the directors, compliance with the prescribed format in respect of the convertible notes would not give a true and fair view of the state of affairs of Burns Philp.The directors consider that the subordinated perpetual unsecured convertible notes represent equity as they:
- are not repayable on a final conversion date;
- can be freely converted into ordinary issued capital;
- are subordinated in right of payment to the claims of all unsubordinated creditors;

and therefore should be disclosed as equity in the balance sheet. Interest paid on convertible notes is charged against operating profit.

k) Investments

i) Associated companies
Investments in associated companies are revalued each balance date in the books of relevant investor companies to their share of the associated companies' net tangible assets. These revaluations are taken directly to reserves and are not included in the statement of profit and loss except when the share of associated companies' net tangible assets falls below the initial cost of investment. Dividends are included in operating profit as they are received.

An associated company is one in which Burns Philp exercises significant influence over the company and the investment is long term. Information prepared on an equity accounting basis is set out in note 25.

ii) Other investments
Quoted investments are carried at market value while all other investments, except for partnership interests, are carried at the lower of cost and recoverable amount. Interests in partnerships are carried at the share of net assets of the partnerships at balance date. Dividends are included in operating profit as they are received.

l) Interest capitalisation
Interest costs on funds utilised to finance the construction of major capital items, including factories, are capitalised as part of the applicable asset cost during the period of construction.

m) Taxation
The liability method of tax-effect accounting is adopted. Under this method, income tax expense is based on accounting profit adjusted for permanent differences between accounting and taxable income.

The benefit of tax losses is brought to account when realised, when realisation is virtually certain or when timing differences give rise to a deferred tax liability that will not be paid while past tax losses are available.

Tax losses not recognised will be realised only if no adverse change occurs in the income tax legislation, Burns Philp derives sufficient future assessable income to enable the benefits to be realised and continues to comply with the conditions of deductibility imposed by law.

Withholding tax is provided on overseas income which is expected to be remitted. No provision is made for earnings anticipated to be retained by overseas controlled entities to finance ongoing operations. Provision is made for Australian tax payable on overseas income assessable under the foreign income accruals taxation system.

n) Inventories
Inventories are valued at the lower of cost and net realisable value. Cost is determined on the basis of first-in-first-out, average cost or standard cost, whichever is the most appropriate for each individual business. The method of assigning costs to inventory in each business is applied consistently from year to year. Selling and distribution costs are estimated to determine net realisable value. Adequate provision is made for slow moving and obsolete inventory (refer note 13).

The cost of manufactured inventory and work in progress includes applicable variable and fixed factory overhead costs, the latter being allocated on the basis of normal operating capacity

o) Provision for employee entitlements
Provision is made for entitlements accruing to employees in relation to such matters as annual leave and long service leave. Provision for long service leave is calculated on the accrued pro rata entitlement at current wage and salary levels of employees who have completed five years service, or in the case of overseas operations, such period as is provided for by local legislation.

p) Retirement benefits
Employees' contributory superannuation and pension funds exist to provide benefits for employees and their dependants on retirement, disability or death. Contributions made to these funds by Burns Philp are charged against profits. Where the assets of a fund significantly exceed the liabilities and where the fund's actuary recommends, contributions may be ceased until such time as the surplus is reduced.

q) Comparative figures
The comparative figures have been adjusted to reflect the presentation adopted in 1992.

Notes to the Financial Statements

Note 33 US GAAP Information

To assist overseas shareholders and analysts with their review of the consolidated financial statements, a reconciliation of the results and shareholders' equity reported in these financial statements with the position that would have been reported if the financial statements had been prepared under US generally accepted accounting principles (GAAP) is provided.

		Profit		
		1992	1991	1990
For the year ended 30 June	Note	**$'000**	$'000	$'000
Consolidated operating profit as reported	1	**92,135**	162,427	53,874
US GAAP adjustments				
· Equity results	3	**2,303**	16,695	16,751
· Depreciation on revalued properties	4	**1,027**	865	940
· Revalued properties sold	4	**1,258**	1,550	737
· Revalued investments sold	4	**1,799**	122	2,265
· Amortisation of goodwill	5	**(1,058)**	(1,058)	(1,058)
· Amortisation of trademarks, tradenames, brandnames and technological assets	5	**(6,539)**	(6,197)	(5,212)
· FITB attributable to tax losses	6	**(13,021)**	(2,977)	(1,663)
· Superannuation (pension) surplus adjustment	7	**(2,440)**	(2,440)	–
US GAAP net profit		**75,464**	168,987	66,634

		Shareholders' equity		
		1992	1991	1990
At 30 June	Note	**$'000**	$'000	$'000
Shareholders' equity as reported	2	**961,356**	857,345	666,307
US GAAP adjustments				
· Revaluation of properties	4	**(30,538)**	(34,371)	(35,921)
· Revaluation of investments	4	**(10,046)**	(1,799)	(1,906)
· Goodwill adjustment	5	**37,226**	38,284	39,342
· Accumulated amortisation of trademarks, tradenames, brandnames and technological assets	5	**(25,165)**	(18,626)	(12,426)
· Revaluation of technological assets	4	**(67,600)**	(67,600)	(67,600)
· FITB attributable to tax losses	6	**(22,725)**	(9,704)	(6,727)
· Superannuation (pension) surplus adjustment	7	**(4,880)**	(2,440)	–
· Final dividend provision	8	**14,590**	14,063	13,145
US GAAP shareholders' equity		**852,218**	775,152	594,214

Notes:

1 Consolidated operating profit after tax and abnormal/extraordinary items attributable to members of Burns, Philp & Company Limited.

2 Shareholders' equity attributable to members of Burns, Philp & Company Limited as per the balance sheet.

US GAAP requirements have necessitated the following adjustments reflected in the above consolidated operating profit and shareholders' equity reconciliation:

3 US GAAP requires the inclusion of equity results.

4 Reversal of asset revaluations. Profits on disposal and depreciation (where applicable) have been adjusted accordingly.

5 Amortisation of all intangible assets over periods up to 40 years. Goodwill written off in prior years has been reinstated to be amortised over 40 years.

6 Reversal of future income tax benefits relating to tax losses. A new accounting standard SFAS109 will allow tax losses to be carried forward to be offset against future profits in certain circumstances. As a result, US GAAP profits are expected to increase in future years.

7 Adjustment for the $30 million surplus received from the Burns Philp Group Superannuation Plan in 1991 which is being recognised in the consolidated profit and loss account in five equal instalments (annual tax effected amount $3,660,000), but which is required to be brought to account over a 15-year amortisation period under US GAAP (annual tax effected amount $1,220,000). As the necessary actuarial valuations were not readily available, full compliance with SFAS87 is not possible.

8 Reversal of final dividend provision, as US GAAP requires dividends to be recorded in the period they are declared, not the period to which they relate.

Statutory Statements

Statement by Directors

In the opinion of the directors of Burns, Philp & Company Limited:

a) The financial statements set out on pages 16 to 62 are drawn up so as to give a true and fair view of the state of affairs at 30 June 1992, and the result for the year ended on that date, of the Company and the economic entity so far as they concern members of the Company.
b) At the date of this statement, there are reasonable grounds to believe that the Company will be able to pay its debts as and when they fall due.
c) The consolidated financial statements have been made out in accordance with Division 4A and 4B of Part 3.6 of the Corporations Law.
d) At the date of this statement, there are reasonable grounds to believe that the Company and the controlled entities identified in note 22 will be able as an economic entity to meet any obligations or liabilities to which they are or may become subject by virtue of the deed of cross guarantee described in note 21.

The accompanying financial statements of the Company and the economic entity are made out in accordance with Statements of Accounting Concepts and applicable Accounting Standards.

Signed in accordance with a resolution of the directors.

P H Finley
Director

A Turnbull
Director
Sydney, 7 October 1992

Independent Auditors' Report to the Members of Burns, Philp & Company Limited

Scope

We have audited the financial statements of Burns, Philp & Company Limited and of the economic entity, being Burns, Philp & Company Limited and its controlled entities for the year ended 30 June 1992, as set out on pages 16 to 63. The Company's directors are responsible for the preparation and presentation of the financial statements and the information they contain. We have conducted an independent audit of these financial statements in order to express an opinion on them to the members of the Company.

Our audit has been conducted in accordance with Australian Auditing Standards to provide a reasonable level of assurance as to whether the financial statements are free of material misstatement. Our procedures included examination, on a test basis, of evidence supporting the amounts and other disclosures in the financial statements, and the evaluation of accounting policies and significant accounting estimates. These procedures have been undertaken to form an opinion as to whether, in all material respects, the financial statements are presented fairly in accordance with Australian accounting concepts and standards and statutory requirements so as to present a view which is consistent with our understanding of the Company's and of the economic entity's financial position and the results of their operations.

The names of the controlled entities audited by overseas KPMG member firms and other auditors are set out in note 22.

The audit opinion expressed in this report has been formed on the above basis.

Audit Opinion

In our opinion, the financial statements of Burns, Philp & Company Limited and consolidated financial statements of the economic entity are properly drawn up:

a) so as to give a true and fair view of:
   i) the state of affairs of the Company and the economic entity as at 30 June 1992 and of the results and cash flows of the Company and the economic entity for the financial year ended on that date; and
   ii) the other matters required by Division 4, 4A and 4B of Part 3.6 of the Corporations Law to be dealt with in the financial statements and in the consolidated financial statements;
b) in accordance with the provisions of the Corporations Law; and
c) in accordance with Statements of Accounting Concepts and applicable Accounting Standards.

KPMG Peat Marwick
Chartered Accountants

G H Bennett
Partner
Sydney, 7 October 1992

BIBLIOGRAPHY

Accounting Handbook 1992, Sydney: Prentice Hall (published annually incorporating all Accounting Standards and Statements of Accounting Concepts).

Australian Accounting Research Foundation, *Subscription Service*, Melbourne: AARF. (The comprehensive subscription package includes all AASB, AAS and auditing standards as well as various reports, discussion papers and monographs.)

Australian Accounts Preparation Manual (four vol), Frequent updates, Sydney: CCH.

Australian Corporations and Securities Legislation (two vol), Latest edition, Sydney: CCH.

Australian Securities Commission (1992) *Annual Report*, Sydney: ASC.

Australian Stock Exchange Limited (ASX) (1992) *Annual Report*, Sydney: ASX.

Bosch, H. (1990) *The Workings of a Watchdog*, Melbourne: Heinemann.

Clark, D. (1990) *Student Economic Briefs 1990/91*, Sydney: The Financial Review Library.

Doing Business in Australia and the United States of America: A Comparison (1990) Sydney: Baker & McKenzie, Price Waterhouse, and Westpac Banking Corporation.

Gibson, R.W. (1971) *Disclosure by Australian Companies*, Melbourne: Melbourne University Press.

Gray, S.J. (1988) 'Towards a theory of cultural influence on the development of accounting systems internationally', *Abacus* 24: 1–15.

Heffernan, M. (1992) 'Australian Economy – 1992/93', in *All Ordinaries Index Companies Handbook*, Sydney: Australian Stock Exchange.

Hilmer, F.G. (1990) *New Games, New Rules.* Sydney: Angus & Robertson.

Hofstede, G. (1987) 'The cultural context of accounting', in B.E. Cushing (ed.), *Accounting and Culture*, Sarasota, Fla.: American Accounting Association.

Jackson, J. and McConnell, C.R. (1988) *Economics* (3rd edn), Sydney: McGraw-Hill Book Company.

Ma, R., Parker, R.H. and Whittred, G. (1991) *Consolidation Accounting*, Melbourne: Longman Cheshire.

McGregor, W. (1992) 'True and fair – an accounting anachronism', *AARF Report*, March, 8–11.

Organisation for Economic Co-operation and Development (1990) *OECD Economic Surveys: Australia*, Paris: OECD.

Pannell Kerr Forster (1990) *The Accounting Profession in Australia*, New York: American Institute of Certified Public Accountants.

Parker, R.H. (1982) 'Why are Australian accounting standards different?', *The Australian Accountant*, August, 424–31.

—— (1989) 'Importing and exporting accounting: the British experience' in A.G. Hopwood (ed.), *International Pressures for Accounting Change*, London: Prentice Hall.

—— (1991) 'Regulating financial reporting in the United Kingdom, the United States, Australia and Canada' in C.W. Nobes and R.H. Parker (eds), *Comparative International Accounting*, London: Prentice Hall.

Paul, J. (1992) 'Statement of accounting concepts SAC 4: background and implications', *AARF Report*, June, 9–15.

Peirson, G. (1990) *A Report on Institutional Arrangements for Accounting Standard Setting in Australia*, Melbourne: Australian Accounting Research Foundation.

Puxty, A.G., Willmott, H.C., Cooper, D.J. and Lowe, T. (1987) 'Modes of regulation in advanced capitalism: locating accountancy in four countries', *Accounting, Organizations and Society* 12: 273–91.

Van Horne, J., Davis, K., Nicol, R. and Wright, K. (1990) *Financial Management and Policy in Australia*, Sydney: Prentice Hall.

Wines, G. (1989) 'The influence of cultural factors on the development of Australian accounting principles', *Accounting Forum* 13, December: 3–15.

Year Book Australia 1992, Canberra: Australian Bureau of Statistics.

11 New Zealand

S. Newby

THE BUSINESS ENVIRONMENT

Government and economic policies

New Zealand is a self-governing nation within the British Commonwealth. The Parliamentary system, legislature and judiciary in New Zealand are based on the British model. The National government came to power in 1990 ousting Labour from its two terms in office since 1984. New Zealand has a sophisticated free-market economy as a result of undergoing major economic reforms in line with deregulated olicies pursued by Labour whilst it was in power, and which are being persevered with under National.

> At the time of its election in July 1984, the new Labour government was confronted with an economy weakened by protectionism, enterprise government intervention and suppressed inflation. Macroeconomic imbalances were severe. Large government budget deficits had been allowed to persist from the mid-1970s, approaching almost 9 per cent of GDP by 1984.
>
> (OECD 1989)

Free-market policies appear to have achieved stronger economic conditions for the longer term. New Zealand is pulling out of the slump of the late 1980s, which followed an initial period of growth in 1985–6. Now New Zealand's deficit compares well with other OECD economies; in 1992/93 at 3.1 per cent it is well below the OECD average of 4.2 per cent, and is beaten only by Japan and Austria. New Zealand's deficit peaked at 3.6 per cent in 1990/91, whereas the OECD average has worsened to the current 1992/93 at 4.2 per cent. Also, New Zealand's average economic growth over the three years to 1994, at around 3 per cent, is amongst the highest within the OECD (National Business Outlook 1993).

Unemployment fell in the March 1993 quarter to 9.8 per cent, 0.3 per cent down from the previous quarter, and 1.7 per cent down from a high of 11.5 per cent a year earlier (Department of Statistics 1993: 31). Long-term interest rates are trending downwards and at July 1993 are between 7 and 8 per cent for a first mortgage housing prime rate for new borrowers

(Department of Statistics 1993: 112). Inflation for the year to March 1993 was 1 per cent with a prediction for the year to March 1994 of around 2.4 per cent (National Bank of New Zealand Limited 1993).

Business survey indicators are increasingly optimistic; July 1993 'results show business confidence, the activity outlook index, investment intentions, and expected export volumes of manufactured goods all achieving strong improvement to be near the record levels achieved in February (1993). ... Economic events over (July) included ... positive building permit data, continued record export receipts, an improvement in the terms of trade and the overseas debt position, and a large drop in wholesale interest rates post Budget. Virtually all responses to the July survey were sent in after the 1993 Budget was released, but before the latest round of mortgage and base interest rate cuts took place' (National Bank of New Zealand Limited 1993).

The extent of reforms since 1984 has been significant, and includes substantial deregulation of the financial system, reduction of tax rates, freeing-up of the labour market and negotiation of pay rates, trimming the welfare state, elimination of government subsidies, reorganization of the state sector including the privatization of state-owned enterprises, relaxation of border protection and the management of international trade.

Overseas trade

New Zealand's small economy is heavily dependent on overseas trade. Traditional primary produce exports such as meat, wool, and dairy products made up approximately 39 per cent of export earnings in 1990, but their importance has diminished from a decade earlier when they contributed the major portion of export earnings: 59 per cent as recently as 1978. Primary produce still makes up approximately two-thirds of New Zealand's export earnings with horticulture and fisheries contributing increasingly. The export of manufactured goods is also of growing importance.

The pattern of trade reflects efforts over the past twenty years to diversify both export products and export markets. Major trading partners are now Australia, Japan, the United States of America and the European Community, accounting for 68 per cent of exports and 75 per cent of imports in 1990. Within these figures exports to the United Kingdom amounted to 7.2 per cent of all exports, and imports supplied were 8.8 per cent of the total. This represents a downsizing and reversal of net trade from the early 1970s when the United Kingdom took more than 40 per cent of New Zealand exports and provided 30 per cent of New Zealand imports. Emerging new markets include the Middle East and South-East Asia (Department of Statistics 1991: Ch. 6).

Table 11.1 New Zealand statistics

	1989 (*'000s*)	*1988* (*'000s*)
Total population	3,312	3,292
Total employed	1,216	1,241
Employed in small enterprises (5 or less people engaged)	231	233
Employed in large enterprises (100 or more people engaged)	594	618
Total number of business enterprises	146	141
Number of small enterprises	120	115

Source: Department of Statistics, September 1989.

Note: Approximately 20 per cent of the labour force is employed in the state sector (*New Zealand Official Yearbook, 1988–89*, p. 75).

Business statistics

The downturn in the economy is reflected in business statistics, summarized in Table 11.1. The statistics illustrate that the New Zealand business environment has large numbers of self-employed and people working in small enterprises. Also, approximately 20 per cent of the labour force is employed in the state sector which is similar to the situation prevailing in the United Kingdom but is somewhat less than in Australia (26 per cent).

As at July 1993, the Justice Department records showed 156,925 registered companies – an increase of 17,000 over the 140,000 companies registered in 1989. Approximately 1,400–1,600 of registered companies in 1993 (actual figures unavailable) were classified as public companies, but of these fewer than 200 were listed on the stock exchange. Therefore a large number of business enterprises in New Zealand are privately funded or funded by borrowings from banks.

Sources of finance

Equity markets

The first stock exchanges in New Zealand were founded in 1869 and were located in Auckland, Dunedin, Reefton and Thames. The development of the exchanges resulted from the gold boom of the 1860s in which many of the discoveries were made by joint-stock companies which needed to raise funds for such speculative ventures. In 1872 the Auckland Sharebrokers Association was formed and in 1897 the Association changed its name to the Auckland Stock Exchange. In 1915 the regional exchanges formed the Stock Exchange Association of New Zealand which eventually became the

New Zealand Stock Exchange. Today the Exchange consists of four regional centres located in Auckland, Christchurch, Dunedin and Wellington, although much of the administration of the Exchange is undertaken at Wellington.

In relation to the size of the country the New Zealand Stock Exchange is as important to the domestic economy as in Australia, the UK and the US (Cameron 1988: 39). The New Zealand Stock Exchange has had an important role in the economic liberalization adopted in the late 1980s and early 1990s not only in the way business is conducted in the market but also in a high level of activity on the market resulting from an upsurge in merger and acquisition activity.

Further details on the role of the Stock Exchange, securities regulations, and performance of the share market in New Zealand are provided later in this chapter.

Financial institutions

There are also well-established merchant banking operations which act as brokers to the capital market, as investment advisers, foreign exchange dealers, underwriters and placers of capital issues. Hire purchase finance for capital items is freely available from the numerous finance companies which obtain their funds through a wide range of secured and unsecured deposits from the public.

Following deregulation there is freedom in financial intermediation in New Zealand; however, almost all financial institutions have sought to be registered as a 'bank'. As at October 1990 there were twenty-three registered banks; these institutions, having moved away from traditional niches, now offer a range of products to cater right across the market from consumer to corporate activities.

Reserve Bank supervision of the banking industry

The banking system in New Zealand is supervised by the New Zealand government through the Reserve Bank which since 1 February 1990 has operated under the Reserve Bank of New Zealand Act 1989. The Act provides that the main functions of the Reserve Bank are:

- to act as the central bank of New Zealand;
- to formulate and implement monetary policy;
- to achieve and maintain stability in the general level of prices;
- to promote the maintenance of a sound and efficient financial system;
- to monitor the prudential soundness of banks;
- to manage the note and coin issue.

BUSINESS ORGANIZATIONS

The types of business organizations operating in New Zealand are very similar to those that exist in the UK. The most economically significant group is the corporate sector. Companies may be limited by shares, limited by guarantee or even unlimited, although, in practice, the most common form of business organization for industrial and commercial entities is to limited liability by shares. Limited liability companies may be public or private (proprietary) and the difference is described below. The procedure for incorporation is as follows:

Approval must be sought for the company name and the following documents must be lodged with the Registrar of Companies:

- *Memorandum of Association*, which states the company's name, the share capital, the initial shareholders, and other basic conditions under which the company is incorporated;
- *Articles of Association*, which state the rules of internal management. Model articles set out in the Third Schedule of the Companies Act 1955 apply where a limited liability company does not register its own articles; however, normally some modification of the model articles is found to be necessary. The articles of a listed company are greatly influenced by stock exchange requirements;
- *Particulars of directors and secretaries*;
- *Address of the registered office.*

There are additional filing requirements for public companies such as the statutory report which gives particulars of shares allotted, cash received and other matters dealing with formation to be presented at a statutory meeting held within three months of commencing business (Companies Act 1955 sect. 134).

Types of companies

Domestic companies

Limited liability companies fall within three main categories: public companies, private companies and overseas companies.

Public companies must have at least seven members including two directors and a secretary, and must file their audited annual accounts with the Registrar of Companies.

Private companies must have at least two members but no more than twenty-five, including a director and a secretary. Private companies are prohibited from inviting a public subscription for shares. It is not necessary for private companies other than non-exempt private companies to appoint an auditor (sect. 163) or file annual accounts (sect. 133).

A private company is classified as 'non-exempt' where:

- it is indebted to any person in respect of any deposit or loan to which the Securities Act 1978 applies; or
- it is a subsidiary of any company or body corporate incorporated outside New Zealand; or
- shares are held by any such subsidiary or any company or body corporate incorporated outside New Zealand or any person not ordinarily resident in New Zealand, if those shares, in the aggregate, carry the right to exercise or control the exercise of 25 per cent or more of the voting power at any general meeting of the company.

(Companies Act 1955, sect. 354(3B))

Overseas companies

Overseas companies are by definition incorporated, formed or constituted in a country other than New Zealand. In order to establish a place of business or a branch in New Zealand an overseas company must satisfy the following requirements:

> Have prior name approval; and within thirty days file with the Registrar of Companies:
>
> - evidence of incorporation (if incorporated overseas);
> - a certified copy of constitutional charter (memorandum and articles);
> - a list of directors and secretary; and
> - the name of a New Zealand resident authorized to act as agent for accepting notices and providing an address for the New Zealand registered office.

Overseas companies are required to file the accounts of their New Zealand operation with the Registrar of Companies but provision is available for their overseas accounts to be filed where they include the New Zealand operations. Certain provisions of the Eighth Schedule of the Companies Act, which sets out minimum disclosure requirements for the financial reports of companies, do not apply but additional disclosure is required of the amount of administration charge unrelated to the New Zealand operation but allocated to it, and of the names of certain New Zealand investees. The accounts must be audited by a chartered accountant approved by the Registrar.

As at April 1991 there were 1,024 overseas companies registered in New Zealand, but not all of them were actively in business; a good proportion seem to have registered for name protection purposes (the actual number of companies registered for this purpose is unavailable).

Consent of the Overseas Investment Commission is required for the following:

- for investment in New Zealand to establish a new business; or

- for investment in New Zealand by way of take-over or acquisition where the cost exceeds NZ$10 million; or
- for any investment (regardless of dollar value) where the investment results in an overseas person(s) controlling 25 per cent or more of any class of shares or voting power in any entity in a specified sensitive sector – currently broadcasting, commercial fishing and rural land.

INTERNAL INFLUENCES ON ACCOUNTING

The main influences on accounting in New Zealand have been company law, the accountancy profession, tax, and the Stock Exchange. Accounting is heavily influenced by the accountancy profession since regulatory direction is scant.

Legislative background: company law

The law relating to the formation and operation of companies in New Zealand is set out principally in the Companies Act 1955 including all subsequent amendments. The Act requires the directors of a company to present to shareholders annual accounts that give a true and fair view. Whilst the concept of 'true and fair' is not defined by the Act it is of great importance and can be used to support non-compliance with accounting rules if compliance would lead to the accounts not showing a true and fair view. Accounting standards are issued by the New Zealand Society of Accountants and they are regarded collectively as defining generally accepted accounting principles in New Zealand. This issue will be discussed later (see pp. 401–12).

All public companies must have their accounts audited and it is the responsibility of the auditor to express an opinion as to whether the accounts show a true and fair view.

Accounting records

Every company is required to keep accounting records in accordance with sect. 151 of the Companies Act 1955. As a general minimum, companies must keep a record of daily cash receipts and cash payments, assets and liabilities of the company, and, where the company's business involves dealing in goods, details of purchases, credit sales, creditors, debtors, and records of stock. Where the company's business involves the supply of services, records are required to be maintained of the services provided and all invoices relating thereto. The accounting records must:

- correctly record and explain the transactions of the company;
- enable the financial position of the company to be determined with reasonable accuracy at any time;

- enable the directors to ensure that any balance sheet, profit and loss account, or income and expenditure account of the company gives a true and fair view of the state of affairs of the company as at the end of its financial year and of the profit or loss of the company for the financial year.

In practice, compliance with the Eighth Schedule and generally accepted accounting principles will satisfy the requirement as to 'true and fair' under law (sect. 153).

Audit

The accounting records must also enable the accounts of the company to be readily and properly audited. Sect. 163 requires every company to appoint an auditor at each annual general meeting. Sect. 354 allows the voting members of a private company (except a 'non-exempt' private company) to pass a unanimous resolution that no auditor be appointed.

Annual accounts

At least once in every year the directors must lay before the company in general meeting a profit and loss account and a balance sheet, as at the date to which the profit and loss account is made up, which satisfy the 'true and fair view' requirement referred to above (sect. 152). The balance sheet must be signed on behalf of the board by two of the directors of the company (sect. 159).

Group accounts

At the annual general meeting, holding companies must present group accounts comprising a consolidated balance sheet and a consolidated profit and loss account for the holding company and its subsidiaries or, alternatively, some other form of group accounts presenting the same or equivalent information where in the opinion of the company's directors it is better to so do (sect. 155). This provision has been utilized, for example, by some large groups in presenting their accounts for a distinct sector such as their finance operations separately from their main group accounts. Group accounts are not required where the holding company is itself the wholly owned subsidiary of another company incorporated in New Zealand (sect. 154(2)(a)).

A subsidiary may be excluded from the group accounts if the company's directors are of the opinion that:

(i) it is impracticable, or would be of no real value to members of the company, in view of the insignificant amounts involved, or would involve expense or delay out of proportion to the value to members of the company; or

(ii) the result would be misleading, or harmful to the business of the company or any of its subsidiaries; or

(iii) the business of the holding company and that of the subsidiary are so different that they cannot reasonably be treated as a single undertaking. (Sect. 154(2)(b))

The approval of the Governor-General in Council is required for exclusion on the grounds that the result would be harmful, or on the grounds of (iii) above, so where infrequently a subsidiary is excluded it is generally on the grounds set out in (i) above.

Statement of Standard Accounting Practice 8 (SSAP 8) dealing with consolidated financial statements acknowledges the legal requirements set out above and states that where a subsidiary is not consolidated it should be included in the consolidated financial statements by applying the equity method (para. 4.19). The general standard under SSAP 8 is that 'subsidiaries and in-substance subsidiaries should be consolidated unless the directors consider that the same or equivalent information can be better presented by application of the equity method. Associates should be accounted for by the equity method' (para. 5.1). SSAP 8 is generally complied with.

Directors' and auditor's reports

Where a balance sheet and attached accounts are presented at an annual general meeting a directors' report is also required to be presented; this must detail the state of the company's affairs, the amount (if any) of recommended dividend and the amount (if any) proposed to be carried to reserves. Also, unless it would be harmful to the business of the company or its subsidiaries, the report should disclose any material change in the nature of the business of the company or its subsidiaries, or in the classes of business in which the company has an interest (sect. 161). The auditor's report must also be attached to the annual accounts (sect. 160).

Filing with the registrar

The accounts presented at an annual general meeting must be filed with the Registrar of Companies within thirty days after the meeting (private companies, other than 'non-exempt' private companies, are exempt).

Company law review

The Companies Bill was introduced to Parliament in September 1990 following a long process of review of existing company law. In December 1992 the Bill was reported back to Parliament following two years of review before the Justice and Law Reform Committee resulting in many minor changes. It is unlikely that the Bill will be passed into law prior to 1994. The major reforms proposed include:

- The Memorandum of Association and Articles of Association are replaced by an optional constitution. No standard form of constitution is provided by the Bill but certain provisions of the Bill are dependent on express powers being granted by a constitution.
- All existing companies will be required to re-register within a three-year period.
- No distinction is made between public and private companies.
- A company may have one shareholder and one director thus 'one-man' companies are permitted.
- An overseas company can transfer its registration to New Zealand (similar to provisions under Australian legislation with which New Zealand is attempting to harmonize).
- Every company is required to include a Statement of Cash Flows with its financial statements in addition to the presently required balance sheet and profit and loss account.
- There is no Eighth Schedule equivalent setting out matters to be disclosed. The Bill provides that financial statements of companies must give a 'true and fair view' and comply with any regulations made under the enacted legislation and the requirements of any other enactment. Specific reference is made to compliance with the accounting standards approved by the Accounting Standards Review Board to be established under the proposed Financial Reporting Act (referred to on p. 434).
- There is a requirement for the directors to ensure that the financial statements are completed within five months of the company's balance sheet date and registered within thirty days after that.
- The definitions of 'holding company' and 'subsidiary company' follow the Australian Corporations Act 1989 and are based on control of the board, control of more than half the voting rights or majority ownership.
- There is a general requirement to appoint an auditor at each AGM, but shareholders may determine by unanimous resolution in each year not to appoint an auditor. This concession would be available to all companies except 'non-exempt' companies and 'issuers' as defined by the Financial Reporting Bill (includes listed companies except companies with equity securities only and with fewer than 25 shareholders, authorized life assurance companies, and unit trusts).
- The auditor's report will be required to describe the work done by the auditor and the scope and limitations of the engagement as well as to make the statements on whether all information and explanations required have been obtained, proper accounting records have been kept, and a true and fair view given, as presently required.

- The concepts of par value and nominal value have been replaced by a requirement that shares be issued for a fair and reasonable consideration (in terms of effect on the company and on all existing shareholders). Thus a share premium account will not be needed. Shares may be of different classes offering different rights.
- There are provisions to enable a company to buy back its own shares.
- Finally, but perhaps of key importance, the bill introduces a solvency test to replace capital maintenance and distribution rules under the present laws. Dividends may be repaid and shares repurchased only so long as the solvency of the company is maintained. This is defined in terms of a liquidity test which requires a company to be able to pay its debts as they fall due, together with a balance sheet test which requires the value of the company's assets to be greater than the value of its liabilities including contingent liabilities. Previously the Bill referred to the 'realizable value' of assets and the 'present value' of liabilities but now 'value' is undefined.

The accountancy profession

Historical background

Accountancy has been practised in New Zealand for about 150 years, since the time of the signing of the Treaty of Waitangi which established New Zealand as a British Colony. The earliest professional accounting organization was founded in 1894. The New Zealand Society of Accountants (NZSA) was established by Act of Parliament in 1908. Today the accounting profession is controlled and regulated solely by the NZSA, which promulgates all accounting and auditing standards and provides guidance on other matters affecting the profession.

The NZSA is in a unique position of influence, being the sole representative body for accountants in New Zealand (both practitioners and non-practitioners). This position is attributed to restriction by statute on the performance of audit work principally to NZSA members (sect. 165(4), Companies Act, 1955). This privilege seemed to lead the other associations of accountants that had formed in New Zealand to eventually amalgamate with the NZSA. Also, only members of the NZSA may use the designation 'chartered accountant'.

Since 1 May 1993 the New Zealand Society of Accountants Amendment Act, which abolished the NZSA fidelity fund, provides that anyone who can demonstrate they are 'suitably qualified' may call themselves an 'accountant' or 'auditor'. Previously these titles were restricted to use by members of NZSA.

Influence on financial reporting regulation

The NZSA promulgations are binding on members, and their accounting standards collectively are generally accepted by the business community as providing a definitive approach to what constitutes a true and fair view. At present there is no regulatory authority that enforces compliance with accounting standards. The NZSA actively monitors published financial reports for instances of non-compliance with accounting standards or of poor reporting and corresponds with company directors and/or auditors on any matters of concern. This is usually in an educative capacity, however, as the NZSA has authority only over its own members and thus has no authority over company directors unless they happen to be members of the NZSA. Further details are given in the section headed 'Compliance with Standards' (see pp. 399–401).

Accounting in New Zealand is very much led by the accounting profession since government direction has been weak. Only a minimal list of items that must be disclosed in the statutory accounts are specified in the 1955 Companies Act, which was modelled on the United Kingdom Companies Act 1948. There is also securities legislation which sets out disclosures to be made in prospectuses.

The legislation does not prescribe a format for financial statements. For listed companies the New Zealand Stock Exchange requires certain disclosures to be made in a prescribed form in Preliminary Announcements. Again, though, there is no prescribed format for the actual financial statements of issuers but there is an express requirement for the financial statements to be drawn up in accordance with the accounting standards issued by the NZSA with any departures from the standards to be disclosed and explained in the published accounts or notes thereto.

Entry to the profession

The effect of the New Zealand Society of Accountants Act 1958 has been that the practice of the profession of accountancy in New Zealand has been under the control and regulation of the New Zealand Society of Accountants alone. Under the Act accountancy services could be offered to the public only by members of the NZSA who held a Certificate of Public Practice (sect. 14A). (The NZSA rules provide that non-practice members may receive fees for public accounting services where the fees are below specified limits and the services are performed outside usual employment or by 'retired' members (NZSA 1988b: 11)). From 1 May 1993 The New Zealand Society of Accountants Amendment Act opens up competition to non-NZSA 'accountants' and 'auditors'; however the designation 'chartered accountant' is still for the use of NZSA members only (sect. 32).

Previously NZSA Rules, together with the requirements of the Act, determined entry to the profession. It is likely that the NZSA Rules will continue to be of considerable importance to those wishing to enter the profession of accountancy. Qualification requirements for membership of the NZSA are concerned with:

- personal qualities (i.e. applicants must be of good character and reputation);
- education, as set out in a prescribed minimum Body of Knowledge;
- practical experience.

Exemption to part or all of the accountancy examination and experience requirements may be granted where an applicant holds overseas qualifications or has already been admitted to a recognized association of accountants overseas.

Accounting education

Generally the education requirements are satisfied by completing an accountancy programme at either a university or polytechnic. The importance of gaining membership to the NZSA has resulted in most accountancy programmes catering for the NZSA examination accreditation.

It appears that many accountancy students prefer to satisfy the education requirements through a university programme because they can then gain both an academic degree and a professional qualification at the same time. Of the 944 new admissions to the NZSA in 1989 70 per cent were university graduates (1972: 42 per cent). Of the total membership, 52 per cent have a university degree (NZSA 1989: 21).

There is, however, intense competition for entry to selected commerce faculties. In 1988, nation-wide, nearly 2,000 candidates were refused entry and the University of Auckland, for example, had 1,488 applicants for 685 places (NZSA 1988a).

All new members admitted after 1 July 1991 must also have sat and passed the Final Qualifying Examination (offered for the first time in November 1989). The examination is an open book examination of three hours duration. From May 1994 the structure will consist of two three-hour papers held over two consecutive days. The examination aims to test a prospective member's knowledge of the following areas:

- the structure of the accountancy profession;
- NZSA and IFAC technical pronouncements;
- ethics and jurisprudence;
- current issues facing the accounting profession.

Practical experience requirements

Generally, prospective members must have completed at least three years' acceptable practical accounting experience – either in the service of a chartered accountant in public practice, or in a public sector or private sector organization.

The experience may be gained concurrently with study or after academic qualification, except that at least twelve months' advanced professional experience involving the exercise of professional judgement at a senior level should be obtained after completion of the examination requirements and during twelve months' continuous employment with the same employer (NZSA 1990a: 28).

Certificate of Public Practice

Conditions for the issue of a Certificate of Public Practice include:

- New Zealand residency;
- intention to offer accountancy services to the public;
- suitable premises from which to operate the practice;
- membership of the NZSA for not less than two years;
- not less than two and a half years' acceptable experience in the office of a chartered accountant in public practice within the preceding ten years;
- attendance at a Course for New Practitioners within the preceding ten years.

Certain of the requirements may be reduced or dispensed with on application, where the NZSA is satisfied there is good reason to do so (NZSA 1990a: 13–14).

NZSA membership statistics at June 1990

Membership of the NZSA reached 17,401 in June 1990 – up 5.5 per cent from 16,485 in 1989, which was up 4.5 per cent from 15,777 in 1988. Nearly 17 per cent (2,948) of the membership resided outside New Zealand – mostly in Australia (778), Great Britain (330) and Malaysia (320). Within New Zealand 32 per cent (5,626) of the total were Auckland members and 18 per cent (3,083) are Wellington members.

Public Practice Certificates were held by 2,531 members – down 20 from 1989. There were 1,192 chartered accountancy practices – an increase of 7 from 1989. Sole practitioners comprised 69 per cent of the total, with 28 per cent in the 2–5 partner size practice. Only 4 firms had 50 or more partners – down from the 6 firms in 1989 (NZSA 1990b: 20). Of the total membership 27 per cent (4,737) worked in public practice, 30 per cent (5,232) worked in the private sector, 7 per cent (1,299) worked in the public sector, 17 per cent (2,948) were overseas (see above), and 16 per cent (2,817) were either retired or not working (NZSA 1990b: 27).

An analysis of trends in the age and gender of membership reveals that over time the proportion of younger members is increasing due to the increasing net growth in membership each year, largely through new admissions by examinations. In 1990 51 per cent of members were in the 20–40 age group, 31 per cent were in the 41–60 age group, and 17 per cent were 61 or older. Also the proportion of women members is increasing steadily each year, reaching 2,404 women members in 1990 – 13.8 per cent of total membership. This represents an increase of 396 per cent over 10 years from the 485 women members in 1980, compared with a 46 per cent net growth in total membership over the same period (NZSA 1990b: 25).

Accounting standards

As part of its statutory responsibility to control and regulate accountancy in New Zealand the NZSA develops, promulgates and reviews accounting standards. This work is undertaken by the Financial Reporting Standards Board (FRSB) (previously known as the Accounting Research and Standards Board (ARSB)) of the NZSA which has in turn established several committees to deal with specific areas such as:

- financial accounting;
- primary sector accounting;
- research.

Types of pronouncements

The FRSB is responsible for the development of various types of pronouncements of differing authority and scope. At the highest level are Financial Reporting Standards (FRSs) (as the most recent standards are referred to) as well as Statements of Standard Accounting Practice (SSAPs). Unless limited scope is indicated SSAPs and FRSs are applicable to all financial statements prepared for other than exclusively internal use. Thus SSAPs and FRSs generally apply to any financial statements issued by entities such as those listed below, for external use (i.e. for use by shareholders or members, the Inland Revenue Department, lenders, creditors and the public):

- public companies;
- private companies;
- sole traders;
- partnerships;
- non-trading concerns;
- estates and trusts;
- public and other business entities.

Examples of SSAPs that have a more limited scope are SSAP 9 which deals with information to be disclosed in company balance sheets and profit and loss accounts, and SSAP 20 dealing with accounting for shares under a dividend election plan; both SSAPs apply to companies only.

The Council of the NZSA has approved a new Explanatory Foreword which will be issued and become operative after the Financial Reporting Bill is enacted. Under the new Foreword accounting standards will be applicable to all 'general purpose financial reports'. The *Explanatory Foreword to General Purpose Financial Reporting* (June 1993) defines general purpose financial reports as 'financial reports which are intended to provide information to meet the needs of external users who are unable to require, or contract for, the preparation of special reports to meet their specific information needs.' The Foreword will apply to both the public and private sectors.

'Interpretations' of SSAPs are issued whenever additional guidance on the interpretation of a particular SSAP is thought necessary. As at August 1993 seventeen Interpretations had been issued of which five were current.

Public Sector Accounting Statements were introduced in July 1987 to prescribe the minimum acceptable level of disclosures required in external financial reports of public sector entities. FRSs and SSAPs continue to apply to public sector entities also.

Technical Practice Aids (TPAs) are issued by the FRSB (ARSB) for the general information and guidance of members. They represent the conclusions of a majority of FRSB members voting but do not have the NZSA Council authority. As at August 1993 seven TPAs had been issued of which five were current.

Research Bulletins on Financial Accounting Practice are published by the FRSB (ARSB) to provide assistance to members on contemporary accounting issues not yet addressed by a NZSA pronouncement. Such Bulletins do not represent official NZSA recommendations; however, they are intended to lead to improvements in standards of practice. As at August 1993 seven Research Bulletins had been issued, three of which were current.

Further details of the particular pronouncements issued and current as referred to above are given in Newby (1989), and also in *The Accountant's Manual* (see Appendix B).

The Professional Practices Board is responsible for the entire Professional Standards and Guidelines series including auditing standards.

Standards-setting process

The standards-setting process at present is wholly controlled by the NZSA, but is consultative in that comments on proposed standards are called for. The process typically involves the following steps:

- identification of projects by the FRSB;
- a draft is then developed for consideration by the Board;

- the draft is reviewed and issued by the ARSB as an Exposure Draft (ED);
- comments on the ED are invited from members of the NZSA and other interested parties;
- comments are considered by the FRSB in preparing the final text of the promulgation.

If the promulgation is to be a FRS or other type of standard it must next be submitted to the Council of the NZSA for approval and issue. The FRSB itself has authority to issue other classes of promulgation such as TPAs and Research Bulletins (NZSA 1988b: 13).

Membership of the committees involved in standards-setting is made up of representatives from practice, industry and academia. In terms of representation for the various constituency groups affected by accounting regulation the reality is that only preparers of financial statements and auditors make a significant input to accounting regulation in New Zealand both through committee memberships and through responding in the standards-setting process. Interpreters and users of financial statements have the opportunity to make representations via the general call for comments but seldom do. Representation has implications for general acceptance of standards and thus compliance (see 'Compliance with Standards' below).

Evolution of standards

The NZSA has instituted a review procedure whereby all SSAPs and FRSs are subject to five-yearly reviews. The Explanatory Foreword to SSAPs and FRSs in New Zealand explains:

> Methods of financial accounting evolve and alter in response to changing business and economic needs. From time to time new accounting standards will be drawn at progressive levels, and established standards will be reviewed with the object of improvement in the light of new needs and developments.
>
> (Para. 4.1)

As at August 1993, eighteen SSAPs have been revised or withdrawn.

Compliance with standards

The NZSA requires members who assume responsibilities in respect of financial statements (for example, by their association with such financial statements in the capacity of director, or as accountant responsible for the preparation of the financial statements, or as auditor) to apply the standards promulgated by the NZSA, and to ensure full disclosure is made in the financial statements of any material departures from SSAPs (sect. 2

of the *Explanatory Foreword to Statements of Standard Accounting Practice*). Under the new Explanatory Foreword a specific responsibility will be placed on members of the NZSA to observe 'generally accepted accounting practice'. This will require that all applicable FRSs have been complied with and where no relevant standard exists, that the practice adopted:

- results in a fair presentation; and
- is appropriate to the circumstances of the entity; and
- has authoritative support within the accounting profession in New Zealand (that support will be derived primarily from application of the Statement of Concepts (June 1993)).

The accounting standards are enforceable only against members, however, and compliance with the NZSA standards, apart from being a stock exchange listing requirement, is not enforceable against companies. Nevertheless the standards are widely accepted as authoritative. Where standards have not been generally accepted, as evidenced by poor compliance, the NZSA has responded by revising the standard or even withdrawing it (e.g. SSAP 17). Another example is CCA 1 which was originally issued in March 1982 as the first of a separate series of standards on current cost accounting. It required listed companies to produce supplementary financial statements showing the effects of current costs. Owing to a lack of compliance – which worsened over three years from only 11 per cent compliance in 1983 to 3 per cent in 1986 (Ryan 1987: 282) – the standard was withdrawn and reissued as a Recommendation in March 1986, and early in 1992 it was withdrawn altogether.

Two ways of evaluating compliance are to look at audit qualifications and to examine published financial statements directly to assess their degree of compliance with FRSs and SSAPs. A survey of the financial reporting practices of the top 100 listed New Zealand companies by Ryan (1989) summarizes audit opinions over a three-year period and reports an increase in the number of companies given a qualified opinion from four in 1987 to eleven in 1989. Of the six 'except for' accounting standard qualifications given in 1989, two were in respect of property revaluations and the treatment of unrealized gains under SSAP 17; two were for non-disclosure of a Statement of Cash Flows under SSAP 10; one was for non-disclosure of turnover under SSAP 9; and one was for the treatment of goodwill under SSAP 8 (Ryan 1989: 272).

A survey of publicly available company financial reports over 1988 and 1989 reveals that the highest incidence of apparent non-compliance is in the areas listed below. The rate of incidence of any one of the practices set out is generally fewer than ten companies.

- *SSAP 7*: the classification of items as extraordinary vs abnormal (particularly involving losses), and an inadequate description of each extraordinary item;

- *SSAP 8*: goodwill not amortized, the write-off of goodwill treated as extraordinary, inadequate disclosure of details of investees, and inadequate disclosure of details required on the acquisition or disposal of consolidated interests;
- *SSAP 9*: inadequate disclosure of interest rates and repayment terms of long-term liabilities, and inadequate disclosures regarding asset valuations;
- *SSAP 10*: insufficient detail of gross flows of major sources and uses of cash;
- *SSAP 21*: translation of transactions at a rate other than the exchange rate in effect at the transaction date, and non-disclosure of the net exchange difference included in profit and loss for the period.

In line with proposals discussed in the section 'Reforms of the Domestic Regulatory Framework' (see pp. 418–22) the NZSA has jointly recommended legislative backing for accounting standards, the formation of an independent Accounting Standards Review Board, and the sharing of standards-setting costs amongst the organizations who utilize and benefit from accounting standards.

Summary of GAAP in New Zealand

The overriding principle as to content and form of accounts is the requirement to give a 'true and fair view'. This is set out in the Companies Act 1955 which states that:

> Every balance sheet of a company shall give a true and fair view of the state of affairs of the company as at the end of its financial year, and every profit and loss account of a company shall give a true and fair view of the profit or loss of the company for the financial year.
>
> (Sect. 153(1))

Section 153 goes on to state that 'a company's balance sheet and profit and loss account shall comply with the requirements of the Eighth Schedule to this Act, so far as applicable thereto'. The Eighth Schedule lists certain disclosure requirements, the normal method of stating assets, etc., but does not really address methodological issues. Also there is no prescribed format for financial statements, either in companies legislation or FRSs/SSAPs. Under the Act it is the directors of a company who have responsibility for the preparation of financial statements which show the information required and present a true and fair view. The Act does not, however, define what a 'true and fair view' means.

Paragraph 1.1 of the current Explanatory Foreword to SSAPs states that accounting standards 'describe methods of accounting approved by the Council of the NZSA for application to all financial statements'. As the NZSA has statutory responsibility to control and regulate accountancy in

New Zealand, FRSs/SSAPs by implication describe generally accepted accounting principles (GAAP) in New Zealand. Paragraph 1.2 goes further in stating, 'accounting standards ... introduce a definitive approach to the concept of what is a true and fair view', and that, 'a true and fair view implies:

- disclosure;
- appropriate classification and grouping of all material items; and
- consistent application of acceptable accounting principles [SSAPs]'.

These notions are reiterated in the new Explanatory Foreword. Thus, FRSs and SSAPs generally define 'true and fair'. This creates something of a dilemma for company directors who are not members of the NZSA and therefore are not bound by SSAPs (unless the company is listed, in which case compliance with accounting standards is a Stock Exchange requirement). Where companies are required to be audited, however, the auditors must be members of the NZSA and are bound to have regard to SSAPs when expressing an opinion on the truth and fairness of the financial statements, which in turn encourages directors to comply in order to receive an unqualified audit report.

A summary of FRSs/SSAPs, and hence GAAP, is set out in the next section. Within this context, SSAP 1, 'Determination and Disclosure of Accounting Policies', explains that the general accounting policies which underlie the preparation of financial statements and which are in common use relate to:

- a historical cost or modified historical cost measurement base;
- the going-concern assumption; and
- the matching of expenses and revenues under accrual accounting.

(SSAP 1, para. 4.2)

Current New Zealand standards

Set out below is a listing of the thirty-one accounting standards on issue in New Zealand as at August 1993 with a brief description of the critical features where there are differences between NZ and US GAAP.

SSAP 1 Determination and Disclosure of Accounting Policies

Disclosure is required of general and particular accounting policies together with any changes of accounting policies during the period. The nature of a change, the reason for the change and its monetary effect should be disclosed. Where no changes in accounting policy during the period have occurred that should also be disclosed.

In the US, except for changes in certain specified accounting principles that are made by retroactive restatement, the cumulative effect of a change in an accounting principle is included in net income of the period and is presented in the income statement net of related tax effects after extraordinary items.

SSAP 2 Accounting for Associated Companies

Withdrawn and replaced by SSAP 8 (see below).

SSAP 3 Accounting for Depreciation

Depreciable assets are required to be depreciated on a 'systematic basis' over their 'useful life' by a method which results in a fair periodic allocation that corresponds 'to the expected pattern of exhaustion of the asset's service potential'. Where an asset is revalued the charge for depreciation should be based on the revalued amount.

Revaluations are prohibited in the US and therefore depreciation relates only to the original cost of fixed assets.

SSAP 4 Accounting for Inventories

'Inventories should be valued at the lower of cost and net realisable value' with cost normally determined using FIFO, weighted average cost, or specific identification. LIFO is not an acceptable method of valuation in New Zealand but in other respects the requirements in New Zealand are consistent with US GAAP.

SSAP 5 Accounting for Events Subsequent to Balance Date

In New Zealand the financial effects of both favourable and unfavourable 'adjustable events' occurring after balance date may be brought to account, resulting in either adjustment of the financial statements or note disclosure of the effect. US GAAP does not permit favourable events to be brought to account because to do so would recognize income prior to realization.

SSAP 6 Materiality in Financial Statements

Separate disclosure (apart from statutory compliance) is determined according to the nature and amount of an item. The New Zealand requirements are consistent with US GAAP.

FRS 7 (Revised) Extraordinary Items and Fundamental Errors

Extraordinary items are defined as being infrequent, outside the ordinary operations of the entity and outside the control or influence of managers or owners. They are to be disclosed separately in the statement of financial performance following the operating surplus. The amount of attributable tax and the individual amounts of each extraordinary item should be disclosed.

A fundamental error is one which is so significant that its inclusion would destroy the fair presentation of the financial report taken as a whole. Errors affecting prior periods are adjusted against the opening equity. Full disclosure of the amount and nature of any fundamental error and the reasons for it must be made. Figures for prior periods should be restated where practicable – this does not appear to be as onerous as in the US where corresponding figures must be restated.

FRS 7 is expected to bring about a significant change in reporting practices in New Zealand where it has been common to find reporting of items classified as 'extraordinary'.

The standard also makes it clear that the effect of a change in accounting policy should be reflected in the result for the current year. Previously any cumulative adjustment applicable to prior periods was accounted for by adjusting opening equity.

New Zealand practice will now be consistent with US GAAP in that the only retroactive restatement allowed for accounting policy changes will be where an accounting standard or statutory requirement specifically requires a direct adjustment against equity.

SSAP 8 Accounting for Business Combinations

The New Zealand Companies Act 1955 and SSAP 8 permit group accounts to be in a form other than consolidated financial statements where the directors consider better presentation is achieved. Thus, it is possible to exclude certain subsidiaries, for example, on the grounds that they are involved in activities dissimilar to those of the main group. Non-consolidated subsidiaries are generally accounted for under the equity method. The equity method of accounting is applied in a manner consistent with US GAAP.

SFAS 94 has eliminated the above treatment in the US. It requires consolidation of all majority owned subsidiaries (except where there is lack of control) for all fiscal years ending after 15 December 1988 with restatement of prior periods.

Consolidation accounting under SSAP 8 is based on the concepts of control and significant influence as distinct to legal ownership. 'Control' is defined as 'the power to govern the financial and operating policies of another entity for the purpose of obtaining the benefits and/or assuming the risks normally associated with ownership', and determines whether an entity is an 'in-substance subsidiary' of another. 'Significant influence' is defined as 'the capacity of an investor to influence the financial and operating policies of an investee', and determines whether an entity is an 'associate' of another. Neither of the above terms is defined in law, but both are generally accepted in practice. SSAP 8 requires that 'subsidiaries and in-substance subsidiaries *should* be consolidated unless the directors (or governing members) consider that the same or equivalent information can be better presented by application of the equity method. Associates *should* be accounted for by the equity method'.

The usual condition for consolidation in the US is ownership of a majority voting interest either directly or indirectly except where there is lack of control.

In New Zealand the purchase method is normally used to account for mergers and acquisitions.

The goodwill/discount on acquisition is determined on a similar basis to US GAAP. Goodwill is required to be capitalized and amortized on a systematic basis over the period of benefit (unlikely to exceed 10 years and should in no case exceed 20 years). Where there is a permanent impairment in value goodwill should be written off to the profit and loss account. A discount on acquisition is accounted for by reducing proportionately the fair values of the non-monetary assets until the discount is eliminated and where non-monetary assets acquired are reduced to zero any remaining discount balance is classified as a gain and taken to the profit and loss account. In contrast, goodwill may be written off over 40 years in the US. Any remaining discount on acquisition after reducing non-monetary assets acquired to zero must be classified as a deferred credit and amortized over a period of benefit (not to exceed 40 years).

SSAP 9 Information to be Disclosed in Company Balance Sheets and Profit and Loss Accounts

SSAP 9 sets out minimum disclosures for the balance sheet, profit and loss account and notes to the financial statements. There is no prescribed format for financial statements in either SSAP 9 or in legislation.

Under the shareholders' funds section separate disclosure is required of reserves arising from the revaluation of assets; these are not permitted in the US. In the profit and loss account specific disclosure is required of audit fees and expenses, and directors' fees.

Specific disclosure is required in the notes of 'information from which it is possible to identify and evaluate exposure to exceptional risks of operating or borrowing in other countries, including the risk of foreign currency rate fluctuations' (para. 4.4(e)). There is a similar provision in SSAP 8.

Disclosures required under the other SSAPs or under US GAAP are broadly referred to within those sections and hence are not dealt with here.

FRS 10 (Revised) Statement of Cash Flows

Changes to the previous SSAP 10 bring New Zealand practice much closer to the US FAS 95 methodology and presentation.

The direct method is still the required method for presenting cash flows from operating activities (whereas in the US the indirect method is also allowed). A new requirement is to include in the notes a reconciliation of the reported operating surplus with the cash generated from operating activities (i.e. the indirect method presentation).

An important change is the treatment of interest and dividends. Interest and dividends received should now be classified as operating activities (previously they were classified as investing activities). Interest paid should also now be classified as an operating activity, except where the interest paid has been capitalized in the construction of an asset – in that case the cash flow should be separately disclosed as an investing activity. Dividends paid should continue to be classified as a financing activity except that dividends paid on capital classified as debt should be included in operating activities.

Another new requirement is for disclosure in the notes of non-cash investing and financing activities, consistent with US requirements.

SSAP 11 Expenditures Carried Forward to Future Accounting Periods

'Expenditures which are expected with reasonable certainty to produce future identifiable benefits sufficient to cover the amount deferred may be allocated to future accounting periods. Other expenditures should be charged to the profit and loss account in the period in which they are incurred.' The New Zealand approach is consistent with US GAAP.

SSAP 12 (Revised) Accounting for Income Tax

The revised standard now requires use of the liability method (previously the deferral method was allowed). Although the comprehensive basis is recommended, a partial approach may be used where timing differences are not expected to crystallize for 'some considerable period ahead'. Disclosure of a schedule of expected reversals of timing differences is not required.

A debit balance in the deferred tax account should be retained and carried forward only to the extent that there is 'virtual certainty' of recovery in future periods (this has tightened up from the previous requirement for 'reasonable certainty').

Income tax benefits arising from income tax losses should be recognized only to the extent of accumulated net credits from timing differences in the deferred tax account unless there is virtual certainty that the tax benefits will be realised.

Requirements accord closely with IAS 12.

SSAP 13 (Revised) Accounting for Research and Development Activities (R&D)

R&D costs are normally expensed as incurred although development costs may be deferred where such costs can be separately identified and can reasonably be expected to be recovered from related future revenues. Generally no deferral of R&D costs is allowed in the US other than certain qualifying development costs of computer software to be sold, leased, or otherwise marketed.

The revised SSAP 13 requires disclosure of the amount of development cost capitalized during the period, and also the balance of unamortized deferred development costs. Another new requirement is for disclosure of total R&D costs expensed in the period including the amount of deferred development costs amortised.

SSAP 14 Accounting for Profit on Construction Contracts

In New Zealand the percentage of completion method is preferred where reliable estimates can be made, otherwise the completed contract method is required. This is consistent with US GAAP.

SSAP 15 Accounting for Contingencies

Requirements in New Zealand are consistent with US GAAP.

SSAP 16 Accounting for Government Grants

Government grants are recognized as income in the profit and loss account once the enterprise has complied with the primary conditions attaching to the grants. Generally, grants received in respect of the purchase of long-term assets are not to be treated as reductions in the purchase price of those assets. Where grants are in recognition of anticipated losses or increased costs they are recognized in the profit and loss account over the period that the anticipated losses or increased costs are to be incurred. This is consistent with generally accepted recognition and matching concepts.

SSAP 17 Accounting for Investment Properties and Properties Intended for Sale

SSAP 17 requires investment properties, other than development properties, to be recorded in the balance sheet at their net current value and not subject to periodic charges for depreciation. Net changes in value may be disclosed either in the profit and loss account following profit after extraordinary items and clearly identified as unrealized, or transferred directly to an investment property revaluation reserve except where the reserve is insufficient to cover a deficit. In that case the deficit should be charged to the profit and loss account as part of operating results. This is inconsistent with US GAAP, where investment properties are treated like any other property and stated at their cost less accumulated depreciation.

SSAP 18 Accounting for Leases and Hire Purchase Contracts

Finance leases are required to be capitalized with certain disclosures required to be made. Requirements in New Zealand are consistent with US GAAP although additional specific guidance is given in the US for leases involving real estate.

SSAP 19 Accounting for Goods and Services Tax

SSAP 19 deals with a tax specific to New Zealand. The preferred method is to state both income and expenditure items net of goods and services tax except where inputs are subject to irrecoverable tax, in which case the tax should be included in the measurement of costs and assets. This accounting treatment does not require adjustment for US reporting purposes.

SSAP 20 Accounting for Shares Issued Under a Dividend Election Plan

A dividend election plan offers shareholders the choice of receiving dividends in cash and/or in shares. Where the company can estimate with reasonable certainty the amount of the dividend that the shareholders will elect to receive in cash then it should record a dividend liability for that amount and may recognize a share election reserve for the balance. This does not conform with US GAAP where normal practice would be to recognize a dividend liability for the full amount.

SSAP 21 Accounting for the Effects of Changes in Foreign Currency Exchange Rates

Foreign currency transactions should be translated at the exchange rate on the date of the transaction except that short-term transactions covered by forward exchange contracts may be measured at the forward rates specified. At each balance date, monetary items should be translated at the closing rate and non-monetary items should be recorded at the exchange rate in effect at the transaction date except where a hedge is involved. All exchange differences relating to monetary items are required to be recognized in the profit and loss account as exchange gains or losses. This is generally consistent with practice in the US.

Foreign operations are classified as either integrated or independent, which determines translation methodology. When translating the income statements of consolidated foreign subsidiaries the closing rate is used in

New Zealand whereas the US requires the actual (in practice, average) rate. Furthermore, the US allows operations to be reported in 'functional currencies' which may differ from local currency. There is no specific commentary on this treatment in SSAP 21. Greater guidance is given under US rules regarding hedging. Accounting methodology is broadly consistent except that the use of revenue streams as hedges is perhaps more readily applied in New Zealand.

SSAP 22 Related Party Disclosure

Disclosure is required of an entity's relationship with related parties and of all material transactions between an entity and its related parties. The value of related party transactions may be expressed either in dollar terms or as a percentage of the value of all transactions of each type for the period. Under US GAAP, the dollar amounts of related party transactions must be disclosed.

SSAP 23 Financial Reporting for Segments

Disclosure is required for each industry and geographical segment of revenue, results, assets, the basis of inter-segment pricing, and abnormal items. In addition, a description of the products and services from which each industry segment derives its revenue and the location of geographical segments should be disclosed. Compliance with SSAP 23 will ensure compliance with IAS 14.

In the US, public companies are required to make additional disclosures in respect of each reportable business segment; for example of:

- depreciation, depletion and amortization expense;
- capital expenditures undertaken;
- equity share of results and net assets of unconsolidated subsidiaries and other associate companies.

SSAP 24 Interim Financial Reporting

SSAP 24 sets out minimum disclosure requirements where interim financial statements are produced. US GAAP requires greater disclosure – for example, information on seasonal revenue, costs, or expenses. Also, US enterprises are required to make at the end of each interim period a best estimate of the effective tax rate expected to be applicable for the full fiscal year. Where a company is listed in the US, there are further detailed reporting requirements specified under the Stock Exchange regulations.

SSAP 25 Accounting for Interests in Joint Ventures and Partnerships

An interest in a joint venture should be accounted for by use of the proportionate method. In the case of an interest in a partnership, a controlling interest should be consolidated as per SSAP 8, a minority interest where there is significant influence should be accounted for by the equity method, and other minority interests should be accounted for at cost or valuation. In the US there is no equivalent standard; however, investments in partnerships and unincorporated joint ventures are commonly accounted for by use of the equity method.

SSAP 26 Accounting for Defeasance of Debt

A debt may be treated as extinguished by defeasance only when certain specified conditions are satisfied. Gains or losses on defeasance of debt should be recognized in income for the same period. Disclosures are required of 'the aggregate carrying amount of assets given up' for the defeasance, 'the aggregate carrying amount of debt extinguished', and the amount of 'net gain or loss on defeasance recognised', together with details of any amounts defeased outstanding, their maturity dates, and of any outstanding guarantees, indemnities, borrowing covenants, etc. given by the debtor.

Requirements in New Zealand are consistent with US GAAP except that in the US a material net gain or loss on extinguishments of debt is required to be treated as an extraordinary item.

SSAP 27 Right of Set-off

Monetary assets and liabilities may be set-off but only if a legally enforceable right of set-off exists, and set-off is acknowledged and intended. This is consistent with US GAAP. Disclosures are required of any risk factors attaching to the assets and liabilities set-off, and of any rights of set-off which have not been exercised, in the financial statements.

SSAP 28 Accounting for Fixed Assets

SSAP 28 deals with accounting for and reporting of fixed assets under the historical cost and modified historical cost systems. The initial cost of a fixed asset is the value of the consideration given to acquire or create the asset (and may include the capitalization of financing costs, as specified).

Revaluation of fixed assets is considered to provide more timely and relevant information for financial statement users and is widely practised in New Zealand. SSAP 28 provides that all assets within a class should be revalued at the same time, and on a continuing systematic basis. Assets should be stated at their 'net current value', and their 'net carrying amount' should not exceed their 'recoverable amount'. At the time of revaluation the related accumulated depreciation should be credited to the asset account, thus depreciation continues to be charged even when assets are revalued annually. The periodic amount of revaluation is credited or debited directly to an asset revaluation reserve for the class of assets.

On sale, the revaluation amount for that asset is transferred directly to retained earnings and the gain or loss on sale is measured as the difference between the net sale proceeds and the net carrying amount. Thus contrary to prior practice the amount of the revaluation gain, even when verified on realization, is not recognized as a gain in the Profit and Loss Account.

Revaluations are contrary to US GAAP, however SSAP 28 accords with IAS 16, Accounting for Property, Plant and Equipment.

FRS 29 Prospective Financial Information

This standard codifies the presentation and preparation of general purpose prospective financial information, with application also to special purpose reports. It excludes generalized comments such as found in management's discussion in annual reports and certain other instances. It sets out guidelines regarding the use of assumptions in forecasts and projections, and disclosure thereof. With regard to presentation, the information should be presented in the same format as prior financial reports, and cover the same periods used historically. Accounting policies should be those to be used in the future with any changes from current policies noted.

FRS 30 Reporting Share Ownership Arrangements Including Employee Share Ownership Plans

This standard requires disclosure of share ownership arrangements and employee share ownership plans (ESOPs) with a view to exposing their extent and materiality. It does not apply to the reports prepared by an ESOP, management buy-outs, registered superannuation schemes, or exempt entities under differential reporting.

Detailed disclosures required to be made concern: share ownership including details of put/call options, control of the ESOP, financial commitments including the amount, terms and repayment dates of advances, and the financial position and results for the period of the ESOP when it is entitled to exercise 5 per cent or more of the reporting entity's voting rights.

FRS 31 Disclosure of Information about Financial Instruments

This standard also focuses on disclosure (since the reporting issues are so complex). It concerns both assets and liabilities on and off balance sheet in relation to financial instruments and, again, is intended to expose the extent and materiality of financial instruments in use. It reflects a concern with the increased prevalence of innovative financial 'engineering' since the deregulation of the economy in New Zealand.

The standard does not apply to entities exempt for differential reporting, nor to financial instruments specifically addressed in other standards such as investments defined in SSAP 8, leases, partnerships and joint ventures and defeased debt.

The standard discusses the types of risks to which an entity is exposed such as price risk (made up of currency risk, interest rate risk and market risk), credit risk and liquidity risk. The disclosures required detailing these risks are designed to inform users of financial reports of the entity's policies to limit and control risk, and to assist in evaluating the entity's exposure.

Standards 29, 30 and 31 have no International Standard comparison.

Tax law

Tax law in New Zealand is set out principally in the Income Tax Act 1976 and Amendments and Regulations under the Act. Other important Acts are the Land Tax Act 1976 and Goods and Services Tax Act 1985. The administration and collection of taxes is undertaken by the Inland Revenue in accordance with the Inland Revenue Department Act 1974. Rates of tax for each fiscal year are established by separate legislation.

Income tax is an important source of government revenue in New Zealand, contributing more than 80 per cent of revenue collected in 1988/89. The net income tax collected during 1988/89 came from individuals (86 per cent), companies (13 per cent) and non-resident withholding taxes (1 per cent). Indirect taxes, principally goods and services tax (GST), are another significant source of revenue contributing some 17 per cent of total tax revenues, although gift and death duties and land taxes are of little importance.

Since 1 April 1988 company taxation has been based on a full imputation system with all registered companies being required to maintain an imputation credit account – that is, an account for memorandum purposes only. All New Zealand income tax paid by 'residents' is recorded as a credit in the imputation credit account and all credits outstanding at 31 March are available for allocation to shareholders. Other credits include those attached to dividends from other New Zealand companies and withholding payments made by the company. Debits consist of those allocated to dividend distributions and refunds of income tax. In addition, debits also arise when a company ceases to be resident in New Zealand or where a 75 per cent shareholder continuity test in relation to the availability of profit distributions is not fulfilled.

The credits must be allocated across all dividends to prevent directing credits to those able to use them. The maximum ratio of imputation credit is determined by the corporate tax rate which for several years has been 33 per cent, giving a ratio of 33:67. If the imputation credit account is in debit at the end of the fiscal year a penalty tax of 10 per cent applies as a deterrent to companies attaching credits in excess of the tax paid. In addition, the account must be brought to balance or to credit.

There is no capital gains tax or wealth tax in New Zealand, although in certain circumstances profits from speculative ventures and transactions in land or investments may be liable to income tax. A consultative document for the taxation of capital gains and indexation of the tax base for inflation released in December 1989 announced proposals for the reform of tax law relating to capital gains. However, these proposals have been deferred indefinitely as part of the government economic statement made in March 1990.

Assessment based on residence

Income tax is assessable on all world-wide income derived while a 'person' (including a company) is a resident of New Zealand. A tax credit, not exceeding the relevant New Zealand tax on the foreign source income, is allowed for foreign tax payable where such tax is similar in nature to New Zealand income tax.

A non-resident is assessable for income tax only on income with a source in New Zealand, which would include income derived from:

- any business wholly or partly carried on in New Zealand;
- contracts made or performed in New Zealand;
- service as an employee or agent in New Zealand;
- the ownership of land in New Zealand;
- investments in New Zealand companies or institutions;
- money lent in New Zealand; and
- royalties deductible by the payer against New Zealand income.

A company is deemed to be a New Zealand resident if:

- it is incorporated in New Zealand; or
- it has its head office in New Zealand; or
- it has its centre of management in New Zealand; or
- the directors, acting in their capacity as directors, exercise control in New Zealand (even if there is some decision-making outside New Zealand).

Income tax is assessed on an annual basis. The income year is normally to 31 March; however, adoption of another balance date may be approved where the business cycle makes it appropriate.

Tax rates

The rate of tax on the assessable income of both public and private companies in 1993 remains at 33 per cent, increased to 38 per cent for non-resident companies. There is not a separate 'corporation tax' as in the United Kingdom.

A flat-rate withholding tax is imposed on certain classes of income derived by non-residents. These include interest, dividends and royalties, also contract payments for construction and installation projects, fees for consulting or technical services, personnel or equipment hire charges, fees for the provision of entertainment. Only in the case of dividends and some classes of interest is this a final tax. A tax credit is available in respect of a non-resident withholding tax previously assessed.

Special tax provisions apply for the grouping of companies in order for tax losses to be transferred between companies.

Differences between book and tax amounts

The influence of taxation on financial reporting is not great and as a result there are a number of differences between book and tax amounts. For example, depreciation provided for in the financial accounts is normally different to that allowed for tax purposes. Some expenses that are accrued in the financial statements are not allowable against tax until actually incurred, and on occasions it is possible for prepaid expenses to be allowed against tax in a period before they are expensed. Other areas where there may be timing differences include interest recognition, payments on construction contracts, profits and losses on foreign currency conversions, and inventory valuations.

SSAP 12 requires use of the liability method for timing differences and stipulates that deferred tax assets should not be carried in the balance sheet unless they will accrue with virtual certainty. Deferred taxes need not be provided for if a liability is not expected to crystallize in the future.

Tax changes

Major tax changes have occurred in many significant areas of taxation legislation in recent years. During the 1988 calendar year five Income Tax Amendment Acts were passed by Parliament and in 1989 a further four major Income Tax Amendment Acts were passed as well as two amendments to the Land Tax Act. Much of this legislation implemented planned taxation reforms dating back from 1987, while some of the changes were necessary to fine-tune the new tax regimes. Up until 1985 the pattern had been that only one or two Amendment Acts were enacted each year. However, there have been rapid and major reforms since then. So much so that in response to protests by taxpayers and tax return preparers the government is now pursuing taxation simplification. A consultative approach is now taken by government in introducing proposed amendments. In response to the call for submissions on simplification the NZSA commented on sixty-seven separate issues of concern in its 128-page submission to the government.

A matter of widespread concern is that draft legislation cannot be relied upon until it is in its final form, and even then there have been frequent 'fine-tuning' amendments. In addition, the date of effect can vary – sometimes being when government first announces a change, sometimes from the commencement of a current income year and sometimes before the Amendment Act receives Royal assent. An environment has been created wherein it is difficult for tax advisers to provide clear advice to clients because of the volume of tax changes, and uncertainties about future amendments and implementation dates.

As this topic is still subject to significant reforms further details of the current regimes are not given here.

Securities laws and the Stock Exchange

The offering of securities to the public is controlled by the Securities Act 1978 and the Securities Regulations 1983. Generally a security may only be offered to the public if accompanied by a registered prospectus or if offered in an authorized advertisement. The Act and Regulations prescribe the form and content of the prospectus for three categories of securities: equity, debt, and participatory securities. The prospectus must include audited financial accounts made up to a date no earlier than nine months before the date of allotment of the security on offer, although additional unaudited interim financial statements may be included to meet the timeliness criteria. Other obligations placed on issuers include keeping registers of securities, keeping proper accounting records and issuing certificates evidencing securities.

A five-member Securities Commission is charged with the responsibility of administering the Act. At present the Commission performs a law and practice review function covering securities law, aspects of company law and other matters, but it only has power to comment thereon. Once proposed reforms (described under *Ministerial Group on Securities Law Reform* on pp. 421–2) are enacted the Commission will have a much more powerful market supervision role.

The Stock Exchange

The New Zealand Stock Exchange is the national corporate body representing broker members. It was established by the Sharebrokers Amendment Act 1981 as the successor to the Stock Exchange Association of New Zealand and has been a full member of the International Federation of Stock Exchanges (FIBV) since 1985 (NZSE 1990: 1). The Exchange is funded from fees paid by its members and by listed companies. A board of directors, made up of brokers and independent business people, has assumed responsibility from the traditional Council and Executive for direction and control of the Exchange since 1 April 1989.

The purpose of the Exchange is to provide and operate an efficient market for the raising of capital for listed companies and the trading of securities, including shares and fixed interest securities such as bonds and government stock. On 1 August 1989 new listing rules were introduced together with policies for better surveillance of listed companies' and broker members' operations.

Electronic trading

From 21 June 1991 automatic screen trading through PCs connected to a central computer in Wellington has replaced the open outcry system, making the present trading floors at Auckland, Wellington and Christchurch redundant. Brokers are able to trade continuously during the hours of 9.30 a.m. to 3.30 p.m. and thus remain open while the Australian exchange is open (*New Zealand Herald*, 22 May 1991). Trading and settlement activities of brokers have been centrally processed on a national computer system since 1988. One of the features of the system is the automatic matching of trades so that contracts between brokers are confirmed only when trade slips entered by the buying and selling brokers are matched. The system nets the deliveries of scrip and transfer authorities between brokers on a daily basis so that each broker makes a cash settlement for only a single amount (Foster 1991: 63).

Share market statistics

The size and activity of the market has steadily declined in recent years, as summarized in Table 11.2. During the year ended 31 December 1990 the value of shares traded decreased by 32 per cent, the volume of shares traded decreased by 25 per cent, and the number of transactions processed fell by 43 per cent, compared with the year ended 31 December 1989. The Gross Index fell by 36 per cent from 802.21 at 31 December 1989 to 514.02 at 31 December 1990. The total number of companies and securities listed declined by 34 per cent in the same period; the main cause for removal of companies from the list was breaches of listing requirements. In 1989 more than half of the decrease in the number of companies listed was attributable to take-over activity. In 1990 only five New Zealand securities were added to the list; 113 were deleted, with just two New Zealand companies newly listed on the market.

Stock Exchange reporting requirements

The Stock Exchange reporting requirements are summarized below:

- There is a general requirement for listed companies to supply all

Table 11.2 Summary of Stock Exchange listings and fund raising

	*31.12.90**	*31.12.89**	*31.12.88**
Number of companies on list			
New Zealand	171	246	295
Overseas	78	120	156
Number of securities on list			
New Zealand			
Equity	146	208	256
Borrowings	47	94	132
Overseas			
Equity	80	124	163
Borrowings	6	10	23
Value of equity raised			
Pro rata cash issue	NZ$255 m	NZ$821 m	NZ$372 m†
New issues	NZ$29 m	NZ$258 m	NZ$335 m†
Value of debt securities issued	NZ$4,442 m	NZ$8,444 m	NZ$10,323 m†

Sources: *NZSE 1991, pp. 17–18; †NZSE 1990, p. 2.

relevant information promptly to ensure that the market is at all times properly informed.

- All listed company financial statements are required to be drawn up in accordance with the NZSA accounting standards (see 'Accounting Standards', pp. 402–12) with any departures from SSAPs are to be fully disclosed and explained.
- A preliminary announcement is required to be made before the release of each set of annual accounts and each half yearly report and must be made within three months after the end of the financial period being reported on. Each preliminary announcement is required to contain the information called for in prescribed forms summarizing income statement, cash flows and balance sheet amounts, as well as the following:
  - A note of any material change in accounting policies together with disclosure of the impact of the change.
  - A note of any major changes or trends in business subsequent to the end of the financial period being reported on, including any material changes in the value of assets, profitability and contingent liabilities.
  - Any facts, figures or interpretative notes that the directors wish to include.
  - Any additional information necessary to ensure that the announcement is not misleading.
  - Where the information has been audited the announcement must state any qualifications that the auditors have made. The contents of each preliminary announcement need not be audited but where not, prior advice should be given to the auditors.

- Within four months of the close of the financial year the company must issue an annual report to the Stock Exchange and to its members. Additional information required is:
  - A listing of the top twenty security holders dated within one month of publication of the annual report.
  - A listing of the shareholdings of directors and associated persons of directors as at the current and preceding balance date with separate disclosure of beneficial, non-beneficial and associated persons shareholdings of each director.
  - Details of securities holders' spread dated within one month before publication.
- Within three months of the end of the first six months of each financial year the company must issue a half yearly report to the Stock Exchange and to its members. The report should include all the information required in the preliminary announcement.
- There are also requirements to inform the market of such matters as take-over offers, calls, dividends, new issues, any changes to the company's constitution or officers, etc., and such other information as the Exchange may request from time to time.

Reforms of the domestic regulatory framework

New Zealand's regulatory framework is presently undergoing sweeping reforms in response to the deregulation changes since 1984. Deregulation was in essence about privatizing risk. The economic justification for deregulation was that it ought to be cheaper for businesses to manage their risks rather than to continue with government intervention in controlling interest rates and exchange rates. Furthermore, the subsidies and other trade protection measures in place effectively insulated businesses from income volatility.

Reduced business risk through intervention had a flow-on effect in reducing the credit risks of banks and other lenders. When the finance sector deregulation measures were introduced lenders had greater freedom to tailor financial products to the market and thus commercial finance was easier to obtain. As a consequence corporate debt levels grew by 50 per cent to the extent that highly geared companies became the norm rather than the exception. Not surprisingly the incidence of company failure increased and this, coupled with the sharemarket crash, triggered a re-regulation response. Measures introduced by government since 1987 include the following:

- a tightening up on the supervision of banks by the Reserve Bank;
- the introduction of insider trading laws;
- the introduction of requirements to disclose substantial shareholdings in public companies;

- the introduction of controls on dealing in futures contracts;
- new regulations on life insurance companies;
- new laws dealing with the offer of interests in contributory mortgages to the public, and management of those interests;
- a new power for the Registrar of Companies to prohibit certain persons from managing companies;
- new powers for the Registrar of Companies to intervene in the affairs of financially troubled companies and to put companies into statutory management;
- the establishment of a serious fraud office;
- proposed new take-over legislation;
- new company law proposals;
- proposed personal property securities legislation;
- enormous changes in taxation legislation; and
- a proposed new regulatory structure to oversee the securities market.

Also, the Stock Exchange introduced new Listing Requirements.

A healthy capital market is regarded as important to New Zealand's economic system. Following the sharemarket crash in October 1987 and its continued poor performance (see 'Sharemarket Statistics', pp. 416–18), coupled with the increasing incidence of business failures, the government initiated a number of inquiries and reviews into the commercial sector.

Sharemarket inquiry

In October 1988 a Committee of Inquiry (known as the Russell Committee) was set up to look into the operations of the sharemarket and to make recommendations to ensure a fair and efficient market. The Committee's recommended solution was that a powerful regulatory enforcement body called a Supervisory Authority (SA) should be set up which would control the public securities markets (except banking, which would be left to the Reserve Bank). The Minister of Justice subsequently set up an establishment unit to consider proposals further and to give suggestions for their implementation. *The Report of the Sharemarket Inquiry Establishment Unit* was released in November 1989 and it recommended that the present Securities Commission be reconstituted as a supervisory body to be known as the New Zealand Securities Commission (NZSC). The function of the NZSC would be to supervise the activities of market participants, to be grouped in a manner similar to those introduced in the UK.

The NZSCs powers would include:

- initial approval of the above market participants;
- ongoing supervision to ensure that the self-regulatory organizations, approved professional bodies and approved investment exchanges and

their members comply with their in-house rules and other statutory requirements; and
- reserve powers of enforcement.

In respect of financial reporting it was recommended that an Accounting Standards Board (ASB) be established to approve accounting standards which would then be legally binding on all public issuers.

Proposed changes in company law

The proposed reforms outlined above would have applied to public securities only. With only 136 New Zealand companies listed on the Stock Exchange at 31 May 1991 the vast majority of New Zealand companies would not have come within the proposals. Calls for regulatory reforms did not focus on additional disclosures for the smaller private companies on the assumption that they would be dealt with by company law reforms.

The reform of company law has been described under 'Company Law Review' above. The Companies Bill does not in fact specify any requirements as to the contents or format of financial statements except that the latest indications are that all companies will be required to comply with applicable financial reporting standards.

Securities Commission report

While the Securities Commission was itself the subject of proposals for reform by the Russell Committee it meanwhile undertook its own review of the law and practice of financial reporting. Its report, *Capital Structure and Financial Reporting in New Zealand*, proposed a tripartite approach to regulating the financial reporting of public issuers based on the assumption that reforms recommended by the Law Commission would be enacted.

The Commission suggested key requirements of financial reporting such as the obligation to present accounts giving a true and fair view and definitions of important terms, would be enacted in legislation. A difference with the Companies Bill proposals was that the Securities Commission would include Notes to the Accounts within the definition of financial reports together with the balance sheet, profit and loss account and statement of cash flows.

Prescriptive disclosures and methodological requirements would be set out in regulations that would have legislative force. This would permit a quicker response to new developments in accounting practices. For example, in contrast to the Companies Bill, the Securities Commission would have set out requirements for group financial statements in regulations.

Third, the Commission suggested that approved accounting standards would fill the gaps on matters not covered by the Act or Regulations. An Accounting Standards Review Board under the jurisdiction of the

Commission was proposed to approve, monitor and amend or revoke accounting standards amongst other proposed functions.

Other matters dealt with in the Report were provisions on auditors and the requirement for audits, and proposals for law reform on capital adequacy.

The Securities Commission concurred with the abolition of the concepts of par value and nominal capital as now provided for in the Companies Bill; however, its proposals differed from the bill by recommending a distinction be maintained between 'contributed capital' and other shareholders' funds. On the question of corporate solvency the Commission recommended that distributions should not be made unless a company's assets, as stated in the most recent financial accounts, exceeded the aggregate of the company's liabilities together with the balance of its contributed capital account.

Ministerial Group on securities law reform

In March 1991 the national government, voted back in at the general election in October 1990, established yet another group to report on securities law reform. The group's brief involved consideration of three reports provided to the previous Labour government: the Russell Committee report of inquiry into the sharemarket, the Securities Commission's report referred to above, and another on take-overs.

An important outcome has been the strong support by the Minister of Justice for the establishment of an Accounting Standards Review Board (ASRB) as put forward in a joint recommendation by the Securities Commission, the NZSA and the New Zealand Stock Exchange. Their proposals were for legislation to establish an independent ASRB and the making of regulations under the Securities Act 1978 which would include prescription of information to be included in financial statements.

The ASRB would comprise five to nine members, of whom 40 per cent would be nominees of the NZSA. It would be funded from both the public and private sector and its various functions would include:

- approving accounting standards applying to all or any class of entity;
- examining qualified audit reports and, in the case of public issuers, referring such reports to the Securities Commission; and
- making recommendations to the Securities Commission on any changes in the law relating to any aspect of accounting and financial reporting of public issuers.

The regulations under the Securities Act would proceed only after going through the statutory public consultation procedure under the Act. They would not contain provisions about 'measurement' as that would be an area to be addressed by approved accounting standards.

Further legislation would require all public issuers to deliver annually to the Registrar of Companies audited financial statements which the Registrar would be authorized to refuse where the financial statements do not comply with the law. Also, the Securities Commission would have power to order the preparation of revised accounts at the cost of the directors responsible where the Commission considers the financial statements of a public issuer do not give a true and fair view or do not comply with approved accounting standards.

The Minister of Justice has since appointed an Advisory Committee on Accounting Standards as a forerunner to the ASRB pending enactment of the Financial Reporting Bill. As at August 1993 it is fully expected that the proposals will come into being. Furthermore, the NZSA is expected to continue to have the primary role in the development of financial reporting standards which will acquire the force of law once 'approved' by the ASRB.

EXTERNAL INFLUENCES ON ACCOUNTING

External influences impact on accounting in two major respects: standards-setting and accounting practice where there is no NZSA pronouncement on a topic. Accounting for financial instruments, for example, has been greatly influenced by US GAAP which first shaped New Zealand practice and then standards on this topic.

Both the development and the review of standards are subject to the influences of overseas accounting standards and practice. International harmonization would seem to be increasingly relevant as New Zealand businesses become more international. Internationalization has led to a greater awareness of accounting practices together with particular reporting requirements overseas. The government has pursued a policy of deregulation since 1984 and has increased opportunities for international economic activity with a corresponding increase in exposure to international investors. This has led to greater freedom for inward investment as well as expanding opportunities for New Zealand companies to obtain a listing of their shares overseas. The international comparability of financial information is consequently of increased importance.

A notable example which illustrates the importance of international harmonization is SSAP 17 'Accounting for Investment Properties by Property Investment Companies'. This standard once required unrealized gains (as well as losses) arising during a period to be recognized in the profit or loss for the period. The standard was withdrawn in June 1988 and reissued as SSAP 17 'Accounting for Investment Properties and Properties Intended for Sale', in 1989 and provided two options: either to include unrealized revaluations 'below the line' in the profit and loss account or to take them directly to reserves. The original SSAP 17 was issued on the grounds that inclusion of revaluations would help investors gain a fuller view of the profitability of property investment companies given that practice for these companies was to hold properties long-term and they were thus unable to establish 'income' from increments in property values through the usual process of realization. A popular argument for non-compliance with the original SSAP 17 leading to its eventual replacement was that it was out of line with generally accepted accounting standards and practice overseas. For example, the *Auckland Star* on 26 October 1988 reported, 'many property companies refused to take these unrealized gains to their profits because their accounts would be discredited overseas'. The Discussion Paper issued with ED 45, the exposure draft of the new SSAP 17, actually gives 'international harmony' as the reason for allowing optional treatment of reporting changes in value.

Interestingly, the Discussion Paper on ED 45 also compares the proposed requirements of the new SSAP 17 with the requirements of the relevant Australian standard. A comment on comparability with overseas standards has become a feature of discussion papers issued with proposed standards in New Zealand. As standards-setting has developed, concerns have been voiced in the business press that NZ has moved against the tide on some issues, suggesting that our standards-setters should look beyond their immediate environment. To quote: the *New Zealand Herald*, on 22 September 1986, reported, 'New Zealand can soldier on alone in her accounting pioneering and try to convince those elsewhere who eschew change. But she has a weight of numbers and regulatory authorities to convert.'

The NZSA has nevertheless resisted the wholesale adoption of standards developed overseas but it is evident from the high degree of commonality that overseas standards have normally been very influential in the development of equivalent New Zealand standards. The extent to which individual countries have influenced the development of standards in New Zealand can only be generalized (due to a lack of publihed research on the topic) to acknowledging significant influence by countries with which we share common ties and economic experience, such as the United Kingdom, Australia, Canada and the US. International Accounting Standards (IASs) are also influential in the preparation of NZSA standards.

International Accounting Standards

The relationship of New Zealand's accounting standards to IASs is set out in the Explanatory Foreword which prefaces all FRSs/SSAPs. As a member of the International Accounting Standards Committee, the NZSA is obliged to incorporate IASs within its accounting standards. Where significant differences arise then the existing New Zealand practice will prevail until such time as the NZSA issues a new or revised standard.

Table 11.3 IASs with no New Zealand SSAP equivalent, as at July 1989

Code number	*Title*	*New Zealand current position*
IAS 18	Revenue Recognition	Research Bulletin R 118 issued
IAS 19	Accounting for Retirement Benefits in the Financial Statements of Employers	Proposed ED in preparation
IAS 25	Accounting for Investments	Issue of Preliminary ED deferred
IAS 26	Accounting and Reporting by Retirement Benefit Plans	ED 68 on Financial Reporting by Superannuation Schemes issued
IAS 29	Financial Reporting in Hyperinflationary Economics	Local economy has low inflation
IAS 30	Disclosure in the Financial Statements of banks and similar financial institutions	No proposals

IASs are not binding on members; however, they do provide guidance on generally accepted accounting practice, particularly where there is no New Zealand statement on the topic. A comparison of pronouncements reveals six IASs with no SSAP equivalent. In addition, there is no New Zealand requirement to separately disclose the methods of providing for pension and retirement plans as required under IAS 5 'Information to be Disclosed in Financial Statements'.

Although New Zealand does not have an equivalent SSAP to IAS 18, practice is consistent with the revenue recognition concepts therein. Also SSAP 1, 'Determination and Disclosure of Accounting Policies', states that a general accounting policy which underlies the preparation of financial statements and which is in common use is that revenue is recognized as it is earned (under accrual accounting).

New Zealand practice and provisions under SSAP 9 on disclosure and the method of stating investments, are generally consistent with the requirements of IAS 25, 'Accounting for Investments'. Some companies have created a provision for investment fluctuation for their long-term investments.

The provisions of IAS 27 and IAS 28 are substantially included within SSAP 8. Major differences are additional IAS disclosures not specifically called for under SSAP 8; for example, IAS 27 requires disclosure of significant subsidiaries by country of incorporation or residence, and any difference between the proportion of voting power and proportion of ownership interest; IAS 28 requires disclosure of contingencies to the investor in relation to an associate, and disclosure of the investor's share of any unusual or prior period items (SSAP 8 mentions only material extraordinary items). Also the international standards specifically require cumulative preference dividends to be provided for whether or not declared, which is not mentioned in SSAP 8.

Major differences between New Zealand and US accounting principles

This is not a comprehensive list of all the differences between New Zealand and US accounting principles but is intended to identify those differences most likely to affect the comparability of New Zealand and US financial statements. It excludes areas of potential differences arising from legislative and specialized industry accounting requirements.

Differences between FRSs/SSAPs and US GAAP are identified in the preceding section summarizing current New Zealand standards. An important difference to emphasize is that New Zealand financial statements frequently include revaluations and other unrealized items. Further differences arise typically because of the more prescriptive nature of US accounting standards. Significant topics on which there are accounting requirements under US GAAP but where there are no equivalents in New Zealand are summarized below. Areas where there is no equivalent New Zealand SSAP on the IAS topic are summarized in the preceding section on International Accounting Standards. In most cases, despite there being no standard on a topic, practice in New Zealand is found to be typically consistent with IAS requirements.

ARB 43 Shares Repurchased by Companies

Repurchased shares (commonly referred to as 'treasury stock') are shown as a deduction from shareholders' equity based upon the price paid for the treasury stock acquired (i.e. not the nominal value). This treatment is also applied to shares held for contribution to an ESOP (Employees' Stock Ownership Plan) until they are contributed to that plan. Repurchase of own shares is presently illegal in New Zealand, but is proposed under the new Companies Bill.

APB Opinion 15 Earnings Per Share

In the US detailed earnings per share information must be given by all entities whose debt or equity securities are publicly traded or by companies required to file with the SEC. New Zealand has only a general stock exchange listing requirement to disclose earnings per share.

FAS 12 Investments (Marketable Securities)

In the US marketable equity securities are classified into current and non-current portfolios for valuation purposes. Practice in New Zealand is to assess stocks individually, not in aggregate.

FAS 48 Sales With Right of Return

In the US revenue from sales transactions where the buyer has a right of return is recognized only once certain specific requirements are met. In New Zealand practice often is to record the sale and create a provision for returns based on historical data.

FAS 87 Pensions

Under FAS 87, the US has defined requirements regarding pension accounting and the actuarial method used to calculate pension assets and liabilities. Pension funding and any residual surplus or shortfall in the fund valuation must be brought to account. There is no specific requirement to do this in New Zealand. New Zealand has an early *Research Bulletin on Financial Reporting for Pension Schemes* and the topic is currently a project of the Financial Reporting Standards Board of the NZSA.

SUMMARY

In New Zealand, the securities markets are as important to the economy as is the case in Australia, the UK and the US. The New Zealand Stock Exchange, along with company law, the accountancy profession, tax and external factors have been the main influences on accounting in New Zealand. Standards of financial reporting have been very much left to direction by the accountancy profession rather than to regulation.

Company legislation stems mainly from the Companies Act 1955 (modelled on the UK's Companies Act 1948) including subsequent amendments. The Act requires the directors to present accounts to shareholders at the annual meeting that show a true and fair view. Major changes have been proposed as part of the Companies Bill.

The NZSA was formed in 1908 and the profession issues all accounting and auditing standards and provides guidance on related matters. The accounting standards form what is generally agreed to be a definitive approach to what constitutes a true and fair view. Like the UK, development of accounting standards in New Zealand is a consultative process and they are subject to periodic review. External influences are important when setting accounting standards and New Zealand looks to the UK, the US, Australia and the IASC for guidance so that its standards are internationally comparable. As well as issuing accounting standards the NZSA has several committees dealing with financial accounting, professional practice matters, taxation issues, primary sector accounting, as well as research.

In addition to the proposed company law changes there are also proposed changes to the domestic securities regulatory framework. The likely outcome of this review is that there will be an increase in regulation in response to the 1987 stock market crash and the high levels of corporate gearing which led to an increase in the failure of companies.

APPENDIX A

Extracts from the accounts of the Fernz Corporation

AUDITORS' REPORT

KPMG Peat Marwick

Chartered Accountants

TO THE MEMBERS OF FERNZ CORPORATION LIMITED

We have examined the accompanying Balance Sheet, Group Accounts and Consolidated Statement of Cash Flows and have obtained all the information and explanations we have required.

We are of the opinion that proper accounting records have been kept by the Company, that the Balance Sheet and Accounts including the Group Accounts give the information required by the Companies Act 1955 in the manner so required and that they give, on an historical cost basis adjusted by the revaluation of certain assets, a true and fair view of the state of affairs of the Company and the Group as at 31 May 1991 and of the results of the Group's business and cash flows for the year ended on that date.

KPMG Peat Marwick

Chartered Accountants
Auckland
17 July 1991

Fernz Corporation Limited

CONSOLIDATED PROFIT AND LOSS ACCOUNT

For the year ended 31 May 1991

	Notes	1991 $000	1990 $000
GROUP TURNOVER		**$299,249**	$321,604
CONSOLIDATED EARNINGS FROM TRADING		**126,568**	140,034
EXPENDITURE	2		
Auditors' Fees		**434**	320
Depreciation		**9,410**	9,617
Directors' Fees		**123**	161
Interest and Exchange Fluctuations		**15,961**	19,482
Leasing and Rental Costs		**569**	1,289
Operating Expenses		**77,939**	80,437
Total Expenses		**104,436**	111,306
OPERATING PROFIT		**22,132**	28,728
Costs of Environmental Action	3	**(7,264)**	-
Other Income	4	**5,333**	4,965
PROFIT BEFORE TAX		**20,201**	33,693
Taxation	8(a)	**5,591**	12,639
		14,610	21,054
Outside Shareholders' Interests		**(150)**	(196)
		14,760	21,250
Share of Profits of Associated Companies	6	**1,560**	1,593
PROFIT AFTER TAX		**16,320**	22,843
Extraordinary Items net of tax	7	**-**	(712)
CONSOLIDATED NET PROFIT FOR YEAR		**16,320**	22,131
Plus: Retained Earnings brought forward		**38,853**	27,295
		55,173	49,426
Less: Appropriations and Transfers	12(a)	**(10,337)**	(10,573)
Retained Earnings carried forward		**$44,836**	$38,853
Represented by:			
Group		**36,034**	31,611
Associated Companies		**8,802**	7,242
		$44,836	$38,853

The Notes on pages 31 to 43 form part of and should be read in conjunction with this Statement.

Fernz Corporation Limited

CONSOLIDATED BALANCE SHEET

As at 31 May 1991

	Notes	1991 $000	1990 $000
AUTHORISED CAPITAL			
100,000,000 Ordinary Shares @ $1 each		**$100,000**	$100,000
ISSUED AND PAID UP CAPITAL	10	**46,993**	46,821
CAPITAL RESERVES	11	**12,906**	12,576
OTHER RESERVES	12	**67,347**	63,156
Group's Share of Associated Companies	13	**11,700**	10,114
TOTAL SHAREHOLDERS' FUNDS		**138,946**	132,667
OUTSIDE SHAREHOLDERS' INTERESTS	14	**406**	732
DEFERRED TAX	8(c)	**4,167**	1,674
TERM LIABILITIES (SECURED)	15		
Borrowings		**60,246**	80,289
Lease Liabilities		**1,029**	270
TOTAL TERM LIABILITIES		**61,275**	80,559
CURRENT LIABILITIES			
Bank Overdrafts (Secured)	15	**8,342**	9,481
Short Term Loans (Secured)	15	**37,120**	33,707
Creditors and Accruals		**50,242**	62,508
Current Portion of Term Borrowings (Secured)	15	**42,417**	587
Provision for Taxation	8(b)	**209**	8,076
Provision for Final Dividend		**5,639**	5,608
TOTAL CURRENT LIABILITIES		**143,969**	119,967
		$348,763	$335,599

The Notes on pages 31 to 43 form part of and should be read in conjunction with this Statement.

	Notes	1991 $000	1990 $000
FIXED ASSETS	16		
Land		**10,439**	10,045
Roads and Drains		**2,143**	2,114
Buildings		**37,826**	36,662
Machinery and Plant		**96,522**	62,847
Capital Work in Progress		**771**	10,432
Leased Plant		**1,216**	769
TOTAL FIXED ASSETS		**148,917**	122,869
TERM INVESTMENTS	17		
Investments in Associated Companies		**26,906**	25,158
Investments in Other Companies		**1,051**	1,149
Other Investments		**14,375**	15,016
TOTAL TERM INVESTMENTS		**42,332**	41,323
CURRENT ASSETS			
Cash and Bank		**2,057**	2,702
Debtors	18	**70,343**	74,518
Inventories - Raw Materials		**43,094**	50,465
- Work in Progress		**433**	394
- Finished Products		**37,343**	39,714
Taxation Benefits Due	8(b)	**422**	287
TOTAL CURRENT ASSETS		**153,692**	168,080
INTANGIBLE ASSETS	19	**3,822**	3,327
		$348,763	$335,599

On behalf of the Board of Directors

Chairman

Managing Director

Fernz Corporation Limited

PARENT COMPANY BALANCE SHEET

As at 31 May 1991

	Notes	1991 $000	1990 $000
AUTHORISED CAPITAL			
100,000,000 Ordinary Shares @ $1 each		**$100,000**	$100,000
ISSUED AND PAID UP CAPITAL	10	**46,993**	46,821
CAPITAL RESERVES	11	**12,896**	12,566
OTHER RESERVES	12	**34,238**	23,570
TOTAL SHAREHOLDERS' FUNDS		**94,127**	82,957
TERM LIABILITIES (SECURED)	15		
Borrowings		**10,000**	10,000
TOTAL TERM LIABILITIES		**10,000**	10,000
CURRENT LIABILITIES			
Bank Overdraft (Secured)	15	**3,113**	5,453
Short Term Loans (Secured)	15	**6,000**	7,000
Creditors and Accruals		**1,154**	1,279
Current Portion of Term Borrowings (Secured)	15	**-**	500
Provision for Final Dividend		**5,639**	5,608
Owing to Subsidiary Companies	18	**-**	7,901
TOTAL CURRENT LIABILITIES		**15,906**	27,741
		$120,033	$120,698

The Notes on pages 31 to 43 form part of and should be read in conjunction with this Statement.

	Notes	1991 $000	1990 $000
FIXED ASSETS	16		
Land		**701**	701
Roads and Drains		**317**	317
Buildings		**6,679**	6,895
TOTAL FIXED ASSETS		**7,697**	7,913
TERM INVESTMENTS	17		
Investments in Subsidiary Companies		**42,005**	64,211
Investments in Associated Companies		**2,837**	15,044
Investments in Other Companies		**1,051**	1,051
Other Investments		**2,878**	12,803
TOTAL TERM INVESTMENTS		**48,771**	93,109
FUTURE TAX BENEFIT	8(c)	**73**	135
CURRENT ASSETS			
Cash and Bank		**9**	1
Debtors	18	**10,903**	14,703
Taxation Benefits Due	8(b)	**3,551**	3,971
Owing by Subsidiary Companies	18	**48,259**	-
TOTAL CURRENT ASSETS		**62,722**	18,675
INTANGIBLE ASSETS	19	**770**	866
		$120,033	$120,698

On behalf of the Board of Directors

Chairman

Managing Director

Fernz Corporation Limited

CONSOLIDATED STATEMENT OF CASH FLOWS

For the year ended 31 May 1991

		1991 $000		1990 $000
CASH FLOWS FROM OPERATING ACTIVITIES				
Cash was provided from:				
Receipts from customers		329,275		357,294
Cash was applied to:				
Payments to suppliers and employees	278,919		296,626	
Taxes paid (including GST)	15,668	294,587	15,383	312,009
Net Cash Flow from Operating Activities		34,688		45,285
CASH FLOWS FROM INVESTING ACTIVITIES				
Cash was provided from:				
Proceeds from sales of Fixed Assets	1,313		689	
Proceeds from Other Investments	1,511		2,068	
Dividends received	3,290		4,010	
Cash was applied to:				
Acquisition of Fixed Assets	40,929		28,571	
Investment in Subsidiaries	153		-	
Acquisition of Other Investments	804		1,904	
Net Cash Used in Investing Activities		(35,772)		(23,708)
CASH FLOWS FROM FINANCING ACTIVITIES				
Cash was provided from:				
Proceeds of long term debt	33,692		18,347	
Proceeds of short term debt (net)	1,442		-	
Cash was applied to:				
Settlement of short term debt (net)	-		4,292	
Settlement of long term debt	778		694	
Interest paid on short term debt	7,505		9,403	
Interest paid on long term debt	8,937		9,848	
Dividends paid	10,300		11,256	
Net Cash Flow from Financing Activities		7,614		(17,146)
Net increase (decrease) in cash held		6,530		4,431
Add: Opening cash brought forward		(13,779)		(17,501)
Exchange rate changes on cash		(36)		(709)
Ending Cash Carried Forward		(7,285)		(13,779)
CLOSING CASH BALANCE COMPRISED				
Bank Overdraft		(8,342)		(9,481)
Cash and Bank Balances		2,057		2,702
Short Term Loans at call		(1,000)		(7,000)
		(7,285)		(13,779)
SUMMARY OF THE EFFECTS OF ACQUISITION OF SUBSIDIARY COMPANIES				
Shares issued for Cash to Minority Interests		(8)		-
Current Liabilities		(22)		-
Minority Shareholding purchased		183		-
		153		-

1. STATEMENT OF ACCOUNTING POLICIES

GENERAL ACCOUNTING POLICIES

The general accounting policies recognised as appropriate for the measurement and reporting of profit and financial position on an historical cost basis have been followed by the Group except that certain land and buildings are included at valuation.

Reliance is placed on the fact that the Company is a going concern. Accrual accounting is used to match revenue and expenses.

PARTICULAR ACCOUNTING POLICIES

The following particular accounting policies which materially affect the measurement of profit and the financial position have been applied:

(a) Basis of Consolidation
The Consolidated Financial Statements include the accounts of Fernz Corporation Limited and all subsidiary companies in which Fernz Corporation Limited either directly or indirectly holds more than 50% of the issued share capital using the purchase method. On the acquisition of a business, fair values are attributed to the net assets taken over.
Goodwill is capitalised and written off pre-tax profit on a straight line basis over a period considered appropriate by the Directors, of up to 20 years.
Sales and profits of subsidiaries acquired during the year are included for the period since acquisition.
Sales between the Group companies and unrealised inter-group profits are eliminated.

(b) Associated Companies
These are companies in which the Group has a substantial shareholding but not a controlling interest and in whose commercial and financial policy decisions it participates.

Equity Accounting
Investments in associated companies are dealt with on an equity accounting basis in the Consolidated Financial Statements.
The significant associated companies included are:

(i) BOP Fertiliser Limited 40%
(ii) Pacific Raw Materials Limited 39%
(iii) McDonald's Lime Limited 20%

Shares in associated companies are included at cost or valuation, adjusted for the Group share of the post-acquisition increases in net assets.

(c) Joint Ventures
Where the Group participates in a joint venture, the Group's interest is brought to account by including the appropriate proportions of the relevant assets, liabilities, revenues and expenditures of the joint venture into the respective categories in the accounts of the investor companies.
The significant joint venture included is:
Nufarm Coogee Joint Venture 80%

(d) Fixed Assets
Land and buildings are recorded at original cost or valuation. Other fixed assets are recorded at cost.

(e) Depreciation
Depreciation is calculated on a straight line basis which writes off the cost and subsequent revaluations of fixed assets (less their estimated residual value where applicable) over their estimated economic lives.
The following economic lives have been established for the principal categories of fixed assets.

Buildings	25-100 years
Acid Plants	15 years
Chlor Alkali Plants	20 years
Other Fixed Assets	10-20 years
Mobile Plant	3-7 years

NOTES TO THE FINANCIAL STATEMENTS (CONTINUED)

(f) Long Term Investments
Shares in other companies and other investments are included at cost.

(g) Current Assets
(i) Inventories Valuation
Inventories purchased for resale are valued at the lower of historical cost, on a first in first out basis, and net realisable value. Cost represents direct acquisition cost.
Raw materials and manufactured inventories are valued at the lower of cost using a weighted average basis, and net realisable value. For manufactured goods, cost is calculated by taking into account raw materials cost, direct manufacturing costs and all factory overheads including depreciation. All valuations include due allowance for obsolete and slow moving inventories.

(ii) Debtors
Debtors are shown at their estimated net realisable value after bad debts have been adequately provided for.

(h) Trade Marks and Technology Rights
Trade Marks and Technology Rights acquired are capitalised and written off pre-tax profit on a straight line basis over a period considered appropriate by the Directors, of up to 20 years.

(i) Foreign Currencies
Foreign currency transactions have been converted to New Zealand currency at the exchange rate ruling at the transaction date. Foreign currency assets and liabilities at balance date are converted at the rate of exchange ruling at that date. Realised and unrealised gains and losses are recognised in the Profit and Loss Account. The financial statements of overseas subsidiaries are converted to New Zealand currency at exchange rates ruling at the balance date. Changes resulting from the conversion of the opening net investment in overseas subsidiary companies at the rate of exchange ruling at balance date are taken up in Exchange Fluctuation Reserve.

(j) Interest
Normally interest payments are charged against profit for the year in which they are incurred. At times when major capital projects are being undertaken an appropriate amount may be capitalised as a project cost.

(k) Taxation
The charge for income tax is the amount of the estimated tax liability in respect of the accounting profit reported for the year. Deferred Taxation is calculated using the partial liability method.

(l) Leasing
Lease rental payments are treated as current operating costs and are charged against current profit.

(m) Development
Expenditure on product research and development is charged in the Profit and Loss Account in the year in which it is incurred.

(n) Maintenance
Expenditure on maintenance, repairs and improvements which do not result in an addition to the value of the Companies' assets or which do not increase the capacity of the asset beyond its original design, is charged against revenue as incurred.

(o) Employee Benefits
Provision is made for benefits accruing to employees for annual leave and long service leave.
Funded superannuation schemes are operated for the benefit of employees and Company contributions are charged to expenses. All contributions to the Schemes plus the income from investments are held in funds administered by trustees and managed by insurance companies independent of the Group's finances.

There have been no significant changes in accounting policies which have been applied on bases consistent with those used in previous years.

APPENDIX B

Sources of information and references

Some useful sources of information are set out below.

Publications of the New Zealand Society of Accountants, including promulgations and the *Accountants' Journal*:
New Zealand Society of Accountants, PO Box 11-342, Wellington, New Zealand.

Ryan, J.B. (ed.), *New Zealand Company Financial Reporting: 1989*, Kerslake Billens & Humphrey Ltd, Levin, New Zealand, 1989. A periodic survey of the top 100 listed New Zealand company annual reports, including examples of presentation; available from:
Mr. M.A. Perkinson, Accountancy Department, The University of Auckland, Private Bag, Auckland, New Zealand.

A useful reference textbook is *Company Accounting in New Zealand* by Robb *et al.*, available from:
John Wiley & Sons, 236 Dominion Road, Mt Eden, Auckland, 3, New Zealand.

Annually updated technical publications such as the *Staples Tax Guide*, *The Accountant's Manual*, and *Model Financial Accounts*, published by:
Centre for Professional Development (NZ) Ltd, Private Bag, Auckland, New Zealand.

The KPMG Peat Marwick *Survey of New Zealand Financial Institutions* and other publications available from:
KPMG Peat Marwick, National Communications Centre, PO Box 1584, Auckland, 1, New Zealand.

Information on the New Zealand share market available from:
New Zealand Stock Exchange, PO Box 2959, Wellington, New Zealand.

Reports of the Law Commission and other Government Committees such as the Russell Committee, also Department of Statistics publications and the *New Zealand Official Yearbook* available from:
Government Printing Office, Private Bag, Wellington, New Zealand.
The reports of the Russell Committee are also available from:
Tribunals Division, Department of Justice, PO Box 10-044, The Terrace, Wellington, New Zealand.

REFERENCES

Cameron, R. (1988) 'The sharemarket', in G. Karacaoglu, *An Introduction to Financial Markets in New Zealand*, Wellington: Victoria University Press.

Companies Bill (1990) Wellington: Government Printing Office, September.

Department of Statistics (1990) *New Zealand Official Yearbook 1988–89*, Wellington: Government Printing Office.

—— (1991) *New Zealand Pocket Digest of Statistics 1991*, Wellington: Government Printing Office.

—— (1993) *Key Statistics July 1993*, Wellington: Government Printing Office.

Foster, W.P. (1991) 'New Zealand Stock Exchange', in *The Interdata Financial Handbook* (6th edn), Sydney: IDP InterData Pty Ltd.

Johnston, T.R. and Edgar, G.C. (1982) *The Law and Practice of Company Accounting* (6th edn), Wellington: Butterworths (and Supplement, 1986).

National Bank of New Zealand Limited (1993) *Business Outlook – July 1993*, Wellington: National Bank of New Zealand Limited.

Newby, S. (1989) *SSAP Update (S 321)*, Wellington: NZSA.

New Zealand Law Commission (1989) *Company Law: Reform and Restatement*, Report no. 9, Wellington: Government Printing Office.

—— (1990) *Company Law Reform: Transition and Revision*, Report no. 16, Wellington: Government Printing Office.

New Zealand Society of Accountants (NZSA) (1988a) 'Pressure for places in commerce faculty', *Accountants' Journal*, April.

—— (1988b) *A-3 General Notes for the Guidance of Members*, Wellington: NZSA.

—— (1988c) 'New Zealand Society of Accountants 80th Annual Report and Accounts for the Year Ended 30 June 1988', *Accountants' Journal Supplement*, September.

—— (1989) 'New Zealand Society of Accountants 81st Annual Report and Accounts for the Year Ended 30 June 1989', *Accountants' Journal Supplement*, September.

—— (1990a) *A-2 Rules*, Wellington: NZSA.

—— (1990b) 'New Zealand Society of Accountants 82nd Annual Report and Accounts for the Year Ended 30 June 1990', *Accountants' Journal, Supplement*, September.

New Zealand Stock Exchange (NZSE) (1990), *Sharemarket Review for the Year Ended 31 December 1989*, Wellington: NZSE.

—— (1991) *Sharemarket Review for the Year Ended 31 December 1990*, Wellington: NZSE.

OECD (1989) *OECD Economic Survey 1988–89: New Zealand*, Paris: OECD.

Robb, A.J., Neal, A., Leo, K.J. and Hoggett, J.R. (1990) *Company Accounting in New Zealand* (2nd edn), Auckland: John Wiley & Sons.

Russell Committee (1989a) *Report of the Ministerial Committee of Inquiry into the Sharemarket*, Wellington: Government Printing Office.

—— (1989b) *Report of the Sharemarket Inquiry Establishment Unit*, Wellington: Government Printing Office.

Ryan, J.B. (ed.) (1987) *New Zealand Company Financial Reporting: 1987*, Wollongong: University of Wollongong Printery.

—— (1989) *New Zealand Company Financial Reporting: 1989*, Levin: Kerslake Billens & Humphrey Ltd.

Securities Commission (1989) *Capital Structure and Financial Reporting in New Zealand*, Wellington: Government Printing Office.

12 Conformity with international accounting standards

IAS		Japan	South Korea	Taiwan	Hong Kong	Thailand	Malaysia	Singapore	The Philippines	Australia	New Zealand
1	Disclosure	✓	✓	✓	✓	✓	A	B	✓	✓	✓
2	Inventories	✓	✓	✓	✓	✓	A	B	✓	✓	✓
4	Depreciation	✓	✓	✓	B	✓	A	B	✓	✓	✓
5	Disclosures	✓	✓	✓	✓	✓	A	B	✓	✓	✓
7	Funds flow	✓	✓	✓	✓	✓	A	B	✓	✓	✓
8	Unusual items	RNC	RNC	✓	✓	✓	A	B	✓	✓	✓
9	R&D	RNC	RNC	✓	PC	✓	A	B	PC	RNC	✓
10	Contingencies	✓	RNC	✓	✓	✓	A	B	✓	✓	✓
11	Construction contracts	✓	✓	✓	✓	✓	A	B	PC	✓	✓
12	Taxes	RNC	RNC	✓	✓	✓	A	B	PC	✓	✓
13	Current assets	✓	✓	✓	PC	✓	A	B	✓	PC	✓
14	Segments	✓	PNC	PC	✓	✓	A	B	PNC	✓	✓
15	Changing prices	PNC	PNC	PNC	PNC	✓	PC	PNC	PNC	PNC	PNC
16	Property, plant	✓	✓	✓	PC	✓	A	B	✓	✓	✓
17	Leases	PNC	RNC	✓	✓	✓	A	B	PC	✓	✓
18	Revenue recognition	✓	✓	✓	PC	✓	A	B	PC	✓	PC
19	Retirement benefits	✓	RNC	✓	PNC	✓	A	B	PC	PNC	PNC
20	Government grants	✓	RNC	PNC	PNC	✓	PC	B	PNC	RNC	✓
21	Foreign exchange	RNC	✓	✓	✓	✓	A	B	B	✓	✓
22	Business combinations	RNC	✓	PC	PC	✓	✓	B	✓	✓	✓

23	Borrowing costs	✓	✓	✓	✓	✓	A	B	PC	✓	✓
24	Related parties	✓	✓	✓	PNC	✓	✓	B	✓	✓	✓
25	Investments	PC	✓	✓	PC	✓	A	B	✓	PC	PNC
26	Retirement plans	PNC	RNC	PNC	PNC	✓	A	B	PC	✓	PC
27	Consolidation	✓	✓	✓	✓	✓	A	B	✓	✓	✓
28	Associates	✓	PC	PNC	✓	✓	A	B	✓	RNC	✓
29	Hyperinflationary economies	PNC	PNC	PNC	PNC	PNC	PNC	PNC	PNC	PNC	PNC
30	Banks	RNC	RNC	PC	PNC	✓	✓	PNC	✓	PC	PNC
31	Joint ventures	PNC	PNC	PC	✓	✓	PNC	PNC	PC	RNC	RNC

Source: *IASC Suvey of the Use and Application of International Accounting Standards* 1993.

Notes:
✓ = separately developed requirement conforms in all material aspects with the International Accounting Standard
A = International Accounting Standard adopted as a national requirement
B = International Accounting Standard used as a basis for a national standard
PNC = no national requirement and practice generally does not conform with International Acounting Standards
RNC = national requirement does not conform with the International Accounting Standard
PC = no national requirement and practice generally does conform with the International Accounting Standard

Index